ON LOOP

ON LOOP

Black Sonic Politics in Oakland

ALEX WERTH

UNIVERSITY OF CALIFORNIA PRESS

University of California Press
Oakland, California

© 2025 by Alex Werth

Library of Congress Cataloging-in-Publication Data

Names: Werth, Alex, author
Title: On loop : black sonic politics in Oakland / Alex Werth.
Description: Oakland, California : University of California Press, [2025] | Includes
    bibliographical references and index.
Identifiers: LCCN 2025008706 (print) | LCCN 2025008707 (ebook) | ISBN 9780520416062
    cloth | ISBN 9780520416079 paperback | ISBN 9780520416086 ebook
Subjects: LCSH: African Americans—California—Oakland—Music—History and
    criticism | Dance music—Political aspects—California—Oakland | Sound—Politi-
    cal aspects—California—Oakland | Funk (Music)—Political aspects—California—
    Oakland | Rap (Music)—Political aspects—California—Oakland | Hip-hop—
    Political aspects—California—Oakland
Classification: LCC ML3477.8.O25 W47 2025 (print) | LCC ML3477.8.O25 (ebook) |
    DDC 780.89/96073079466—dc23/eng/20250521
LC record available at https://lccn.loc.gov/2025008706
LC ebook record available at https://lccn.loc.gov/2025008707

Manufactured in the United States of America

GPSR Authorized Representative: Easy Access System Europe, Mustamäe tee 50,
10621 Tallinn, Estonia, gpsr.requests@easproject.com

34   33   32   31   30   29   28   27   26   25
10   9   8   7   6   5   4   3   2   1

publication supported by a grant from
The Community Foundation for Greater New Haven
as part of the *Urban Haven Project*

For Mom and Dad, the dancer and the writer.

Contents

Illustrations

Preface: Slaps and the City

OAKLAND HAS A SOUND. It's sparse, spacious, intense, like the city. The sickness and the cure, it vibrates with tension but moves bodies to release. Low in tone, high in tempo, it's like a temple erected to the gods of "the deep."[1] "Slow down / you know you can't catch me," raps Clyde Carson of the Team over driving 808 claps. "I move too fast on the gas / don't chase me."[2] Built from propulsive bass lines, big drums, and lyrics that express the power of, well, *expression* more than semantic meaning ("yadadamean?"[3]), it's made to deliver maximum feeling with minimum resources. In the map of Black American dance music, Chicago has house. Detroit has techno. And Oakland has "slaps"—a signature style of party rap that's identified by its somatic and emotional impact (as in: "that song *hit* me!") more than its musical form. There's no section labeled "slaps" in the record store. Just a loose collection of tracks—created by rappers, singers, and producers from around the San Francisco Bay

Area—with the power to make people mob to the boulevard or dance floor.

In both name and sound, slaps harken back to the slap-bass style developed by Larry Graham, the bassist for Sly and the Family Stone. Born in Beaumont, Texas, but raised in Oakland, Graham got his start gigging with his mother Dell, a singer and pianist, and Ruben Kerr, a drummer, as the Dell Graham Trio. Originally the guitarist, he was tasked with providing the smooth melodies typical of early 1960s soul. But he soon discovered the power of "the bottom" during a stint at one of their regular venues, where there was an organ on stage. Still on guitar, he learned to work the bass pedals with his feet, giving the trio a more well-rounded sound—until the organ broke down. In need of a substitute, he rented a bass guitar to shore up the low end. Then, need struck again. Dell decided to economize and drop the drummer. Graham, just 15, started to thump and snap the strings of his bass to mimic the rhythmic conversation, now missing, between the kick and the snare. "I didn't think I was developing anything new," he recalled. "It was just out of necessity. Just trying to do the gig right, make it sound good and feel good."[4] Like I said: maximum feeling, minimum resources.

Heard on records like Sly and the Family Stone's "Thank You (Falettinme Be Mice Elf Agin)" (1969) and Graham Central Station's "The Jam" (1975), this technique infused the emerging sound of funk music with a fun, in-your-face, and forcefully danceable West Coast vibe.[5] The impact was indelible. Organizing songs around the bass line instead of the melody, Graham set the tone for the bottom-heavy sound of the Bay Area's Hyphy Movement and LA's gangster rap. For decades to come, East Bay hip-hop artists like Digital Underground—whose anthem "The Humpty Dance" (1990) is fueled by samples from Sly and Parliament Funkadelic—excavated records from the 1960s and '70s to give their songs what the music historian and radio DJ Rickey Vincent calls "that slap."[6]

But Oakland's funk culture didn't just slap. It slapped *back*. In the late 1960s, young Black migrants—who, like Graham, moved out from the U. S. South and Southwest during the Second Great Migration—led a sonic and political attack against the city's homegrown regime of Jim Crow. Since 1966, when residents Huey Newton and Bobby Seale formed the Black Panther Party for Self-Defense (BPP), Oakland has become inseparable from the popular imagination of Black Power. Graham's sound might have resonated with the energy of the revolution, and vice versa, but it's the *images* of the 1960s and '70s—the leather jackets, naturals, and berets, the fists, balled and raised—that have come, ironically, to memorialize "the movement."

So, in 2016, it seemed as though every cultural organization in Oakland mounted a visual art show to commemorate the BPP's golden anniversary. The most notable of these events, "All Power to the People: Black Panthers at 50," took place at the Oakland Museum of California (OMCA). A monument to architectural modernism, the OMCA emerges, almost geologically, from the civic center on the south side of Lake Merritt. It sits between the Alameda County courthouse, where Newton was once imprisoned and tried, and the Oakland Auditorium, where, in 1968, H. Rap Brown and Stokely Carmichael rallied 5,000 supporters to call for his release. These and other scenes from Oakland's Black Power Era were, of course, captured in the exhibit. When I visited, participants wandered in between the visual installations, whispering in the hushed tones expected of a museum. They paused to read the BPP's Ten-Point Program and view the agitprop illustrations made by Minister of Culture Emory Douglas. They peered at the images of impassioned speeches produced by the throngs of photographers who flocked to Party rallies. And they posed for Instagram in a replica of the iconic rattan chair, where, in 1967, Newton was stoically pictured in full regalia, rifle and spear by his side.

"The reproduction of this photograph [at the time]," writes the Black studies scholar Leigh Raiford, "reveals that the Panthers understood that their ideas, their image . . . [and] their physical persons were under attack." In response, she writes, they "staged their opposition . . . through spectacle." If their politics were intensely visual, in other words, it wasn't a matter of vanity but *strategy*. According to Raiford, the BPP waged a tactical campaign of visibility to counteract racist images of Black people in the media, depict resistance as real and attractive, and redefine Blackness—the very meaning of which was rooted in the notion of race as visible difference—on their own revolutionary terms.[7] "Photography," confirms the visual studies scholar Tina Campt, "is an everyday strategy of affirmation and a confrontational practice of visibility."[8]

So, it's no surprise that "All Power to the People" was, by and large, a collection of images. Apart from a pair of headphones—where I spent most of my time listening to a "Black Power Playlist," including anthems like James Brown's "Say It Loud—I'm Black and I'm Proud" (1968) and Marvin Gaye's "Inner City Blues (Make Me Wanna Holler)" (1971)—the sound of revolt was muted by the museum.[9]

What, then, did Black Power sound like in Oakland? How did it resonate in not just the musical recordings of the time, which became instant classics, but also the city's streets, parks, and nightclubs? How did these sounds enable young people to experience the more existential aims of the movement—the ideals of freedom and power—in their bodies and everyday practices? And how did the authorities react to this attack on the sonic order of White Power? Was this a thing of the past—an inert artifact of culture and politics, to be catalogued and remembered in this time of retrospectives? Or did it ripple, still, through the lives and social movements that make Oakland a perennial site of struggle over the unfinished work of Black freedom?

I ruminated on these questions as I strolled from the OMCA to Samba Church—an Afro-Brazilian dance class that, befitting its name, was my regular devotional practice on Sundays. Somewhere along Fourteenth Street in Downtown Oakland, I was snapped out of my reverie by the slap of the bass rattling from the trunk of a "scraper" as it rumbled past (see ch. 5). Then, I noticed the distant din of the *bateria*, or drum corps, warming up at the cultural center where I was headed. I paused, allowing the sound to wash over me. There were cranes and construction sites rising all around—part of a wave of investment in high-end housing that heralded the coming of what the geographer Brandi Summers calls, in a tragic riff on Parliament, the "post-Chocolate City."[10] Clearly, Oakland's social and urban fabric had been torn up and pieced back together since the 1960s. But the air still quivered, decades later, with the audible echoes of the Black Power Beat. The sonic record of revolt might not live in the museum, I realized, but it reverberated in the street.

It wasn't just the museum or popular memory that missed the sonic dimensions of Oakland's otherwise celebrated saga of struggle over rights to the city and racial justice. In academia, too, the fields of urban studies, planning, and geography—which are rooted in visual tools and methods (think: the architectural plan and the map)—tend to literally overlook the ways that popular music and sound cultures animate the brick-and-mortar politics of race and space. In the process, both popular culture and social science have silenced a truth at once palpable and ignored: Black dance music doesn't simply "represent," in hip-hop patois, our racialized cities. It's not merely a soundtrack to or record of urban struggle. It's an *active force* that inspires movements and countermovements of freedom and control, fueling a contest over the laws, spaces, and practices that comprise the urban environment. In other words, Black dance music works to remake the very cities it seems to "represent."

On Loop takes a different approach. It listens for the intersections between Black dance music and urbanism in Oakland—a city long "seen" as central to both the sound and politics of Black Power, but rarely at the same time. Drawing upon musical, archival, and ethnographic research, and a decade of personal experience as a DJ and dancer, it argues that Black dance music—from blues to funk, hip-hop to hyphy—has animated the looping struggles over development, dispossession, and self-determination that have come to define Oakland. In the process, it reveals that we can't understand the most enduring problems and pleasures of American urban life—segregation, gentrification, social movements, policing, nightlife, and more—without attuning to the multitudes of Black dance music and sound cultures as pervasive but invisible sites of resistance and repression. Permeating the visible city, there is a Black sonic politics.

INTRODUCTION

On Black Sonic Politics

<hr>

"BLACK NOISE MATTERS, TOO"

As the winter rains wash over the Oakland Hills, the waters run down the *arroyos*, the grooves, that mold the rolling terrain until they reach Lake Merritt. There, in the middle of the city, they mingle with estuarial tidewaters that, in time, retreat to San Francisco Bay. This ecological mix, at the edge of land and sea, makes "the Lake" attractive to cormorants, egrets, and geese. But for most of the people who are drawn to its shores, the water—which once served as the area's sewer, and still tends to smell a little rank—isn't really the pull. It's the three-mile circuit of parks and trails, teeming with the intersecting energies of the city, that's the allure. Whether people are there to circulate, or watch those who do, to dwell at the Lake is to linger in the loop.

According to the ethnomusicologist Michael Veal, who has studied the techniques of Jamaican dub reggae producers, looping is a means to make music transcend the constraints of mainstream culture and social oppression. Blurring the line between start and end, now and then, it creates an expansive and emotive atmosphere that produces mystical experiences rather than measurable commodities. It makes room for what he calls a holy trinity of Black "reverb, remembrance, and reverie."[1] In fact, in the words of the Jamaican cultural theorist Sylvia Wynter, this emphasis on looping—as opposed to linear patterns—has long defined the "subversive quality" of Black popular music: "its assault on [a colonial] sense of time, its freeing of time from a market process, its insistence on time as a life process."[2]

These words echo in my mind whenever I walk the loop around the Lake. When I moved to Oakland in 2009, I made it my practice to return to this circuit month after month, season after season, starting my stroll in the same spot, and cruising in the same direction. This ritual of repetition made me feel at once anchored in the constant march of time and free to veer off into more imaginative realms. This mix of freedom and constraint might seem contradictory. But it's not. "Without an organizing principle of repetition," writes the literary scholar James Snead, of Black music and culture, "improvisation would be impossible, as an improvisator relies upon the ongoing recurrence of the beat."[3]

One Saturday in 2017, I prepared to start my loop, per usual, at the pergola near the Grand Lake Theater. Some Black residents referred to this site as Congo Square West—a citation that, crossing time and space, connected Lake Merritt to the one spot in antebellum New Orleans where enslaved Africans were permitted to meet, drum, and dance, making it an invaluable site of cultural survival and invention.[4] Indeed, as I approached, I was met with the sound of a drum circle, where a group of musicians synced and syncopated their rhythms, and a few spirited dancers connected with the grooves. I smiled, spotting some of my friends from Samba Church, their moves perfected during the climactic *roda*, or dance circle, that ended each week's class (see Preface).

I peered at my watch and felt a pang of worry, remembering the packed day of errands that I had mapped out that morning. But I soon felt this sense of urgency dissipate amid the intricate, polyrhythmic loops. From the edge of the circle, I started to clap along on the 3–2 clave. "The hand and the voice and the body," writes the poet and cultural critic Hanif Abdurraqib, "the sweetest of instruments. The instruments from which all other instruments are born."[5]

After what felt like five minutes, but was probably twice that, I managed to remove myself from the circle and start my walk—"clockwise," as always—around the water. As I set out on the path, I found myself walking, nodding, even thinking in time with the beat. The sound of the drums began to waver in and out as I moved through a changing environment of music, chatter, traffic, and trees. Oddly, though, when I arrived at the amphitheater at the far end of the trail, the beat seemed to crescendo. Almost a mile from the drum circle, the high-pitched tones had waned, but the low-pitched rumble of the bass rolled across the water, reaching my body like soft thunder.[6]

If Lake Merritt is often called the "heart" of Oakland, then here was its potent and contested pulse. Permeating the air, the rhythm produced an unseen but inescapable sense of Black cultural resonance.[7] Soaring across the water—with no perceptible source, and no clear limit—the sound of the drum was like the telltale heart that refused to forget the city's Afro-Diasporic ancestors.[8] No wonder it incited so much disquiet about acts of silencing and suppression.

The amphitheater at the southern end of the Lake was no stranger to these struggles. In September 2015, on the night of a total lunar eclipse, members of SambaFunk! (SF!)—the cultural group that ran Samba Church—gathered to celebrate this cosmic event and the upcoming birthday of artistic director (and ardent Libra) "King" Theo Aytchan

Williams.[9] Formed in 2009, SF! often brought its mix of Afro-Brazilian samba and Oakland funk to local parks, protests, and public events. So, on the night of the eclipse, a group of "Funkquarians"—most, but not all, Black and Latine—packed up their percussion and struck out, like the rest of the region's astrological enthusiasts, for the Lake. Once they reached the amphitheater, they circled up and began to drum the celestial energy of the "Blood Moon" down to the earthly plane.

For the drummers, time dissolved amid this ritual of rhythm and repetition. But for the neighbors, the loops only seemed to reinforce the need for control. At 9 p.m., residents of 1200 Lakeshore Avenue, a nearby apartment tower, started to plead with the Oakland Police Department (OPD) for relief. Rising like a citadel above the flatlands, or "flats," of this low-rise city, 1200 Lakeshore is a local landmark. In the 1970s, Huey Newton—who once made it his mission to recruit working-class "brothers on the block" as rank-and-file revolutionaries for the Black Panthers (see ch. 2)—took up residence in the penthouse. Stepping onto the wraparound belvedere, he could gaze down at the Alameda County courthouse, where he had been jailed and tried three times between 1967 and 1971 on charges of killing the OPD officer John Frey. (Newton's conviction was eventually overturned. Frey, on the other hand, was a notorious antagonist among Black Oaklanders: a dangerous cop, even by OPD standards.[10])

During the prosecution, which carried the potential of capital punishment, the posh apartments of 1200 Lakeshore echoed with cries of "Free Huey!" and "Off the Pigs!" But on the night of the Blood Moon, the call went out not to "off" the police so much as unleash them. "Somebody's got to come over and shut [the drumming] down," fumed one resident to 911. "It's impossible to sleep." According to the caller, the music was now intermingled with the sound of someone "screaming" at the musicians. "We're to the point where we want to go [protest], too," he said. "But it's Oakland, you know, and everybody here's got a gun." Given news of the confrontation, if not the racially coded reference to violence, the dispatcher elevated the incident to a "disturbance" and sped officers to the scene.[11]

Indeed, as the Blood Moon rose, a resident named Sean McDonald stormed out of his apartment at 1200 Lakeshore to lay down the law among the drummers. At first, he demanded to see a permit for their gathering. When they ignored his request (no one had a permit to be at the amphitheater that night), he attempted to silence them by snatching King Theo's drumsticks. Once the other musicians swooped in to defuse the situation, McDonald, who is White, called the police to report he had been "attacked." "Do you need an ambulance, sir?" asked dispatch. "I don't need an ambulance," he replied. "I need police response, and preferably more than one unit. There's like ten people down there, and they're aggressive and violent . . . when all I did was tell them to stop banging on their drums."[12] Soon, a dozen officers arrived on the scene. Based on McDonald's account, they cited King Theo and two other *bateristas*—all three of them Black, despite the diversity of the group—for battery.[13]

Once word of the incident got around, Black Oaklanders and their allies—mobilized by the Black Lives Matter Movement, which got its start in the city in 2013—condemned McDonald and the OPD for sonic and racial profiling.[14] Now against the ropes, McDonald insisted that his actions were not a reflection of White privilege or anti-Black policing. Instead, he saw the issue in terms of a race-neutral difference in values—a conflict between neighborliness and nuisance, decency and disrespect. "This is about being a good neighbor, and nothing more," he deflected. "I promise that my lifestyle will never negatively impact that of my neighbors or community."[15] (Apparently, this vow didn't apply to the drummers. For McDonald, it seemed, calling the cops on musicians of color didn't violate so much as restore the norms of civility and care.)

But the Funkquarians refused to act as though all rights are "civil." Holding a drum circle outside of City Hall, they disrupted the solemn rites of government to call attention to the ties between biased parts of the municipal code and racist policing. At a city council meeting later that week, Paul Cobb—the long-standing civil rights activist and now publisher of the *Oakland Post*, an African American newspaper—connected the incident at the Lake to noise complaints made against a Baptist church in his native West Oakland. Both, argued Cobb, were an attack on the rights of Black residents to make what he called, in the Christian tradition, a "joyful noise." "When we're talking about Black lives," he said, "it's good to remember that Black noise matters, too."[16]

In response to this outcry, Oakland's Parks and Recreation Advisory Commission (PRAC) held a series of meetings to air issues about music at Lake Merritt. At one that I attended in September 2016, SF! members called for the City to pass a law that recognized a "right to drum." But it turned out that the language of "rights" was a double-edged sword. "They say that drumming is a 'right,'" replied an older White man, his tone somewhere between skepticism and scorn. "But it's not my right to go in front of your house . . . and go [*boom, boom, boom*]!" he said, pounding his fist on the lectern. "That's all we hear up on the hill for eight hours straight!" This, he explained, was a curse of topography, as the hills that surrounded Lake Merritt created a "natural amphitheater." "The acoustics are such that you can walk two blocks one way and not even hear it. And you can walk five or six blocks the other way, straight up the hill, and it's like it's in your living room."

One resident after another testified to the unsettling movement of sound around the Lake. It wasn't the music that was the problem, they maintained, but rather the surprising ways that it circulated. One resident of 1200 Lakeshore explained that, at their height above the water, he and his neighbors only heard a "limited part of the sound spectrum." It wasn't the "good part," he added, indicating a disdain for the bass frequencies. "I can feel it in my chest. It's like assault and battery." "It has nothing to do with . . . not liking someone's culture," said another resident, parrying charges of racial discrimination. "It's physically an issue of survival." "It's a living hell," agreed her husband. "We're being driven out of our homes."[17] In a curious reversal of privilege, then, the very thing that gave these residents access to unrivaled views and a sense of remove—living in an exclusive apartment tower— now left them defenseless against the depredations of the drum.

But sound, it seemed, wasn't the only thing to warp a linear sense of time and space. Rather, like the ring of the drum that ricocheted across the water, legacies of racial violence and Black cultural repair reverberated in the struggle over Lake Merritt's soundscape. "My drums were taken away," said a Black dancer and steelpanist. Her remarks were met with a knowing round of *mmm hmms*. In fact, in many parts of the Americas, colonists and slave owners prohibited Black and Indigenous people from gathering and drumming to prevent cultural resistance to colonization and, ultimately, rebellion. In this sense, the speaker invoked the experiences of ancestors who lived and died centuries ago. But amid the present debate, it was as if the wounds were her own. "I say 'sorry, not sorry' about my culture if it annoys you," she continued. "It may not be at the frequency of love that you can hear." While McDonald's idea of a "good neighbor" required sonic individualism and separation, she called for an alternative civitas of mixture and mutual exchange—a Black sonic politics. "I challenge you to hear that frequency," she concluded. "Let the drums, singing, clapping, dancing, and movement fill your spirit—fill your soul—so that you can connect with your neighbors."[18]

SOUND AND POLITICS

Listen for a moment. What do you hear? The roar of cars, trains, or machines. The rippling of leaves in the trees. A siren. A cicada. The sound of pop music or reggaeton or rap. Voices. Loud ones. Soft ones. Ones you understand. Ones you don't. Cheering. Chanting. Silence.

Who are these people? What are they up to? What sort of environment is this? You probably began to imagine answers, involuntarily, before I even asked. Sound, it would seem, promises to tell you something—to reveal some important truth—about the space and people around you.

What do you feel? Excitement or irritation? Intimacy or estrangement? Do you belong here? Do they? The answers likely depend on who you are and how you have been taught to listen. These impressions might seem immediate and personal. But in fact, they resound with entrenched ideas that have been produced, historically and culturally, to serve or subvert the prevailing social order. How you hear, in other words, doesn't just *reflect* social categories and relations. It *reifies* them. Listening, writes the musicologist Nina Sun Eidsheim, "actively produces meaning." It is thus a "political act."[19]

The idea that sound is political might remind you of the connection between music and social movements. It might summon a roster of activist musicians like Harry Belafonte, Nina Simone, Bob Marley, and Pete Seeger, or call to mind the lyrics of famous protest anthems—songs that openly address issues of power and inequality—from "Give Peace a Chance" (1969) by the Plastic Ono Band to "Fight the Power" (1989) by Public Enemy.[20] To be sure, these intersections of music and politics are important—and well documented.[21] But *On Loop* invites us to listen for more than the intentional aims and explicit messages of musical recordings and performances—what the ethnomusicologist Matt Sakakeeny calls music as a "political text."[22] Instead, it urges us to attune to an expanded field of relations between sound and power, or what scholars call "sonic politics." Mixing ideas from Black studies, urban studies, and sound studies, *On Loop* starts from the belief that struggles over race and space in cities like Oakland are shaped by the cultural meanings, affective impacts, and institutional responses to a range of sounds. This might include the lyrics or symbolic parts of music. But as revealed in the case of SambaFunk!, it also often extends to the nonrepresentational aspects of sound—such as tone, volume, repetition, and reverberation—which are the locus of conflict and regulation.

Indeed, the political nature of listening is most apparent in the appraisal of "noise." While its meaning might seem evident, there is no standard or scientific definition of noise. Rather, according to the sound studies scholar Lilian Radovac, it denotes the "final verdict in a process of aesthetic judgment that is always and necessarily social."[23] The City of Oakland's own Noise Element—the part of the General Plan dedicated to governing the sonic environment—defines noise as "unwanted sound."[24] A soundwave, in this sense, is politically neutral. It comes into the world innocent, free of moral or legal judgment. It's only once it crosses over a line from appealing—or, at least, acceptable—to disturbing to a particular person that it becomes registered and regulated as "noise." But as witnessed in the debate over drumming at Lake Merritt, one person's pain is another's pleasure. Despite repeated attempts to create a precise, often numerical, measure to define this limit, there is no impartial means to separate the "good" sounds from the "bad." Instead, in the absence of a universal norm, the definition of noise tends to be determined by discriminatory ideas about race, class, gender, and other forms of social difference.

According to the sound studies scholar Jennifer Lynn Stoever, in the United States, the meaning of noise is inseparable from the racist association of Whiteness with reason and Blackness with unruliness. In other words, the conceptual divide between sound / noise has long been constructed in tandem with other racialized dichotomies— quiet / loud, proper / improper, order / disorder—that lend an acoustic quality to what she calls the "sonic color line."[25] The musicologist Matthew Morrison attributes the sonic character of America's racial order to the nineteenth-century minstrel show. The visual tropes of "blackface," like skin color, clothes, and gait, are all well known. But White minstrel artists—working-class immigrants, mostly Irish, who corked their skin to perform caricatures of African Americans—also mimicked Black music and speech. This created a "sonic complement" to blackface, which Morrison calls "Blacksound." Blacksound, as a set of racist scripts, "served as an aesthetic basis for the civic enactment, performance, and formation of race and its hierarchies."[26] "The sonic color line," agrees Stoever, "enabl[es] us to hear race as well as see it."[27] So, if you thought that you heard "Black music" or "White voices" a minute ago, it might be tempting to think that people from different races make different sounds. But it's actually this automatic and unconscious act of categorization that reinforces "race" as a cultural construct in the first place.[28]

This isn't to say that there aren't real and meaningful differences in oral, musical, and sound cultures across communities. To the contrary, ethnic and geographic distinctions have given rise to different instruments, tones, textures, and timbres that, in America, have taken on a racial cast (or caste).[29] Captured and transported across the Atlantic, for instance, enslaved people carried their native performance practices from Central and West Africa. In the Americas, colonizers used violence to maintain reading and writing as a privilege of Whiteness. So, enslaved people relied upon their music and voices to preserve their cultures and cosmologies, communicate across linguistic groups, and orchestrate rebellion. According to the Black studies scholar Alexander Weheliye, music and orality thus became the "two main cultural techniques in African America."[30] Pragmatism aside, sound cultures also became important sources of what the cultural studies scholar Paul Gilroy calls "individual self-fashioning and communal liberation" around the Black Atlantic.[31] In this sense, the specific roots and routes of Afro-Diasporic communities mean that there are a range of distinctive, but diverse, Black sounds, even as they are caricatured, captured, and commodified through Morrison's "Blacksound." These sounds continue to reverberate as sources of cultural survival and resistance in the sonic practices that animate cities like Oakland. So, on the night of the eclipse, SambaFunk!—whose sound reflects a mix of dance music from Brazil and the United States, two distant parts of the African Diaspora, reunited in Oakland—infused Lake Merritt with Black modes of participation, celebration, and ceremony.

Importantly, the political impact of music—in particular, dance music—exceeds its semantic content. The liberatory drive of Black dance music can be recognized in the anti-oppressive lyrics of genres like 1960s "message music" and 1970s roots reggae. But according to the American studies scholar Gayle Wald, music is a "medium not only of meaning but also of *feeling.*"[32] This, writes Julian Henriques of Jamaica's reggae sound system, is because sound can't exist apart from the matter—the air, water, solids, and other "sonic bodies"—through which it propagates. In Jamaican "bass culture," he continues, pleasure is experienced through immersion in high amplitude, low frequency sounds that literally "touch" the bodies of dancers. In this context, "the audible becomes haptic and the intangible tangible."[33] In fact, at a microscopic level, soundwaves produce a somatic sensation of pressure and vibration that—when transmitted in an open space—can integrate people into a vast web of interconnection. At Lake Merritt, for instance, when a drummer strikes the surface of a *djembe* or *repinique*, the rattling of the skin disturbs the air molecules around the drum, sending invisible waves soaring across the water. In time, these waves crash into individual bodies—drawing people, for better or worse, into a field of collective occurrence. "Bodies resonate together in space through vibrations," writes Wald.[34]

The sensation of being touched by musical sounds can be positive, reparative, empowering. Building upon the work of Sylvia Wynter, the geographer Katherine McKittrick writes that "black waveforms"—"the beats, rhythms, acoustics, notational moods, and frequencies that undergird black music—affirm . . . modes of being human that refuse anti-blackness."[35] In other words, the energetic waves produced by Black dance music, like the beat of the *bateria*, can generate a feeling of connection between musicians, dancers, and environments—a sense of grooving together in unity and community—that animates people and motivates them to act in concert. "Music can't topple regimes, break chains, or stop bullets," admits the popular music scholar Josh Kun. "But it can keep us alive." "Music gives us the feelings we need to get where we want to go."[36]

At the same time, the experience of being impacted by soundwaves can inspire negative and repressive reactions. The virtue of sound, then, is also its vice. The very same attribute that can create connections—a sound's capacity to cross social, spatial, and corporeal boundaries, to get "under our skin"—can arouse campaigns to reinforce separation. In American cities, the sense of foreign sounds as a noxious invasion or nuisance—a form of "assault and battery," for a resident of 1200 Lakeshore—is fortified by the dominant logic of private property. This system divides space into separate units for the exclusive control of individual owners—and, to a certain extent, tenants—who are entitled to protection from unwanted intrusions. While this set of rules is rooted in the regulation of private property, it has come to extend to public space, too, where people are expected to act in ways that minimize their impact on the people around them. In fact, one of the primary functions of local government is to control these interactions in a manner that maintains the sovereignty of private property and personhood. So, when Sean McDonald commanded the drummers to present a permit, called the police, and defended his actions as those of a "good neighbor," he was reiterating this system of deep-rooted cultural and political norms. In the Conclusion, I describe these norms as constitutive of White sonic politics.

While our perception of sound is contoured by the "sonic color line," it's important to note that people's attitudes toward specific sounds can't be presumed based upon their racial identities. Instead, according to Matt Sakakeeny, people tend to experience sounds in ways that depend, idiosyncratically, upon their "orientation" in any particular moment.[37] In the example discussed earlier, I was pleased to find that the familiar sound of the drums removed me from the routine of my ramble around the Lake—drawing me into the circle, setting the pace of my step, and stirring thoughts and memories. But for the tenants of 1200 Lakeshore, including several Black residents who spoke up at the PRAC meeting, those same sounds might have disturbed their attempts to work, watch a movie, or take a nap.

Still, race and racism become central to the regulation of urban soundscapes when it comes to the ways that people and institutions tend to respond to this sense of disturbance. When sounds trespass upon the constructs of private property and personhood—which, in America, are rooted in the processes of colonial conquest and chattel slavery—people with privilege call upon the state to restore the norms of separation and control that are core to the geography of property.[38] (After all, regardless of who was upset about the drum circle, it was McDonald who "took matters into his own hands" and called the police.) Moreover, in cities like Oakland, which are ordered by hierarchies of race and class, these actions give rise to crusades to crack down on sounds, people, and spaces that are perceived as "out of control" or "out of place" in ways that reproduce those very same inequalities.[39] Sound can thus incite a relay of reactions—a series of percussions and repercussions across scales—that connect intimate sensations to institutional campaigns. Just as the personal is political, when it comes to sonic politics, the molecular is municipal.

ON LOOP(S)

By attuning to the role of sonic politics in contouring the city's cultural landscapes, *On Loop* provides an account of the last century of struggle over Black freedom in Oakland. It thus describes an arc of tremendous social, cultural, economic, and geographical change. But this often isn't a story of total transformation so much as what the writer Amiri Baraka (then Leroi Jones), in his work on African American music, famously called the "changing same."[40] Indeed, repetition is a recurring feature of the city's cultural and political terrain. The stories contained within these pages, like the struggle over drumming at Lake Merritt, reveal the ways that mainstream anxieties about and attempts to control Black sounds loop from one period to the next. In this sense, conflicts over the urban soundscape—and Black sonic politics, in particular—are never new. Instead, they are imbued with meanings, memories, and control measures that reverberate across four centuries of anti-Black oppression and resistance. "Sounds," writes Jennifer Lynn Stoever, "have histories. If we listen, we can hear resonances with other times and places."[41] But the pages to come also point to the ways that Black residents repeatedly revive Afro-Diasporic cultural practices—including, importantly, different forms of looping, from grooving to funk music to spinning donuts in their cars—that reclaim space for freedom and joy. Paradoxically, then, repetition is central to both Black suffering and survival in Oakland. *On Loop* is a nod to the circular rhythms that animate not only the city's Black cultural practices but also ongoing struggles over its Black geographies.

My interest in repetition is inspired, in part, by ideas about looping time from Black feminism. According to Saidiya Hartman, for instance, the present moment of the African Diaspora is freighted with the "afterlife of slavery."[42] Building upon Hartman's work, the performance studies scholars Soyica Diggs Colbert, Douglas Jones, and Shane Vogel note that the notion of "afterlife" allows us to identify "continuities that may be obscured by the logic of progress, revolution, rupture, or reform."[43] And this nonlinear sense of time may be more suited to understanding Black lives and landscapes that, according to Katherine McKittrick, are "not comfortably situated in the past, present, or future."[44] Importantly, this braided experience of time isn't simply a burden of Blackness. It's also a means to disrupt what the urban studies scholar Anna Livia Brand describes as an overly prescriptive model of "continuous dispossession and displacement." When "time is collapsed," she writes, "resistant imaginaries are folded into the present, threading a new future of possibilities."[45]

This act of remixing the past in order to surpass its imperial imprint on the present is also a hallmark of Black dance music and DJ culture. In fact, Black cultural critics have long considered the play of repetition one of the traits that distinguishes African and Afro-Diasporic musics— if not expressive cultures, as a whole—from the canon of European "art music."[46] According to James Snead, in the wake of the Enlightenment, European culture became infatuated with change over time. Musically, this worldview was reflected in the organization of sound around the progression of melody and harmony into a final, pleasing end. But it also underwrote self-serving ideas about cultural "progress," or supremacy, and capitalist growth. From this point of view, change was the precondition of culture as such. To repeat, by contrast, was to be unproductive. It was to be stuck, stagnant, or "backward." Or simply, in the writing of the German philosopher G. W. F. Hegel, African.[47] In response to the racist dismissal of repetition as a cultural and cosmological value, Snead notes that the loop is not a lack. Instead, African and Afro-Diasporic cultures—in fact, many of the folk cultures occupied by European empires, including European ones—intentionally embrace a cyclical concept of time, nature, and the cosmos, in which meaning is made through recurrence and return rather than incessant change. And for Snead, this aesthetic strategy reaches its apex in Black performance—"rhythm in music and dance and language."[48]

Like Snead, scholars have long noted that, in contrast to the emphasis on harmonic progression and resolution in European art music, the power of African and Afro-Diasporic music lies, primarily, in the dense and complex arrangement of rhythm. While the former accentuates the movement of linear time toward its telos, or end, the latter works to make the experience of linear time dissolve into a more expansive present. Still, explains Snead, repetition doesn't *preclude* change in Black culture; it's simply the *prerequisite* for change. Building a continuous groove, performers create the backdrop against which virtuosic variations and improvisations in rhythm, melody, and timbre can stand out.[49] Repetition, agrees the sound studies scholar Julian Henriques— as, for instance, in reggae "versioning" and dub remixing—is the "linchpin of progress, rather than its antithesis."[50] Indeed, the "peculiarity of black music," writes Snead, is that it "draws attention to its own repetition" as a medium of meaning, movement, and pleasure.[51]

Woven into the cultural practices of Black communities throughout the Americas, these African aesthetics began to reach mainstream audiences in the nineteenth and twentieth centuries through the spread of styles like mambo and jazz, which combined elements of European, African, and Indigenous musics. Starting in the 1960s and '70s, however, the importance of repetition became even more pronounced among a series of groove-based, and later electronic and sample-based, dance musics, which went on to reshape global popular culture and consciousness. In Jamaica, for instance, which won its independence from Britain in 1962, musicians, music producers, and DJs created the emancipatory culture of the reggae sound system. Like the funk music that would take root in Oakland (see ch. 2), but slower, reggae turned up the volume—literally—on the entrancing groove of drum and bass, keeping postindependence dancers rocking together as if colonial time had dissipated once and for all.

Later, recording engineers and producers like King Tubby and Lee "Scratch" Perry revolutionized reggae through the advent of the dub remix. Using the mixing studio as an instrument of its own, these producers stripped popular songs down to their core *riddims* and then rebuilt them out of fragmented snippets of melodies and vocals, which, processed through echo and reverb machines, seemed to rocket to the outer edge of sonic space. Dub thus deepened reggae's immanent potential for dance, trance, and transcendence. Designed for public sound systems, where DJs created extended dance experiences, dub contributed to what Michael Veal calls the "revolution of the *songscape* over the *song.*"[52] Whether in terms of the use of echo or the "wheelback," in which DJs rewound a popular record back to the start, the reverberating *riddim* of dub music amplified a looping sense of time. "In the moment of the wheelback," writes the DJ and music scholar Mark Campbell, "time is made to stand still . . . The future is then composed from a repetition of a past."[53]

As Veal notes, this use of new sonic technologies to warp the temporal structure of popular music—turning the singular song into a continuous songscape that could motivate extended and ecstatic experiences among dancers—was repeated in 1970s New York City by the DJs who developed the performance practices that would become hip-hop and disco. In order to attract and impress other teens at parties in the South Bronx, the Jamaican American DJ Kool Herc took the most percussive parts of uptempo soul, funk, and rock tunes—called "the breaks"—and cut back and forth between two copies of the same record to loop these sections on repeat. For Herc, this technique— which he called the "merry-go-round"—was meant to satisfy dancers, who "always wanted to hear breaks after breaks after breaks after breaks."[54] "Forget melody, chorus, songs," writes the hip-hop historian Jeff Chang, noting the rupture with Euro-American norms, "[the break] was all about the groove, building it, keeping it going."[55]

Of course, hip-hop didn't invent the groove. Instead, it mined it, like a raw mineral, and crystallized it within the mix. In this sense, it was predicated on the fact that artists like James Brown, Earth, Wind, and Fire, and the Fania All Stars had already introduced the cyclical, polyrhythmic sensibilities of African and Afro-Latin musics into the soundscapes of American cities.[56] The hip-hop loop, writes the ethnomusicologist Joseph Schloss, thus mixed a "traditional African American approach to composition," one rooted in repetition, "with new technology to create a radically new way of making music." "As breaks are torn from their original context and repeated, they are reconceived . . . as circular, even if their original harmonic or melodic purposes were linear . . . Theme and variation, rather than progressive development, becomes the order of the day."[57] "The loop," agrees the performance studies scholar Patricia Herrera, "manipulates musical temporality into a different flow." It isn't a "simple mode of repetition." Instead, it produces a "new compositional logic that disrupts the linearity of the past with indefinite movement."[58] In other words, sampling and looping allowed hip-hop DJs and producers to take the past—interred, inertly, in the wax of an old record—and revive it as a resource for futuristic, even revolutionary, movements. More immediately, hip-hop created moments of catharsis and play, providing young people of color an escape from the devastation of the South Bronx and denouement of Black and Brown Power. It turned the present from a time of precarity into one of reprieve. "The break," muses the musicologist Mark Katz, "was, indeed, a break."[59]

At the same time, in the discos and underground dance clubs of Manhattan, another group of DJs used a similar mix of songs, technologies, and techniques to create spaces of social and sexual freedom. Channeling the energies of the Civil Rights and Gay Liberation Movements, not to mention psychedelic drug culture, selectors sought ways to elevate and transport dancers through wave after wave of collective euphoria. According to the cultural historian Tim Lawrence, Downtown DJs like Francis Grasso and Nicky Siano were experimenting with techniques to extend the peaks of a hot record around the same time that Herc mastered the "merry-go-round" in the Bronx.[60] They also developed the art of the "nonstop disco mix," or the use of two turntables, slip cueing, and a crossfader to create a seamless stream of songs that, in the words of DJ and cultural studies scholar Oliver Wang, "[build] the floor toward . . . moments of climax and collective effervescence."[61] Record producers like Walter Gibbons and Tom Moulton, in turn, promoted the use of the 12-inch single to prolong the vocal vamps and rhythmic grooves of popular records through expansive remixes that were expressly designed for the disco dance floor.[62]

Veal describes these different strategies of elongation—in essence, of looping—as the "Africanization" of dance music.[63] In fact, while many of the earliest disco DJs were White, their penchant for soul, funk, and other groove-based musics from around the Black Atlantic, and their investment in the ritual power of rhythm, revealed a deep debt to Afro-Diasporic sound cultures. Moreover, many of the people who attended these parties—spreading the practice of expressive dance and setting the sonic expectations for the DJs—were queer people of color. These Black and queer aesthetics were further developed by DJs like Larry Levan and Frankie Knuckles, who mixed underground dance cultures from New York and the Midwest when he became the resident DJ at the Warehouse in Chicago in 1977. In the process, they established the genetic code for what came to be called house music and its prolific descendants across the world of electronic dance music (EDM).[64]

Since the middle of the twentieth century, then, the loop has gone global. Rooted in the rhythms and rituals of Central and West Africa, it has become vital to the aesthetics—the mixing and production techniques, sonic textures, and listening pleasures—of an evolving lineage of Black dance music. In the process, it has instilled a nonlinear orientation toward time, which provides occasions for rupture and reparation, in everyday cultural practices across the African Diaspora. To be sure, not all loops are liberatory. The stories in *On Loop* are replete with forms of repetition—intergenerational poverty, repressive policing, incarceration—that have trapped Black Oaklanders in a state of recurring loss. Repetition, in this sense, can be violent. But at the same time, it serves as a sonic, temporal, and even spiritual resource that is routinely called upon to release Black residents—however momentarily—from the strictures of structural oppression. Returning to Snead, the use of looping in Black dance music isn't a *failure* of creativity. It is an *intentional creative strategy* that actively contests the anti-Black racism of Western musical and historical time. "The beat," James Baldwin once wrote, "recognizes, changes, and conquers time." The loop, in other words, affords a refuge from the hostility of history so that "time becomes a friend."[65]

THE MIX

These ideas—which recur, on loop, in the pages to come—provide us with a new, more acoustically attuned perspective on the ongoing Black freedom struggle in Oakland. Chapter 1 starts with World War II, when the mass migration of African American workers to Oakland from the U.S. South and Southwest was met with new forms of cultural and residential segregation. The moral panic over migration often focused on opposition to the cultural practices of Black Southerners, causing regulators to crack down on working-class entertainment venues and commercial districts. This tension between movement and containment, freedom and a familiar feeling of disenfranchisement, gave rise to a melancholic style of popular music that local record producer Bob Geddins billed the "Oakland Blues."

The blues provided Black migrants with a critical source of economic opportunity, communal identity, and pleasure. But as demonstrated in chapter 2, in the 1960s and '70s, the next generation of migrant youth rebelled against the social, spatial, and sonic constraints of West Coast Jim Crow. Fed up with the conventions of the blues, and the conditions that gave rise to it, young people from around the Black Bay Area created a repertoire of "social movements," including new styles of music (funk) and dance (boogaloo), which allowed them to embody personal freedom and communal connection. Whether involved with the Black Panthers, or indirectly aligned with the spirit of Black Power, these artists used the percussive power and transportive grooves of funk culture—the "black waveforms" of musicians like James Brown,

Sly Stone, and Larry Graham—to propel the era's political mobilization. Converting revolutionary ideals into an exciting and accessible part of everyday life, they enabled young Black people to embody the enthusiasm and togetherness that motivated social movement organizing.

As revealed in chapter 3, however, in the 1970s and '80s, the social movements that swept across Oakland during the Black Power Era crashed into the strategies of governance and development promoted by a rising cohort of Black political elites. Tragically, Oakland became a "Chocolate City," one whose population and politics were predominantly Black, at the precise moment that it became racked by disinvestment, unemployment, and crack cocaine. Amid rising pressure from a new social movement of homeowners of color, the administrations of mayors Lionel Wilson and Elihu Harris revamped the city's regulations and police practices to crusade against "crime and grime." By reorienting policing around cultural comportment and style—including sonic practices—rather than race, the resulting "war on nuisance" advanced the turn toward "colorblind" forms of discrimination typical of the post–Civil Rights Era. In other words, it continued to target young Black Oaklanders, and especially men, but now under color of law.

The next several chapters trace the sonic politics of Oakland's war on nuisance into three distinct but related cultural landscapes: rap concerts, renegade car parties called "sideshows," and downtown nightclubs. Chapter 4 demonstrates that, by creating a conceptual tie between the sound of rap music—its looping, high-volume, bass-heavy beats—and "crime and grime," regulators and venue owners rolled out new restrictions that culminated in a de facto ban on rap concerts. This crackdown, which impacted everything from music venues to boomboxes, disrupted opportunities for local artists to develop their microphone skills and market at the very moment that rap came to dominate American popular music. After serving, in the late 1980s and '90s, as an important site for the mainstream success of hip-hop through the funk-driven sounds of MC Hammer, Digital Underground, and Tupac, the city was forced to retreat into a more provincial scene. This wasn't just because its music-industry infrastructure was lacking, as was the case for the Oakland Blues, but also because of repressive public policies. Building upon the work of hip-hop scholar Tricia Rose, this chapter shows that the cultural criticism of rap music as "Black noise" intersected with a governmental war on nuisance in urban neighborhoods in ways that exposed young Black Oaklanders, and particularly men, to broken-windows policing.

Next, chapter 5 explores how this crackdown on hip-hop artists and audiences inspired the increasing rowdiness of the sounds and sideshows that came to characterize East Bay rap. In the late 1990s and 2000s, the Hyphy Movement—led by rappers like E-40, Mac Dre, and Mistah F. A. B.—turned unconstrained and uncontrollable fun into a sonic aesthetic and a style of embodiment. These practices—like moshing, stunt driving, and pumping bass-driven slaps from the trunk of a scraper—ratcheted up the tension between young men of color and the police. Just as young people responded to their experiences of repression with more rebellious forms of expression, the authorities reacted with more intense regulations, causing the cycle to repeat. Under Mayor Jerry Brown's crusade against sideshows, the City continued to police young men of color over their cultural practices, and particularly their sounds. This further confined members of the East Bay rap scene to the margins and prevented their music from busting out of its regional bubble.

Chapter 6 reveals that, after Oakland's 1990 "rap ban," local hip-hop artists, promoters, venue owners, and officials coalesced around the idea that more intense security measures were the way to manage, rather than suppress, rap concerts and dance parties that attracted Black people and other young people of color. So, in the 1990s and 2000s, at the same time that the City sought to turn disinvested parts of Downtown Oakland into an Arts and Entertainment District, it adopted new regulations and police practices that were meant to control an apparent scourge of nuisance and crime in and around Black-owned nightclubs. Given the entrenched association of rap artists and audiences with recklessness and noise, in particular during the hyphy era, these security measures—which were supposedly "race-neutral"—installed racist ideas about contemporary Black dance music into the day-to-day mechanisms of governance. After the moratorium, then, Oakland's strategy of an outright ban evolved into more subtle, but no less discriminatory, practices that made it prohibitive for Black club owners to book Black dance music. In the 2010s, as investment in nightlife flooded Downtown Oakland, fueling the narrative of a long-awaited "renaissance," almost all of these venue owners were pushed out. This process of displacement might seem like a familiar form of gentrification. But this chapter reveals that—even more than economic changes—the dispossession of Black nightlife was driven by the mundane and bureaucratic regulation of Black crowds and sounds.

Finally, chapter 7 shows how an orientation to looping rather than linear histories opens up a perspective on contemporary struggles for rights to the city that is more attuned to both the recursive nature of anti-Blackness and the continuous revival of Black freedom practices in Oakland. The chapter starts in 2018, when a White woman called the police on two Black men for barbecuing at Lake Merritt. Media reports on what came to be called "BBQ Becky" interpreted the incident as the epitome of gentrification, which, in the decade since the foreclosure crisis, had reached a fever pitch. But longtime Black Oaklanders knew that this was nothing new. Following the nonlinear routes of their memories, this chapter traces the echoes and connections across three periods of struggle over Black spacemaking at Lake Merritt: picnics at Lakeside Park in the 1960s and '70s, cruising on Lakeshore Avenue in the 1980s, and Festival at the Lake in the 1990s. This looping account reveals that both BBQ Becky's actions and people's responses resuscitated ideas about Black "noise" and conduct, regulations, and forms of resistance that became entrenched through repetitive conflicts over Black sonic presence at Lake Merritt decades before the onset of gentrification.

The Conclusion then reveals that, as in previous decades, residents continue to draw upon a deep reservoir of musical and movement practices—like mixing amplified sounds in open air and circulating around the shore—to reclaim the Lake as a Black terrain. Rather than try to reimpose a sense of separation and sovereignty, which are characteristic of the White sonic politics of property, these practices tend to embrace the relational and immersive qualities of sound. They propagate a Black "frequency of love" that is nondualistic, nonhierarchical, and nonlinear.

PARTIAL PERSPECTIVES

As someone who picked up a book about Black sonic politics in Oakland, you have a right to understand my relationship to these cultural practices, experiences, and spaces. In other words, you have a right to consider how I came to know what I know. Knowledge is necessarily partial in the double sense of being both personal and incomplete. So, in this final section, my intention is to give you a sense of my deep investment and involvement in this research and, by the same token, my inevitable limits as an author.

I grew up far from Oakland, both culturally and geographically, in a college town in Western Massachusetts. Like many White millennials, my introduction to Black sound cultures was mediated through the marketing schemes of the popular music industry, which pushed rap, R&B, dancehall, and other genres of Black and Afro-Latin dance music to me and my suburban peers.[66] By middle school, I was hooked. The pages of my massive CD binder were meticulously organized by record label, artist, and release date. I filled it with the albums of luxury rappers—by the 2000s, the section devoted to the roster of Roc-A-Fella

Records was particularly extensive—and more politicized artists like Talib Kweli and A Tribe Called Quest. Whenever these artists performed at local campuses, like Smith College or UMass, I would scrounge up my savings, camp out for a ticket, and crowd near the stage to soak in the energy of their sound. (On reflection, my first encounter with Northern California rap was when Blackalicious, a core member of Oakland's Quannum Projects, opened for Jurassic 5 at Amherst College in 2002.) At the time, my relationship to hip-hop culture was encouraged by the exploitative tactics of an entertainment industry that saw, in White America's cultural obsession with Blackness, a market for records that were at times raw, at times lavish, but almost always made me move. Still, however engineered, my early affinity for hip-hop ingrained in me a rhythmic sensibility, orientation toward samples and loops, spirited relationship to movement, and interest in words for their meter and cadence, not just their meaning, that continue to animate these pages.

In college, my affection for the sounds and ethics of Black dance music expanded from hip-hop to soulful house music thanks to Afro-Sonic, a weekly party at the Black Repertory Company in Providence, Rhode Island. On Thursday nights, I would trek down Westminster Street through the snow and the slush, the winter air blustering off of the Providence River, and take my place amid the steamy, often spacious dance floor for the ensuing spiritual workout. Immersed in the polyrhythmic grooves provided by the resident DJs Mike Delick and BlackDove, and a revolving ensemble of West African master drummers, I would emerge, after midnight, renewed from this purification ritual of sound and sweat. (Sodden, the walk back up College Hill was even more bitter than the one down. But my mood couldn't be better.)

Graduating with a degree in urban studies, I moved to Oakland in 2009, lured by a romantic relationship and the sense that many of the cultural and political movements that stirred my soul seemed to start in the San Francisco Bay Area. I arrived at a ripe moment, a sort of inflection point, in the city's nightlife. Decades of disinvestment and the over-the-top regulation of nightclubs, especially those owned by or catering to Black residents, had decimated Downtown Oakland's once-thriving entertainment venues and forced many DJs and dancers into underground spaces (see ch. 6). But starting in the late 2000s, the City of Oakland's long-simmering campaign to redevelop the area began to bear fruit. Downtown saw a sudden rush of investment in a new crop of restaurants and nightclubs, which created a surge of opportunities for DJ crews, who were needed to program an increasing number of party nights. Coming from Providence, I was drawn to thePeople, which started at the Oasis and moved to the New Parish. Eventually curated by DJs Cecil, Cali, and heyLove, and graced by a rotating cast of visiting artists, these events provided a temporary moment of *détente* across divisions of race, class, gender, and age—schisms that grew more intense as the city was riven by the pressure of gentrification and displacement. In the spirit of the original underground discos of New York, thePeople created a Black sonic container—laced with notes of jazz, funk, gospel, hip-hop, and house—in which we, as dancers, could practice an imperfect ethics of kinship that neither denied nor petrified our identities.

In this context, I started to build relationships with local artists and other members of the scene, who introduced me to the city's vibrant Afro-Diasporic dance communities. I became a regular at several studio classes, where I was blessed to study with a series of warm and talented teachers. Downtown Oakland is home to the Malonga Casquelourd Center for the Arts, which houses resident performing arts organizations and visiting instructors. Named for the Congolese drummer, dancer, and choreographer—one of many African artists who moved to Oakland, a mecca of the Black Arts Movement, in the 1970s—the center is a brick-and-mortar embodiment of the city's enduring contributions to African dance in the Diaspora.[67] There, working with King Theo, I joined SambaFunk!, marching at carnaval in San Francisco and Oakland and, for a time, participating in a performance group. I also attended Diaspora Dance with Alicia Langlais (aka the Dance Dragon Slayer), where we partied to Afrobeats, soca, and dancehall. On other nights, I headed down Fourteenth Street to In the Groove Studios, where Rashad Pridgen (aka Soul Nubian) taught Afro-house. At peak, I was sweating through my clothes at two to three classes a week and then going out to nightclubs or day parties on weekends. The laundry was endless.

It was during this time that I started to DJ. While I had dabbled in hip-hop and electronic music production since high school, DJing allowed me to direct my love for dance into new modes of mobilizing community and solidarity through sound, especially funk, disco, and soulful house music. Inspired by parties like thePeople and Sol House, which combined music, dance, visual art, and food to bring people together, I launched an event series called Good Culture with the artist Jasmine Fuego. From 2017 to 2019, Good Culture ran like a cross between a performing arts showcase, which elevated artists of color, and dance party. During this time, I also spun at several of the venues described in the pages to come, like the New Parish, Rock Steady, and Starline Social Club.

But DJing and dance weren't the only things that I studied during this period. In 2012, I started a PhD program in geography at UC Berkeley. Like many graduate students, I spent the first couple of years on campus reading social theory and cycling, anxiously, through a rash of potential research topics. Outside of school, I felt my attachments deepening to people and places within Oakland's dance music and cultural organizing scenes. But at school, where "going out" seemed like more of an unserious distraction than a legitimate course of study, I often felt disconnected from my body, spirit, and community. Eventually, I released this self-doubt and relented to my passion. I decided to take my extracurriculars and make them my curriculum. "Free your *ass*," writes the anthropologist Jafari Allen, reversing the name of the 1970 Funkadelic record, "and your *mind* will follow."[68]

And why not? I realized that much of what I was studying in graduate school—the racial politics of property and policing, production of urban space, and right to the city—flowed through impassioned moments of struggle over Black dance music and soundscapes, like the SambaFunk! incident at the Lake, in ways that truly mattered to the people around me. Amid growing activism against gentrification and police violence, it was as though all of the political feelings of the era— the grief, rage, and refusal—if not the entire tragedy of anti-Black racism in America, telescoped into a noise complaint about a drum circle. That, it seemed, was worth listening to.

I used the time, resources, and access provided by my graduate studies to delve into the questions that emerged from the cultural work that I was connected and committed to. I spent entire weeks at local archives reading up on struggles over now-vanished cultural venues and events, like downtown nightclubs and Festival at the Lake. I conducted public records requests and pored over the reports, emails, and meeting notes that documented the back-and-forth between regulators, venue owners, and event producers. I interviewed over 50 people—including DJs, dancers, public officials, police officers, and club owners—who could offer different vantage points on the history, geography, politics, and *sound* of Black dance music in Oakland. Indeed, to my delight, I listened to music—a lot of it.

So, through my cultural practices as a DJ, dancer, and event producer, and also my sustained research as a graduate student, I developed—over time—a level of intimacy with much of what I discuss in this book. Still, it's important to recognize that my involvement in Oakland's Black cultural production and politics was necessarily fraught with paradox. As a White Jewish man from Western Massachusetts, I was, ineradicably, an outsider—to some, I'm sure, an interloper. On top of that, I arrived at a moment that—as I'll discuss more in chapter 7—was deeply dislocating for Black Oaklanders. The 2000s witnessed intense political and economic shocks, as Mayor Jerry Brown

(1999–2007) discarded the last vestiges of the community development policies from the Civil Rights and Black Power Eras in favor of redevelopment and policing strategies meant to court White artists, entrepreneurs, and "techies" from San Francisco. The decade ended, tragically, with the foreclosure crisis—the mass transfer of wealth from Black and Latine residents, who were displaced in droves, to speculators and newcomers, many of them White.[69]

In this context, my migration to North Oakland, an historically Black neighborhood that had been targeted for foreclosure and antigang policing strategies, was inseparable from a rising wave of gentrification that continues to displace Black residents. And to the extent that nightlife and cultural events attracted me to the city, I was actualizing the aims of local planners and developers, who, since at least the 1980s, sought to entice more affluent, and often White, people to move to Oakland by marketing its Black cultural landscapes.[70] Good intentions and work aside, the simple fact of my presence in the city's Black spaces ran the risk of fueling the processes of dispossession that I critique throughout this book. I tried to counter these harms through redistribution and solidarity. I paid for and promoted artists' classes, performances, and parties. I connected them to gigs and promotional opportunities. I volunteered at their events. Still, I lived for more than a decade in Oakland and Berkeley with the irresolvable tension between structural inequities and a personal ethics of relationship building, love, and repair. Of course, there's only so much that individual care can do in the face of systemic oppression. It would be foolish to believe that love, alone, is the answer. But it seemed to me that to deny or suppress that love, or to not try because of long odds, would be similarly unsound.

The perspective in *On Loop* is shaped by my emplacement in Oakland. It's contoured by my race, class, gender, and geographical location. It reflects my academic training, cultural predilections, and political commitments. It arises from my personal passions and relationships. Coming from one perspective, it inevitably misses many others. Here, it feels important to name a few of those so that you understand what this book is not.

First, the narrative of this book ends prior to the COVID-19 pandemic. This reflects the fact I completed my research and graduated from UC Berkeley in 2019. At that point, I decided to step back from academia to deepen my political work in Oakland. I was serving as an advocate for antidisplacement and housing justice policies when the pandemic—and later, parenthood—turned things upside down. Reeling from these two ruptures, my partner and I moved back to the East Coast in 2022 to regain our footing with the support of family. I remain involved in the Bay Area antidisplacement movement, working on tenants' rights research and campaigns. But my connection to the city's on-the-ground cultural scenes has admittedly waned in recent years.

This is significant because the pandemic had massive impacts on Oakland's cultural spaces and politics. The public health restrictions pushed social, cultural, and economic activities into the streets and parks—in particular, Lake Merritt—which revived familiar struggles over noise, nuisance, and safety, only now in a climate of intense fear and racial reckoning. After a decade when it seemed as though Downtown Oakland had turned the corner from a "ghost town" to a round-the-clock hub of commerce and nightlife, employers sent people home, venues went out of business, and vacancies surged. Officials now worry, as they did in the 1980s and '90s, that the area has sagged back into a state of semi-abandonment, making it feel dangerous and depressing to consumers (see ch. 3). And amid an increase in crime and anxiety—spurred by the precarity of the pandemic—local and state politicians, business owners, and the media have returned to characterizing the city as "out of control," causing the pendulum of public opinion to swing from defunding the police to a resurgent law-and-order mindset. In many ways, it feels like time has been spinning back-ward, reinforcing the need to see struggles over Black freedom in Oakland in terms of loops rather than lines. Readers who want a more detailed account of this most recent period should pick up the geogra-pher Brandi Summers's *Oakland Echoes* (forthcoming).

Second, this book centers on Black / White racial politics. Oakland is a deeply multiracial metropolis. According to the 2020 Census, the population is roughly split between Black, White, Latine, and Asian American / Pacific Islander people. (There's also a lot of overlap among and diversity within each of these categories.) Still, I focus on Black sonic politics for historical, political, and personal reasons. Historically, the mass migration of African Americans around World War II, and their cultural and political impact during the time of Black Power, meant that, by the late twentieth century, Oakland had become one of the nation's most iconic "Chocolate Cities." Even as it becomes more diversified and gentrified, contests over the city's cultural landscapes continue to resonate with the notion of Oakland as a site of Black free-dom and rebellion. Politically, this is especially true regarding the sonic issues at the center of this text. On one side, young people and artists from across communities have gravitated to Oakland's hip-hop, house, and other Black dance music scenes—imbuing the soundscape with Blackness, if not always by Black people. On the other—due, in part, to the racist association of Black culture with crime, deviance, and "noise"—regulators and police officers have acted in a singularly repres-sive way toward sounds and styles that are coded as Black. And person-ally, as I've explained, my practices as a DJ and dancer drew me to parties, classes, and creative collaborations that centered on Black dance music and Afro-Diasporic performance.

While rooted in these realities, this attunement to Black sonic poli-tics means that I inevitably miss a number of other important cultural practices and experiences. To be clear, *On Loop* isn't meant to be a com-prehensive account of sonic politics or social movements in Oakland.

As a result, it doesn't say very much about the presence and politics of the city's other communities of color, especially Latine ones, except insofar as they have become entangled in the struggles described in the pages to come due to their perceived proximity to Blackness. This incomplete point of view runs the risk of further marginalizing Latine people from the city's history, identity, and representational politics. "The memorialization of Oakland as a site of Black protest and aestheticized Black space," writes the geographer Juan Herrera, "has produced historical amnesia about the city's Chicano and Latino mobilizations." While I don't solve that dilemma in this book, I do insist on being honest about the parameters of my "perspectival approach" and challenging what he calls "an analytical desire to produce comprehensive and truthful representations of place."[71] For readers who want to learn more about Latine politics in Oakland, and the Fruitvale District in particular, I strongly recommend that you check out Herrera's *Cartographic Memory* (2022).

Third, this book focuses on the actions and experiences of cisgendered men. Again, this is true for political and personal reasons. Politically, *On Loop* is concerned with aspects of urbanism—the music industry, car culture, public space, property ownership, policing—that have been historically dominated by men. Indeed, the power to shape and control urban space—including, importantly, through its soundscape—has been purposefully maintained as a prerogative of masculinity.[72] This is certainly true when it comes to the cultural practices and scenes that I write about, such as funk music, hyphy rap, and the sideshow. Personally, as a White man who interacted with and relied upon a lot of men of color to complete this research, I think that the perception of our shared identity as cisgendered men often allowed me to build trusting relationships across otherwise meaningful boundaries of race, class, and age. The upshot of this gendered orientation is that the sonic politics of Black women and trans people—their experiences, cultural work, and political visions—are muted in the pages to come. For readers who want to learn more about the politics of relation and care being constructed by Black women in Oakland, often in private or interior spaces, I recommend the geographer Kaily Heitz's *Oakland Is a Vibe* (forthcoming).

And finally, fourth, this book isn't a comprehensive history of Black dance music in Oakland. In fact, it isn't really a work of musical history at all. Instead, given my training in urban studies and geography, it's a story about the looping nature of struggles over Black belonging and freedom in Oakland through the city's cultural landscape. Within this ongoing space of contestation, it argues that Black dance music and everyday sonic practices, while often overlooked, have in fact been integral to efforts to shape and reshape the city. Here's an example of what I mean: Oakland's rap music scene is significant for a range of reasons. But it's relevant for *On Loop* because, amid a crusade to combat disinvestment, it intersected with public anxieties about nuisance and noise in ways that contributed to the popularity of broken-windows policing. For readers who want a more comprehensive overview of local artists—including the underground hip-hop scene—or the troubled relationship between East Bay rap and hip-hop culture at large, I recommend *Rap and Politics* (2020) by the political scientist and DJ Lavar Pope and *That's My Word*, an online resource created by the journalists Eric Arnold, Pendarvis Harshaw, Nastia Voynovskaya, and Gabe Meline for KQED. There are certainly many artists and songs that I "left out" of the pages to come. Not because they were less important, but rather because others were more central to the specific story about the geography of the Black freedom struggle that I wanted to tell. I only hope that their fans will forgive me!

1

OAKLAND BLUES

Migration and Melancholy

Hey, you, you ol' funky Oakland town
How come you such a cold and brutal city?
DAVE ALEXANDER, "Hey, You Old Oakland Town" (1974)[1]

WHITE POWER

Oakland was established in 1852 on land twice stolen, first from Indigenous Ohlone people and then Spanish *rancheros*, fast on the heels of the American invasion of California during the U.S.-Mexico War.[2] Over the next century, White Power—not Black—defined the city's expansion, politics, and public culture. African Americans didn't arrive en masse until the outbreak of World War II, when the Bay Area became what the San Francisco Chamber of Commerce called, with only a bit of bluster, the "greatest shipbuilding center the world has ever seen."[3] Building the nation's naval arsenal required an industrial army unmatched in size. So, recruiters from the Moore Dry Dock in Oakland, Kaiser Shipyards in Richmond, and U.S. War Manpower Commission swept across depressed areas of the country in search of labor. They met their most ardent takers among African

Americans in the South and Southwest, who, given the grinding conditions of economic exploitation and racial violence, were so eager to seek a better life that three-quarters of the Black migrants who moved to the Bay Area at the start of the war did so without encouragement from recruiters.[4] Instead, once word of decent work and a moderated color line made its way to towns like Palestine, Texas and Monroe, Louisiana, Black people packed into cars, busses, and trains and struck out for the West Coast.

Those who took to the rails would get their first apprehensive look at Oakland—a land at once foreign and rife with promise—as the train rumbled into the Southern Pacific station at Seventh Street and Broadway. Here, along the main artery of this budding metropolis, they might peer out the window and marvel at the modest grandeur of the area's hotels, restaurants, and entertainment venues. To the north, along Broadway and Telegraph Avenue, were art deco movie palaces, department stores, and row after row of tidy single-family bungalows, which sprouted along the streetcar lines that radiated, fan-like, across the flats. But Black folks wouldn't be going north. They would be going west.

Once the White passengers descended the steps, and the doors slammed shut, the train would continue to crawl down Seventh Street to West Oakland. Wedged between the city's industrial waterfront and commercial core, the neighborhood was originally developed by prosperous Victorians, who sought a more spacious and pristine environment than San Francisco—the cramped, vice-ridden capitol of the Gold Rush economy—apparently afforded. But its status as a commodious suburb was put to an end in 1869, when the City Fathers convinced the Central Pacific (later bought by the Southern Pacific) to select West Oakland as the western terminus of the transcontinental railroad—the spectacular, if temporary, end to Manifest Destiny. Located at the intersection of agriculture and extraction in California's Central Valley and Sierra Nevada, continent-spanning railroads, and an emerging port that pointed out toward the Pacific Ocean, the next edge of empire,

West Oakland became an irresistible site for industrial development.[5] This, in turn, drove the emigration of workers, primarily from Northern Europe, who settled within walking distance of the shipyards and manufactories that mushroomed throughout the district.[6]

It wasn't long before the arrival of the railroad spurred African American migration, as well. In the 1860s, at the same time that Oakland was selected as the end of the line, the Pullman Company popularized sleeping cars as a way to make transcontinental travel more comfortable for the affluent Whites who could afford it. At the end of the Civil War, when millions of African Americans became "free" to sell their labor as one of the most devalued segments of the waged working class, George Pullman mandated that his cars be served by Black male porters. Porters—and later cooks, waiters, and other roving service workers—soon came to reside in Oakland between trips. In order to ensure that they were ready for service on short notice, the Central Pacific required workers to live within minutes of the yards. So, while Oakland was yet to formally segregate African Americans— it was different for Chinese Americans, then the most populous community of color—this system of corporate control made sure that most of the city's first Black residents lived west of Adeline Street.[7] At the end of the nineteenth century, then, Black Oaklanders entered emancipation in a nominally "free state" under conditions of separation and servitude that were ominously familiar.

Most of this book addresses the sonic and spatial struggles that emerged during and after the Black Power Era. But in order to understand the political context, cultural appeal, and psychic impact of Black Power in Oakland, we need to wind the record back to World War II. We need to remember the city built by and for White Power. During the 1940s and '50s, the wartime migration of African Americans from the U.S. South and Southwest was met with intensified forms of segregation. The moral panic over migration often turned on an antipathy to the cultural practices of Black Southerners. In response, city officials rolled out new modes of regulation and policing that targeted working-class entertainment venues and commercial districts. This paradoxical experience of movement and containment gave rise to a melancholic style of popular music that local record producer Bob Geddins billed the "Oakland Blues." The blues provided Black migrants with a critical source of economic opportunity, communal identity, and pleasure. But it would soon be surpassed by the more muscular and optimistic sonic politics of the funk, which sounded the call for Black Power.

OUT SOUTH

Disembarking from the train amid the bustle of Seventh Street, or the beaux-arts Central Station at Sixteenth and Wood, wartime migrants entered a neighborhood that had been made, in part, by previous waves of Black settlers and strivers. But this West Oakland was as multiethnic as it was working class. It was Mexican, Italian, Greek, and—until the war—Japanese.[8] Oral histories reveal that African American residents remembered the prewar years as a period of residential and, to a lesser extent, social mixing with other groups—"pre-segregation," in the words of Betty Reid Soskin, co-owner of a record store in South Berkeley.[9] Still, a mix of overt and covert policies ensured that Black residence, religion, culture, and commerce were constricted to the westernmost part of the East Bay. In the late 1930s, the U.S. Home Owners' Loan Corporation redlined almost all of the land west of Grove Street (later renamed, paradoxically enough, Martin Luther King Jr. Way). In turn, local real-estate agents, mortgage lenders, and landlords diligently restricted Black, Mexican, and—except for Downtown's Chinatown—Asian American residents to the most degraded areas along the industrial waterfront.[10]

As was common in segregated communities across the nation, Black Oaklanders—there were only one thousand in 1900—seeded their own crop of civic and religious organizations to create a separate, but aspirationally equal, version of the good life in the Golden West. Groups like the Brotherhood of Sleeping Car Porters, the first Black union recognized by the American Federation of Labor, served as a vehicle for Black political activity, economic development, and mutual aid. They also encouraged the growth of a small middle class, which sought to escape the increasingly overcrowded and rundown conditions of the neighborhood. But trapped amid redlining's grip, Black people who wanted out were forced to move north along the water to North Oakland or South Berkeley—where, by the 1920s, a higher percentage of Black residents owned their homes than did Whites.[11]

This social and spatial arrangement would be upset by the coming of world war. In 1941, President Franklin Roosevelt's declaration of open military conflict in the Pacific Theater introduced new forms of capital, labor, and governance that remade the East Bay. At the time, Oakland politics were the domain of Joseph R. Knowland—owner, editor, and publisher of its main newspaper, the *Oakland Tribune*, and de facto chief of its Republican Machine. During the Depression, Knowland, formerly a five-term congressman, managed to maintain economic growth by securing massive federal investments in military facilities like the Oakland Army Base, Oakland Naval Supply Center, and Alameda Naval Air Station.[12] So, with the onset of combat in the Pacific Ocean, the region's bases and shipbuilders were strategically poised to reap the windfalls created by the new economic geography of war.

In 1930, the federal budget totaled approximately $3 billion; but between 1940 and 1946, the U. S. spent $35 billion in California alone.[13] Much of that streamed into Bay Area shipyards, which cranked out an astonishing 1,400 naval vessels over the course of the conflict.[14] At the same time, many of the region's White male workers were drafted for service, sparking a rush to recruit replacements from across the country. The population of the Bay Area boomed with the influx of over 500,000 migrants—the most conspicuous of whom were Southerners, both Black and White, from Oklahoma, Texas, Arkansas, and Louisiana. Many of them settled in the East Bay, where, as of 1943, around 40 percent of the region's industrial army—including an estimated 10,000 Black residents—toiled at one of a dozen shipyards that dotted the shoreline between Alameda and Richmond. In Oakland, which received a third of all African American migrants to the region, the Black population grew from around 8,500 to 22,000—a 250 percent increase—between 1940 and 1944.[15]

Gathering their belongings and exiting the train, Black migrants encountered a hardening color line that came to mirror what they had trekked so far to leave behind. While most would find work, often at wages that beat sharecropping, they were consigned to the lowest paid and most dangerous roles. And if they managed to land a spot in the new war worker housing, they were confined to the least desirable units along the train tracks. Those who were less "fortunate" were forced to compete for increasingly scarce, crowded, and decrepit apartments in West Oakland—where workers would rent "hot beds," catching a bit of rest while another tenant was on shift, or just crash in the hall.[16] The simultaneous growth in population and segregation meant that, by midcentury, West Oakland no longer looked like the "melting pot" of yore. Instead, it came to resemble the apartheid pattern of other American cities, from Nashville to New York. In 1940, Black people made up 16 percent of West Oakland. By 1950, when around 85 percent of Black residents lived in the neighborhood, that number had exploded to 62 percent.[17]

The round-the-clock clammer of cranes and hammers. People curled up to sleep in odd corners of cafés and movie theaters. These represented seismic changes in the everyday landscapes of prewar residents. But the old-timers reserved their most visceral reactions for the ways that migration seemed to upend the city's social and cultural order. The exigencies of the war created unprecedented opportunities for marginalized workers, emboldening the presence of young people, women, and Southerners in the public realm. But unsurprisingly, it was the sight and sound of Black migrants—in particular, those who agitated against the more de facto system of segregation that prevailed before the war—that attracted the most venomous attacks from civic elites. The *Oakland Observer*, a conservative weekly, for instance, condemned Black migrants for contesting "their place" in the caste order— for "butting into the white civilization instead of keeping in the perfectly orderly and convenient Negro civilization" forged by prewar residents.[18]

In fact, it wasn't just White people who were menaced by the "strange" mannerisms that Black migrants introduced to the city's streets, trollies, and commercial spaces. Black old-timers, too, were often aghast at the presence of their rural kin, who seemed to endanger whatever stability and standing prewar residents had managed to carve out from amid the regime of White Power. As in cities across the North and West during the Great Migration, this anxiety about assimilation triggered struggles over Black "respectability."[19] Migrants, said some of the old-timers, who would begrudgingly shoulder the burden, required training in modern urban mores by the "better element of their own race."[20] In *The Warmth of Other Suns*, for instance, the author Isabel Wilkerson notes that the Chicago Urban League went door-to-door, passing out leaflets that told migrants not to "carry on loud conversations in street cars and public places" (among other directives). In this way, writes the sound studies scholar Jennifer Lynn Stoever, middle-class African Americans "disparaged migrants from exercising newfound freedom to sound, listen to, and audibly inhabit public space."[21]

In the East Bay, these struggles over culture and comportment were often centered on the entertainment venues that cropped up in response to the deluge of defense spending. With the dry docks running around the clock, the growing armies of workers punched out with pockets that, unlike the Depression, were now swollen with the wages of war. "There were no more weekends or nights," recalled Stanley Nystrom, a resident of Richmond. "It was just twenty-four hours a day, seven days a week."[22] In this context, soldiers, workers, and other socially dislocated migrants sought out immediate indulgences amid the bars, poolrooms, and amusements that proliferated across the East Bay. In response, prewar residents and politicians condemned these spaces—and their occupants—for "ruining" the region. In Oakland and Richmond, authorities rolled out a string of venue regulations meant to suppress an alleged migrant-fueled "crime wave."[23]

In the 1940s, the press, police, and city officials attributed the supposed increase in social disorder to what they described as the cultural deficiencies and criminal dispositions of migrants from the South and Southwest—the "quality rather than the quantity" of the newcomers, in the words of one police lieutenant.[24] This, of course, was more stereotype than statistics. According to the historian Donna Murch, the African Americans who moved to Oakland from Louisiana—compared, for instance, to those who moved to Chicago from Mississippi or New York from North Carolina—tended to come from cities, where, since the late nineteenth century, many of them had participated in skilled trades and labor organizing.[25] Indeed, by the 1930s, notes Wilkerson, nearly two out of three Black migrants came from the towns and cities of the South rather than rural areas, often with education levels that rivaled those of African Americans living in the North and West.[26]

But these facts were of no concern to the White newspapermen and moral crusaders who campaigned, successfully, for the government to increase funding for law enforcement around the East Bay's military bases and shipyards. Given concerns about vice and violence, these regulations and police patrols targeted the region's boomtown business districts. Richmond, for one, authorized its Merchants Committee to arm private security guards, while Oakland recruited over 2,300 auxiliary officers into the ranks of the Oakland Police Department (OPD).[27] Between 1940 and 1950, the number of uniformed officers in the OPD ballooned from 400 to 600.[28] At the same time, the city council rushed to impose new permit requirements and fees on movie theaters, cabarets, carnivals, jukeboxes, and buskers—seemingly anything that might attract pleasure-seeking migrants. In a prelude to the ways that Oakland would come to use special permit fees to fund police campaigns against African American sideshows and nightclubs in the 1990s and 2000s (see chs. 5 and 6), the City recycled these entertainment taxes back into its law-and-order campaigns.[29]

While the *Tribune* and *Observer* might rail, on occasion, against the transgressions of "Okies," a catchall for rural Whites, the brunt of the billy club fell upon Black residents. During the war, the OPD ran continual sweeps of West Oakland—which, with its concentration of itinerant military men, migrant workers, and Black people, became indissolubly linked to the public imagination of crime. Using draft-card checks as a means of "systemic harassment," and a precursor to stop-and-frisk, the OPD arrested hundreds of Black men for the supposed crimes of draft evasion and vagrancy.[30] The OPD had never taken kindly to Black residents. But the war marked a turning point in the intensity of police repression. Walter Green, a migrant from Mississippi, recalled that, as the OPD grew, it recruited Southern White "Crackers" to patrol the city's new social and sexual color lines.[31] Jim Crow too, it seemed, had hitched its way to the West Coast, causing migrants to decry California as the land of his more dressed-up but no less devilish twin: James Crow.[32]

For this reason, the sociologists Marcus Anthony Hunter and Zandria Robinson call the West Coast cities that attracted African Americans during the Second Great Migration, from Seattle to San Diego, "Out South." Charting a "chocolate map" of the United States, they take inspiration from Malcom X's renowned speech "The Ballot or the Bullet"

(1964). "Stop talking about the South," X exhorted the crowd at Detroit's King Solomon Baptist Church. "As long as you South of the Canadian border, you South."[33] Building upon this idea, Hunter and Robinson argue that Black American life is "best understood as occurring wholly in 'The South'—one large territory governed by . . . practices of racial domination." But it wasn't just racism that made Oakland "Out South." "Black migrants," they continue, carried " 'The South'—Black regional customs, worldviews, and cultures—with them to their new homes in destinations across urban America."[34] In fact, the latter turned Oakland from a cultural and political outpost of White Power into what the local author Ishmael Reed would call, lovingly, "Blues City."[35]

BLUES CITY

In the 1950s, as the wartime boom began to wane, Oakland set out to convert the section of its aging, industrial waterfront that bordered Downtown into a modern shopping and entertainment district meant to contend for the suburban dollar. Considering the competition from commercial destinations in emerging cities like Concord and Walnut Creek, planners for what's now called Jack London Square lamented the condition of Oakland's nightlife. "Legend has it, when the Palace Theater in New York was the national capital of vaudeville," they wrote, "there was a sign backstage that read, 'The worst three weeks in the year are Christmas, Easter, and Oakland.' "[36] Clearly, the Palace Theater crowd had never been to Sweet's Ballroom, at Broadway and Twentieth, let alone Seventh Street, West Oakland's "Harlem of the West."[37]

Indeed, even before the war sent the city's entertainment economy into overdrive, Oakland had become home to a swinging but segregated nightlife. As streetcar lines from around the East Bay converged on Broadway, twisting together like a braid, they deposited a steady stream of pleasure-seekers into the streets of Downtown, where they could revel at everything from smoky dancehalls to soaring concert venues. On the south side of Lake Merritt, the Oakland Auditorium, opened in 1914, attracted up to 13,000 people to dance the jitterbug, black bottom, and other crazes to the swing-era big bands of Lionel Hampton and Cab Calloway. An archival recording of one of Hampton's concerts at the Auditorium in 1944 alternates between crooning cheek-to-cheek ballads and throbbing, uptempo romps in which raucous melodies, belted out by a chorus of horns, resolve into mellow vibraphone solos.[38] Broadcast on the radio, the roiling excitement of the show reached an audience of thousands more. On a smaller scale, the Sweet Brothers— William and Eugene—built their first of four ballrooms on Broadway in 1920. For under a dollar, dancers could twirl to the music of Duke Ellington, Ella Fitzgerald, and Frank Sinatra or stare down upon the swirling crowd from the ornate mezzanine. Oakland, in the words of the drummer Earl Watkins—who toured the nation with the great jazz pianist, and notable resident, Earl "Fatha" Hines—was "one of the greatest dance towns in the country."[39] Palace Theater be damned.

But in order to participate in this vivacious nightlife, dancers and musicians of color had to navigate an intricate system of segregation. For instance, while the Sweet Brothers booked the most popular Black touring acts from Harlem, Chicago, and Los Angeles, they maintained a strict regime of racial separation. People of color might get a chance to lindy hop to the likes of Ellington, or a local talent put on by the eminent Black promoter Johnny Burton, but only on Mondays—the least desirable night of the week.[40] The Auditorium, by contrast, was at least initially open to Black and mixed-raced audiences. But the presence of Black people was always precarious. According to a report in the *Oakland Sunshine*, an African American newspaper, the manager of the city's marquee concert hall was reluctant to rent it out for all-Black events because he "very well knew that colored people like to shoot and cut one another at their dances . . . and thus by keeping a continual war they might disgrace the building."[41]

But violence was the effect of segregation, not the cause. In 1944, a race riot erupted after a Cab Calloway dance at the Auditorium. Calloway and his orchestra had appeared at Sweet's Ballroom the previous night for an all-White audience. So, the promoter, William Sweet, added a second night at the Auditorium for African Americans. Barred from seeing the maestro of Harlem's famed Cotton Club in most settings, 15,000 Black people from all over the region converged for their chance to dance. But once the venue reached capacity, an estimated 5,000 revelers were turned away. Frustrated and stranded, with nowhere else to turn in Downtown Oakland, many crammed onto a streetcar to return to San Francisco. When a White sailor attempted to force his way onto the crowded car at Twelfth Street and Broadway, a melee broke out, spreading to some 2,000 servicemen and civilians. The OPD, swamped, called in the Navy Shore Patrol and Army Military Police to quell the unrest.[42]

The problem, surmised the *Oakland Observer*, was one of too *much* freedom rather than too little. The disturbance, insisted the paper, stemmed from the invasion of "socially-liberated or uninhibited Negroes." Instead of remaining out of sight and sound, like prewar residents, the newcomers "insist[ed] on barging into the white man."[43] From this point of view, more segregation was needed to keep the peace, not less. Black audiences were soon officially relegated to Mondays at the Auditorium, as well.[44]

Like dancers, Black musicians were barred from Downtown Oakland's nightlife by White venue owners and union bosses from the San Francisco Chapter of the American Federation of Musicians (AFM). Formed in 1885, and chartered as AFM Local 6 in 1897, the union offered musicians a range of benefits, from reduced hours and increased pay in the boom times to mutual aid in the busts. But only if they were White. It wasn't until 1923, after years of organizing among Black artists, that Local 6 allowed African Americans to form their own "colored" union—one of more than 50 such groups across the AFM, where racial segregation was the norm.[45] Based in Oakland, Local 648 could now set its own pay scale and negotiate contracts for Black musicians throughout the Bay Area.

Still, everywhere they turned, musicians of color found themselves curtailed by the AFM's racial cartel. According to the musicologist Leta Miller, in the Depression, Local 6 ramped up its efforts to protect the privileges of White musicians. In an unprecedented maneuver, it lobbied the national union to put every club in the Bay Area on the AFM's "forbidden territory" list. While this tactic was typically reserved for one or two venues that tried to avert union rules, Local 6's preemptive approach meant that, from Santa Rosa to San José, any club that hired Local 648 members would face reprisal. Miller notes that this put Black musicians in a bind. As in other sectors of the American economy, the only way that Black artists could compete with Whites was to work for lower wages. But now, if Black musicians underbid the union scale, Local 6 could automatically boycott the club and bully management back into line.[46] Describing this dilemma, the editors of *The Spokesman*, a newspaper for Black San Franciscans, put it thus: "If they work, they are traitors to labor; if they remain idle, they are traitors to their stomachs."[47]

These were no empty threats. In the early 1930s, Local 6 went after several venues in San Francisco that hired Black musicians, including popular jazz pianist and bandleader Wilbert Baranco.[48] In the East Bay, the drummer Earl Watkins recalled that the AFM managed to prevent all but the most famous Black touring acts from performing Downtown or along East Fourteenth Street, where there were several Italian- and Portuguese-owned restaurants and nightspots.[49] The union remained divided until 1960, when it was forced to integrate by the State of California following the passage of the Fair Employment Practices Act (1959), which outlawed segregated unions.[50] By then, the national organization had turned against the Jim Crow locals. In 1957, President James Petrillo ordered San Francisco to integrate from the stage of the AFM Convention in Denver. "Either do it," he growled, in front of the delegates, "or we'll force you to."[51]

These restrictions meant that, at midcentury, Downtown Oakland was unreceptive to both Black employment and enjoyment. As in other cities across the United States, Black residents responded by building up their own customs, institutions, and economies.[52] West Oakland became the body and soul of this apartheid terrain, and Seventh Street its dancing, swinging, striving heart. Here, segregation was, predictably, unequal. While Black people were prevented, for the most part, from exiting the neighborhood, the opposite was true for White people from the rest of the city. All along the strip, residents of the area's apartments, rooming houses, and hotels intermingled with outsiders who came to work at the shipyards and military bases, catch the ferry to San Francisco, or go "slumming" amid the racially and sexually charged attractions.[53]

Accustomed to carving opportunity from constraint, Black West Oaklanders turned their location at the crossroads of the region's economic and transport networks into an occasion, however restricted, for entrepreneurial endeavor. In 1929, Oakland was home to more than one hundred Black-owned businesses, most of them barbershops, beauty parlors, restaurants, and poolrooms. By the 1950s, as newcomers continued to stream into the neighborhood, Seventh Street alone came to house dozens of Black-owned bars and clubs.[54] According to Miller, the wartime migration of African Americans, which fueled the growth of music venues in segregated neighborhoods like West Oakland, finally allowed artists of color to break through the barricade that the AFM had built around the region's nightlife. After decades of competing with White musicians for gigs at White venues—a contest they couldn't win—Black, Mexican, and Filipino artists could now count on an ever-expanding set of opportunities to play for audiences of color.[55] Increasingly, these crowds were made up of migrants who—excited by their new surroundings and homesick for the old—didn't want to hear the Dixieland review served up for White folks in San Francisco. They wanted to hear the low-down country blues.

This wasn't the first time that migration and music combined to contour the culture of Black Oakland. The cultural historian Willie Collins notes that, at the turn of the century, when most concerts in the city consisted of conservatory-taught "art music," the Pullman Porters and other "railroad men" were instrumental in introducing Oakland to jazz. These itinerant workers were conduits of taste; before there was a national distribution system for "race records," they carried copies of this new, syncopated sound on return trips from New Orleans or Chicago as early as the 1910s.[56] But more than that, they were one of the main sources of income in the community. In 1925, when the Brotherhood of Sleeping Car Porters was formed, railroad workers made up a third of Black wage earners in Oakland.[57] On their nights off, they recycled these earnings into the neighborhood by hiring a band for a dance or attending clubs like the Creole Café—an interracial "black and tan" on Seventh Street where, in the early 1920s, Jelly Roll Morton and Kid Ory further schooled East Bay artists and audiences on the sounds of the Crescent City.[58] "Black railroad men," concludes Collins, "in large part, sustained African American music and musicians in the Bay Area."[59]

The railroad revamped the soundscape of Oakland, once again, during World War II by transporting migrants who were raised on the country blues. Soon, cabarets and rent parties around West Oakland rang out with the raw, earthen vocals of backwoods barrooms and Black Baptist churches. Those sounds were ephemeral, however, the stuff of small moments of communion and pleasure, until Bob Geddins began to record them.[60] Born on a plantation near Marlin, Texas, Geddins migrated to Los Angeles in 1933, where he opened a record store that catered to the tastes of other recent arrivals to the West Coast. But his ambitions soon turned to the East Bay when, on a visit to his mother, who had moved to West Oakland, he became captivated by the crowds—and prospects—that swelled along Seventh Street. "I never seen so many people in all my life," he recalled. "[It] was so crowded you couldn't hardly walk down the street unless you bumped into somebody." "There were people from everywhere," he continued, "Louisiana, Alabama, Georgia, Mississippi, Texas, Oklahoma, Tennessee!" It was as if the neighborhood had become a crossroads of the Black Belt. But while the population was now Southern, through and through, it seemed to Geddins that the local music industry had yet to catch up. "I said to myself, 'This could be a record heaven,'" he remembered, "because there was no blues records to be heard here in the Bay Area."[61]

During the war, Geddins moved to West Oakland, where he found work as a burner and welder at the Kaiser Shipyards in Richmond and a buyer at Wolf's Records on Seventh Street. After a period of importing records, he began to scout fresh talent at the churches and nightclubs that popped up around the burgeoning Black East Bay. Opening the first record pressing plant in West Oakland, at Eighth and Center Streets, in 1944, Geddins could now capture the fleeting sounds of local blues musicians—most of whom, like him, were recent migrants—on wax. Over the next two decades, he would go on to produce hundreds of singles on labels like Big Town, Down Town, and Art-Tone, earning him the title "Godfather of the Oakland Blues."[62]

Unlike its more famous cousin from Chicago, which was created by migrants from the Mississippi Delta, and tended to include more electrified instruments and hard-driving rhythm sections, the Oakland Blues was grounded in the country sounds of the Southwest. Geddins wasn't much of a musician or singer. But his ability to communicate the mood of the migrant experience—a mix of folk culture and racial malaise—would be the key to his artistic success. His early recordings often featured a dragging beat, drawn-out vocals, and mournful tone.

According to the music journalist and historian Lee Hildebrand, Geddins would encourage artists to extend their phrasing by imitating his crawling Texas drawl. "I try to make everything I record sound as sad as possible," explained Geddins. But if the sound of sorrow reflected his cultural roots, it also revealed a commercial instinct to connect with Black consumers. "When black folks go to buyin' blues," he said, "they want to buy something that gives them the feeling of the old things that they went through when they were having troubles and difficulties . . . You got to make the story sound as if the singer was really in this mood of distress or went through these problems. All the people that have had similar problems are the ones that like that stuff and are gonna buy those records."[63]

This carefully refined aesthetic of sadness comes across, loud and clear, on "Three O'Clock Blues" (1948), which Geddins arranged for Lowell Fulson. Born on Choctaw land south of Tulsa, Oklahoma, Fulson was exposed to the Oakland Blues while stationed in the city as a sailor during World War II. He soon met Geddins, after finishing a tour in Guam, when he heard music coming from the Big Town pressing plant and went to see what was going on. Geddins signed him on the spot. "Three O'Clock Blues," which reached number six on *Billboard's* "Most-Played Juke Box Race Records" chart, became Geddins's first national hit.[64] Sung in a melismatic and miserable tone, the song tells of a man who is sick with insomnia over the departure of his love interest. The vocal lamentations engage in a call-and-response with equally mournful guitar licks. The narrator warns that, if his missing lover doesn't return within the day, he's "gonna jump overboard and drown."[65]

Sonically, the song—essentially, a musical suicide note—is raw. It consists of just three elements: Fulson's crooning, moaning guitar solos, and clipped chords played by his brother Martin. In fact, according to the music writer Michael Point, most of Fulson's early recordings were "country-tinged guitar duets" with Martin. But by the 1950s, his sound became more urbane. In 1951, when he started touring on the strength of this early single, he put together a full band, including a young Ray Charles on piano.[66] With "Three O'Clock Blues" now on rotation on Black radio across the nation, a little-known artist named B. B. King recorded his own rendition in a makeshift studio at the Memphis YMCA. King's version, which spent five weeks at the top of the R&B charts in 1951, would be the breakout moment of his career.

Like the original, the cover is built around the slow and aching conversation between the vocals and the (now-electric) guitar licks. But pitched up from A to C, allowing King to sing at the top of his range, and floating over cymbal rides that highlight the song's mellow swing, it sounds decidedly less despondent. He even modified the lyrics to make it about a man who calls it quits on his unreliable lover, rather than the other way around. Instead of threatening to "jump overboard and drown," the narrator announces that he's "going down to the bowlin' ground"—a spot, as King explains in a useful ad lib, where "the mens hang out."[67] As "Three O'Clock Blues" left Oakland, then, it turned from a story of despair and self-destruction into one of defiant and masculine cool. Fulson would go on to notch a few more hits. King would become a legend.

This was another side of the Oakland Blues: the real money was always somewhere else. You had to move out to move up. Geddins had a knack for recruiting artists and producing records that appealed to postwar Black audiences, but he lacked the capital, and perhaps the canniness, to profitably market these sounds. While he launched his career on Big Town, Fulson soon departed for Los Angeles because Geddins's main methods for distributing records—hand-delivering them to radio stations and record stores during road trips down South, or hawking them out of the trunk of his car—weren't big time enough.[68] In order to take advantage of more professional marketing networks, writes Hildebrand, Geddins had to cut deals with larger companies like Imperial in LA and Chess / Checker in Chicago.[69] These deals often turned out badly for Geddins and his artists. Time and again, songs that were recorded and popularized in Oakland were covered—with little credit or compensation—by musicians and labels with national reach.

In one prominent case, Big Mama Thornton—who came to the East Bay at the invitation of Jimmy McCracklin, another musician who was scouted by Geddins but scooped up by Chess / Checker—recorded "Ball and Chain" with Oakland's Bay-Tone Records. The song was never released, but Thornton incorporated it into her live act. It was during one such concert, at a bar in San Francisco, that Janis Joplin and James Gurley of Big Brother and the Holding Company heard the tune and asked Thornton to cover it. Performing their own version of "Ball and Chain" for mostly White audiences at concerts like the Monterey Pop Festival in 1967, they rocketed past Thornton to the vanguard of the Bay Area scene. This, of course, came after Elvis Presley covered Thornton's "Hound Dog" (1953)—which she recorded in LA with Berkeley-raised musician Johnny Otis—selling 20 times as many copies, and anointing him the White "King" of rock 'n' roll.[70]

In the end, many of the artists who Geddins recruited and groomed, turning them into incarnations of the Oakland Blues, including McCracklin and Sugar Pie DeSanto, decamped for more prominent labels. "I got cheated out of so much money," he lamented in the documentary *Long Train Running: The Story of the Oakland Blues* (1981). In fact, by the time he was tracked down for an interview, Geddins had called it quits on music. The filmmakers, Marlon Riggs and Peter Webster, then graduate students at UC Berkeley, found the "Godfather" running a car radiator shop on Foothill Boulevard in East Oakland.[71]

Geddins might not have had the money or muscle to retain local talent. But he built up a rich community of blues musicians and listeners, who fueled the growth of nightlife in West Oakland during the 1940s and '50s.

With their songs disseminated by DJs Bouncin' Bill Doubleday and Don Barksdale on KWBR, which began to target Black listeners in the 1940s, artists like Johnny Heartsman and L. C. "Good Rockin'" Robinson attracted flocks of revelers to Seventh Street's rollicking nightspots.[72]

These clubs ran the gamut from the high end to the low. At the top of the heap was Slim Jenkins' Club.[73] Harold Jenkins, who, at 6'5", earned the nickname "Slim," was born in Monroe, Louisiana. He moved to West Oakland after serving in World War I, part of the first wave of migrants that would turn the city into the largest community of African Americans from Monroe, ranging from Huey Newton to basketball legend Bill Russell, on the West Coast.[74] At the time, Jenkins was so that poor he rode the rails to California as a stowaway on a Pullman car, hidden with the help of friendly porters.[75] After working as a waiter to learn the nightlife trade, he opened his own club—it started as a liquor store, but evolved into a restaurant and cabaret—next to the old Creole Café at the end of Prohibition in 1933. With white tablecloths, uniformed waiters, and art deco banquettes, it soon earned a reputation as the classiest venue in the Black East Bay (see fig. 1).

Jenkins, in turn, became the de facto "Mayor of West Oakland." Catering to members of the White Power structure, like Joseph Knowland and Mayor Clifford Rishell, he acquired a position of relative importance within the city's Republican Machine.[76] But his attempt to attract ruling-class Whites tempered the tone of his dance floor. "He didn't want any of that down home blues," remembered the drummer Earl Watkins. It wasn't that local artists were barred from performing on Jenkins's venerated stage. To the contrary, when it wasn't hosting concerts by Miles Davis or the Ink Spots, the venue presented an important source of work for members of the Black musicians' union. It was just that Jenkins would enforce exacting standards of respectability. "If you had a jazz band," explained Watkins, who worked the venue with Wilbert Baranco in 1946, "he would have a singer . . . [because] he wanted more of a cabaret style."[77]

Figure 1. Two bartenders at Slim Jenkins' Club on Seventh Street in West Oakland, 1953. Credit: African American Museum and Library at Oakland.

While celebrated as the peak of entertainment in West Oakland, then, Slim Jenkins' Club still operated within the system of sonic surveillance that the sound studies scholar Jennifer Lynn Stoever calls the White "listening ear."[78] For a more unrestrained experience, working-class African Americans might cross the street to visit Esther's Orbit Room. Born in Palestine, Texas, Esther Mabry was no stranger to the violence of Jim Crow. Her father, who worked on an oil rig, was a recurring victim of racial terrorism; resentful of his modest success, White men poisoned his mules, poured sugar in his gas tank, and, eventually, torched the family's house. Esther escaped to California in the 1940s, finding work as a cook at Slim Jenkins'. In 1950, she opened a club of her own, which, in contrast to Slim's, served up chitlins and the shouting and blasting of California's postwar rhythm and blues.[79]

Indeed, the sad, stripped-down, country sounds of Geddins's early records only represented one side of the Oakland Blues. He also produced songs like Jimmy Wilson's "Tin Pan Alley" (1953) and Jimmy McCracklin's "Too Late to Change" (1963). Still slow and emotive, like "Three O'Clock Blues," these songs feature sustained horn blasts, which harmonize with the vocals like a wailing chorus, and moaning countermelodies performed by the electric guitarist Lafayette "Thing" Thomas. Even Fulson evolved to meet the emerging desires of audiences at clubs like Esther's. "They wanted to be able to dance off the blues," he recalled. Willie Collins points out that in "Blue Shadows" (1950), released two years after "Three O'Clock Blues," Fulson's country guitar is replaced by the bright and tinkling sounds of piano and saxophone. With the drums and bass maintaining a swinging 4 / 4 rhythm, it got the crowd at Esther's moving, alright.[80]

Popular memories and, to a lesser extent, written histories about renowned venues like Slim Jenkins' Club and Esther's Orbit Room have managed to withstand the effects of time. But the more mundane soundscapes of the Oakland Blues—the ways that the music, whether recorded or performed, pervaded the everyday lives of Black migrants—are harder to capture. That, according to the ethnomusicologist Christina Zanfagna, is not an accident. Excluded from property ownership, and targeted by White vigilantes and police, Black Americans have been precluded from building enduring cultural institutions, forcing them to repurpose everything from parks to apartments into sites of musical communion. Just mapping brick-and-mortar spaces, like cabarets and recording studios, that managed to survive in this inimical environment, she writes, "does not account for the multiple uses and conversions of urban space that (have had to) occur behind walls, after hours, and therefore, out of sight."[81]

Indeed, formal venues were only one of the spaces in which West Oaklanders came together to listen to music, forge connections, and forget—if only fleetingly—the burdens of segregation. The neighborhood was replete with rent parties, military dances, and social halls like the Elks Lodge, where unions and voluntary associations would sponsor events.[82] The record "Johnny's House Party, Parts 1 & 2" (1957) by Johnny Heartsman gives us a sense of what these forgotten frolics might have sounded like. Heartsman, born in Houston, migrated to West Oakland by way of Southern California. As a teenager, he started to work as a session musician for Geddins, playing bass on "Tin Pan Alley." On "House Party," an instrumental track, he finger-picks and arpeggiates his way all over the heavy swing of the drums and walking bassline. What really gives the record its verve, however, is the ad libs: the chorus of shouts, screams, and calls of "c'mon!" that registers the excitement of the crowd.[83] While recorded at South Berkeley's Music City, "House Party" hints at how Black revelers contributed to the soundscape of everyday romps through their own spontaneous participation and affirmation.

This more diffuse topography of sonic pleasure, inaudible to us today, meant that Black music was woven into the fabric of the East Bay. The sounds of the Great Migration poured out of not just nightclubs but also record stores, car radios, and jukeboxes. Johnny Otis, the Greek American musician and record producer who scouted Little Esther Phillips and Etta James, recalled that his lifelong love affair with Black music began when he heard a blues record through the window of a neighbor—a Pullman porter—in South Berkeley.[84] It was quite possible to be touched by sound, changed even, on a stroll to the corner store.

Not everyone was pleased. Given the crusade against the cultural practices of Black migrants, and increasing racial violence of policing during World War II, the OPD intensified its nighttime patrols in West Oakland. These men were "cold blooded," recalled Watkins. "They'd beat your butt . . . within an inch of your life." This aggression, he explained, was like "law enforcement in the South"—not only in terms of its brutality but also its obsession with restricting liaisons along racial and sexual lines.[85] In his research on Chicago, the geographer Rashad Shabazz argues that patrolling interracial sex at black and tans fueled the growth and consolidation of "carceral power" on the South Side.[86] In Oakland, the cops might avoid well-connected interracial spots like Slim Jenkins' Club—where, otherwise, they might run across their boss on a tryst—but they regularly surveilled run-of-the-mill venues that attracted a mixed crowd. Watkins recalled a gig with the singer Connie Jordan at the Wolf Club in the 1950s where the OPD stopped White women, issued citations, and reported them to their partners or parents for "coming over to this colored club and associating with Black men." (The cops, he noted, weren't nearly as concerned when they spotted a Black woman consorting with a White man.) But the harassment didn't stop there. When their intimidation tactics didn't do enough to discourage racial mixing, the police raided the venue, scaring and interrogating the customers, to punish its owners for promoting such unsavory encounters in the first place.[87]

DEFREMERY, PT. 1

Like their parents, young people, too, experienced West Oakland as a site of both cultural expansion and repression during the blues era. In fact, the regulation of Black migrant youth became even more deeply entrenched in the spaces of everyday life, as the OPD extended its reach into the realms of youth recreation. In 1944, amid a moral panic over migration and "juvenile delinquency," the OPD more than doubled the size of its juvenile detail and began to assign special officers to dance halls, movie theaters, and other leisure spaces that were popular among young people.[88] Creating park patrols and agreements with venue operators to keep teens away from late-night amusements, the police introduced new modes of youth control that repeated, on loop, for decades to come.[89] And the City decided that DeFremery Park, located at the heart of West Oakland, was the ideal test site for this experiment in governing migrant youth.

It's easy to miss the DeFremery Recreation Center (DRC) today. This powder blue Victorian manor, encircled by redwoods and oaks, is tucked back from the intersection of Eighteenth and Adeline Streets, surrounded by an expanse of grass that always seems to be scorched by West Oakland's near-year-round sun. The building tends to be over-shadowed by the grounds, which host a beloved skate park and annual events like Life Is Living and the Black Cowboy Parade. But this modest estate once served as a literal stage for the epic of Black Power.

Originally the domain of James DeFremery, founder of the Savings Union Bank in San Francisco, the property was purchased and converted into a park by the City in 1907. As West Oakland transformed into a working-class community, the park—one of the only open spaces in an increasingly congested and industrial precinct—became one of the main gathering spots among the region's prewar Black residents. Its role as a center of Black social and cultural life continued to expand during World War II, when the United Service Organizations added an auditorium, where it promoted concerts and dances for service-members, to the back of DeFremery's villa. But in the wake of the wartime crusade against migrant recreation, and especially the 1944 race riot, the City decided to remodel the space into a rec center designed to reform the conduct of working-class youth.

In 1947, the DRC opened under the direction of an African American social worker named Dorothy Pitts (née Seel). Its aim, explained Pitts, was to "minister" to young people through cultural activities—like charm classes for girls and escort classes for boys—meant to promote "acceptable social standards." Early in her tenure, she assessed the etiquette of the city's youth by attending a concert by Johnny Moore and the Three Blazers at the Oakland Auditorium. She was appalled by the ways that young men rubbed up against women during a dance and then abandoned them at the end of a song. To attend a DRC dance, she decided, the youth would need to receive instruction from a teacher who could instill the proper "social graces."[90] That person turned out to be the dancer and choreographer Ruth Beckford, who developed the first recreational modern dance program in the United States. (As a student of Katherine Dunham, the "Queen Mother of Black Dance," Beckford would introduce an entire generation of Oakland youth to Afro-Diasporic movement through her African-Haitian Dance Company.[91])

The DRC's programming was thus meant, in the words of one participant, to make the "country kids" more "city civilized."[92] This corrective mission was often cultural. But it could be coercive, too. In the postwar period, for instance, as the OPD stepped up surveillance of African American nightspots, the police cracked down on West Oakland youth by installing bright lights and probation officers at DRC dances. Like the Wolf Club, the OPD would turn away cars of young White women to, in Pitts's words, "prevent trouble." At times, cops would simply crash the events.[93] These tactics soon spread from the DRC to other gathering spaces, fueling a 55 percent rise in youth arrests between 1960 and 1965.[94] In response, argues the historian Donna Murch, schools, parks, rec centers, and other places where young people were policed became "essential to their growing racial and class consciousness."[95] So, it's no surprise that, in the late 1960s, young activists reappropriated those very same spaces—including, iconically, DeFremery Park—converting them from sites of repression into ones of Black power, pleasure, and play (see ch. 2).[96]

In the 1940s and '50s, as the East Bay was remade through militarism and migration, Oakland doubled down on the spatial politics of White Power. Confronted with increasing segregation and regulation, Black migrants combined their country roots and metropolitan opportunities to craft a melancholic sound called the Oakland Blues. The cultural practices of Black migrants were used, in turn, as a pretext to increase the policing of West Oakland nightspots, Downtown entertainment venues, and youth spaces like the DRC. In the 1960s and '70s, however, at the dawn of Black Power, the next generation of migrant youth discarded the social and sonic conventions of the blues, creating exciting new styles of music (funk) and dance (boogaloo) that fueled the city's famed "social movements."

2

SOCIAL MOVEMENTS

Sounding the Call for Black Power

And so, in a larger sense, we must then ask: how is it that black people move?

STOKELY CARMICHAEL, speech at Black Power Conference, UC Berkeley (1966)[1]

Beat is there to make you move.
Sound is there to help you groove.

SLY AND THE FAMILY STONE, "I Want to Take You Higher" (1969)[2]

THE COMING OF THE PANTHER

On October 29, 1966, Stokely Carmichael spoke at a Black Power Conference that was organized by Students for a Democratic Society at UC Berkeley. Taking to the stage of the Greek Theatre, a performing arts venue nestled in the hills above campus, he addressed what he called, teasingly, "the white intellectual ghetto of the West." "We are engaged in a psychological struggle in this country," he told the crowd of some 3,000 students. "And that is whether or not black people have the right to use the words they want to use without white people giving their sanction to it." "Whether they like it or not, we gonna use the word 'Black Power,'" he continued, to rousing applause. "We are not going to wait for white people to sanction Black Power. We're tired of waiting."[3]

An activist with the Student Nonviolent Coordinating Committee (SNCC), Carmichael entered the 1960s Civil Rights Movement as an acolyte of Martin Luther King Jr. and his patient, faith-based, long-arc-of-the-moral-universe approach to reform. By 1966, however, Carmichael had become the country's foremost messenger for the more assertive politics of Black Power. "Black Power," he wrote, with the political scientist Charles Hamilton, the next year, "is a call for black people in this country to unite . . . It is a call for black people to begin to define their own goals, to lead their own organizations and to support those organizations. It is a call to reject the racist institutions and values of this society."[4]

As he toured cities and campuses across the nation, Carmichael touted the Lowndes County Freedom Organization (LCFO) as an example of Black Power in practice. In 1965, residents of Lowndes County, Alabama—where there was only one Black registered voter, despite being 80 percent Black—organized, with SNCC's support, an independent political party to resist the rule of the state's all-White Democratic Party. Running Black candidates for local office, the LCFO adopted the panther as its logo. As Carmichael told the audience at the Greek: "We chose . . . a black panther—a beautiful black animal—which symbolizes the strength and dignity of black people. An animal that never strikes back until he's backed so far into the wall he's got nothing to do but spring out. And when he springs, he does not stop." Indeed, Carmichael's charge was to inspire Black communities, from coast to coast, to pursue self-determination by creating their own political institutions that, like the LCFO, were designed to address local concerns. "The political parties of this country do not meet the needs of the people on a day-to-day basis," he said. "The question is: how can you build political institutions that will begin to meet the needs of Oakland, California?" "And," he added, "the needs of Oakland,

California is not one thousand policemen with submachine guns. They don't need that. They need that least of all."[5]

We don't know whether Huey Newton and Bobby Seale were in the audience at the Greek that day. But as students at Merritt College in North Oakland, two miles to the south, they got word of Carmichael's "call" for Black Power nonetheless. Born in Louisiana and Texas, Newton and Seale arrived in the East Bay amid the wave of African American migrants from the South and Southwest during World War II (see ch. 1). At the time of Carmichael's visit, they were both deeply involved in the ferment of Black radical thought that had taken root across the region's college campuses. At Merritt, they were first introduced to the writing of authors like W. E. B. Du Bois, James Baldwin, and Malcolm X by Donald Warden, who started the Afro-American Association, a Black nationalist study group, as a student at UC Berkeley. (Becoming a mentor to James Brown in 1964, Warden would influence the politicization of soul music.) By the time of the Black Power Conference, however, Newton and Seale had tired of Warden's tendency to prioritize talk over action and his advocacy for Black capitalism. They turned their attention, instead, to the Soul Students Advisory Council, a campus front group for the more militant Revolutionary Action Movement (RAM), where they encountered the anticolonial ideas of Frantz Fanon and Mao Zedong.[6]

As a member of RAM, Newton wrestled with the contradiction between the group's academic tendencies and revolutionary ideals. How, he wondered, could organizers appeal to working-class "brothers on the block," for whom oppression and violence were grinding realities rather than intellectual concerns? According to the historians Joshua Bloom and Waldo Martin, the answer came in August 1966, two months before Carmichael's visit, when Newton read about the Watts Community Alert Patrol (CAP) in a SNCC newspaper. In 1965, following the Watts Uprising, which was prompted by police brutality, residents organized CAP to monitor the activities of the Los Angeles Police

Department. Eventually, they attached the black panther logo to their cars as they cruised around the neighborhood "sousveilling" the police.[7] Indeed, inspired by the LCFO, African Americans had started to organize their own "Black Panther Parties" in New York, Los Angeles, and Philadelphia. In the Bay Area, RAM members formed the Black Panther Party of Northern California. But in CAP's courageous and confrontational approach, Newton and Seale saw a means to connect the internationalism of RAM's revolutionary views to the everyday experiences of marginalized youth, who saw the Oakland Police Department (OPD), which had expanded its tactics of youth control in reaction to Black migration, as an occupying force. Forming their own group, the Black Panther Party for Self-Defense (BPP), Newton and Seale organized young people into armed patrols and began to "police the police."[8]

Inspired by national and international currents, then, the BPP's initial activities were resolutely local. Driving around North and West Oakland with a small cache of weapons, and stopping to monitor the interactions between residents and the OPD, they soon caught the attention of community members across the East Bay. The first time that most Americans learned about the BPP, however, was May 1967, when 30 young militants staged an armed demonstration at the State Capitol in Sacramento to protest a law sponsored by Assemblymember Donald Mulford, a Republican from Piedmont. The "Mulford Act" was designed to undermine the Panthers by banning the open carry of firearms, which they had used as an effective means to provide security against police violence. Then, in 1968, the BPP attracted a mass following, as young people, college students, and radicals looked to the Party for guidance on how to respond to the murder of Dr. King. By the end of the year, the Central Committee in Oakland had helped open 20 chapters across the country. (At peak, in 1970, the BPP had offices in 68 American cities and an International Section, led by Eldridge and Kathleen Cleaver, in Algiers.[9])

As the movement grew, so did its priorities, expanding from policing the police to grassroots social services, or "survival programs." This new stage of BPP activity started in January 1969, when the Party created a free breakfast program at St. Augustine's Episcopal Church in North Oakland. (Originally, the program was run by Ruth Beckford, director of the youth dance program at the DeFremery Recreation Center [see ch. 1]. Beckford was recruited by one of her Afro-Haitian dance students, LaVerne Williams, who was Newton's girlfriend.[10]) The program was so popular—especially with middle-of-the-road residents, who might have looked askance at the gun-toting but approved of feeding children—that it spread to virtually every chapter. By the end of the 1968–69 school year, the Party reported that it fed 20,000 students. On top of that, local chapters launched a raft of programs to address community needs that had gone neglected by the authorities, ranging from sickle cell anemia tests to rental aid and ambulance services.[11] This, too, resonated with Carmichael's call for self-determination.

Between 1966 and 1970, the BPP transformed from a small group of migrant youth working to protect Black East Bay residents from police abuse to the vanguard of a national movement for community care, anticolonialism, and armed resistance to White supremacy. But the revolutionary spirit that spread during the Black Power Era wasn't simply limited to community organizing and militant struggle. It also sparked significant changes in Black cultural expression. In terms of local histories, the ways that Black residents combatted the racial segregation and subordination that gave rise to the Oakland Blues—from organizing against urban renewal to creating survival programs—have all been extensively studied and rightfully revered.[12] But except for the funk historian and radio DJ Rickey Vincent, most scholars have overlooked the ways that young people who participated in Oakland's Black Power Movement revamped its popular music, street dance, and soundscapes—which, in their own vital ways, revolutionized the city's racial and spatial order.

Indeed, alongside the rifles and rallies taken up to tackle the power structure, young Black Bay Area residents developed a number of what I call "social movements," including new styles of music (funk) and dance (boogaloo), that allowed them to embody personal freedom and communal connection. In her writing about the author and artist Toni Cade Bambara, the sociologist Avery Gordon argues that there is a "sensuality of social movement"—a "day-to-day practice of instantiating an instinct for freedom."[13] In the late 1960s and early 1970s, a new generation of Bay Area musicians, dancers, and radio DJs ensured that there was no space more apt for practicing the principles of freedom than the funky dance floor. Whether involved with the Black Panthers, or indirectly aligned with the spirit of Black Power, these artists propelled the era's political movements by converting their revolutionary ideals into an exciting and accessible part of everyday life. Returning to Carmichael, this chapter embraces the idea that the "call" for Black Power was a sonic event. Ringing out from radios and bullhorns, it prompted, in turn, a range of sonic and kinesthetic responses.

THE BLACK POWER BEAT

In 2017, Rickey Vincent and I stared out over the sweeping view of San Francisco Bay from the sixth floor of what was then Barrows Hall at UC Berkeley—a stone's throw from where Stokely Carmichael had issued the call for Black Power in 1966.[14] As a lecturer in the Department of African American Studies, Vincent taught his signature course, "The History of Funk," to students and residents alike. He wasn't teaching it that term. But when I invited him to talk music and politics, he suggested that we meet in an office that he used from time to time. The location turned out to be auspicious. It provided a panorama of the places that mapped out his musical and biographical tracks through the East Bay.

Vincent grew up in Berkeley during the 1960s and '70s. His mother was a member of the Black Panthers and his father, who was White, was a scholar of Black radical politics at Merritt College, where he encountered Huey Newton.[15] Graduating from Berkeley High in 1979, Vincent attended UC Berkeley, where he started out studying astronomy before switching to ethnic studies. (His eventual interest in the cosmology of funk music, and his identification as a "funkateer," would seem to be the perfect marriage of these two pursuits.[16]) He went on to get a master's from the legendary College of Ethnic Studies at San Francisco State—which, arising from the struggles of the Third World Liberation Front, became the first academic program of its kind in 1969—and a doctorate from the Department of Ethnic Studies back at Cal. In the 1990s, he became one of the Bay Area's most pervasive public intellectuals, teaching classes on Black popular culture, funk, and hip-hop at local colleges and universities. But his ability to commune with the masses reached a new level in 1997, when he became a DJ on independent radio station KPFA. From Barrows, we could see the studios in Downtown Berkeley, where, every Friday night, he would spin what KPFA's website described as "two hours of the strongest, stankiest, uncut fonk anywhere on the airwaves."

Over the course of our conversation, it became clear that, for Vincent, geography and biography, music and politics, culture and consciousness coalesced in the spaces around us. Gesturing toward the sprawling, low-rise neighborhood of his youth, he explained that the area that ran from UC Berkeley in the north to West Oakland in the south created a potent "conduit of exchange" among cultural and political rebels.[17] In the 1960s, the redlined neighborhoods of the East Bay became a space in which Black unionists, civil rights activists, and migrant youth intermingled with White members of the anti–Vietnam War movement and counterculture, turning this stretch of the flats into what the historian Robert Self calls "one of the most vibrant political landscapes anywhere in the nation."[18]

On top of that sociological map, Vincent added something spiritual. He pointed to the west, where the sun descended toward the endless expanse of water beyond the Golden Gate Bridge. Here, on the edge of "infinity," he said, Black Power required more than equal rights and opportunities. It required a transformation of the body and soul. And for Vincent, it was the increasingly out-of-this-world music that emerged from the region in the 1960s and '70s that made this sense of limitlessness—of expanding beyond the continental shelf, if not the planet itself—come alive. Emboldened by exciting new sounds, styles, and street dances, he and his peers took the landscape of segregation and turned that mother out.[19] In the process, the music of the Bay Area came to resonate with the emancipatory imagination of Black Power, and vice versa. In the 1940s and '50s, the record producer Bob Geddins might have connected with Black migrants by marketing them ballads about their "troubles" (see ch. 1). But young people like Vincent soon became disillusioned with the carefully crafted gloom of the Oakland Blues. "I was tired of that old, slow moan," he told me. "I wanted the beat!"[20]

It wasn't that the blues didn't contest White Power. To the contrary, according to the geographer Clyde Woods, the blues was not only a musical genre that resonated with the trauma of slavery and segregation but also a Black "epistemology," or way of understanding the world, that organized "communities of consciousness" against racism.[21] Indeed, the historian Donna Murch has shown that it was rural migrants and their children—the same people who brought the blues to Oakland—who eventually discarded the respectability politics of the prewar era for the militancy of Black Power.[22]

Still, that didn't stop young people like Vincent from desiring and developing new sound cultures that embodied a more vigorous sense of empowerment. The "beat," he said, blended the longing and struggle of gospel and blues with the rhythms of commercial dance music—infusing R&B with not just a message but a *feeling* that was unapologetically pro-Black. It thus made dance music more explicitly and energetically political.[23] And as a confluence of antiracist organizing and countercultural revolt, the Bay Area led the charge to create a sound that not only mirrored but mobilized these social movements. According to Vincent, artists crossed social and sonic boundaries—drawing on everything from Miles Davis to James Brown, the acid-fed rock of the Grateful Dead to the Latin *ritmos* of Carlos Santana—to create something expressive, expansive, and unforgivingly funky. "It had the power that a lot of us wanted in our music," he explained, matter-of-factly.[24]

Power, whether political or vibrational, was a recurring theme in our conversation. Most of the time, the two meanings seemed interchangeable. This made sense. As was the case in Vincent's family, there was often little separation between the organized politics of Black Power and neighborhood life. "Every Black person knew someone in the Black Panthers," he told me. "I wasn't unique." But for Vincent, the Panthers were only one of many figures of Black—and often masculine—strength that made an impression on him as a kid. They were part of a cast of local characters that included musicians like Sly Stone, members of the Oakland Raiders ("the meanest SOBs in the league . . . they played in East Oakland, for God's sake"), and the pimps that inspired the blaxploitation film *The Mack* (1973).[25]

At the same time, as a scholar, Vincent was responsible for researching some of the most careful connections ever made between Black popular music and the Black Panthers. While in graduate school at UC Berkeley, he wrote his dissertation on the Lumpen, a soul band made up of rank-and-file Party members, after receiving a tip from Boots Riley, front man of the local anticapitalist rap troupe the Coup. (When he finally turned this research into a book, Vincent named it *Party Music* in honor of the Coup's 2001 album of the same name.[26]) Vincent revealed that, while the BPP is often viewed as an organization that took up guns, survival programs, and political organizing in pursuit of self-determination, it also promoted the strategic use of music, and cultural politics in general, to mobilize the masses. The BPP's war of words (and sometimes munitions) with more overtly cultural groups like the US Organization—founded by Maulana (Ron) Karenga, another former member of the Afro-American Association—was well known. But while most scholars of Black Power reproduced this division between the "revolutionary nationalist" and "cultural nationalist" wings of the movement, in the Lumpen, Vincent came upon empirical evidence of what he knew, personally, to be true: you could be "funky and a revolutionary at the same time."[27] Indeed, for many Black Oaklanders, this both / and breakdown of the bounds between music and struggle was a given. When I talked to Greg Bridges, a DJ on KPFA and KCSM, who grew up in East Oakland, he stressed the importance of Vincent's revelations for the nation at large. "But," he said, "it wasn't a surprise to us around here that there was a band in the Black Panthers. Music was a part of our everyday fabric."[28]

The three original members of the Lumpen—William Calhoun, Michael Torrance, and Clark Bailey—met as student activists at San José State University and San José City College in the late 1960s. They were later joined by James Mott—one of the leaders of the BPP Sacramento Chapter, and partner of Ericka Huggins, who ran the Oakland Community School. As rank-and-file revolutionaries, their talent and commitment as militants were appreciated by the Party command. But their musical gifts soon became apparent, as well. Minister of Culture Emory Douglas heard them singing, humming, and harmonizing with soul tunes on the radio while readying stacks of the BPP newspaper, the *Black Panther*, for distribution. Douglas—who, more than anyone else, was responsible for creating the BPP's iconic visual identity through illustration, collage, and printmaking—became convinced that music, too, could serve to educate and recruit local youth.

Douglas enlisted the support of Chief of Staff David Hilliard. Together, they persuaded the Central Committee to purchase a piano, microphones, and speakers so that the Party's musical communiques could be heard in hi-def. Hilliard came up with the name the Lumpen—a spin on the notion of the *lumpenproletariat*, or "underclass," in the writings of Karl Marx—to emphasize that the BPP saw underemployed and overpoliced young people, rather than the industrial working class, as the vanguard of the revolution. And these "brothers on the block," in Newton's words, were more likely to be moved to action by a soulful dance band than a strident union organizer. So, Calhoun was tasked with writing songs to create a compelling, but essentially didactic, means of communicating the Party's messages at concerts and rallies with the aim of recruiting young people to the cause.[29] (Indeed, the Lumpen's backing band was called the Freedom *Messengers*.)

The Lumpen was active for a short but productive period between 1970 and 1971, when they were dispatched to warm up the audience at political speeches and, eventually, headline their own shows. At the same time, their 45 RPM single, which included the songs "Free Bobby Now" and "(Won't Be) No More," was promoted in the *Black Panther* and sold at rallies to raise consciousness and cash. The band took the record to Oakland's KDIA and San Francisco's KSOL, the two most popular Black-serving radio stations in the area. But the DJs refused to play songs that encouraged listeners to "get guns to defend our community," no matter how much they mimicked, sonically, the R&B chart-toppers of the era.[30] Without the reach of radio, the group had to rely upon live performances to make an impact. Storming the stage at the Oakland Auditorium, Showcase Club, Merritt College, and UC Berkeley, they energized the soundscape across a range of spaces—some commercial, others educational—that were vital to the emerging politics of Black Power.[31]

According to Vincent, the Lumpen used these performances to mix "the politics of pleasure with the politics of revolution."[32] While their record contained original melodies, their concerts incorporated covers that infused popular soul and funk tunes with an overtly militant message. At a performance at Merritt College in November 1970, for example, the Freedom Messengers revved up the crowd with a rendition of Sly and the Family Stone's "Dance to the Music" (1967) that replaced the familiar and infectious chorus of the original with the refrain "pow-er to the peo-ple!" When the singers finally emerged to a roaring ovation, they were decked out in the dazzling costumes that were de rigueur among popular artists like the Temptations. Still, the Lumpen put a subversive "spin" on the conventional song-and-dance routine. "Our choreography was not just about spinning," explained Torrance. "It was part of the story. So with our steps you would see us throw grenades, you would see us pump shotguns . . . We did all that with dance."[33]

These performance techniques were essential to the Lumpen's political aims. The musicians saw their main goal as spreading BPP ideas through "relevant" lyrics. This, after all, was a time when "message music" was in its prime. In our conservation in 2018, Greg Bridges recalled that, as a teenager, songs like "We're a Winner" (1967) by the Impressions and "Respect Yourself" (1971) by the Staple Singers were more than mere pop tunes. They were "blueprints" for how to be Black. "[The music] became instructional," he told me, his deep, sonorous radio voice rippling over the phone.[34] The Lumpen made use of this mold, too. They just pushed the message from self-respect to organized rebellion. At the concert at Merritt College, for instance, they aroused the most excited responses from the audience when they sang about the audacity of insurrection. In "People Get Ready," a cover of the popular and prophetic gospel-soul tune, written by Curtis Mayfield for the Impressions, the band crooned: "People get ready / revolution's come. / Your only ticket / is a loaded gun. / Now wait my people / have faith, be strong. / We'll put the pigs / where they belong." If the original became a quintessential anthem of the Civil Rights Movement—with its moral message that virtue and devotion were the path to the promised land—then the Lumpen's revamp insisted that armed revolt was the true "ticket" to deliverance from oppression.[35]

But words were one thing. Action was another. In order to convince the prospective revolutionaries in the crowd to put their faith in collective resistance—a choice that carried the potential of death, as the poignant "dedication" to fallen comrades before "People Get Ready" revealed—the Lumpen needed to embolden people on a somatic and spiritual level. They needed to ignite a fire in people's bodies—to raise their temperatures and hasten their heartbeats—rather than just implant ideas in their heads. Their repertoire was calibrated to do just that. On "Power to the People," their cover of "Dance to the Music," the musicians ramped up the tempo from 128 to 148 beats per minute, sending the already fast-paced tune into an even more fervent state. They also took the three-minute length of the original song, which had been designed for radio airplay, and repeated it twice, extending the excitement by a minute and a half. Making their version faster and longer, they created a sonic vehicle that invigorated the crowd with embodied enthusiasm, creating a felt sense of what it meant to seethe and sweat together, in ways that somaticized the message of unity and strength.[36]

REVOLUTIONS IN RHYTHM

Indeed, by the late 1960s, young Black Oaklanders had come to desire and demand a new kind of electrifying energy, unifying force, and—most of all—fun from their popular music. The template for this sound was created, first and foremost, by James Brown, whose eighteen-piece orchestra appeared at both the Oakland Auditorium and newly constructed Oakland Coliseum in 1967. Brown would write one of the most iconic protest songs of the era: "Say It Loud—I'm Black and I'm Proud" (1968). But his most profound impact on popular culture was, arguably, his innovations in rhythm. According to Vincent, Brown revolutionized American dance music by rearranging songs around the downbeat—the first pulse in a four-beat bar of music—or what Brown called, with transcendent overtones, "the One."[37] This mysticism was spot on. Rather than move a song through a series of changes—a linear progression from A to B to C—the recurrence of the downbeat marked a return to the start. Within this looping form, the downbeat gave each individual musician a common point of orientation. This allowed them to find space within the groove to complement each other's rhythms and melodies—creating tension between the different elements, while still maintaining a tight sense of togetherness. The results were mesmerizing.

In the early 1960s, R&B tunes—like pop songs in general—were organized around a predictable verse-chorus structure that featured catchy melodies and prominent vocalists. In 1965, for instance, when "Papa's Got a Brand New Bag"—often credited as one of the first funk songs—was the sixth-most popular record of the year on *Billboard's* R&B Chart, Brown came in a few spots ahead of "My Girl" (1964) by the Temptations. Released just seven months earlier, "My Girl" sounds like it's from a different epoch. The song is locked into the marching pulse of its 4 / 4 time signature, like a metronome, with the bass line and melody landing on the one and three and the rhythm guitar responding on the two and four. In the pre-chorus, the horns and vocals step up together, almost ploddingly, on the beat, further cementing the song's obedience to a regular rhythmic structure. It then repeats the same pattern of verse-pre-chorus-chorus two more times, creating an inevitable sense of progression and resolution through the addition of symphonic strings and, ultimately, a key change.[38] In this way, "My Girl" reflects the linear arrangements typical of European music (see Intro), which defined most popular songwriting prior to the mid-1960s.

"Papa's Got a Brand New Bag," by contrast, finds pockets of syncopation throughout the 4 / 4 structure to insert pops of sound. It pronounces its reorganization around "the One" with prominent horn blasts on the first beat, which are counterposed with more discreet guitar chops on the two and four. Meanwhile, the bassline meanders around the beat, messing with the metrical conventions of a song like "My Girl." The result is a looping, bouncing, propulsive groove.[39] When the song came out, dancers responded in kind. While Brown had been popular among African American audiences since the release of "Please, Please, Please" in 1956, "Papa's Got a Brand New Bag" became his first crossover hit, reaching the Top 10 on the Pop Chart and earning him his first Grammy Award.

The influence of this new sound was profound. By the end of the 1960s, songs came to be appreciated less for their meaning or melody than their ability to produce what the ethnomusicologist Michael Veal calls a captivating "songscape."[40] In recordings like "Get Up (I Feel Like Being a) Sex Machine" (1970), "The Payback" (1973), and "Papa Don't Take No Mess" (1974), Brown's singles became extended and repetitive meditations on rhythm that were designed to work dancers into a state of euphoria. This, according to Vincent, reflected the increasing influence of Afro-Diasporic music in Brown's funky arrangements—or what Vincent calls "the spiritual element of music-making, the necessity to bring about trance, to raise rhythm to a cosmic level."[41] Brown, in fact, began to insist that his entire band exploit their instruments for their percussive potential. Horn, guitar, bass, grunt. They all became means to increase the rhythmic tension and intensity of the groove. "I was hearing everything, even the guitars, like they were drums," he later explained.[42]

In the East Bay, funk musicians took their cue from Brown's revolution in rhythm and ran with it. Sylvester "Sly Stone" Stewart led the charge. Stewart was born to a musical and religious family in Denton, Texas, who, after World War II, joined the exodus to the Bay Area. They settled in the North Bay city of Vallejo, where the Mare Island Naval Shipyard served as a magnet for migrant workers. The Church of God in Christ, where an uncle ministered, became the center of the children's musical cosmos. The oldest among them, including

Sylvester, formed a gospel singing group called the Stewart Four, recording a 78 RPM single that the family sold on return trips to Texas in the 1950s. "My kids were always singing," recalled their mother, Alpha. "After dinner, during dinner, before dinner, in the car, on the way to church, after church," agreed Vaetta (Vet), the youngest.[43]

As a teen, Sylvester turned from gospel to pop music, participating in a number of local, mixed-race singing groups. Eventually, he moved to San Francisco, where, as DJ Sly Stone, he captivated listeners on the upstart "race station" KSOL. (He would go on to spin records on KDIA, too.) At KSOL, the station managers counted on the cutting-edge young tastemaker to be the "vanguard of music," according to owner Alan Schulz.[44] Interestingly, however, when he went out to recruit a band of his own, Stone tapped musicians who cut their teeth in the gospel and blues scenes that, by the mid-1960s, had already been eclipsed by the more progressive sounds that he spun on the radio. Larry Graham, for one, was still performing jazz and R&B standards with his mother at clubs like Esther's Orbit Room, the Showcase, and the Sportsman in Oakland (see Preface). Cynthia Robinson, on the other hand, played trumpet in backing bands for Lowell Fulson and Jimmy McCracklin (see ch. 1). In fact, according to Robinson, Sly and the Stoners—the precursor to Sly and the Family Stone—was "literally made up of Johnny Heartsman's old band."[45] The Oakland Blues, it seemed, would be at once embraced and vanquished by this new musical experiment.[46]

Like the Lumpen, Sly and the Family Stone wasn't immune from explicit political messages—as, for example, in songs like "Everyday People" (1968) and "Stand!" (1969).[47] But more often, their politics—which tended toward the emancipatory potential of pleasure and playful self-expression—reverberated in the very waveforms of the music and the ways that diverse crowds moved to it. The band personified the social and cultural intersections that made the Bay Area such a progressive milieu in the 1960s. In contrast to most R&B acts at that time, Sly and the Family Stone was made up of a mixed-race and mixed-gender roster of musicians, who each appeared in their own unique, attention-grabbing costumes. This combination of individualism and integration staged a form of solidarity that resisted the segregationist order of White Power and the separatist aims of many Black nationalists. On "Dance to the Music" (1967), their breakout single, the band bucked the conventions of contemporary soul performance. Rather than retreat to the background, ceding center stage to the star vocalist, the musicians each introduced and expressed themselves through a funky solo.[48] In the process, they sounded a new and more equitable relationship between the individual and the group—or what the dancer and performance studies scholar Naomi Macalalad Bragin calls "moving" and "grooving"—which converted the dance floor into a space for practicing the sociality of social movements.[49]

Musically, Sly and the Family Stone combined the rhythmic force of James Brown, who they covered early on, with the incomparable low-end sound of Larry Graham. In fact, at the time when Stone recruited Graham, after a performance in Haight Ashbury, Graham was still accompanying his mom's piano. It wasn't until he became a member of the Family Stone that he was able to put the slap bass and the drums—two essential ingredients of the funk—together.[50] This recipe can be savored on "Thank You for Talkin' to Me, Africa" (1971). A sloweddown reprise of "Thank You (Falettinme Be Mice Elf Agin)" (1969), the song begins with a mix of slap bass and drums that's at once sparse and absorbing. Soon, the organ and guitar enter the recording, their sharp and syncopated sounds accentuating the space in between the pounding 4/4 beats. It's nearly two minutes into the seven-minute song before the familiar lyrics emerge, now doused in reverb. By that time, the listener has already become engrossed in the expansive, repetitive groove. And as stated in the title, the band thought that this transportive musical dialect spoke straight from the motherland.[51]

Michael Veal notes that, in the 1970s, musicians from around the African Diaspora adopted new technologies and mesmerizing grooves to create liberatory sound cultures—from funk in the U.S. to dub reggae in Jamaica—that connected mythic notions of Africa to the imagined freedom of outer space.[52] Still, Sly and the Family Stone incorporated distinctly national and regional features into their sonic UFO. "I Want to Take You Higher" (1969), for instance, starts with a conventional verse-chorus structure. But after a break at the three-minute mark, the song departs on an extended gospel vamp—a "combination of repetition and escalation" characteristic of gospel songs—in which a chorus of voices sings "higher!" over and over, translating the semantic meaning of the word into a somatic experience of transcendence. Meanwhile, the musicians trade solos that resonate with the blues-inspired psychedelic rock then gripping the Bay Area. Here, the Stewart children's mastery of the looping vamp, which the minister and musicologist Braxton Shelley calls a Black Christian "ritual technology," returns to transform the soul of the congregation via a dance floor version of the holy ghost.[53]

This exemplifies what the Black studies scholar Tony Bolden means when he writes that "funk comprises a secular counterpart of 'the spirit'" in African American culture. Indeed, as a recognizable category of music, funk can be identified by certain genre-defining sounds, like slap bass and syncopation. But according to Bolden, it also indicates a genre-*defying* tendency that cuts across different styles of Black music. Like "swing" in jazz and "flow" in hip-hop, "funk" refers to an ineffable force—a kinesis—that enters into and unifies the bodies of musicians and audiences. As with the significance of motion and emotion in "sanctified" forms of African American worship, the affective power of this "funk / spirit" to "take you higher" reaches its realization in dance.[54]

THE POWER OF THE POP

In the context of Black Power, and the creation of songs like "I Want to Take You Higher," the dance floor served as an arena in which Black Oaklanders could experience deliverance into new forms of community and consciousness. As the dance studies scholar Imani Kai Johnson writes, dance music involves an inextricable connection between sound and movement. In this "aural-kinesthetic" relationship, the meaning of a song exists in the collective embodied response, rather than the individual listening experience, of the people who groove to it.[55] So, as funk artists pushed the sounds of the Bay Area in new directions, young people invented dances that incorporated the power and ethics of the music into their everyday corporeal movements. In Oakland, they called it boogaloo.

Remixing the name of a 1960s soul (and later Latin) dance craze, the innovators of the Oakland boogaloo replaced the smooth motions that mirrored the mellifluous sound of soul music with more staccato ones— or "pops"—that matched the percussive force of the funk. This signature move, in which dancers contract their muscles in time with the beat of a song, started to appear in the street dance performances of young Black East Oaklanders around 1965. The visual culture of the postwar era provided ample inspiration for the "punchiness" of the pop: stop-motion sci-fi films, comic books, industrial machines. But it was also, fundamentally, an aural-kinesthetic response to the percussiveness of funk music. The pop, in this sense, was like the embodied equivalent of the slap—a way for a bolt of energy, a wave of Black power, to shudder through muscle, ligament, and bone. (According to the music writer and journalist Eric Arnold, young people originally called this move the "Oakland Hit." But as boogaloo culture spread to Richmond as "robotting" and San Francisco as "strutting," and then eventually to Southern California via the Central Valley, it was uprooted from the soil of its genesis, becoming known, more generically, as "popping." As it left the Bay Area, popping became one of the main tributaries of hip-hop dance.[56])

In Oakland, young Black people practiced and circulated these movements through street dance battles, talent shows, and, eventually, televised performances. In a precursor to the sideshow (see ch. 5), young people from around the region would converge on the basketball courts at East Oakland's Sobrante Park or the amphitheater at North Oakland's Mosswood Park. As the sun went down, they would circle up their cars, turn on their lights, and reveal their newest moves in a person-to-person "face off."[57] These battles provided a space for dancers to experiment with and expand upon the boogaloo repertoire. People competed for fun and bragging rights. But when it came time for a talent show, where there might be prize money, dancers got serious. They took what was largely an individual means of expression and turned it into a coordinated spectacle of dazzle and grace. Choreographing complex performances, crews of young people refined their routines in the privacy of bedrooms and garages before revealing them to excited crowds at rec centers and school auditoriums. The most successful of these groups, the Black Resurgents, even managed to enjoy a modest career as entertainers.[58]

In 1971, the Black Resurgents formed to compete in a talent show at East Oakland's Elmhurst Middle School. (Their routine was set to "Super Bad" by James Brown.) In 1974, they won the Black Explosion talent competition at the Oakland Auditorium. Connecting with the musician, and fellow Castlemont High student, D'Wayne Wiggins, they began to perform at Black-owned clubs around Oakland, opening for the Pointer Sisters and Tower of Power, to music by Wiggins's Alpha Omega. (Wiggins would go on to form the popular R&B group Tony! Toni! Toné! with his brother Raphael Saadiq and cousin Terry Christian Riley.) In 1975, while still seniors, the Resurgents opened for Graham Central Station—the band fronted by Larry Graham after he left Sly and the Family Stone—which resulted in a touring gig that raised their profile around the region. After connecting with the record producer Harvey Fuqua, who used to run A&R at Motown, and signed Sylvester to Fantasy Records, the group even opened for San Francisco's queer disco icon. But the acme of their career arguably came in 1977, when they danced their way out of the P-Funk Mothership to the screams of thousands of fans at the Oakland Coliseum.[59]

Whether in the middle of an improvisational dance circle, or on stage during a talent show, the boogaloo—like the funk music that inspired it—provided young people with opportunities to practice new modes of social movement. If you went to Sweet's Ballroom or Esther's Orbit Room in the 1950s, you would have seen couples swinging, dipping, flipping, and grinding (see ch. 1). But whether more acrobatic or erotic, these dances would have been performed in pairs. In fact, for most of the twentieth century, African American and European American social dance involved variations on partner dancing. Funk dance departed from the rules of partner dance—the relatively set patterns of steps, the defined roles of leader and follower—freeing people to explore a more personal form of expression. According to Naomi Macalalad Bragin, however, this focus on soloing wasn't solipsistic. To the contrary, improvisation required dancers to be at once responsive to the individual *and* the group. The two became, paradoxically, inseparable. In this sense, funk dance marked a return to a tradition of "feeling together in movement" that survived from Central and West African performance practices. In the process, it informed a repertoire of social dances that taught young people to move both apart and together—to rehearse the cooperative spirit of social movement—through an idiom that she calls "*Soul Train*-ing."[60]

In the few videos of performances from the 1970s that survive in the archives, the members of boogaloo crews tend to start out in a line and move through a series of orderly formations. At times, they perform identical steps, often either staggering their movements in a wave-like motion or interlacing their limbs to stress the intricacy of their coordination. Other times, they create symmetrical counterpoints to each other's positions (e.g., one goes low, one goes high). These complex choreographies demonstrate the dancers' abilities to move through their differences as a single, synchronized organism. Eventually, one of the dancers will step forward to improvise a solo. The soloists often look like marionettes, their motor force originating in some uncanny source beyond their bodies. The overall stiffness of their movement

Figure 2. The members of boogaloo dance crew the Black Resurgents with Jay Payton, host of KEMO's *Soul Is*, 1973. Credit: African American Museum and Library at Oakland.

creates exciting moments of contrast when they release one part of their body into a more fluid state: a little wiggle of the leg or swivel of the head. But even as the soloists do their own thing, they remain integrally connected to the rest of the group through their shared movement grammar and orientation to the hard-hitting funk beats. No matter where they are in space, the dancers pop or pose in time with the drums. As with the looping groove of funk music, then, the rhythmic structure of the pop provides each of the dancers with a cohesive time grid, permitting them to invent as individuals while still contributing to the common aims of the collective (see fig. 2).

The complex coordination among East Bay funk dancers was taken even further by robotting groups from Richmond. Crews like the Criminons and Lady Mechanical Robots took up the tight, interwoven choreographies from boogaloo routines, where dancers appeared to move as precisely calibrated machines. But they made the moves faster, sharper, and more compact. Looking for ways to stand out from the pack, robotting groups started to speed up the records that they danced to from 45 to 78 RPMs. On the one hand, this allowed them to cram nearly twice as much choreography into time-constrained talent competitions. But on the other, it took the futurism of the funk and made it sound even more otherworldly. Robotting crews also tightened up their formations so that they touched arms, shoulders, and hips. "You had to be uniform," said Renée Lesley, a member of the Lady Mechanical Robots. "You had to go to the ground and do something offbeat, [but] when you came back up you had to make sure that you were touching . . . When you separated you had to pop back up together." Macalalad Bragin calls this a "collective practice of being in touch that bonds the dancers in rhythm."[61]

In the shadow of Silicon Valley, where revolutions in aeronautics and computing were underway, midcentury critics worried that space-age technologies would spell the end of liberal individualism. And in a sense, they were right. But the future that was staged by robotting crews wouldn't just produce mindless conformism and corporate control. Instead, when remixed by young people of color, machines inspired the creation of complex collectivities, flowing, spectacularly, as one. Despite their apparent distinctions, then, Richmond crews like the Androids and Asteroids expressed a similar cultural politics to Oakland crews like the Black Resurgents; emerging from the P-Funk Mothership in 1977, the Resurgents made it clear that everything from rebels to robots served as an invitation to invent revolutionary forms of social movement.

In the late 1960s and early 1970s, boogaloo dancers were surrounded with the ideas, ethos, and style of Black Power—a milieu that was reflected in names like the Black Resurgents and Black Messengers. While these allusions could be metaphorical, the connections to revolutionary politics were often material, if not always militant. The BPP's Community School, for one, regularly organized talent shows, where youth culture and style, including boogaloo, could mingle with Party messaging. And in between commercial gigs, the Resurgents rallied crowds at BPP events.[62] Like the Lumpen, then, they came to serve as cultural ambassadors for the Black Panthers, attracting teens to the movement and creating affective connections between embodied style and insurgent politics. These performances communicated to a mass audience that Black Power involved certain ways of moving and grooving, not just marching and debating. In the 1970s, tens of thousands of teens attended boogaloo shows or tuned in when the Resurgents performed on KEMO's *Soul Is*—a local version of *Soul Train* that was hosted by the emcee and entertainer Jay Payton. In the process, young people imbibed—and, in many cases, imitated—new and empowering ways of inhabiting a Black body that embedded the muscular optimism of the moment in their everyday social movements.

DEFREMERY, PT. 2

At the end of chapter 1, I noted that, in the late 1960s, young Black Oaklanders reclaimed the terrains where they encountered the constraints of Jim Crow, converting youth spaces from sites of oppression and policing into ones of Black power, pleasure, and play. Certainly, this was true of educational spaces—from the school cafeterias, where boogaloo crews wowed their peers, to Merritt College, where revolutionary ideas kindled the creation of the BPP. But no place signified this transformation of urban space quite so much as DeFremery Park in West Oakland.

In "All Power to the People: Black Panthers at 50" at the Oakland Museum in 2016 (see Preface), images of DeFremery Park popped up throughout the exhibit. It's now well known that the Panthers used this space as the staging ground for survival programs, from grocery giveaways to sickle cell anemia tests. But its importance among Black residents didn't emerge out of nowhere in the 1960s; it had served as a prominent site for picnics, concerts, and military and youth dances since the start of the twentieth century (see ch. 1). The politicization of the park during the Black Power Era didn't erase this legacy of liveliness. It rather incorporated these amusements into the movement. Still, it was hard to sense these sonic politics at the exhibit. So, when I spotted a second pair of headphones along the wall, I rushed over to find a screen playing *Black Panthers* (1968), a documentary by the French filmmaker Agnès Varda. Here, I hoped, amid the silence of the archive, I might finally find a trace of the everyday soundscape of Black Power in Oakland.

At first, I was delighted. The film begins with a focus on music, sound, and social movements. Opening with a rally at DeFremery Park, it simmers with youthful excitement as an unnamed band (it was shot before the formation of the Lumpen) performs an uptempo soul tune with a militant message outside of the DeFremery Recreation Center. "We got to free Huey!" goes the refrain. But the call for liberation isn't limited to the imprisoned minister of defense. As it rings out from the amplifiers and ripples across the grass, it's taken up by the crowd of young people—including many children—who sing and clap, sway and two-step, in time with the band (see fig. 3).

But this attention to pleasure is soon discarded by Varda in favor of more "serious" concerns. "This is no picnic in Oakland," states the narrator. "It is a political rally organized by the Black Panthers." While this grim pronouncement treats a "picnic" as the antithesis of politics, at the time, this distinction would have made little sense to the throngs of young Black people who gathered at DeFremery Park. Still, this moment of aural-kinesthetic connection between the sound of the music and movement of the crowd serves as a mere prologue to a series of more overtly "militant" images. In the process, the film pivots to

Figure 3. Young women and children dance along to a band at a Black Panther Party rally at DeFremery Park in West Oakland, from the film *Black Panthers*, 1968. Credit: Ciné Tamaris.

focus on a familiar set of visual tropes. In one scene, BPP recruits rehearse military-style marches on the basketball court while Bobby Seale and Stokely Carmichael look on, like generals, in review. In another, a captain recites the Ten-Point Program. But rather than attend to the sound of his voice, the camera zooms in on his Africanist necklace. Indeed, the film can't seem to resist focusing on the black uniforms, black glasses, black naturals, blue flags, red books, and other colorful displays of militancy that defined the Party's image. There are several shots of the West Oakland streetscape, too. But rather than stop to attune to its everyday vibrations, the footage is taken from a moving car, converting the street into a silent canvas for the presentation of BPP posters and other visual propaganda.[63]

In Oakland, the iconic images of Black Power like those captured in *Black Panthers* are now canonized in everything from museum retrospectives to contemporary streetwear. In the process of reproducing the BPP's politics of "insurgent visibility," the *vibe* of these freedom practices is routinely missed.[64] This, I think, is a mistake. The Panthers themselves understood that neither Black people nor their allies came to the rallies at DeFremery Park out of raw need or revolutionary zeal alone. Instead, they came to groove to the Lumpen, move like the Black Resurgents, and satisfy their collective desire to build a better world. They came to feel this revolutionary idea of "freedom" in their neighborhood, their bodies, their bones. They came, that is, because these events were *fun*. And listening for the sounds of Black Power offers a way to tune into what the Black studies scholar Robin D. G. Kelley calls, in a riff on P-Funk spin-off Parlet, the "pleasure principle" of Black cultural politics.[65]

While politicians and social scientists (we could add documentarians) tend to treat Black cultures as "expressions of pathology" or "creative 'coping mechanisms' to deal with racism and poverty," writes Kelley, they ignore the importance of "aesthetics, style, and pleasure" to Black communities.[66] "Though often mischaracterized as a *lack* of rationality," adds Tony Bolden, "the pleasure principle should be understood as an alternative *form* of rationality."[67] This misreading, which is rooted in racist ideas about Black people's supposed lack of moral reasoning, means that the sensuous intelligence of Black cultural practices is often discounted—or worse, derided—in favor of more "proper" or "legitimate" forms of political organizing, like protests and policy campaigns.

But there's no action without attraction, no movement without desire, no community without communion. In the 1960s and '70s, funk culture was instrumental to creating opportunities for collective action in Oakland. Emerging in response to the social and sonic conditions of the Oakland Blues, it embedded a felt sense of power and potential in people's everyday lives. But these social movements didn't go uncontested. To the contrary, Black dance music animated not only new freedoms but also forms of control that came to define the urban environment after Black Power. As the excitement of the 1960s and '70s gave way to a pervasive sense of crisis in the 1980s and '90s, the sound cultures created by young Black Oaklanders were met with new modes of regulation meant to stamp out "nuisance," and especially "noise," in ways that intensified the policing of Black youth.

3

INTO THE CRACK

The War on Nuisance

A TALE OF TWO WILSONS

By 1972, the Black Panthers (BPP) were in crisis. Under President Richard Nixon, the FBI's Counterintelligence Program (COINTELPRO) had waged a relentless campaign to infiltrate, discredit, and divide progressive social movements, in particular Civil Rights and Black Power organizations. And the BPP—which FBI Director J. Edgar Hoover, afraid of the popularity of their free breakfast program, called the "greatest threat to the internal security of the country"—had been their number one target. Of the countless COINTELPRO attacks against Black radicals, almost 80 percent had been directed at the Panthers.[1] Using misinformation and disinformation, the FBI had propagated suspicion and conflict among supporters. In 1972, Huey Newton and Bobby Seale were reunited in Oakland after years of being bogged down in politicized court trials and prison terms. But more and more, they found themselves at war with would-be allies rather than the state.

This struggle reached its peak when Newton renounced Eldridge Cleaver over the timing of insurrection. While Cleaver called for an immediate assault on the state, Newton insisted on building popular support, brick by brick, through the Party's survival programs. So, in July 1972, Newton declared Oakland the "base of operations" for a more incremental approach to the revolution. After years of national growth, he called upon the rank-and-file from other cities to close their chapters and move to Oakland, where they could concentrate on creating a model for Black Power through social service programs and electoral politics. By seizing the reins of local government—by 1970, the city was 35 percent Black—Newton envisioned a path to "survival pending revolution" via the redistribution of public jobs, taxes, and services—a sort of municipal socialism with a mission of racial justice.[2]

In 1973, seven years after Stokely Carmichael urged the crowd at UC Berkeley to "build political institutions . . . to meet the needs of Oakland" (see ch. 2), the BPP ran Bobby Seale for mayor and Elaine Brown for city council.[3] They both came up short. But activists turned out in droves to register voters of color across the flats—some 35,000 in 1973 alone.[4] This massive increase in registration meant that when a more moderate African American political leader named Lionel Wilson ran for mayor in 1976, there were enough voters mobilized to end the reign of White Power to put him over the top. Under Brown, who became BPP chairwoman in 1974, every remaining Panther was deployed to get out the vote. "The streets of Oakland were being harvested [for Wilson]," she later recalled.[5]

Wilson's win represented a radical change for local politics. But he was no radical. Born to a Creole family in New Orleans, he migrated to West Oakland on the advice of a relative who had secured work in the shipyards during World War I. A member of this earlier group of Black residents, he went on to rack up a series of "firsts." In the 1930s, he became one of the only Black students at UC Berkeley—part of a cohort of up-and-coming political leaders, such as Tarea Hall Pittman, Byron Rumford, and Ron Dellums—where he studied economics. "While there was far more discrimination and . . . segregation in the South," he recalled, of Oakland's Jim Crow (see ch. 1), "there was an awful lot of it here [too]." When he and his wife bought a home, they had to use a White surrogate to skirt the segregationist tactics of local realtors and mortgage lenders—even though, as a member of New Orleans's Creole community, he was light-skinned enough to be mistaken for White when he entered the Army during World War II.[6] Angered by this mistreatment and emboldened, like many Black servicemembers, by his tour of duty in Europe, he went on to earn a law degree from UC Hastings in San Francisco. In the 1950s, during the rise of the Civil Rights Movement, he worked with the NAACP and East Bay Democratic Club to dismantle the de jure conditions of racial discrimination. Then, in 1960, Governor Pat Brown appointed him the first Black superior court judge in Alameda County.

In the 1960s, Wilson began to pivot into politics. He chaired the Oakland Economic Development Commission during the federal War on Poverty. Savvy and centrist, he navigated the waves of the city's Black Power revolt by promoting economic opportunity in its Black neighborhoods. All of this made him one of the city's most prominent, and palatable, Black political figures. In 1976, then, when Mayor John Reading, the last of the Knowland Machine Republicans, announced that he was stepping down, a rare coalition of Black moderates, liberals, and radicals implored Wilson to run.[7] He alone, it seemed, was pro-Black enough to appeal to the city's contentious grassroots and pro-business enough to appease its tottering corporate establishment.

The election of Lionel Wilson thus inaugurated a new political, but not necessarily economic, era that the political scientist Adolph Reed once called a "Black urban regime."[8] As in Chicago, Detroit, Washington, DC, and dozens of other cities across the nation, Black Oaklanders marched through the gates opened by the Civil Rights struggle and took control of local government. ("We didn't get our 40 acres and a mule," rapped George Clinton on "Chocolate City," Parliament's 1975 ode to the District of Columbia, "but we did get you, CC."⁹). Indeed, by 1980, Black, Latine, and Asian American residents had seized most of the seats on Oakland's Port, Civil Service, and Planning Commissions, which positioned them to direct employment and contracting opportunities, long the spoils of White Power, to communities of color. Meanwhile, Mayor Wilson pursued many of the same economic development aims that he had fought for during the War on Poverty. He attempted to stem the ravages of disinvestment and expand the pie for business owners and workers of color by championing a series of overzealous redevelopment schemes that were put forward by his predecessors. As a ring of racially restrictive suburbs removed more and more jobs and tax revenue from the city, accelerating its apparent descent into poverty and crime, Wilson eschewed progressive proposals in favor of an all-out campaign to restore a sense of public safety and attract capital back downtown.¹⁰

In an unexpected twist, then, Lionel Wilson's administration came to align with the reactionary politics of another prominent Wilson. James Q. Wilson was a political scientist and public intellectual, who, over the course of his five-decade career, became a champion of neoconservative ideas about government, morals, and especially crime. Jim, as his familiars called him, grew up in a working-class home in Long Beach, California. The first in his family to go to college, he received a PhD in political science from the University of Chicago in 1959. There, he was mentored by Edward Banfield, a staunch critic of "root cause" theories of social problems and government antipoverty programs. From Chicago, Wilson trailed Banfield to Harvard, where he taught for 25 years.

In the mid-1960s, as director of the Harvard-MIT Joint Center for Urban Studies, Wilson turned his attention to poverty, crime, and the role of the police in urban life. This resulted in *Varieties of Police Behav-*

ior: The Management of Law and Order in Eight Communities (1968), which compared policing practices and political cultures across a mixture of mid-sized cities, including Syracuse, New York, Highland Park, Illinois, and Oakland. For Wilson, Oakland was significant because it epitomized a "legalistic" style of policing; the Oakland Police Department (OPD) required officers to enforce the letter of the law—even, or especially, in the case of minor crimes—without leniency or discretion. As a result, arrests for everything from traffic violations to vice soared in comparison to the other cities in the study. In Oakland, for instance, 16,000 arrests were made in 1965 for public intoxication—five times as many per capita as Syracuse, another allegedly "legalistic" community. "Whereas a patrolman in another city will wait until someone complains of a drunk or until he sees one creating a disturbance," explained Wilson, "an Oakland patrolman . . . will often stop and investigate any person he sees who appears to have been drinking."[11]

Of course, it was impossible for the police to be everywhere at once. So, inevitably, arrests were highest in working-class neighborhoods of color, like East and West Oakland, where the OPD concentrated its patrols. Coming to Oakland between 1965 and 1967, at the exact moment the BPP emerged to monitor the everyday terror of the OPD (see ch. 2), Wilson didn't see racist state violence. ("To be sure," he wrote, dismissively, "Oakland has had a few highly publicized cases of alleged brutality . . . But taken together they do not suggest systematic or routine abuse."[12]) Instead, he saw the makings of an "equitable" but "zealous" form of law enforcement. It wasn't that young people, poor people, or people of color didn't bear the brunt of this policing. But according to Wilson, that was because they were responsible, perhaps even *predestined*, for most of the crime. "Because such persons are more likely than certain others to commit crimes," he argued, of "Negroes, drunks, and the like," "the law will fall heavily on them and be experienced as 'harassment.'"[13]

In the 1960s, as the nation was rocked by urban revolts against anti-Black policing and discrimination, Wilson's research made waves in government, garnering him a role in President Lyndon Johnson's Commission on Law Enforcement and the Administration of Justice. (Wilson eventually panned the commission's report on the grounds that it cited racism and poverty—rather than individual moral character, his preferred explanation—as the root cause of crime.[14]) But the impact of *Varieties* would be eclipsed by the article that he went on to pen in the *Atlantic* with the criminologist George Kelling. Published in 1982, "Broken Windows: The Police and Neighborhood Safety" presented a turning point in the policing of Black and Brown communities across the U. S. Wilson and Kelling argued that, in order to reduce crime and increase a feeling of safety, the police shouldn't prosecute only the most serious criminals. Instead, they should crack down on people who commit minor violations of the law—"panhandlers, drunks, addicts, rowdy teenagers, prostitutes, loiterers, the mentally disturbed"—because they corrode the "sense of order and civility" among law-abiding "citizens." This, reasoned Wilson and Kelling, would signal that the neighborhood wouldn't stand for any troublesome behavior. Otherwise, criminals-in-waiting would see the signs of social and moral decay—the proverbial "broken windows"—and run amok. The solution, suggested the authors, was to return to the era of the "beat cop," who would walk the neighborhood, addressing the mundane, street-level concerns that could make or break the "quality of community life" among its more upstanding residents.[15]

This idea, now called broken-windows policing, took off in the 1980s and '90s as cities across the country sought to counteract a creeping fear of lawlessness among middle-class residents, business owners, and African Americans, who were fed up with the waves of drug-fueled crime and violence crashing into their communities. William Bratton, head of the New York Police Department under Mayor Rudolph Giuliani, considered Wilson his "intellectual mentor." He was so taken with "Broken Windows" that he toted copies of the article to conferences, pressing it into the palms of other top cops, like an evangelist.[16] Giuliani was a disciple, too. Losing to David Dinkins in 1989, he consulted with Wilson and Kelling—a two-man "Rudy University"—about how to make inroads with the increasingly anxious electorate.[17] In 1993, he ousted Dinkins, the first Black mayor, in a rematch.

Bratton and Giuliani, who oversaw the rise of the racially abusive practice of "stop-and-frisk," are now remembered for making New York City the capital of broken-windows policing.[18] But many of the tactics associated with their reign—including a zero-tolerance approach to misdemeanors, quotas for citations and arrests, and data-driven management—were detected, decades earlier, by Jim Wilson in Oakland. And as Lionel Wilson sought to right the city's reputation and economy as it reeled from racialized neglect, he came to rely, increasingly, on the quality-of-life policing strategies attributed to his improbable counterpart. Cracking down on both streetcorner drug dealers and neighborhood nuisances, he tried to demonstrate that Oakland could have it all: law *and* order. And this put him at odds with the liberatory sound cultures of Black Power.

In the late 1970s and '80s, the wave of sonic and social movements that swept across Oakland during the Black Power revolt (see ch. 2) crashed into the strategies of governance and development that accompanied the rise of the Black urban regime. Mayor Wilson attempted to cement the economic gains of the Civil Rights Era, which saw desegregation and upward mobility, by incorporating people of color into the mechanisms of political and corporate power. At the same time, however, a series of compounding crises—public and private disinvestment, mass unemployment, and crack cocaine—seemed to threaten these tenuous wins. In the wake of Black Power, Oakland came to be seen as a volatile and violent space of ruin—a "ghost town." The racist overtones were clear. Still, this fear of economic and moral decay inspired new modes of policing that were meant to restore order in working- and middle-class communities of color.

In the 1980s and '90s, spurred by a new social movement of homeowners of color, the administrations of Lionel Wilson and Elihu Harris retooled Oakland's regulations and police practices to crusade against "crime and grime." In line with changes in racial politics that occurred across the country in the post–Civil Rights Era, this "war on nuisance" reorganized policing around cultural comportment and style, including sonic practices, rather than race. In other words, it continued to target young Black Oaklanders, and especially men, but now under color of law. With the rise of broken-windows policing, then, residents weren't seen as predestined for crime, as Jim Wilson had written in the 1960s, because they were Black; they were predestined for crime because their modes of expression were unruly and unmanageable. And as we'll see in each of the remaining chapters, this war on nuisance— which targeted Black youth culture, including Black dance music and soundscapes—would loop through struggles over Oakland's cultural landscape, from streets and parks to concerts and nightclubs, in ways that fundamentally transformed the city's urban environment.

INTO THE CRACK(S)

During the Black Power Era, as street chants and car radios echoed across Oakland, the cries of revolution were even more conspicuous amid a landscape in which the sounds of hammers and steel had, since World War II, stilled to a hush. The war remade the city in ways that ripple to this day. But the actual eruption of military-industrial activity that set those waves in motion was exceedingly brief. The shipyards began to fire workers as early as 1944, and between August 1945 and February 1946, manufacturing jobs plummeted by 70 percent. By the end of 1946, the number of industrial jobs had already returned to pre-war levels; only now, there were tens of thousands more residents in need of work.[19]

This rollback hit African American migrants the hardest. Given the segregation of most military industries, along with union rules ("last hired, first fired"), many of the Black workers who found jobs along the water lost them before the war was even over.[20] Black residents, wrote Huey Newton, in his memoir, were "once again kicked off 'the plantation' and left stranded with no place to go in an industrial society."[21] Moreover, in contrast to other migrant communities, many of which relocated again after the war, 85 percent of African Americans remained on the West Coast—becoming, like the sleeping car porters before them, links in an ongoing process of chain migration. Between 1944 and 1950, as Oakland's boom turned out to be a bubble, its Black population ballooned by 118 percent.[22]

This economic crisis soon became racial and spatial, too, as manufacturers retreated behind the color lines that came to divide the East Bay's cities from its emerging suburbs. Between 1951 and 1964, for instance, industrial investment in Alameda County created a whopping 41,000 new jobs in manufacturing. But given that suburbs like Fremont courted companies with open land, minimal taxes, anti-union policies, and a comparatively White demographic, most of these opportunities whistled right past Oakland.[23] By the 1970s, the city's portion of industrial jobs had dropped from 50 to 30 percent of the county total.[24]

In theory, Black people could have followed the jobs. But as the legal scholar Richard Rothstein argues, they were prevented from doing so by explicit governmental policies that maintained the suburbs as an exclusively White space.[25] Between 1949 and 1951, when 75,000 building permits were issued for private homes across the Bay Area suburbs, only 600 were in neighborhoods that were open to African Americans. And according to a study from the early 1960s, of the 350,000 homes built in Northern California during the postwar period, people of color ended up purchasing less than a hundred.[26] So, Newton was being literal when he said that Black Oaklanders were "stranded with no place to go." As in other metropolitan regions across the country, working-class people of color became confined to overcrowded and underserved neighborhoods that were being forsaken by capital for a racially restrictive ring of suburbs. By 1960, one study found that two thirds of the city's residents of color were living in conditions of "deprivation" or worse.[27]

But the other third were doing better than ever before, as the postwar expansion of public education and employment, coupled with Civil Rights and Black Power organizing, strengthened the political and economic muscle of middle-class communities of color. The California Master Plan for Higher Education (1960), for instance, paved the way for a new generation of young people of color to pursue advanced studies. According to the historian Donna Murch, by the end of the 1960s, the Bay Area had one of the highest rates of college attendance among young people of color anywhere in the United States.[28] Armed with their degrees, a rising number of Black East Bay residents secured professional work amid the massive, but temporary, expansion of the postwar welfare state during the War on Poverty. From 1958 to 1968, public-sector employment in Oakland rose by 30 percent. And given the ingrained nature of corporate racism, and NAACP-led campaigns to integrate the civil service, government work became the main avenue into the Black middle class. By the late 1960s, around one third of Black workers in Oakland were employed by the public sector—garnering wages unimaginable to the previous generation of waterfront welders, let alone Victorian Era porters and maids.[29]

The growth of the Black middle class accelerated the struggle to tear down the walls of residential segregation. The U.S. Supreme Court had struck down racial covenants, which required that millions of new homes be sold to White people in perpetuity, in *Shelley v. Kraemer* (1948). But Oaklanders of color were still barred from most single-family neighborhoods by homeowners who refused to sell, bankers who refused to lend, and realtors who steered buyers to certain areas of the city according to their race.[30] Things started to change, however, during the era often referred to as "White Flight." Like their employers, White people—who, thanks to the racial largesse of the federal government, were granted low-cost, low-risk mortgages—began to abandon Oakland for the suburbs after World War II. Between 1955 and 1966, around 163,000 White residents left Oakland. (The city's total population barely topped 367,000 in 1960.[31]) Soon, White sellers couldn't find White buyers, so they began to sell to middle-class people of color. What was once a rare transgression, punished by social and economic sanctions, turned into an exploitative industry called "blockbusting." Drumming up worries of a racial "transition," realtors scared White people into selling their properties at reduced rates and then resold them to people of color, who, excluded from homeownership in most parts of the region, were often compelled to pay twice the price. While racist and manipulative to its core, this process meant that many Black residents decamped from rundown apartments in West Oakland to modest bungalows in East Oakland, North Oakland, and South Berkeley—where, according to a 1968 survey, 86 percent of Black households owned their own homes.[32]

This was the milieu in which Lionel Wilson emerged as a mainstay of Black politics in Oakland. It created a sense of momentum toward, if not freedom, then at least improvement—an optimistic mood that was cemented in his ascent to City Hall. But this sentiment turned out to be passing. Upon election, he encountered an unprecedented and unenviable series of problems. It was as if the city was facing a firestorm of retribution for the defiance of its Black Power revolt—one orchestrated at the top levels of government. While the postwar welfare state set the stage for the growth of the Black middle class, in the 1970s the massive increase in public spending that occurred during the War on Poverty— as of 1968, Oakland received around $100 million, almost twice the city budget, in federal funds—evaporated amid a conservative counterrevolution that has come to be seen as the onset of "roll-back" neoliberalism and rise of the carceral state.[33] According to the geographer Ruth

Wilson Gilmore, this period didn't represent a simple retreat from government spending on poverty. Rather, it involved the redirection of resources from programs that supported the poor—in particular, empowerment programs that had spurred an uprising in cities like Oakland—to ones that punished them.[34]

This reactionary movement was led by a cabal of California Republicans, including Richard Nixon, Ronald Reagan, and Edwin Meese—who, after serving as deputy district attorney in Alameda County, went on to become President Reagan's attorney general. These men advanced their careers by whipping up White backlash against Black Power. In 1968, for instance, Nixon took the White House back from Great Society Democrats by tying his political opponents to divisive issues like the Civil Rights and anti–Vietnam War Movements through the racially coded idea of "law and order." He then criminalized and disrupted those movements through the advent of the "War on Drugs." As former aide John Ehrlichman admitted in 1994, by associating anti-war activists and African Americans with illegal drugs, the Nixon administration could "arrest their leaders, raid their homes, break up their meetings, and vilify them night after night on the evening news." "Did we know we were lying about the drugs?" he added. "Of course we did."[35] Finally, Nixon replaced the federal government's antipoverty programs with the comparatively impotent Community Development Block Grant (CDBG). The CDBG program reduced the overall investment in combatting poverty, allowed funds to be moved from poor communities to middle-class ones, and ended the troublesome mandate for poor people's participation—which, during the War on Poverty, had seeded the growth of a new crop of political leaders, like Wilson.[36]

The rollback of public resources at the national scale was soon repeated at the state level with the passage of Proposition 13 (1978). Driven by White, antitax suburbanites—the very same people whose exodus from cities like Oakland had been underwritten at all tiers of government—the regressive measure radically capped property taxes for those who were privileged enough to own their own homes.[37] Given that cities, especially those with eroding economies, tend to depend upon property taxes to bankroll public services, Prop 13—which was predicted to cause a $7 billion drop in revenue across the state—promised to bleed Oakland and other communities abandoned by White companies, consumers, and capital. Paul Cobb—a veteran civil rights activist, and member of Wilson's inner circle—called it "white folks' message to us that we are going to have to do it ourselves."[38]

Indeed, Black voters, who opposed Prop 13 more than any other group, could read the writing on the wall (or the "Notice of Possible Closure" that went up on rec centers and libraries throughout Oakland that election season). It read that people of color had "stolen" the central cities; so now, as punishment, White people were going to take their wealth and barricade it behind the suburban color line. Across the state, voters approved Prop 13 by a margin of two to one. But the numbers were flipped upside down in the flats, where people of color voted no by the same ratio. In the end, Oakland was one of the only cities in the state to reject the measure.[39] Lionel Wilson barely had time to set foot in City Hall before facing the fallout. In Oakland, the property tax reassessment prompted by Prop 13 required an immediate drop of $14 million in city spending (14 percent of total).[40] This translated to cuts in gardeners, park rangers, and recreation workers; cuts in street sweeping and weed abatement; cuts in library services; and the closure of an arts center in East Oakland.[41] Cuts, cuts, and more cuts. Oakland was in the grips of a reckoning.

But these aspects of the conservative counterrevolution were just the tremors of one of the most tragic and traumatic chapters in the city's history—one often summed up in a single word: *crack*. Indeed, it did, opening up million-dollar markets, rupturing communities, breaking bodies, and fracturing the terrain of local politics. In Oakland, crack is often remembered as the unraveling of Black Power. In many accounts, the entire period from the 1960s to the 1990s is succinctly compressed into these diametric moments in the saga of Black urban life (and death). And not without good reason; Newton, for one, who once wrote that "neglect destroys us . . . much more often than the police revolver," managed to survive decades of skirmishes with the OPD only to be murdered, in 1989, by a drug dealer on the streets of West Oakland.[42] In fact, during the Reagan Era, more and more aspects of life in Oakland—its policies, priorities, and repute—seemed to slip into the rift, fall into the crack.

While the city's experience of the crack epidemic is important, it's not exceptional. In the 1970s and early 1980s, U.S. cities became inundated with potent cocaine from Latin America—much of it with the awareness, if not assistance, of Reagan's CIA. This caused the price to fall, creating a mass market for a drug that had, up until then, been a luxury of the elite. At the same time, dealers experimented with a chemical process to turn cocaine from a powder into a "rock" to be smoked, which made the product both cheaper and more addictive. As a result, demand skyrocketed.[43]

Crack users came from many communities. But the racial and spatial contours of disinvestment made sure that most of the dealers—certainly, most of the people who were criminalized amid the growing War on Drugs—were Black. In Oakland, Wilson expanded opportunities for government work among people of color, but the factories weren't coming back, and the doors to the city's corporate offices remained barely cracked. So, in 1980, when the unemployment rate among Black and Latine residents was 14 and 12 percent, more than twice the rate among Whites, 60 percent of out-of-work residents were Black. This increasingly structural unemployment hit young people the hardest. Studies revealed that Black youth experienced more discrimination in the job market than other young people, regardless of education. As a result, in 1980, Black Oaklanders between the ages of 16 and 19 suffered from the worst unemployment rate at 34 percent.[44] In

this context, selling crack was one of the only avenues of economic survival available to young, working-class Black men.[45]

Only not everyone survived. At the time that crack hit the streets,
Oakland's illegal drug economy was undergoing a complete revamp.
In the early 1980s, the U. S. Attorney's Office took out the city's three
biggest heroin pushers. This left the market open to a new generation
of street entrepreneurs, who, given the cheap and copious nature of
crack, only needed a little start-up cash (and a lot of mettle) to take over
a corner and set up shop. This rush, in turn, meant an increase in violent competition over territorial markets.[46] "You had people fighting
over blocks where they didn't even own their homes," said radio DJ
Greg Bridges, who grew up in East Oakland, his voice heavy with
grief.[47]

By 1991, at the height of a crack-fueled wave of violence that rocked
cities around the country, Oakland had the fourth-highest murder rate
in the United States. Of course, not every murder stemmed from the
drug game. But the economics of the market, and the sudden increase
in guns as tools of the trade, incited deadly rounds of street-level corporate conquest and retaliation—or what residents called, in a tragic twist
on the communal ethos and culture of Black Power, "fonk."[48] And
given the pipeline between disinvested schools, unemployment, and
the drug trade, this devastation was visited overwhelmingly on young
Black men. Between 1982 and 1992, the murder rate for Black Oaklanders, ages 10 to 24, grew by a frightening 165 percent, while it fell by 50
percent for Whites.[49] In 1992, when murders reached an all-time high,
175 people were killed in Oakland.[50]

This, too, was death by neglect. But as Democrats and Republicans
raced to condemn young men of color as "wild animals" and "super-
predators," the epidemic tearing through the flats was treated as a
moral panic that required more police and prisons, rather than a moral
crisis that merited public support.[51] The sociologist Tanya Maria
Golash-Boza calls this "carceral investment."[52] As Reagan's attorney

general, Ed Meese, who was born and raised in Oakland, made the city into a test case for these tough-on-crime tactics. Another acolyte of James Wilson, Meese—who derided the notion that crime stemmed from poverty as "sociological mumbo-jumbo"—directed federal law enforcement dollars to Oakland.[53] According to investigative journalists Ali Winston and Darwin BondGraham, during the Lionel Wilson administration, the OPD parlayed these resources into the creation of special drug units. In a local form of stop-and-frisk, plainclothes officers used the pretext of low-level crimes to stop Black and Latino men and search them for contraband.[54] Suddenly, being stopped for looking "suspicious" could mean being arrested on a drug charge that—given mandatory minimum sentencing guidelines, and a rabid attitude among prosecutors and judges—might carry years, even decades, behind bars.

As in other American cities, then, Oakland's War on Drugs introduced more severe forms of criminalization and control that were racist to their core. While, according to the legal scholar Michelle Alexander, most of the people who used illegal drugs during this period were White, 75 percent of those imprisoned for drug crimes were Black and Latine. From 1983 to 2000, the national incarceration rates for Black and Latine drug offenders increased 26 and 22 times over.[55] In Oakland, the juvenile courts saw a 2,200 percent increase in drug cases between 1980 and 1990.[56] And by 1996, over 90 percent of the young people booked on drug-related charges were Black.[57] Mayor Wilson's own son, Stevie, was charged for cocaine trafficking in 1988.[58] Anyone, it seemed, could stumble into the crack.

GHOST TOWN

The crack epidemic contributed to a creeping sense of concern, a sort of civic angst, that Oakland was spiraling into economic, physical, and moral decay. The city, it seemed, was dying, and Downtown was its diseased heart. The explosion of entertainment activity during World War II (see ch. 1) turned out to be the last spurt of vitality before the area was drained of its lifeblood, torniquet-like, by the expiration of war wages and the exodus of working- and middle-class Whites. Between 1925 and 1955, the value of real estate in Downtown Oakland fell by 50 percent. Then, between 1955 and 1960, it did so again, only in one-sixth the time. These exponential losses alarmed the Knowland Machine, which, in the postwar period, consisted of Downtown's financial, retail, and real-estate magnates. So, in 1954, Joseph Knowland gathered the city's most powerful men at the Athenian-Nile Club, an all-White social club where many of them were members (see ch. 6), to form the Oakland Citizens Committee on Urban Renewal. This organization evolved two years later into the Oakland Redevelopment Agency (ORA), which hastened to designate a wide swath of land around Downtown—including all of West Oakland—"blighted."[59] "The landscape of East and West Oakland is depressing," confirmed Huey Newton in 1973. "[It] resembles a crumbling ghost town, but a ghost town with inhabitants, among them more than 200,000 Blacks, nearly half the city's population."[60]

In this context, the ORA's at-times singular mission was to convert Downtown Oakland into a postindustrial reserve of service-sector workers and suburban consumers. Given its proximity to the "ghostly" residents of West Oakland, however, it wasn't enough to turn the center of the city into a citadel of office towers; prophylaxis would be needed, as well, to protect it from the spectral population stalking its edges. With City support, the State of California constructed the moat-like Interstate 980 to resegregate Downtown from West Oakland (see fig. 4). At the same time, the ORA sought to "revive" the most neglected parts of the neighborhood through residential redevelopment. But the agency never seemed to make as much housing as it took. Between 1960 and 1966, it oversaw the destruction of almost 10,000 housing units in the area, forcing some residents to East Oakland and others into the streets.[61]

Figure 4. An aerial view of Interstate 980, which separates Downtown and Lake Merritt from West Oakland, 1978. The image also shows the path of the BART train and Interstate 880, the "Nimitz Freeway," in West Oakland and the land cleared for the City Center redevelopment in Downtown. Credit: California Department of Transportation.

In a cruel twist, the City condemned many of these homes—which Black residents had bought, through tremendous travail and courage, during White Flight—to make room for roads and rails to serve the same suburbanites who had deserted the city in the first place. In 1965, for instance, the Port of Oakland granted the new Bay Area Rapid Transit (BART) District the right to run trains between Downtown Oakland and Downtown San Francisco along the route of the former Southern Pacific Red Line. BART, in turn, inserted imposing, elevated tracks right down the middle of Seventh Street (see ch. 1). BART was designed to connect the Bay Area's scattered commercial districts. But while no expense was spared to conceal the intrusive tracks as they ran through the centers of Oakland, Berkeley, and San Francisco, no such accommodations were made along Seventh Street in West Oakland and Grove Street in North Oakland—at the time, two of the most important commercial and cultural corridors in the Black East Bay. Whereas, during World War II, streetcars had carried a continuous stream of commuters through the heart of West Oakland—fueling the growth of Black businesses—BART would now speed workers and consumers to their destinations without ever touching the ground. In the end, what remained of this once-vibrant Black-owned commercial district would succumb to "urban renewal" as Seventh Street was converted into a colossal construction site and then suburban flyover.

The scale of destruction in West Oakland would only be duplicated Downtown. In 1964, a Black urban planner named John B. Williams was named director of the ORA. In the waning days of the White Power administrations of mayors John Houlihan and John Reading, Williams became one of the most influential African Americans in local government. (Indeed, Lionel Wilson noted that, until he died from cancer in 1976, after 12 years running the ORA, Williams was a likely mayoral contender.[62]) While Williams was driven, like Wilson, to ensure that residents of color received a proportional share of the economic opportunities created through urban renewal, he was also motivated by a mission to revamp Downtown Oakland, which he referred to as "brutally ugly and economically wasteful."[63] The City Center redevelopment was the cornerstone of this aggressive renovation scheme. Under Williams, the ORA used copious doses of eminent domain to seize and demolish 15 blocks—an ironic 40 acres of land—southwest of Fourteenth Street and Broadway to pave the way for new office towers, department stores, and a hotel and convention center. While, in the 1970s and '80s, the ORA managed to attract a smattering of service-sector amenities, like the convention center, the plan—which would have doubled the city's supply of office space—turned out to be too ambitious. In the long interval of waiting for new development, the scars of demolition remained for decades a souvenir of dispossession for the more than one hundred businesses and scores of poor people who had been evicted.[64]

As the ORA's attempts at renewal seemed, time and again, to come up short, civic leaders started to blame their stymied campaigns on Oakland's alleged "image problem"—a doggedly racist, thinly veiled trope that viewed the city as poor, violent, and corrupt.[65] In the mid-1980s, for instance, the ORA courted the Rouse Company—the darling developer of downtown-saving projects like Boston's Faneuil Hall and New York's South Street Seaport—to construct a $300-million mall on the site next to the abandoned Fox Theater. In a speech on economic development at Holy Names University, Rouse president Michael Spear assured his audience that Oakland's technical, political, and economic "infrastructure" was as good as anyone's. "What is lacking," he went on, "is what I will call perceptual infrastructure." The company, he reported, was struggling to attract anchor tenants because national retailers maintained a view of the area that was "negative in the extreme." Some, he reported, even expressed that Downtown would be an ideal site to tap into the East Bay's growing retail market—if only the ORA could "erase the word 'Oakland' from the map."[66]

"Oakland's reputation as a crime-ridden ghetto does not encourage peace of mind," confirmed an urban economist from UC Berkeley in 1987. Despite $200 million in ORA spending since 1968, decades of decline had stamped Downtown Oakland with a "deadly reputation of dowdiness and a depressed inner-city feeling."[67] This disrepute was especially damaging at night, when not only white-collar workers and suburban housewives but hard-bitten residents of the flats reported feeling wary—if not downright scared—roaming the streets after dark. In 1985, amid the turmoil of crack, a survey asked Oakland residents whether they were willing to walk at night. "The answers were overwhelmingly negative," stated the report. "With few exceptions, no one walked willingly or without trepidation."[68] "It was a ghost town—a straight up ghost town," recalled Theo Aytchan Williams, artistic director of SambaFunk! "At the end of the workday, everybody was out," he said, whistling like a rocket. "Sometimes, I'd be the *only* person Downtown."[69]

On this, then, a wide range of residents could agree: Oakland was a "ghost town." But what was there to do about it? For Newton, calling the city a "ghost town with inhabitants" served to critique the intentional and racist process of disinvestment that turned the flats into a "crumbling" environment. For elected officials, however, it rationalized decade after decade of redevelopment and policing campaigns designed to resurrect property values in Downtown Oakland and neighborhood commercial corridors.

CRIME AND GRIME

In 1984, at the invitation of Mayor Wilson, delegates from ten government agencies met at the Lake Merritt Sailboat House to discuss ways to contain the spiraling drug trade. "Oakland's problems are not unique," Joseph Kreuger, special agent with the U.S. Drug Enforcement Agency, told the crowd of prosecutors, probation officers, and prison administrators. But, he admitted, "[it's] difficult, if not impossible, to sell the constituency and the media on this reality." Still, given its stepped-up campaign to control heroin and crack, Oakland had a "very positive story to tell." "It should give thought to ways of capitalizing on its successes," he said.[70]

Indeed, by the time of the conference, Wilson had identified the need to restore a sense of social order in neighborhoods across the flats as his top concern.[71] Oakland, after all, was in the midst of a cascading series of crises, each one compounded by the next. And given the vindictive retreat of public and private capital, nothing imperiled his redevelopment goals more than the racialized narrative of communities out of

Figure 5. Mayor Lionel Wilson and pop singer La Toya Jackson at a community rally meant to encourage young people to "Just Say No," 1988. First Lady Nancy Reagan coined this slogan, which became a centerpiece of the federal response to the crack epidemic in the 1980s, during an event at Longfellow Elementary School in North Oakland in 1982. Credit: African American Museum and Library at Oakland.

control. The City had already spent $133 million on urban renewal schemes, most of it Downtown. But this deluge of public spending had done little to attract private development or improve unemployment— the worst in the region at that time.[72] It thus seemed as though Oakland's "image problem"—its inability to "sell the constituency and the media" on the fact that it was more than a violent, drug-ridden "ghost town"— reigned supreme. In addition to redevelopment, then, Wilson doubled down on a law-and-order mode of policing meant to promote a sense of security among not only outside corporations, investors, and tourists but also a new social movement of middle-class residents of color (see fig. 5).

In the post–Civil Rights Era, people of color came to predominate in working- and middle-class neighborhoods throughout the flats and some parts of the prosperous hills. At the same time, after a prolonged period of Black / White political struggle, Oakland became a thoroughly multiracial metropolis. With the relaxation of U.S. immigration restrictions in 1965, it saw a rapid increase in migrants from Africa, Latin America, East and Southeast Asia, and the Pacific Islands. By 1990, when the Black population peaked and then began to drop, the proportion of Latine and Asian American / Pacific Islander residents reached 13 percent and 15 percent.[73] (Those numbers have since continued to rise.) And given the growing economic stratification, or "cracks," discussed above, the recomposition of the city's racial and spatial order was accentuated by the increasing importance of age, class, and style as dividing lines within its communities of color. Whereas, during the Black Power and Third World Liberation Movements of the 1960s and '70s, the city was a seedbed of cultural and anticolonial nationalism—politics rooted in race—the rifts that opened up in the post–Civil Rights Era gave rise to new identities and solidarities.

One of those new forms of association was the increasing identification of middle-class residents of all races with the privileges and priorities of property ownership. As more and more residents of color scaled the walls of residential segregation, they demanded the same protections against urban disorder and declining property values that White homeowners had long considered a right. At the same time, as the children of immigrants began to mingle with African American students in the public schools, the city saw the growth of a multiracial, but Black-centered, youth culture that was increasingly alienating to parents, property owners, and politicians. "Youth," writes the anthropologist Jennifer Tilton, who studied struggles over young people in Oakland, thus became an "almost racial category."[74] Young Black men continued to confront the violence of policing at exceptional rates. But increasingly, other young men of color—in particular, those who expressed an affinity for working-class Black youth culture through their sonic and sartorial style—became tagged as "gangbangers" and "thugs" and targeted amid the War on Drugs.[75]

The rising emphasis on age, class, and style—in addition to race—within struggles over urban space reflected the changing legal and social realities of the time. In the 1940s, in response to African American migration during World War II, the OPD recruited White Southern "Crackers" to control Black people through Jim Crow–style policing (see ch. 1). This approach, with its roots in the politics of segregation and racial caste in the U. S. South, was applied with brutal uniformity. The "law of the nightstick," in the words of the reporter Emerson Street, barely distinguished between men, women, and children, young and old.[76] Black people were criminalized because they were Black. But this one-size-fits-all approach came under attack during the Civil Rights Era, when the state and federal government outlawed policies and practices, including policing tactics, designed to discriminate by race. In the decades to come, Oakland's political terrain grew increasingly fractured. With Black people running City Hall and, as of 1993, the OPD, and Black property owners calling for more crime suppression in the flats, it was no longer tenable, legally or politically, to target Black residents as a monolithic block.

In this moment of rupture, reorienting Oakland's regulations and police practices around "nuisances," rather than conventional racial categories, provided a way for officials to ramp up control of young and poor men of color—who seemed to threaten the city's redevelopment aims—in public space. In theory, nuisance was defined in terms of conduct, not race, meaning it would pass muster with antidiscrimination laws. In practice, however, broken-windows policing enabled officials to "micromanage" the lives of Black and Brown youth by increasing contacts with the police, which fed into the maw of mass incarceration. Even more, write the policing scholars Alex Vitale and Brian Jordan Jefferson, this system of intense and invasive regulation actually turned low-income neighborhoods of color into "prisonlike spaces themselves."[77] In line with the selectively "post-racial" creed of the time, then, it represented a turn toward what the Black studies scholar Robin D. G. Kelley calls "color-blind violence."[78]

In Oakland, the war on nuisance started in the 1970s. But it was consolidated during the national turn toward "community policing" in the 1990s. According to Tilton, this turn occurred in response to a renewed crisis in the legitimacy of policing after years of tough-on-crime policies, which degraded relations with urban communities of color, and the LA Uprising. The 1994 Crime Bill—authored, in part, by then Senator Joe Biden—authorized the federal government to invest in 100,000 community policing officers across the nation. Under Joseph Samuels, its first Black chief of police, Oakland used this funding to add 50 of these officers to the force.[79] Then, in 1996, Mayor Elihu Harris, who succeeded Lionel Wilson as the head of the city's Black urban regime, completed the OPD's conversion to a model of community policing.

In Oakland, this conversion involved a change in both the aims of policing and the structure of police / community relations. In terms of aims, community policing centered on responding not only to crimes but also more quotidian "problems" that were identified by neighborhood residents. This reorientation actually began in 1967, right after James Wilson completed his research in Oakland, when—in response to Black organizing against police violence—a reformer named Charles Gain was appointed to lead the OPD. In addition to abolishing the quota system, which reduced stops and arrests in Black neighborhoods, Gain called for a philosophical shift toward "service-style" policing.[80] If the OPD's legalistic approach operated through a strict opposition of "lawbreakers" and "law enforcers," then service-style policing reframed residents as well-meaning people with mundane "problems" and police officers as empathetic "problem solvers." There would be a resurgence of more militaristic strategies under Chief George Hart and Lionel Wilson during the 1980s. But the emphasis on improving police / community relations through responsiveness to neighborhood nuisances, rather than just crime control, remained a staple of the post–Civil Rights Era department.

In terms of structure, community policing involved creating over 50 neighborhood beats (the number has since dropped to 35), each of which was managed through the cooperation of a Neighborhood Crime Prevention Council (NCPC), Neighborhood Services Coordinator, and Community Policing Officer.[81] By participating in the NCPC, residents could communicate directly with officials about the nuisances that plagued their blocks—from illegal dumping and open-air drug markets to disturbing noises. The Neighborhood Services Coordinators and Community Policing Officers, in turn, were supposed to be accountable to these neighborhood activists—aligning municipal services, like code enforcement, with police activities to "clean up" the streets. In this sense, Oakland's approach to community policing codified the cooperation between residents and beat cops in a crusade against urban disorder that was the hallmark of broken-windows policing.[82]

Certainly, residents and politicians of color continued to fight for a more equitable distribution of jobs, housing, and education in Oakland. But two decades of disinvestment and drug-fueled disorder had instilled a real sense of fear and desperation among some flatland residents—in particular, homeowners of color, who, between their mortgages and the ongoing racial segregation of the city and region, were often trapped in neighborhoods that were becoming increasingly precarious. In the process, many homeowners of color—who, according to Tilton, predominated in the NCPCs—came to see equitable protection of their persons and properties against disorder as a "civil right."

This new social movement didn't just arise from evolving attitudes among middle-class residents of color; it was encouraged by economic and political changes, too. First, Prop 13—which resulted in massive cuts to more run-of-the-mill municipal programs and services—ensured that the ever-funded OPD was, at times, the only agency available to respond to community concerns. Second, the creation of the NCPCs prompted residents to advocate for government support in terms of discrete, site-specific nuisances, rather than the structural critiques of oppression that had prevailed during the Black Power Movement. And this recentered the relationship between residents and the City on the policing of what Tilton calls *"problem people* or *problem places* instead of economic or racial inequalities."[83] In the process, Oakland's insurgent homeowner groups came to be seen as a new cadre of "urban guerillas"—not, like the Black Panthers, for their fight against capitalism and colonialism, but for their crusade against "crime and grime."[84]

SOUND BANDITS

The celebrated novelist, musician, and poet Ishmael Reed wasn't born in Oakland. Rather, this son of Buffalo, New York, moved to teach at UC Berkeley in 1967, making him a member of the mass migration of cultural and political luminaries to the East Bay during the Black Power Era. Indeed, by the time that he and his wife, Carla, purchased a large Victorian in North Oakland in 1979, Reed had become, in his own words, the "first patron" of the city's Black Arts Movement.[85] But he wasn't a strict cultural nationalist. Instead, as a professor of English at Berkeley, he became a trenchant critic of Anglo-American cultural dominance and champion of literary multiculturalism. And Oakland—which, thanks to growing immigration, now reverberated with not only funk and blues but also cumbia and Cambodian pop tunes—was like his urban muse.

Eventually, Reed turned his pen to the town with *Blues City: A Walk in Oakland* (2003). Written after the election of Mayor Jerry Brown, a moment that seemed to mark the end of the Black urban regime (see ch. 5), Reed defended the city from what he called "Jerryfication" by providing a personal account of its diverse cultural scenes. "Oakland is a city where identities blur," he wrote. "Where one encounters hip-hop dancers at a festival in Chinatown; where the mistress of ceremonies at a Kwanzaa celebration is a white woman in Yoruba dress; where . . . about a fifth of the audience at a Native American powwow is black." The city, for Reed, was thus a rich and resistive "cultural stew," a finger in the eye of White America's fixation with racial purity and separateness, a sort of reflection of his own gumbo poetics. But despite all of this mixture, it was still, indelibly, a Black town, synonymous with the sound of its Southern roots. "Oakland is Blues City," he wrote, "husky and brawling."[86]

So, for Reed, resisting "Jerryfication" meant preserving the diverse, and especially Black, character of Oakland's soundscapes. But apparently, his appetite for Black sounds ran aground when it came to the next generation of Oakland's bass-driven slaps. In 2004 and 2005, he wrote a series of op-eds in the *Tribune* that inveighed against the invasion of his block by "sound bandits." Reed—ever a rabble-rouser, an agitator against canonical commonsense, whether in the media or academia—was no stranger to neighborhood disputes. In the late 1980s, as the street became rocked with drug dealing and shootouts, he rallied other homeowners to the cause, forming a neighborhood watch and calling for the demolition of vacant houses.[87] In this sense, he became a commander of the "urban guerillas" on the rise at the time.

Then, in the mid-2000s, Reed took up his pen again to advocate for action against neighborhood youth "whose chief purpose in life seems to be competing in some strange contest to determine who can play the stereos in the trunks of their cars the loudest." These men, he said, were "addicted to The Beat." (In this, he inadvertently echoed his satirical take on mainstream concerns about Black dance music in *Mumbo Jumbo* [1972], in which "Jes Grew," an "anti-plague," infects Black people with not a deadly disease but rather an invigorating desire to express themselves outside of White Christian norms.) "My neighbors and I have done more than any citizen should be required to do to bring this crisis to the attention of those in charge of our safety," he wrote, recounting his involvement in the local NCPC. "We have attended meetings, written e-mails, made phone calls and written letters." But to no avail. "My neighborhood," he seethed, "has been ceded to lawbreakers."[88]

If, in the 1960s and '70s, Black dance music had spurred social movements in Oakland, then, starting in the 1980s, it became embroiled in increasingly desperate campaigns to combat the city's reputation as a "ghost town." Amid the ravages of disinvestment and drug-related violence, and epochal changes in the city's population, politics, and economy, middle-class people of color and members of the Black urban regime embraced law-and-order measures to rid the flatlands of "crime and grime." In the ensuing war on nuisance, young Black Oaklanders, especially men, became targeted for their cultural comportment and style, including their sonic practices. Indeed, as revealed in the next chapter, residents and regulators turned their attention, with increasing frequency, to "noise" as the nuisance par excellence. Intersecting with the rise of rap music, this cemented a tie, among officials, between crime, grime, and *rhyme* in ways that intensified the policing of Black youth.

4

BLACK NOISE

Crime, Grime, and Rhyme

> [I] am surrounded by crime and lots of drug dealing, but the most intrusive and offensive activity throughout the area is loud car (and sometimes home) stereos . . . If I could change just one thing in my neighborhood above all else, I would eliminate the excruciating noise from boomboxes. The noise has robbed us of any good quality of life. I can close the blinds and not see the marauding teens and the drug dealing, but there is no way to shut out the boombox cacophony.
>
> MARGURITE FULLER, resident of East Oakland, letter to the *Oakland Tribune* (2005)[1]

HEY MR. DJ

The screech of the BART trains, scraping along the tracks on Seventh Street, would sound the death knell for West Oakland's once vibrant music venues. Certainly, by the late 1960s, most young Black Oaklanders were more attracted to the power of the funk than the pathos of the blues (see ch. 2). But the erosion of the neighborhood through displacement, desegregation, and urban renewal (see ch. 3) had severed the spatial connection between Black artists and audiences that kindled West Oakland's nightlife during and after World War II. On top of that, according to the drummer Earl Watkins, as White residents and revelers deserted Oakland,

White venue owners began to court Black artists and audiences as their economic salvation.[2] In addition, the integration of the American Federation of Musicians (AFM) opened up even more opportunities for musicians of color. But union wages made it more difficult for Black venue owners to book the jazz and blues artists who once gave them their distinctive sound. Caught between competition and economic decline, most of the clubs in West Oakland either closed down or converted to dives.[3]

On top of these local changes, there were more general cultural, technological, and economic transformations afoot that would revamp the nightspots that survived the onslaught of Oakland's restructuring. Principally, with the acceptance of disco and its descendants, like boogie and house, by the social and sexual mainstream, dance music became recorded music, and DJs its high priests (see Intro).[4] This revolution in popular music, writes Steven Waksman, in a comprehensive account of live music in America, "recast the relationship between 'live' and 'recorded' music more dramatically than at any time since the popularization of sound recordings during the early jazz age."[5]

There were several catalysts for this shift. First, recorded music was a lot more flexible and affordable than live music. As a club owner, you could hire a single DJ to spin records for the night, rather than an entire ensemble of musicians, whose wages and work conditions were often regulated by the AFM, and customers would still come out to dance. According to the dance music historian Tim Lawrence, the top rate for a disco DJ in New York in the 1970s was 50 dollars—much less than for a unionized band.[6] Next, there was the matter of fidelity. Bands could be unpredictable, performing their repertoire with more or less precision and verve, depending on the night. DJs, on the other hand, played records that, at least in theory, sounded the same as they did at home or on the radio—or, with the advent of sound systems, audio effects, and 12-inch singles made especially for nightclubs, even better.[7] Records were also easier to mix for live sound. According to Lee Hildebrand, a longtime concert promoter, music critic, and historian, Oakland's Black-owned clubs—which suffered from the same redlining as the rest of Black neighborhoods—often had "lousy sound systems." Owners soon realized that, in addition to being cheaper, DJs tended to sound better, too.[8] Some venue owners switched over to recorded music. Others simply got out of the game. "That was a pretty tough time," recalled Edward Hawthorne, drummer for the Soul Messengers, which backed everyone from Etta James to Rufus Thomas when they packed the Showcase and the Sportsman. "For a while, disco really hurt live music."[9] In the 1970s, as bands were replaced by DJs at larger venues, agrees Hildebrand, the blues "moved underground" to the West Oakland "beer-and-wine joints . . . where it had begun."[10]

Finally, as with the rise of earlier genres, the sounds of the city's dance floors were responsive to a new mood—a new set of cultural and political priorities—among residents. While the blues and the funk resonated with the experiences of previous generations, venue owners now had to cater to crowds that craved recorded dance music—and especially rap—or else fall, fatally, out of step with the trends. In fact, by the mid-1980s, it was clear that rap had seized the hearts, minds, and wallets of young people of color across the East Bay, making it one of the first regions outside of New York—the crucible for the rise of hip-hop as a multifaceted youth culture in the 1970s—to embrace rap music.

As seen in chapter 3, in the 1980s and '90s, mayors Lionel Wilson and Elihu Harris, the leaders of Oakland's "Black urban regime," sought to stem fears of moral and economic decline by investing in new regulatory and policing measures to address "crime and grime." One of their main targets was "noise." Oakland, it was said, again and again, had an "image problem" that stymied redevelopment. But this period of the city's history reveals that, among residents and regulators, it had a "sound problem," too.

The timing of this war on nuisance couldn't have been worse for an up-and-coming generation of Black musicians and audiences. In the

1980s, young Black residents turned the East Bay—home to MC Hammer, Digital Underground, and, for a time, Tupac—into one of the most important nodes in the national emergence of hip-hop culture. Creating a conceptual connection between the sound of rap music and the threat of "crime and grime," however, regulators and venue owners rolled out a series of restrictions that culminated in a de facto ban on rap concerts. Tragically, this crackdown on everything from music venues to boomboxes disrupted opportunities for local artists to develop their microphone skills and market at the precise moment that rap came to dominate American popular music. Just as fast as it emerged, then, Oakland lost its influence and esteem in the national rap game, retreating into a more regional scene.

In some ways, this was an echo of the Oakland Blues; many of the most successful artists recruited by Bob Geddins, like Jimmy McCracklin and Sugar Pie DeSanto, had to leave Oakland to advance their careers (see ch. 1). But during the 1950s and '60s, this was often because local record labels lacked the capital, distribution, and industry standing to vie with out-of-town competitors. In the 1980s and '90s, however, it was because the very spaces and practices that Black musicians relied upon to reach their audiences were under sustained attack. Paradoxically, then, amid Oakland's conversion into a "Chocolate City," antipathy to rap became a matter of sound public policy.

The title of this chapter is a nod to pathbreaking hip-hop scholar Tricia Rose, who, in 1994, published *Black Noise: Rap Music and Black Culture in Contemporary America*. At the time, Rose noted that—given the aesthetic priorities of prominent drums, thumping bass, and looping, hypnotic beats—the earliest rap records and performances were derided by mainstream music critics and cultural institutions as mere "noise."[11] Building upon her important work, this chapter reveals how the notion that rap music was noise intersected with an emerging war on nuisance in urban neighborhoods in ways that made young Black Oaklanders, and especially men, a target for broken-windows policing. In this sense, the treatment of rap as noise was more than just a favored metaphor of conservative critique. It was a material practice that became entangled in concrete political economies of property and policing in cities like Oakland.

THE RAP BAN

In the 1980s, the city was ripe for rap. In terms of its sound, samples, dance styles, and emphasis on the pleasure of self-expression, hip-hop culture built upon the foundation of the funk that emerged from Oakland and the surrounding Bay Area (see ch. 2).[12] In this sense, hip-hop's DNA was embedded in the East Bay, making it a mecca and ready market for the next iteration of groove-based Black dance music. Shock G, the frontman for Digital Underground, for instance, was raised between New York and Tampa, Florida. Introduced to hip-hop in the late 1970s, while living in Queens, he formed a mobile DJ crew, the Master Blasters, when he returned to the South. But he soon realized that New York hip-hop, which could be heady, didn't get the dance floor moving; George Clinton and P-Funk did. His ensuing love affair with funk music was part of what drew him to the East Bay, where he routinely tuned in to Rickey Vincent's radio program on KALX at UC Berkeley. As the producer of their most popular songs, Shock G inserted the essence of the funk into Digital Underground's anthems and antics. Their debut album, *Sex Packets* (1990), was imprinted with the sounds of Sly and the Family Stone, the Ohio Players, and Prince. But the top spot went to Parliament-Funkadelic, whose samples appeared a dozen times on the record.[13]

Shock G was also instrumental in turning Tupac Shakur into a national name. Tupac is now claimed by several cities on the map of American rap culture—including New York (where he was born), Baltimore (where he went to a performing arts high school), and Los Angeles (where, as a member of Death Row Records, he became an emblem of West Coast rap and its deadly beef with the streets of his childhood). But his career as a rapper actually began in the improbable climes of Marin County—a wealthy, mostly White enclave north of San Francisco—where he moved in 1988. While living in Marin City, the county's only Black community, and attending Tamalpais High School in Mill Valley, he made outings to Oakland, where he had ties through his upbringing in the Black Panthers. (His mother, Afeni Shakur, was tried as part of the Panther 21 for an alleged plan to attack police stations in New York, and his godparents included the political prisoners Assata Shakur and Elmer "Geronimo" Pratt.)

In Oakland, Tupac met Shock G and the rest of Digital Underground. After serving as one of the group's roadies and backup dancers, and rooming, for a time, with crew member Saafir, he appeared on "Same Song" (1991), which lifted its hook from Parliament's "Theme from the Black Hole" (1979). Then, under Shock G's mentorship, he recorded his debut album, *2Pacalypse Now* (1991), at Starlight Sound Studios in Richmond, where *Sex Packets* had been recorded. The album featured several songs produced by Shock G and cameos by local rappers Raw Fusion and Ray Luv. And one of the biggest hits of Tupac's early career, "I Get Around" (1993), which was laced with samples from Zapp, Prince, and the Honey Drippers, was actually produced by Shock G for Digital Underground before he decided to give it to his mentee instead.[14]

While Tupac's music reverberated with the pleasurable sounds of the Black Power Era, his lyrics and public persona also represented a strain of Black militant politics that made sense for a Panther cub who came of age, artistically, in Oakland. In 1991, as broken-windows policing was becoming the norm, resulting in increased racial profiling of young Black and Brown people (see ch. 3), he was accosted and assaulted by police officers for allegedly jaywalking across Broadway. At the same time that his rebellious debut, *2Pacalypse Now*, was released, he sued the Oakland Police Department (OPD) for $10 million in damages.[15] (The case was settled for $42,000.)

Clearly, the musical and political legacies of the "social movements" that animated Oakland in the 1960s and '70s echoed in the work of its hip-hop generation.[16] But the geographical spaces of the East Bay also formed an indispensable ingredient. The music writer and journalist Eric Arnold, author of *Hip-Hop Atlas of the Bay* (2018), has mapped out the role of the region's cultural landscapes—from streets to schools, basement recording studios to big concert venues—in cementing the city's place, literally, in the rise of rap culture.

Take MC Hammer, for example. Born in 1962, Stanley Kirk Burrell was raised in a cramped, government-assisted apartment off of High Street in East Oakland. Like other working-class African Americans who came up in the flats in the 1960s and '70s, he found opportunities to overcome the restraints of disinvestment by dancing in the neighborhood's streets and open spaces, where he replicated the moves of the soul musicians that he saw on television and boogaloo crews that he saw in school (see ch. 2). (The members of the Black Resurgents recall Burrell hanging around their rehearsals, absorbing their style.[17]) According to Arnold, he put these moves to work at the Coliseum—the sports complex in East Oakland that was home to the Oakland Athletics, Oakland Raiders, and Golden State Warriors. In 1973, Athletics owner Charlie Finley spotted an 11-year-old Burrell—who scalped tickets and danced for tips—doing a James Brown routine outside the stadium. Impressed, Finley gave him a job in the clubhouse. (According to local lore, Burrell was given the name "Hammer" by the slugger Reggie Jackson, who thought Burrell looked like "Hammerin'" Hank Aaron.) Later, after a stint in the Navy, and a Christian rap group called the Holy Ghost Boys, the now rechristened MC Hammer started independent record label Bust It Productions with seed money from team members Mike Davis and Dwayne Murphy.[18]

Hammer recorded his first single, "Ring 'Em," and—like other local musicians, from Bob Geddins to Too Short—began to sell copies out of the trunk of his car.[19] Around that time, he started to collaborate with the producer Felton Pilate, former member of the Vallejo band Con Funk Shun. In 1986, Hammer re-recorded "Ring 'Em" as the lead single on his debut album *Feel My Power* in the closet of Pilate's homespun recording studio. The track, like many of the songs that Pilate produced, consisted of stripped-down drum-machine sounds peppered with notes of the funk. (The beat for "Ring 'Em" is punctuated by the syncopated pop of a slap bass in the third bar of every four-bar loop.) "After 10:00 p.m.," Pilate told *Rolling Stone* in 1990, "the old woman upstairs would pound on my ceiling with a broom any time she heard anything."[20]

In addition to these immensely public and intimately private spaces, Hammer's path into the pop music pantheon also depended on the East Bay's surviving nightspots. He recruited members of his notoriously massive dance crew among the crowds of young people at clubs like Silk's, a popular disco in Emeryville.[21] And he was courted by Capitol Records after Joy Bailey, an A&R executive, saw him recording the music video for "Let's Get It Started" at a venue called Sweet Jimmie's on San Pablo Avenue (see ch. 6). Because of that chance encounter at a Black-owned nightclub in Downtown Oakland, writes Arnold, "hip-hop blew up."[22] Recording *Please Hammer Don't Hurt 'Em* (1990)—which, thanks to Pilate, continued to combine spare drum-machine beats with samples from Prince and the Jackson 5—for a mere $10,000, Hammer went on to move over 18 million copies, becoming the first rapper to notch a diamond record.[23] This mouth-watering math made record and radio industry executives take note. In Oakland, a marriage of residual funk, swaggering sexuality, and a knack for the spectacular took hip-hop's countercultural force and turned it into a crossover commercial dynamo.

As artists like MC Hammer started to gain national and international recognition, they encountered a rising war on nuisance among local regulators and venue owners, who clamped down, like a vise grip, on the spaces where rappers developed their musicianship, artistic net-works, and markets. One by one, Oakland's most prominent concert venues implemented a total moratorium on rap music—starting with the Coliseum.

In addition to instigating MC Hammer's career, the Coliseum was responsible for raising rap's profile with East Bay audiences. According to Arnold, in the 1980s, rap artists struggled to reach listeners because, except for college stations like KALX at UC Berkeley and KUSF at the University of San Francisco, Bay Area radio stations refused to play these raw, unvarnished sounds. (Indeed, even KMEL—one of the first stations in the country to popularize an "urban," meaning rap-heavy, format—didn't dedicate significant daytime airplay to rap music until 1992.) The Coliseum thus served as one of the few spaces where rappers could circumvent mainstream media censorship to reach a mass audi-ence.[24] In 1984, at the start of what Steven Waksman calls the "golden age of arena rap," hip-hop disciples descended upon the Coliseum to rock with Kurtis Blow, Whodini, and Run-D. M. C. at Fresh Fest, the first national arena tour with all hip-hop acts.[25] In 1986, Timex Social Club—which, after forming at Berkeley High School, reached number one on the R&B and dance charts with "Rumors" (1986)—opened for L. L. Cool J and the Beastie Boys on Run-D. M. C.'s Raising Hell Tour. And in 1987, the same year he went national with the release of *Born to Mack* on Jive Records, Too Short got an important boost when he opened for L. L. and Whodini on the Def Jam Tour.[26]

So, in 1989, when MC Hammer went on tour with Heavy D and the Boys to mark the success of his multiplatinum *Let's Get It Started* (1988), it was only right that his stop at the Coliseum was heralded as a home-coming of epic proportions. The celebration turned sour, however, when Heavy D took issue with the venue over its policy of leaving the lights on during rap concerts as a supposed security measure. The audi-ence, siding with the rapper, turned restless. As the mood grew tense, a group of gang members began to tear through the crowd, attacking concertgoers and sending the rest running for cover in what a reporter described as a "stampede."[27] Eventually, recalled the music writer Lee Hildebrand, who ducked into Heavy D's dressing room to escape the commotion, the OPD arrived, the crowd settled, and Hammer managed to do his set. But by then, the arena had practically emptied of his hometown crowd.[28] In the end, a reported 30 people were hurt, one of them shot.[29] Then, in December, concerts at the Kaiser Center (formerly the Oakland Auditorium) with L. L. Cool J and 2 Live Crew were marred by reports of violence. In response, the Coliseum and Kaiser Center—the two biggest music venues in Oakland—enacted a total ban on rap concerts. The moratorium then spread to mid-sized venues like the Omni, which started to close down or cut ties with rap promoters, too, as public opposition continued to rise.[30]

This crackdown couldn't have come at a worse time. In 1990, the *Oakland Tribune* reported that, with approximately 150 hip-hop recording artists, the Bay Area was home to the largest number of rap acts outside of New York.[31] MC Hammer and his crew—which, according to *Rolling Stone*, included fifteen dancers, twelve singers, seven musicians, and two DJs, thus making it the "most elaborate live show ever mounted by a rap entertainer"—were touring 60 cities in support of *Please Hammer Don't Hurt 'Em*.[32] And Too Short and Digital Underground were at the top of their game, each moving millions of records thanks to recent contracts with national labels. As Arnold writes, 1990 was quite simply a "peak year for Bay Area hip-hop."[33]

But the "rap ban" threatened to upend all that. For the artists at the top of the charts, it was an insult. While MC Hammer was welcomed with open arms by crowds in Europe, Australia, and Japan, he was effectively barred from performing in his own hometown. For the artists who sought to match this success, however, the moratorium was even more punishing. Restricting access to smaller nightclubs and community-oriented music venues, which had long served as a proving ground for new talent, it threatened the rap community at its roots.

This crackdown wasn't unique to Oakland. Acts of violence like those at the Coliseum and Kaiser Center inevitably occurred at some rap concerts—just as they did at some non-rap concerts. But between 1986 and 1990, local authorities, music venues, insurance companies, and the media created a moral panic over so-called "rap-related violence."[34] One important ingredient of this process was increasing public outrage over gangster rap, which, according to critics, not only glorified, but *engendered*, crime and violence. In 1989, for instance, in response to N. W. A.'s "Fuck tha Police" (1988), the Fraternal Order of Police—a nationwide union of law enforcement—called for its members to "refuse to . . . provide security for concerts by any group advocating violence against police officers." Indeed, police opposition led to the disruption or cancellation of N. W. A concerts in Cincinnati, Detroit, and Washington, DC.[35] (Tupac would later be targeted, too. In 1992, after a Black teenager shot a Texas state trooper, who pulled him over while he was reportedly listening to *2Pacalypse Now*, Vice President Dan Quayle called upon Interscope Records to remove the album from stores on account that it promoted violence.)

In one sense, the notion that rap artists and audiences were predisposed to violence was a warmed-over version of an age-old stereotype about Black men. In the context of the War on Drugs, however, which came to center on the suppression of gang-related crime, the panic over gangster rap encouraged public and private institutions to take new and extreme measures to control the circulation of rap music in cities across America. Insurance companies, for instance, ratcheted up their rates for rap concerts. According to one promoter, who produced a tour for Public Enemy, the cost of insuring rap events increased by 300 percent, from 30 to 90 cents per person, between 1988 and 1990. (Rock shows, by contrast, only cost 30 cents.[36]) By eating away at the profit margin, rising insurance rates discouraged promoters from putting together all-rap lineups. In 1988, at the height of arena rap's "golden age," *Billboard* noted that hip-hop tours were among the highest earners. Soon, almost no one would sponsor them. Promoters started to pair rap artists with rock bands—who, the thinking went, would draw more White people and women—as a way to sidestep inequitable insurance and booking practices.[37] In 1990, the same year as Oakland's moratorium, there were no rap concerts at Madison Square Garden or the Nassau Coliseum in New York, as well.[38]

In the East Bay, rap proponents sought to recuperate a space for hip-hop as a music and movement by shifting the conversation from violence to security. "Remember," wrote members of Digital Underground, in an op-ed opposing the threat of another moratorium at the Berkeley Community Theater, "the key word at any large gathering of any kind is security."[39] (The ban was proposed after a reported stabbing at a rap concert, but was overturned thanks to community resistance.) Confronted with increasing repression, these advocates argued that it was better to use fine-grained security measures than a flat-out ban. At UC Berkeley, law students formed the Group for Rap Industry Protection (GRIP), which issued a manual to concert promoters on security strategies that were more *discriminating*, perhaps, than discriminatory.[40] In the process, advocates reorganized the contours of public debate; it wasn't a split between rap and other genres of music that mattered, they argued, but one between "good" and "bad" crowds, which could be managed with security. In this sense, they targeted a small group of "troublemakers" to save the scene as a whole. "We're not going to let a very, very small percentage of thugs destroy it for . . . the rest of the crowd," stated Gene Winer, Kaiser Center director of facility and sales. But it wasn't just people in power who took a vindictive view of the supposed "thugs." "Don't just slap their wrists when [people] start trouble," said Concord rapper Chill E. B., who agreed that a more punitive approach was needed. "Put them in jail where they can sit until the concert's over."[41]

The moratorium was eventually reversed in late 1990. By this time, however, the call for more security had become a matter of consensus. In December, the Kaiser Center agreed to ease its rules so that Bill Graham—one of the most famous concert promoters in the country, and one of the sponsors of the original rap revues at the Coliseum—could put on a show with N. W. A.'s Ice Cube and Too Short. Graham worked with the OPD, GRIP, and a host of community groups to create a security plan, which called for metal detectors, pat-downs, and a 30 percent increase in personnel. "We've been working on this for a long time," said Erroll Jackson, a promoter who partnered with Graham, in a seeming reference to Operation Desert Shield. "We'll have the tightest security this side of Saudi Arabia."[42] Indeed, as the area swarmed with OPD helicopters and motorcycle patrols, the *Tribune* reported that the Kaiser Center "looked more like a fortified embassy in some hostile country than a concert hall." "Just another Saturday night dance," quipped Graham, sarcastically. "We want to let the negative element know we're here to take care of things."[43]

In the end, the event went off without a hitch—at least, that is, if you didn't see the militarization of live music as a "hitch"—and the morato-rium was lifted. But this only cemented the idea that more security was the key to averting "rap-related violence." By 1996, according to promoter Sean Kennedy, who spoke to a reporter at the time, security would account for more than half the cost of producing a rap event in Oakland.[44] Club owners and concert promoters might be saving money on unionized bands, compared to the funk era. But they were soon required to reinvest those savings into security technologies and police patrols, at least if Black artists and audiences were involved (see ch. 5).

MOBILE MUSIC

Nightclubs and concerts only represented one part of Oakland's rap culture to come under attack during the war on nuisance. In 1990, the same year as the moratorium on rap concerts, the city council issued new regulations on the use of boomboxes in public space. This preoccupation with public "noise" was nothing new. The sound studies scholars Karin Bijsterveld and Lilian Radovac show that, around the turn of the twentieth century, upper-crust social reformers in Europe and the United States sought to regulate the sounds of peddlers, street musicians, and other members of the poor to reinforce the social and spatial distance between the ruling class and the rabble.[45] Indeed, by 1912, the OPD called for officers to cite anyone who "maliciously and willfully disturbs" the public by "loud or unusual noise" for the crime of "disturbing the peace."[46] But the campaign to control the sound-scapes of marginalized urban communities took on new intensity amid the depths of disinvestment and rise of rap music thanks to a set of cultural, technological, and legal changes that swept American cities in the 1970s and '80s.

From the start, hip-hop culture depended upon broadcasting music in public space. Excluded from more sanctioned venues by a mix of race, class, and age, the young people of color who birthed the movement in New York in the 1970s were forced to use rec rooms and neighborhood parks—spaces that weren't wired for live music—to throw parties. The hip-hop sound system, like the reggae sound system that inspired it, thus required importing towers of speakers into the public realm. This practice gave Black and Brown youth—who were expected by the authorities to remain silent and invisible—the power, in the form of wattage, to take over their neighborhood soundscapes.[47]

Then, with the spread of cassette tapes, which were more compact and mobile than records, companies like Philips and Sony began to make consumer stereos that were portable, as well. The boombox—which arrived in America in the late 1970s, at the exact same moment that hip-hop was on the make—took the sonic power of the mobile sound system and crammed it into a device that was small enough for a teenager to tote around on their shoulder. Powered by a brigade of batteries, rather than an electrical outlet, the boombox could be transported into new environments, like subway stations and cars, that completely upended public expectations about where music could (and should) be heard. And at what volumes. The ever-increasing size of the speakers and the inclusion of an equalizer allowed users to put out more sound, and particularly bass, in ways that were perfectly tuned to the aesthetics of rap music. (In addition, the cassette recording function made it possible to circulate tapes of home recordings and live performances from person to person, neighborhood to neighborhood. The boombox was thus instrumental in disseminating the sounds of hip-hop DJs and emcees before they could rely upon radio airplay.[48])

The widespread use of the epithet "ghetto blaster" made it clear that this manner of sounding in public carried the stigma of racial and spatial otherness. There was a congruity between the fact that boomboxes appealed to working-class youth of color—who were so often treated as a nuisance—and amplified music in a way that trespassed on mainstream norms and environments. Both were seen as inherently "out of place" in proper society. Of course, this confrontational stance was part of the boombox's allure. For people who were systematically stripped of the right to take up space, the boombox was attractive precisely because it allowed them to "stake a claim" on the city. "The ability to exercise control over space," write the ethnomusicologists Joseph Schloss and Bill Bahng Boyer, "allowed boombox owners . . . to foster spaces of familiarity and comfort out of thin air."[49] The Sony Walkman, which reached American markets in 1980, right after the boombox, offered users a similar opportunity to retune public space to their liking. But while the Walkman permitted people to retreat from the acoustical commons, creating a fortress of audio privacy, the boombox was embraced because it provided the opposite: a sonic means to scale the walls of solitude, to draw people, willingly or not, into relationship.[50]

Most people, it turned out, were not willing. In Oakland, public resentment around amplified sound grew in tandem with the war on nuisance from the late 1970s to the 1990s. In 1976, in response to incessant complaints about bongos and congas emanating from funk musicians at Lake Merritt, the city council passed a law that banned playing instruments in the park without a permit (see ch. 7). Then, in 1978, the *Tribune* ran an editorial railing against the scourge of residents with portable radios. "Somewhere along the way," fumed the paper, "they failed to learn that everyone has a right to his own peculiarities—including the right not to listen to someone else's radio." Insisting upon an individual "right" to live free of other people's sounds, the editors invoked the logic of nuisance, extending it from property law to the public realm. "Why don't they understand it?" mused the editors, tying sonic taste to moral and intellectual merit. "Lack of education? Lack of proper upbringing? Simple stupidity? It's probably a little of all three." "After all," they added, as if the racist and classist tenor of their critique wasn't clear, "did you ever hear anybody with a transistor radio listening to Mozart?"[51] In response, the city council revised its noise ordinance to prohibit using a stereo in public without a permit. Finally, in 1990, when changes in youth culture and technology made congas in the park seem idyllic and quaint, the city council amended the law again to crack down on "boomboxes" in particular.[52]

If the "boombox ban" seemed like an attack against the hip-hop generation, that's because it was. In fact, the entirety of Oakland's noise ordinance codified a set of dominant cultural norms that were hostile toward Black dance music, and especially rap. For one, the ordinance—which was introduced in 1971 by Joshua Rose, Oakland's first Black city councilmember—sought to regulate all "unnecessary, excessive, and annoying noises" as "nuisances."[53] Rather than set a numerical limit on volume, then, it relied upon nebulous, even biased, categories of discernment that—given the racist association of Blackness with noise—rendered Black people vulnerable to discrimination. Beyond that, the ordinance defined any sound marked by a "repetitive pattern . . . including loud music" as an "annoying noise."[54] While apparently neutral and innocuous, this emphasis on repetition and loudness opened the door to targeting Black dance music, which, as discussed throughout this book, uses looping grooves and sonic pressure to build ritual, community, and pleasure. And rap, with its focus on circular samples and prominent beats, took these aspects of Black musical aesthetics and turned them up to ten. This put young people of color who made and listened to the music at odds with not only the cultural but the legal measure of legitimate sound.

Finally, the 1990 amendment to the noise ordinance outlawed any sound that could be heard "fifty or more feet from the source of the amplification."[55] On one level, this was classic nuisance law; in land use, a thing—whether a sound, smell, or some sewage—didn't become a nuisance until it traveled across a lot line, disturbing a neighbor.[56] But on another level, the insistence that public sounds be, in fact, private served to undermine the way that amplified music was used to draw people together into new geographies of connection. It criminalized the ways that rap fans used boomboxes to revamp urban space in service of young people of color's collective pleasure. In the words of Schloss and Bahng Boyer, it "made the very practices that people depended upon for community formation illegal."[57]

If, in the minds of regulators, boomboxes encouraged sounds to intrude where they didn't belong, then car stereos seemed to make the trouble even worse. Oakland had a long history of automotive cruising. But in the 1990s, as more and more residents complained about the aggravating impacts of car stereos and roving parties called "side-shows" (see ch. 5), the City copied a tactic from New York called "Operation Soundtrap." Starting in 1991, in a sonic variation on the "speedtrap," members of the New York Police Department and Department of Environmental Protection would ride out together, patrolling communities of color in the middle of the night, to screen for booming car stereos. Running overnight operations in Washington Heights and the Bronx, the police would impound cars, impose fines, and—if a record check turned up an outstanding warrant—arrest drivers for alleged crimes.[58] While this tactic was a sonic component of New York's turn to stop-and-frisk, its proponents insisted that it was needed to respond to resident concerns about their quality of life. "You get more complaints about noise than you do about drugs," said Assemblyman Denny Farrell, who represented Upper Manhattan. "Drugs don't keep you up at night."[59]

Oakland soon followed suit. In 1996, it spent thousands of dollars on decibel meters so that the OPD could monitor noise levels at cruising "hotspots."[60] Of course, it was impossible to patrol every street in the city. So, as in New York, the OPD targeted the spaces where Black and Brown drivers tended to congregate, creating a form of racial-cum-spatial discrimination that was typical of the war on nuisance. In theory, Oakland's new noise ordinances were written in a race-neutral manner. But in practice, sonic acts never seemed to rise to a policeable offense without the presence of Black and Brown bodies and sounds.

UNCIVILIZED SOUNDS

The "rap ban" wasn't the first (or last) time that Black musicians and fans experienced excessive regulation in Oakland. As seen in chapter 1, amid the tumult of wartime migration, the OPD patrolled the streets and nightspots in West Oakland to police the social and sexual color line in the 1940s and '50s. Still, this level of policing was light compared to the measures that were introduced in the 1980s and '90s. Among the older musicians, promoters, and DJs who I interviewed, none recalled seeing the OPD inside of the old soul and blues clubs. In fact, when I asked Edward Hawthorne and Carl "Sweet Meet" Greene of the Soul Messengers about regulation during the Black Power Era, they corrected me, noting it was the musicians' union, not the municipality, that controlled the scene. "I don't ever remember the police busting into the club or being outside," said Hawthorne. "The worst thing that'd happen was the union man would come in and you don't have a union card or there's no [union-approved] contract." "They'd pull you off the stage," added Greene, recounting when a union rep caught them gigging on the sly.[61]

What, then, explained the dramatic increase in the policing of Black nightlife during the rise of rap? I put this question to Ed Blakely one morning over coffee and eggs in Downtown Oakland. The setting, right across the street from the Marriott and Convention Center, was fitting. In the 1980s and '90s, as a professor of urban planning at UC Berkeley's College of Environmental Design, Blakely advised mayors Lionel Wilson and Elihu Harris on downtown renewal. By then, the Oakland Redevelopment Agency had begun to abandon the slash-and-burn approach of City Center (see ch. 3) in favor of a new focus on architectural preservation, residential development, and cultural tourism. Indeed, Blakely—who still recalled fond memories of staying out late on Seventh Street, listening to music alongside luminaries like Wilson and Ron Dellums—ran for mayor in 1998, in part, on the idea of promoting a jazz district across from where we sat in Old Oakland. (Blakely would come in second to Jerry Brown, marking the end of the Black urban regime, but go on to serve in Brown's administration.) "At 4:30 p.m.," said Blakely, echoing other residents, "the city had no life! So, we needed to create that Downtown. And we saw this area here as an entertainment zone."[62]

Given his love of music, and conviction that nighttime congregation was needed to save Downtown, I was surprised by Blakely's response to my question about the intense regulation of nightlife in the 1990s. "It was the *crowd*," he said, decisively.

> People like you and me, when we go to hear jazz, we go to *hear jazz*. We don't go to do a drug deal or talk or meet our friends. When you're in a jazz club, it's a very quiet, cool place. Even the clapping is polite. But when you go to hip-hop clubs—*aaaaaaahhhh* [mimics shouting]! . . . It's been the change in the crowd. Oakland—a little bit down on its heels—draws a crowd from Richmond to Stockton who are lowlifes. And that's only happened recently, in the '90s . . . Outside, there'd be a whole bunch of people yelling to one another. They could've talked civilized, but they didn't seem to. Maybe they were high on something.[63]

In this account, Blakely differentiated Oakland's Black soundscapes along the lines of time (pre- vs. post-1990s), space (inside vs. outside the venue), and genre (jazz vs. hip-hop). While the former was "civilized," the latter was not. In the process, the frame of his analysis moved from race to class in a manner characteristic of the post–Civil Rights Era. He grouped the two of us into the same category through statements like "we" and "people like you and me" under the assumption that, as a middle-class White man in grad school at UC Berkeley, I had the same sonic sensibilities and sense of sophistication as a Black man fifty years my senior. In contrast to the "lowlifes" from Richmond and Stockton, two cities coded as poor and Black, he implied, each of us was accustomed to "polite"—even "cool"—ways of sounding in public. For Blakely, then, sound was the crux of the distinction between high-class and low-class crowds. Whereas the jazz crowd was respectable because it listened with quiet intent, the rap crowd was rowdy because, rather than sit and listen, or talk "civilized," it made senseless noises.

In this way, Blakely's words reminded me of Tricia Rose's writing on the ways that rap music was dismissed by critics when it first emerged. She notes that rap was met with immense and immediate controversy as mainstream listeners decried its allusions to Black nationalism, male sexual chauvinism, and violence. But out of all of these issues, what seemed to incense critics the most was the insistence that rap music was indeed *music*. To the Eurocentric ear, which considered melodic progression and resolution as the measure of musical excellence (see Intro), rap sounded like nothing more than the *lack* of melody and harmony. Instead, rap's tendency to push rhythm, rupture, and vibration to their maximum expression registered, to the arbiters of musical taste, as mere noise.

But as Rose explains: "Rap's rhythms . . . are its most powerful effect. Rap's primary force is sonic." She goes on to note that, like funk (see ch. 2), and indeed all Afro-Diasporic musics, including Blakely's idealized jazz, rap prioritizes "rhythmic and percussive density and organization" as a source of musical complexity and pleasure.[64] The condemnation of rap as noise, then, was racist in terms of its reprise of old stereotypes—e.g., the idea of jazz as "jungle music"—and disdain for Black sonic traditions. But for rap artists and audiences, these "noises" were entirely the point. The beat. The bass. The breaks. The high-pressure volumes and encompassing sounds. The public setting of its broadcast and reception. This, according to Rose, accounted for rap's "sonic power and presence."[65]

For the authorities tasked with recuperating Oakland's "image problem," however, it was a "nuisance" or worse. Given the associations between the hip-hop generation, crack dealing, and gang violence, local officials, police officers, and venue owners assumed that rap music either attracted or incited crime. Rather than see rap concerts and audiences as a means to revive the city's nightlife, then, regulators associated them with the disorder and desolation that gave Oakland—widely described as a "ghost town"—such an eerie vibe. In the drive for redevelopment, it seemed, it wasn't just crowds but their complexions and sounds that mattered. Creating a conceptual tie between crime, grime, and rhyme, officials cracked down on the sonic spaces and practices needed for the hip-hop ecosystem to thrive. This reveals that the notion of rap as "Black noise" represents more than racist reaction and conservative musical critique. Indeed, it's more than musicological. Instead, in the context of struggles over urban disinvestment and social disorder in cities like Oakland, it incites a very real set of regulatory practices—in this case, the policing of rap concerts, boomboxes, and car stereos—that contribute to the marginalization of young people of color.

Today, if you asked fans which cities are driving hip-hop culture in the twenty-first century, few would say Oakland. In fact, people from outside of the region might find it tough to name even one up-and-coming East Bay rapper. The local rap community is acutely aware of this obscurity. There's a persistent sense among artists, audiences, and critics that, while the East Bay has had an outsized impact on national rap culture ("the soil them rappers be getting their lingo from," according to E-40), it hasn't gained the recognition, respect, and commercial opportunities it deserves.[66] Andrea Smith, for instance, a scholar of ethnic studies, who came up in the East Bay rap scene, identifies a number of reasons for this relative insignificance. These include outside cooptation, a lack of homegrown record companies, and an "iconoclastic" and "independent" streak among artists and fans, which has made them hesitant to compromise on content in ways that major labels and radio stations demand.[67]

These insights about the relationship between East Bay rap and the cultural industry are all crucial. However, when we situate these dynamics within specific post–Civil Rights Era struggles over law, order, and urban space in Oakland, one more reason for the stunted growth of the rap community comes into view: the repressive practices of local authorities. As the next chapter demonstrates, this process went into overdrive in the 2000s, when officials attempted to control the sounds and sideshows associated with a new youth culture called the Hyphy Movement. But rather than suppress hyphy, this attack on young people of color's musical and movement practices pushed East Bay rap into more marginal and rebellious realms, which, in turn, only redoubled the drive to regulate them.

5

THE SIDESHOW

Getting Hyphy at the Margins

The moon is full.
Look at the dark clouds.
Sittin' in my scraper
Watchin' Oakland goin' wild.
Tadow!
E-40, "Tell Me When to Go" (2006)[1]

SPINNING IN CIRCLES

The sound of screeching tires, sudden and startling, sent me speeding to the kitchen windows. Outside, in the intersection of Fifty-Ninth and Adeline Streets in North Oakland, I saw a car—modest and unremarkable, but for the fact that it was sliding sideways across the asphalt—spinning donuts. Its nose remained pinned in place as its rear swung around in wild circles, sending its weight careening to the curb, like a centrifuge. I was riveted, caught between the excitement of this astonishing sight and concern that the driver would spin out and crash into my car, which was parked nearby.[2]

Adeline, it seemed, was ideal for such a stunt. Until the middle of the twentieth century, the strip had carried a stream of streetcar commuters, including Black workers from North Oakland and South Berkeley, to labor along the waterfront (see ch. 1). But with the mechanization of the Port of Oakland in the 1960s, this overwide transportation corridor—now emptied of both the streetcars and commuters—became something of a relic. Around the time that I moved to that corner, in 2015, Oakland began to revamp the streetscape for the postindustrial era by replacing space for cars with bike lanes—changes that, according to the geographer John Stehlin, served as both a sign and a vehicle for the neighborhood's gentrification.[3] But it was the wideness and emptiness of Adeline that made it so attractive for spinning donuts. So now, mere weeks after the City repaved the street, this adept driver slipped into the intersection and began to spin. Then, just as suddenly as he appeared, he was gone. All that remained was the stench of smoldering rubber, thrill of uncertainty, and graffiti-like tire marks that redecorated the immaculate asphalt (see cover).[4]

These marks can be seen all over Oakland. Intersections. Interstates. Anywhere that an act of architectural grandeur or accident of urbanism imparted a space capacious enough for cars to circle up and dance. The streetscape of East Oakland, in particular, is knotted with these spaces. In the early twentieth century, the patchwork neighborhood development process created a crazy quilt of street patterns that—crosscut by corridors like MacArthur and Foothill Boulevards—resulted in oversized intersections wherever several streets converge or cross at diagonals. It created, in other words, a network of open spaces in a neighborhood that, through disinvestment and disregard, would come to lack them. Unsurprisingly, then, whenever I drove through East Oakland, I noticed that these scissor-like intersections and tire marks went together with predictable precision.

Seen from the air, these marks—which resemble the discs on a pair of turntables—inscribe a record of struggle over time, space, and race. As discussed in the Introduction, the straight line, that deceptively simple sign of the "march of progress," is one of the ordering ideas of capitalist and colonial time. In cities like Oakland, this sense of time is imposed onto the terrain of the street through stripes that striate currents of people and vehicles into segregated travel lanes. Within this structure, turns, crossings, and occupations are strictly regulated.

But the marks imparted by a spinning car read like a residue of looping, rather than linear, time—each layer representing the accumulation of life energies reclaimed from the clock, the grid, the law. In this way, spinning donuts is similar to the DJ practice of the "rewind," where the selector at a Jamaican sound system spins a popular record all the way back to its start and releases it again (and again) to stoke the pleasure of the crowd. In the words of the DJ and music scholar Mark Campbell, this practice refuses the "linearity" of the song in response to the "audience's insistence on enjoying the repetition of the track." "Market time," he writes, "is made to yield to the consciously extended moment of Black joy."[5] For the revelers who spin cars, not records, the street—like the song—is more than just a passage to move through; it's a place to loiter and linger, to congregate and play, to circle, not circulate, in ways that etch an alternative geometry of Black life upon the asphalt. "You probably drive straight ahead," says the rapper Too Short. "We do it sideways."[6]

In Oakland, spinning donuts is one of the essential ingredients of renegade car parties called "sideshows." In the 1990s and 2000s, the sideshow became integral to the city's hip-hop culture and rap music, serving as an inspiration for songs and music videos as well as a venue where those records were played and popularized among young people of color. As seen in chapters 3 and 4, this was a time when middle-class residents and regulators sought to stem disinvestment and a sense of social disorder through law-and-order policing strategies that pushed young people of color deeper into the social and spatial margins. This experience of marginalization, in turn, became reflected in the increasing rowdiness of the sounds and sideshows of East Bay rap. Led by a new generation of artists, like E-40, Mac Dre, and Mistah F. A. B., the

Hyphy Movement turned unconstrained and uncontrollable fun into a popular style of music and embodiment. If the commercial appeal of MC Hammer and Digital Underground characterized the East Bay's emergence on the national rap scene, then, after a period of intense repression, hyphy represented the region's retreat into a more provincial, eccentric, and antagonistic era of slaps.

This call-and-response between young people of color and the police became a circular process. Just as young people responded to their experiences of repression through more rebellious forms of expression, the authorities responded through more intense forms of regulation, causing the cycle to repeat. Under Mayor Jerry Brown, in particular, Oakland doubled down on its war on nuisance by mounting a crusade against sideshows—and, by extension, the people and cultural networks that gathered there—as public enemy number one. The City thus continued to police young people of color based on their cultural practices, and especially their sounds, in ways that further confined members of the East Bay rap scene to the margins and prevented their music from busting out of its regional bubble.

ON THE SIDE

I first met Yakpasua Zazaboi at a café in Old Oakland, around the corner from my office, on a sunny day in 2022. "I'll be the guy in all green," he said, over text. Sure enough, when I arrived, I spotted a man wearing a single shade of green, from his hat to his Adidas shelltoes, the tint an exact match for the avocado on his toast. Born in "Frisco" and raised in Daly City, he came up across the water (it might as well have been the world) from East Oakland. But he was so obsessed with the idea of mobility that he bought a car at 15, before he could legally drive it. On the night that he turned 18, in 1995, he and his friends decided to cruise to Oakland in search of an adventure. "We didn't know anything about Oakland," he told me. "The only thing we knew was Too Short. Short was always rapping about the 'Foothill Strip.' So, we said: 'Let's go find the Foothill Strip!'"

It took them a while, without smartphones or maps, but eventually they stumbled into Foothill. Within minutes, they ran into a sideshow. It was a marvel. There were people playing music, selling T-shirts and rap tapes, and passing out flyers for events. But more than anything, Zazaboi remembered the smiles. Black people smiling. A lot of them. More than a thousand, he guessed. It opened his mind to new possibilities of Black freedom and pleasure. "I had *never* seen Black people hanging out like that," he told me. "I was instantly sprung." Smitten, he and his crew began to come back every weekend.

The 1990s were a troubled time for Zazaboi. Coming of age amid the tail end of the crack epidemic, he—like most of his friends—tried his hand at selling drugs. "Everyone I ran with was selling rocks," he told me. Starting at 15, he cycled in and out of the carceral system: first juvie, then jail. Eventually, his mom—a White woman from Cape Cod—sent him to live with his dad, who was from Liberia, in Oakland. But Zazaboi's involvement in the drug trade ran its course by the time he turned 21. "That was my last time going to jail for actually doing something," he told me. At the time that we met, in 2022, he was running for an open city council seat in Oakland's District 6. The race, which he lost, would leave a sour taste in his mouth. But in retrospect, he recalled that his arrest in 1999 would be his first real introduction to the unpleasantries of electoral politics. At the time, San Francisco mayor Willie Brown was running for reelection. According to Zazaboi, Brown, who's African American, told the police to drum up a lot of drug arrests to prove that he was tough on crime. Caught in a sting operation, Zazaboi told an undercover officer where he could score some crack. He was eventually convicted to six months behind bars.

When he wasn't on the street or at the sideshow, however, Zazaboi was in the classroom at Oakland's Laney College, where he studied film. He had meant to study music. "Like everyone else back then," he recalled, "I wanted to make beats." So, when he saw a course on "production," he signed up without realizing that it was for *video* production. He decided to stay anyway. That semester, he was nabbed in San Francisco. While locked up, he saw a news report about a police raid against a sideshow that he had attended the previous weekend. The segment made him sick. "The news was calling us 'barbarians,' 'dangerous,' 'disrespectful.' It hit me like: 'Yo, you've got access to all this equipment. You can actually *do something* about this.'"

Released after three months, Zazaboi returned to his studies. Borrowing equipment from Laney, he began to document his beloved events. In 2000, he produced his first film—a five-minute short called *Sydewayz*—as a school project. It was a hit. It received a standing ovation from his classmates, who asked whether they could buy a copy. That gave Zazaboi an idea. Like the entrepreneurs selling T-shirts or tapes, he started selling copies of his video at the sideshow—"five dollars for five minutes," went his pitch. It was so popular that he started to carry a camera with him at all times. In the early 2000s, it was still rare for a young person—at least, a young person in East Oakland—to have access to video equipment. So, Zazaboi became the de facto documentarian of the scene. In 2001, he released a second version of *Sydewayz*—this one, $20 for 32 minutes of footage—which was again eagerly received. He estimated that he sold a couple thousand copies hand-to-hand. But the film, which was widely bootlegged, reached the screens of several thousand more. (In 2006, he cut a deal with Destroy Entertainment, a subsidiary of Rhino, to market a full-length DVD to national audiences.)

Still, for Zazaboi, it was never just about the money. It was about providing a counterpoint to the civic narrative that demonized the sideshow as nothing more than a nuisance or, worse, menace. "We were representing ourselves," he told me. Zazaboi would become a go-to source for reporters who wanted to see things from the point of view of sideshow enthusiasts. But only *after* the popularity of his videos forced them to reckon with it. "The news never came to talk to us—*ever*—until after I put those documentaries out," he said.[7]

Back in 2022, Zazaboi and I discussed the roots and routes of this now notorious part of Oakland's cultural landscape. The sideshow could be traced back to the city's postwar car cultures. In the wake of World War II, the car became the apotheosis of consumer citizenship and personal sovereignty. For Black Americans, whose movements had been regulated since slavery, however, it came to represent a literal vehicle of fugitive freedom. According to the critical race scholar George Lipsitz, Black people "created cultural forms"—everything from musical records to car clubs—"that celebrated movement in defiance of segregationist constraints and confinement."[8] In addition to this cultural significance, the car might be the only private space—the only private *property*—available to working-class African Americans. In Oakland, for instance, the drummer Earl Watkins recalled that, amid the city's Jim Crow, it was common for White businesses to sell Black people cars but not homes.[9] Black car culture, like the blues, thus emerged as a self-determined source of pleasure in opposition to Oakland's regime of racial domination (see ch. 1).

In the 1960s and '70s, as more and more Black, Latine, and Asian American families moved to East Oakland (see ch. 3), this proto-suburban landscape became the ideal space for young people of color to create automotive identities and communities. Emptied, like Adeline, of streetcars in 1948, corridors like Foothill Boulevard and East Fourteenth Street became transformed into popular "strips" for cruising. Cougars, Mustangs, and Falcons. It was like a cavalcade of muscle cars. Motorists from around the region would parade up and down the street, or post up at the 76 Station or San Antonio Park, to peacock their prowess, creativity, and capital (see fig. 6). The cruise became a place for young people of color to see and be seen, or sound and be heard. In the 1950s, as car radios became more common, the car turned into what the sound studies scholar Brandon LaBelle describes as an

Figure 6. Young people hang out in their car during a cruise at Mosswood Park in North Oakland, 1965. Credit: African American Museum and Library at Oakland.

"intensely sonorous machine"—a vehicle for amplification, or resonator, that "boosts the presence of the beat through its particular acoustical properties." "The car," he notes, "affords musical expression an added kick already embedded in music's promise of movement."[10]

The cruise, like the sound that resonated from car stereos, was often one of the only ways for working-class residents of color to cross the racial and class lines that divided the region. Members of Oakland's car clubs would ride throughout the Bay Area, meeting and mingling with motorists from San José to Walnut Creek. But it wasn't long before suburban cities retreated, yet again, behind the color lines that had come to define the region's social terrain. In the mid-1980s, amid an increasing emphasis on restoring a sense of social order through measures to regulate public space (see ch. 3), one city after another passed anticruising policies. It was like a game of whack-a-mole. Hit the cruise in Fremont, it returns in Walnut Creek. Knock it out in Danville, it's back in

Dublin next week. The more remote the suburb—the wealthier, the Whiter—the faster it moved to nip these "nuisances" in the bud.[11] And as more and more doors slammed shut—extending, it seemed, the legacy of the region's "sundown towns"—the parade of revelers was routed back to Oakland, where the police department (OPD) was waiting (see ch. 7). For Black Oaklanders, then, the car embodied both freedom and its enduring limits.

The crackdown on cruising was yet another instance in which the recreational space available to young people of color was curtailed. In chapter 3, we saw that, as the War on Poverty was replaced with the War on Drugs, disinvestment stripped Oakland of the public and private capital needed to sustain its once lively landscape of commercial entertainment. In the long economic decline that followed World War II, many of the city's art deco movie theaters, music venues, department stores, and roller rinks went dark. These closures were tempered, for a time, by a spate of state-funded programs, including recreation centers, talent shows, and sports leagues. But the rollback of public spending in the 1970s soon led to their demise, as well. This process of intentional neglect pushed more and more social and cultural activities among working-class youth of color into unsanctioned spaces, like streets and parks, where they were exposed to new forms of policing that targeted their very presence as a nuisance and portent of crime. In the 1980s and '90s, caught between the dangers of the crack wars and the OPD, many young people of color simply decided to stay inside.[12] But for others, like Zazaboi, the drive for some measure of social connection, excitement, and reprieve from the struggles of everyday life was strong enough to brave the street. And this put the car at the center of an increasingly contentious conflict between young people and the police over the control of public space.

The sideshow, explained Zazaboi, emerged out of this cultural and political milieu. Originally, the term referred to the ways that drivers would recline and lean to the side as they cruised in a style of masculine cool known as "sidin'" or "high sidin'."[13] But the term also said something important about the *geography* of these impromptu gatherings—the spatial relationship between the margin and the center, or the sideshow and the main event. In the 1980s, rather than suffer the rigmarole of admission and security, which was then on the rise, many working-class residents of color started to congregate with their muscle cars and souped-up stereos on the outskirts of sanctioned commercial spaces, like carnivals and sports games. This spot on the periphery provided an arena of self-determination for people who wanted to be in on the action, but were too young, poor, or fed up with being surveilled by venue management to participate in a permitted manner. The early sideshow thus served as a site on the margins where residents could create their own spaces of communion and pleasure. Upending the rules of participation, the sideshow became the main event. This partition process reached an important milestone in the 1990s, when, after years of being attached to other events, the sideshow became a standalone attraction at East Oakland's most conspicuous site of capital flight: the Eastmont Mall.

In cavernous spaces, silence makes a peculiar sound. The sporadic eruption of noise sends vibrations ricocheting off of reflective surfaces that are far apart. The echoes—which take a long a time to run their course, or "decay," in acoustical terms—fill the space with an atmospheric din that, oddly, signifies emptiness. Originally built to the standards of midcentury American shopping centers, the Eastmont Mall consists of 600,000 square feet of commercial space. But whenever I visited, in 2017 and 2018, it felt more like a mausoleum. It had all of the trappings of a typical mall: soaring atria, spacious corridors, and spotless floors. But rather than beckon consumers with the names of popular brands, the signs that lined the walls advertised the safety-net services of the

Oakland Head Start Program and Alameda County Self-Sufficiency Center—signs of poverty, that is, rather than prosperity.

In the late 1960s, in a rare case of private investment amid the exodus of capital, jobs, and tax revenue (see ch. 3), the Eastmont Mall was built on the site of a shuttered Chevrolet plant. For a time, it served as an important source of employment and pride among East Oakland's growing communities of color—a convenience that marked the area as something other than the margin of the margin within the postindustrial marketplace. It became the sole monument to commerce and recreation in an area increasingly stripped of investment. But East Oakland's economic crisis eventually came for the mall, too. In 1993, the middle-of-the-night departure of Mervyn's, a department store, left it without an anchor tenant or even a single national retailer. Confronted with an enormous space and a vacancy rate of 30 percent, a new team of owners—Jack Sumski and Bob Bridwell—decided to take the mall in a new direction. Convinced, it seemed, that there was always a dollar to be made on poverty, they recruited social service agencies to replace the clothing stores and movie theaters that had abandoned the neighborhood. In 1996, the mall was rebranded the Eastmont Town Center—no longer a commercial space, but a hub of community services. In the process, writes the sociologist Cristina Cielo, the mall became a site that was, from its tenants to its name, "unmistakably marked by the departure of capital."[14]

Most consumers got the message and followed suit. But among East Oakland youth, the opposite was true. The mall, after all, had long been central to the cultural geographies of young Black residents. According to the music writer and journalist Eric Arnold, the cable television station Soul Beat—which, starting in 1978, recorded performances by funk acts and ran music videos by up-and-coming rappers and R&B groups—was filmed at a studio on site. In the 1980s and '90s, when local rappers were by and large barred from mainstream radio and television stations—and, increasingly, music venues (see ch. 4)—Soul

Beat transmitted their sounds from the mall to living rooms around East Oakland. Fans, in turn, would come to the mall to visit a record store called T's Wauzi, where E-40 and Too Short, who were still distributing their own music, sold tapes on consignment.[15] Eastmont, in this sense, performed a similar role to Southern California's swap meets in the rise of West Coast rap. According to the critical race scholar Gaye Theresa Johnson, aspiring musicians in LA, like Eazy E, sidestepped radio censorship by using their car stereos to reach the ears of working-class audiences at the swap meets. These "'guerilla' radio stations," as she calls them, seeded a market for independent rap tapes from the ground up.[16]

In Oakland, too, the region's rap culture, community, and economy emerged from a rich soil tilled by independent recordings, impromptu performances, and young people's meetups at the Eastmont Mall. Here, amid the vast and vacant parking lots, the sideshow seemed to arrive at a permanent home, enacting a version of what Johnson calls "spatial entitlement," in which "working-class communities and individuals secure or create social membership, even when the neighborhoods and meaningful spaces of congregation around them are destroyed."[17] Caught between the closure of recreational venues and chaos of the street, the mall became one of the few spaces where young Black Oaklanders could enjoy themselves with a modicum—however partial or precarious—of freedom and safety.

Today, longtime participants remember the era of the Eastmont sideshow as a time of comparatively tame and creative expression among neighborhood youth. The gatherings got wild from time to time. But according to proponents, attendees tended to care for the sideshow because it was one of the only spaces where young people of color—stripped of property, and the rights that come with it—had de facto, if not de jure, control. "It was all about celebration," explained Zazaboi. "It was about showing off your car. People didn't come with any beef."[18] "You used to see people stop fights at a car show," he said, "because that was almost like the sanctuary out there—the place you used to go to have fun, and not have to worry about the day-to-day struggles you'd be going through. People didn't want to see that messed up."[19]

The youth, perhaps. But the mall management had other ideas. In their attempts to revive the "Town Center," Sumski and Bridwell recruited Leopold Ray-Lynch to serve as Eastmont's general manager. Ray-Lynch had earned a reputation for turning retail centers in economically distressed Black neighborhoods into islands of profit. Prior to Eastmont, he ran the Baldwin Hills–Crenshaw Plaza in South LA—which, according to Mike Davis, the radical urbanist, was resurrected through its "security-oriented design and management strategy."[20] But while Davis might have seen the retail center as a prison-like environment, among older and middle-class Angelenos, it was the place that Ray-Lynch—a West Indian immigrant—made "welcoming" again. So, Sumski and Bridwell hired him to do the same for Eastmont. To the owners, the sideshow wasn't a sanctuary of community and creativity. It was racialized nuisance, another form of "Black noise," that threatened to keep well-to-do consumers—already a rare sight—ensconced in the suburbs. "We want the mall to be for everyone," declared Ray-Lynch, "but we don't want anyone to be uncomfortable. We will be asking young people to leave."[21] Young people, it seemed, thus marked the margins of the "everyone" imagined by mall management. For "everyone" to feel at ease, Black youth—at least those tied to the sideshow—would need to vamoose.

Indeed, any sense of the sideshow as a safe space for youth was put to an end when the OPD moved in—literally. In the 1980s, when the parties began, East Oakland's patrol officers were based out of OPD headquarters in Downtown Oakland. But in the 1990s, as part of the move to community policing, which included a return to neighborhood-based beat cops (see ch. 3), the OPD began to shift operations back to Deep East Oakland. And out of all the potential sites, it chose the mall as its outpost, eventually taking over the space vacated by Mervyn's. At 64,000 square feet, the Eastmont Precinct became not only the Town Center's new anchor tenant but also one of the largest police stations in the state. While young people had seen the mall's massive parking lot as an opportune spot to party, the OPD—which, importantly, made Eastmont the home of its Traffic Section—saw it as the perfect place to stash row after row of police cruisers. By 2002, when the station renovation was complete, the OPD had moved 140 officers—half of its total patrol force—out to the mall.[22]

In an act of police gentrification, young people of color were evicted. This moment is often remembered as a turning point in the struggle over the sideshow. Once the meetups were pushed from the mall parking lot, where they were somewhat contained, into surrounding neighborhoods, it set off a three-decade game of cat-and-mouse that continues today. By scattering young people to scour the streets in search of other spaces to call their own, the displacement of the sideshow redoubled its identity as a fugitive practice. It turned revelers into renegades and intensified the generational struggle between Black youth and the OPD. In time, the focus among sideshow participants shifted from partying to flouting the police. In practice, the two became one and the same.

REDIRECTING TRAFFIC

"We used to cruise for hours," recalled Gino Pastori-Ng. "We'd all chip in a dollar for gas. We'd put four bucks in the tank and drive around all night." When we connected by Zoom, in 2023, Pastori-Ng was—true to his name—living in pastoral Napa County. But he was raised in the Fruitvale neighborhood of East Oakland. His parents met as volunteers at Berkeley's Leftist La Peña Cultural Center in the 1970s. Soon married, the couple started to look for a home. The realtor "took one look at them," explained Pastori-Ng, and steered the mixed-race Italian and

Chinese American pair to a deteriorating part of the flatlands. Born in 1982, at the onset of the crack epidemic, he was instructed to stay indoors. "It was intense," he recalled, of the disinvestment, dealing, and guns that racked the neighborhood. "Violence was normalized."

So, in middle school, Pastori-Ng took refuge in the makeshift recording studio of a neighbor, where he composed his first rudimentary beats and raps on a karaoke machine and keyboard from Radio Shack. As mentioned in chapter 3, this was a time when Latine, Asian American, and Pacific Islander teens intermingled with second- and third-generation African American migrants to form a multiracial youth culture. Living in East Oakland and attending public school, Pastori-Ng developed relationships with Black peers that revolved around Black cultural practices like hip-hop music and style. In the studio, he and his crew started by recording an instrumental line from the keyboard into the first cassette deck of the karaoke machine. Then, while replaying the tape, they recorded another line of music or vocals into the second cassette deck and repeated this process, layer-upon-laborious-layer, until the track was complete. "The results were very grainy," he admitted, with a grin.

As they got older, Pastori-Ng and his friends set their sights on the ultimate escape from the grim realities of the neighborhood. "The most important goal that I had as a teenager was acquiring a car," he said, echoing Yakpasua Zazaboi. As soon as he hit the legal driving age, Pastori-Ng started working—running errands, washing dishes, loading trucks, all "horrible jobs"—to squirrel away enough cash to purchase a vehicle. His perseverance paid off. After a stint behind the wheel of his parents' 1989 Toyota Corolla—nicknamed "The Bucket," for its dilapidated look—he managed to save up enough for a 1990 Nissan Maxima with 12-inch subwoofers in the trunk. The first of his crew to own a car, he finally had a ride that was ready for prime time. He just needed somewhere to take it. For people his age, though, there was nowhere to go that was both fun and safe. There were no movie theaters in the neighborhood. No youth programs to nurture his interest in music. "It was a complete wasteland," he sighed. "We'd just drive around, smoke weed, and listen to music. I spent so many hours sitting in random places in parked cars." At least, that is, until the cops arrived to harass them and move them along.

Caught between the police, their parents, and their peers, young people of color like Pastori-Ng had to learn, at a young age, how to navigate a complex and dangerous terrain of risk. In the 1990s, the flatlands were carved into minute turfs that reflected the factionalism of the drug trade. "It was provincial," he explained. "I pretty much never went to West Oakland or North Oakland because I didn't know anyone there. I didn't know what streets to avoid. Every ten blocks, it was like a different nation." "Were there any spaces that were neutral?" I asked. Now a meditator, Pastori-Ng sat for a moment in silent contemplation. "Downtown felt kind of neutral," he said, "just because there was no one there." "And the sideshow," he added, after a beat. "That was probably one of the most neutral places." This, he explained, was because the sideshow—now evicted from Eastmont—would constantly change locations, making it impossible for one neighborhood or crew to claim ownership. And this convinced young people to venture across the geopolitical lines that divided one set from the next. "It was expected that people from all over the city would be there." (This convergence mirrored the centripetal pull of the nighttime meetups and talent competitions that reigned during the boogaloo era [see ch. 2].)

So, while the authorities would come to condemn the sideshow as inveterately reckless, for young people like Pastori-Ng, it was relatively secure. Violence might have been "normalized" in other spaces, from the streets to the schoolyard, but—out of the 30 or so that he attended—he only recalled one sideshow where a fight occurred. "Everyone came there for a common purpose," he said, "to have fun, see the cars, and listen to music."[23] (In the past two decades, media coverage of the sideshow has become single-mindedly focused on reports of violence.

These reports can be racist. The label of "sideshow," which is coded as Black, serves to tag an event as criminal or dangerous in ways that can be sensationalist. Still, some residents concede that more violence has crept into the scene. This account is thus focused on the 1990s and early 2000s, when my interviewees were in their teens and twenties.)

The night would go something like this: Pastori-Ng and his crew would gas up the Nissan and set out on the streets. They would drive, park, drive, park, turn around, drive again—listening, all the while, to the latest records from local rappers, which would loop through the 12-CD changer. "I pretty much only listened to East Oakland gangster rap," he told me. "People who talked about things in our exact neighborhood." I asked him whether he would play some memorable songs from that era. He put on "City of Dope" (1998) by Yukmouth, one half of the rap duo Luniz. The song is thick with menace. It starts out with the contrast between a cascade of high-pitched piano eighth notes and a plodding bassline, creating an eerie sense of tension. These sounds provide the background to a dramatic narrative about the history of the drug trade in "Crack City," East Oakland. But in between lines that celebrate his own criminal exploits, Yukmouth criticizes the federal government for introducing crack to the city as a way to "get rid of these revolutionary Black Panthers" and praises the community for converting these punitive conditions into a source of neighborhood capital. "Buy rocks then we buy blocks," he rhymes.

The appeal of gangster rappers like Yukmouth, said Pastori-Ng—his head nodding, solemnly, to the beat—was that they talked about "things me and my friends saw happening around us." It was "thrilling" to hear someone from the neighborhood boasting about Oakland, even if it was for things that he found threatening. The artists that he loved—like Too Short, Dru Down, and 3X Krazy—took the city's outlaw reputation and wore it as a "badge of honor." "As a young person, I was afraid and powerless in the world," he told me. "But Oakland was feared and respected. These rappers made being from Oakland feel powerful." Driving around and bumping tracks like "City of Dope" made him and his crew feel like they could tap into that power, too, "even if it wasn't for the most positive reasons."[24]

Eventually, on a good night, the group would run into a sideshow. In the wake of eviction from the Eastmont Mall, this itinerant version of the sideshow wasn't planned or promoted. In the 1990s, drivers didn't have cell phones or social media to coordinate their movements. Instead, the events would emerge spontaneously out of collective action and attraction wherever people craved some fugitive fun. "It was organized vehicular chaos," wrote the journalist Pendarvis Harshaw in his memoir. "After zigzagging across both lanes throughout the eastern portion of the Town, the crowd would commandeer an intersection and an automobile that weighs thousands of pounds would begin to dance."[25]

According to Zazaboi, the original sideshow wasn't centered on stunts. Instead, as a cousin of the cruise, it was a space where drivers—mostly men—showed off their custom cars. As time went on, however, the next generation sought ways to distinguish themselves, to take the culture to the next level, through displays that were even more spectacular, more attention-grabbing, than those of their predecessors. So, after Eastmont, *how* you drove became more important than *what* you drove in making an impression at the sideshow. Besides, stunt driving was "exhilarating." "The attention you get from it is like a drug of its own," said Zazaboi. For young men with few opportunities for social recognition, spinning donuts to the delight of a crowd felt something like value or valor. "It's like being an artist on stage with 30,000 fans singing your song," he told me.[26]

But the next generation's desire to leave its mark on this outlaw culture meant their automotive antics became increasingly rebellious and risky. In addition to donuts, sideshow drivers created an entire movement repertoire—a set of automotive dances—that included individual and collective routines such as "zigzagging," "three-man weaving," and "ghostriding the whip," which gained notoriety through music videos like E-40's "Tell Me When to Go" (2006). If Oakland was a "ghost town" (see ch. 3), why not ghostride it? The move involved putting the car in drive so that it cruised along while its occupants—the driver included—danced on or around the car as it continued to coast. Ghostriding, like most stunts, derived its performative pleasure from reveling in the tension between the risk of danger and the talent to avert its realization (at least, most of the time). The anthropologist Pascal Menoret, who studied the culture of joyriding in Saudi Arabia, describes this as a dance between surrender and skill—a process of "losing control to regain control."[27] At the sideshow, young people just called it having "bars" (as in "handlebars").

It should be noted that many of the forces driving this culture—the association between automotive and sexual prowess, the adoption of a daredevil stance in response to marginalization, and the desire for attention—were all deeply entangled with dominant masculinity. As parties, sideshows tended to attract young men and women. But the drivers were overwhelmingly male. In Zazaboi's *Sydewayz*, for instance, the subjects—the interviewees, motorists, and people egging them on—are almost all men. The camera only briefly centers on women, and often in sexualized ways. In this sense, the film reflects the heteromasculine gaze. Importantly, these expressions of outlaw masculinity are celebrated across American culture, including Whiteness. But they are also embedded in the figures of male power that animate some genres of contemporary Black dance music, like the pimp or drug kingpin in rap or "bad man" in Jamaican dancehall.[28]

Along with the stunts, the second-generation sideshow created its own automotive aesthetic, which centered on the "scraper"—a middle-of-the-road sedan, like a Buick Regal or LeSabre, with custom paint and colossal rims. According to Zazaboi, in the 1990s, the OPD started to target the classier cars that dominated the early days of the sideshow under the assumption that they were paid for with drug money. So, dealers started to drive more nondescript ones—the kind associated with their grannies—to move about under the radar. Eventually, they passed those cars on to other kids in the neighborhood, who would pack them with friends and, weighted down, "scrape around" East Oakland.[29]

In the early 2000s, young people started to develop ways to distinguish these otherwise dull rides, like adding bright coats of iridescent paint and massive rims, from those of their peers. In this era, the name came to refer to the fact that the rims—a sign of mock elegance—were so massive that the wheels would "scrape" against the car as they turned. Indeed, the scraper came to be defined by its oversized sound as much as its look. It often featured a souped-up stereo and, for a time, "whistle tip"—a device that, inserted in the tailpipe, made the car scream like a steam train. In this way, the scraper scorned the White, middle-class norms of "good taste." It took the elements of mainstream consumerism (e.g., aftermarket accessories, GM cars) and flipped them into something outrageous—an eye- and ear-popping provocation. In a kind of ode to marginality—what Roberto Bedoya, the writer and former cultural affairs manager for the City of Oakland, calls *rasquachismo*—it took an unregarded and unremarkable car and made it unmissable.[30]

The scrapers. The stunts. All of this added up to a raucous soundscape. At the center of the sideshow, drivers would spin donuts, releasing the sound of screeching tires into the night air. On the sides, the audience would create a ring of cars, like an arena, each slapping with songs by neighborhood rappers like Yukmouth and 3X Krazy. There was never a "DJ car," said Pastori-Ng. The music, like the sideshow, didn't have a conductor. Still, there would often be one car with "four 15's in the trunk"—a reference to 15-inch subwoofers, as celebrated in the eponymous song by Berkeley rapper Sirealz—that simply dominated the rest.[31] "It was all about the bass," recalled Pastori-Ng. Local producers, he explained, would test out their beats by driving around to see how the soundwaves felt rumbling out of their cars. That exciting sensation, that "out-of-body experience," was a "mandatory element" for any track that would become popular among him and his peers. "The sound of a rattling trunk is one of my most common memories from childhood," he said. "It was often so strong that it'd shake the pictures off the walls."[32] In this sense, the sideshow took the sonic and spatial struggles over "Black noise" in Oakland (see ch. 4) and cranked them up to new extremes.

As the Black studies scholar Alexander Weheliye writes, the relationship between Blackness, sound, and modern technology involves Black people both "consuming" sonic devices, like car stereos and subwoofers, and "being consumed" by them.[33] This aspect of Oakland's sideshow culture is rendered in loving detail in the first episode of the surrealist television series "I'm a Virgo" (2023), directed by the rapper Boots Riley. Cootie, the main character, is kept cooped up by his parents, who want to protect their teenage son—Black, male, and 13 feet tall—from a city that will inevitably meet him with fear and violence. Eventually, he's discovered by a group of young people from his neighborhood in East Oakland, who help him escape from the confines of his backyard.

This experience of freedom and fugitivity is represented, tellingly, by Cootie's relationship to cruising and rap music. On his first ever night out, the crew celebrates by driving around Downtown Oakland in a convertible and attending a sideshow, where they impress the crowd with not only their "bars" but their giant. At one point in the night, Cootie rests the side of his head against the trunk of the car, which rattles with the sound of "Big Subwoofer" (2022) by Mount West-more—a supergroup that includes East Bay "founding fathers" E-40 and Too Short. "I love bass!" he shouts, his words quaking along with his lips and teeth. On his next outing, Cootie cozies up against a stack of subwoofers at a club. Closing his eyes, he sinks into the rhapsody of the vibrations produced by Mac Dre's "Feelin' Myself" (2004). Bass, says Cootie, in a manner reminiscent of Weheliye (if not Dre), "can help you feel the inside of yourself and the rest of the world at the same time."[34]

In the late 1990s and 2000s, the soundscape of the sideshow left an indelible imprint on East Bay rap, and vice versa. While the funky, upbeat, danceable sound of MC Hammer and Digital Underground defined the first wave of local rap to reach commercial success, in the 1990s the scene became epitomized by a grittier set of gangster rappers, who favored a more brooding, synthesized, bass-driven style called "mobb music." The record "Keep It on the Real" (1997) by East Oakland's 3X Krazy exemplifies this sound. Produced, in part, by Tone Capone—who also made the beat for the zoned-out East Bay classic "I Got 5 on It" (1995) by Luniz—the track consists of a smooth, super-low bassline, ethereal synths, and booming drum machine sounds, including the iconic cowbell from the Roland TR-808. Laced with references to cars, cruising, and "high sidin'," the song became a sideshow anthem for the mobb era.[35]

At the turn of the millennium, however, some of the same artists who were active in the 1990s, like Mac Dre and E-40 from Vallejo, took the deep, dark, dragging sound of mobb music, sped up the tempo, and infused it with a youthful drive for defiance and fun. Their songs became the soundtrack to a new youth culture called the Hyphy Movement. "Hyphy wasn't about the basslines per se," recalled producer Trackademicks, drawing a distinction with mobb music. "It was more about the slap and pound in your face."[36] In this sense, hyphy was defined less by its sound—its specific drum samples, vocal delivery, and so on—than its *feeling*. "It's not a clap sound or ghostriding whips and all that," he explained. "It's pure energy."[37] In fact, a Black vernacular twist on "hyper," the word referred to an experience of unbridled excitement that bordered on unruly. While, in the 1990s, Keak Da

Sneak of 3X Krazy used the term to refer to local rap, it didn't derive from the record industry. Instead, according to the ethnic studies scholar Andrea Smith, who grew up amid the Hyphy Movement, "it was simply a slang term to express a style, a feeling, an energy . . . known to Bay Area hip hop."[38] "We put music to it," admitted rapper Mistah F. A. B., "but it wasn't about music."[39] Hyphy, in other words, started as a spirited form of affect and embodiment that was endemic to the cultural landscapes of Black youth. Only later was it codified into a marketable category of music and movement.

Like the funk, then, hyphy resonated with corporeal pleasure and catharsis rather than intellectual ideals (see ch. 2); its party and its politics were indivisible. At the same time, hyphy emerged at a unique moment of political struggle among young Black Oaklanders. As discussed in chapter 3, during the post–Civil Rights Era, young people of color became increasingly policed on the grounds that their conduct and style, rather than their race, rendered them an out-of-control "nuisance." In this context, "getting hyphy" or "going dumb" allowed them to reclaim the unruliness that was ascribed to them and redirect it toward their own pleasurable ends. Like the sideshow, it permitted them to flip their position on the margins into a new center of identity.[40]

At the same time, this regime of antinuisance policing targeted the social and sonic presence of young people of color in public space. So, in response, rap artists—who were, themselves, from the generation that experienced this crackdown—made rebellion against the spatial constraints imposed by the OPD and assertion of their right to the streets central to hyphy's musical and movement vocabularies. This wasn't the first time that local rappers addressed the oppression of the police in their music. But according to the political scientist and DJ Lavar Pope, it represented a departure from the "warfare" messages of mobb music. "While police were still key figures in hyphy music, rappers' responses were more about taunting them, rather than direct violence."[41] And nothing captured this orientation toward rebellion and reclamation, this play of provocation, quite like the sideshow, which became hyphy music's main inspiration and motif. Rappers would reference these fugitive festivities in their lyrics and music videos. Drivers, in turn, would bump tracks like "Sideshow" (2006) by Too Short and Mistah F. A. B. out of their cars at the next event.

"Sideshow" was created by Traxamillion, a rapper and producer from San José, for his all-star hyphy compilation album *The Slapp Addict* (2006). At 105 beats per minute, the uptempo track knocks with 808 kicks and claps designed to rattle the trunk of a scraper. "I need bass / make it fast," raps Short. But the element that really marks the song as of its cultural and political moment is the second verse, in which Mistah F. A. B. explains that it's the OPD's repressive response to the sideshow that motivates the party in the first place:

The sideshow / they wanna shut us down.
But we a'swang something / on e'ry corner in the Town.
Police mad / the streets is wild.
3 o'clock in the morning / and the beats is loud.
Man, it don't stop / won't stop, never would.
Somebody gon' swang something / in e'ry hood.[42]

In these six bars, Mistah F. A. B. concisely captures the way that contesting and provoking the police, including through loud music, was inextricable from what made the sideshow so popular "in e'ry hood." In this way, the space, sound, and regulation of the sideshow fueled each other in a triangular process of intensification.

Clearly, commandeering the street to spin donuts—doors open, bodies hanging out of windows and sunroofs—was a high-profile way to go "wild." But daredevil driving was only one of the ways that young people of color reclaimed the spaces in which they were policed by performatively contesting the circumscribed movements that were expected of them. In the 1990s, alongside the sideshow, residents developed a new

Figure 7. A member of the Turf Feinz, a turf dance crew, performs at the Fruitvale BART Station in East Oakland, from the short film "RIP Oscar Grant," 2010. Credit: YAK Films.

style of street dance called "turfing." A reference to "taking up room on the floor," but also an assertion of territorial pride and control, turfing revived the precise corporeal articulation and pantomime of the Oakland boogaloo (see ch. 2). On top of these lighthearted moves, however, turf dancers introduced more acrobatic—even extreme—forms of contortion that, according to the dancer and performance studies scholar Naomi Macalalad Bragin, reflected the constraints of a more carceral era.⁴³ This spatial politics of reclamation can be seen in the fact that, in addition to parties and battles at recreation centers like Youth UpRising, turf dancers often performed and recorded videos in sites of anti-Black policing. The members of Turf Feinz, for instance, created videos in the streets of East Oakland, on BART trains, and at the Fruitvale BART Station, where Oscar Grant III, an unarmed 22-year-old Black man, was murdered by a transit cop in 2009 (see fig. 7). This, too, was about catharsis and escape. A member of The Architeckz, one of the original turf crews, called it "lettin' your body go." "You just doin' you," he explained. "It's like you in your own world."[44]

But you didn't have to be a formal savant to "let your body go." Quite the opposite. If turfing represented the technical apex of the Hyphy Movement, young people of color developed a more popular style of dance that mirrored the seething currents of a mosh pit. Dancers would bounce, sway, and whip their heads (or, in the words of E-40, "shake them dreads") around in an exaggerated way.[45] Rather than maintain their personal space within the collective, as was the case in the funk era (see ch. 2), hyphy dancers would collide with the crowd, generating more and more energy, until the room was moving as one swirling, convulsing mass. Smith calls it a "controlled riot"; Harshaw, a "tantrum on beat."[46] If the precise coordination of boogaloo reflected the organizational drive of Black Power, then the rowdiness of hyphy dancing marked a turn toward a more disordered movement politics that was indicative of the time. Still, at a moment when rappers from other regions, like Fat Joe, saluted the *refusal* to dance as a sign of masculine toughness, artists and audiences in the East Bay leaned toward wild forms of dancing as a source of collective pleasure and play.[47] "Those tempos make you forget about trying to act too cool," reflected rapper Droop-E, E-40's son. "The 808s and the drums get you moving like this. And then, from there, the energy, it spreads—and everybody's moving."[48]

As a cultural-political "movement," then, hyphy involved a repertoire of individual, collective, and automotive choreographies that reclaimed spaces of domination—from the streets to the club—so that young people of color could have fun. In 2006, these movements reached a national audience through the video for E-40's "Tell Me When to Go," one of the few hyphy records to gain mainstream recognition outside of the Bay Area.[49] The song, which features Keak Da Sneak, was produced by Lil Jon, Atlanta's "King of Crunk."[50] In the early 2000s, artists like Lil Jon popularized the crunk sound, causing

"Dirty South" rap to overtake East Coast and West Coast hip-hop as the nation's principal party music. While hyphy never achieved the same measure of commercial success, "getting hyphy" and "getting crunk" both relied upon club-ready beats that conveyed and encouraged a feeling of freedom-in-abandon.[51] So, on his breakout *My Ghetto Report Card* (2006), E-40 tapped Lil Jon to produce half of the tracks while reserving the rest for Fairfield's Rick Rock.[52]

"Tell Me When to Go" thus steamed "from the Bay to the A" like a transcontinental crunk train. The music video—which was filmed, in part, in the Southern Pacific Railroad Station on Sixteenth Street in West Oakland, the arrival point for so many Black migrants during World War II (see ch. 1)—served as a review of the hyphy generation's movement politics, with crowds of Black residents, mostly young men, moshing, turfing, and twirling cars and motorcycles. After the vocalists trade verses, the track features an extended dance break in which E-40 calls out a series of regionally specific moves and gestures for dancers to imitate. "Now, let me direct traffic for a minute," he says, before instructing the audience to "ghostride the whip," "go stupid," and "go dumb."[53]

In this vocal performance, E-40 ties together several strands of traditional and contemporary Black cultural practice. In the mid-2000s, many of the most popular crossover rap and R&B acts released music videos that centered on participatory dance breaks, which cemented the appeal of those songs among DJs and partygoers. "Tell Me When to Go" thus emerged within a movement that included "Yeah!" (2004) by Usher, Lil Jon, and Ludacris, "Lose Control" (2005) by Missy Elliott, Ciara, and Fatman Scoop, and "Get Me Bodied" (2006) by Beyoncé.[54] These recordings represented the most recent take on the tradition of the hip-hop emcee—or MC, as in "master of ceremonies" and "mover of the crowd"—who works to unify and conduct the energies of a live audience. At the same time, they revived an even older convention from American folk dance in which a "caller" shouts out the steps and signals the change in dance figures. These dances, like cotillions and quadrilles, were imported to the colonies by European settlers. But they were modified by the Black custom of calling, which, in the call-and-response tradition of many people of African descent, was introduced as a way to orchestrate slave dances that didn't rely on the formal instruction at dance schools that was available to many Whites.[55]

In addition to these national and historical strands, however, E-40's insistence on "direct[ing] traffic" gives the dance break in "Tell Me When to Go" a significance that's specific to Oakland. His call for the audience to participate in hyphy movements echoes the ways that the sideshow pirates the street, creating a break in the prescribed order of motion and presence typically the prerogative of the police. In the process, he reroutes the flow of bodies and cars in ways that contest the OPD's ongoing campaign to reassert control over the public domain.

TAKING BACK THE STREETS

In the 2000s, the increasing popularity of the sideshow and hyphy rap was met with a moral panic among local media, property owners, and public officials. In one particularly vivid account, the journalist J. Doug-las Allen-Taylor parodied the fear that came to color the evening news: "Cars whirling in madness as if living beasts. Smoke rising like hell's fires, as if from the tortured streets." While connecting these concerns to contemporary struggles to revitalize "Oakland's image and economy" (see ch. 3), he also noted that the tendency to demonize the sideshow resonated with old, colonial tropes. "The images call up . . . visions out of Euro-America's worst nightmares," he wrote, "savages, drunk and dancing, natives rising in the jungle, a frenzy that must surely end with the burning of homes and the murder of sleeping settlers." "God help us," he added, ironically, "it's the Oakland sideshows."[56]

"Going dumb" might have given young people of color a playful way to antagonize the authorities who sought to govern them. Among older residents and regulators, however, activities like the sideshow represented the ultimate nuisance—an intolerable threat to their dogged but delicate attempts to resuscitate the city's reputation as a terrain that was safe for redevelopment. In the words of the anthropologist Jennifer Tilton, the mandalas of tire tracks that marred the flatlands "literally marked" these areas as too poor and out of control to receive an investment in anything but more police.[57] If Oakland had an "image problem," as it was often said, then here was its anarchic archetype. By taking over commercial strips and retail centers ruined by the retreat of capital, and filling them with Black bodies, Black marks, and Black noise, the sideshow seemed to make some neighborhoods ungentrifiable. Officials responded in kind, doubling down on their embrace of broken-windows policing.

Like other attempts to control "crime and grime," the antisideshow campaign started under Oakland's Black urban regime (see ch. 3). But it ramped up in the late 1990s and early 2000s with the rise of Mayor Jerry Brown. According to the political scientist Robert Oden, the incorporation of residents of color into the administrations of Lionel Wilson and Elihu Harris had failed to address the enduring disparities of poverty, education, and crime that weighed upon flatland neighborhoods. So, Brown—who served as governor from 1975 to 1983, and boasted that he alone had the political clout to bring home the bacon—courted disenchanted voters with visions of economic development in working-class communities of color.[58] At the same time, over the course of the 1980s and '90s, early waves of African American displacement and international immigration had weakened the electoral base of the Black urban regime. Brown, who is White, managed to navigate this molten terrain—marshaling a mix of civic vision, cultural pandering, and personal celebrity to rally a multiracial coalition to his side. The Black urban regime, it seemed, had given up the ghost.

Once he took his oath, however, Brown did little to address neighborhood concerns. Instead, like Wilson and Harris, he took up the torch of downtown redevelopment, courting investors with financial incentives and redoubled support for the police. In the midst of the Dot-Com Boom—which, in the late 1990s, set off a land rush in San Francisco and Silicon Valley—Brown doled out subsidies to developers who, after decades of neglect, were now scouting a real-estate frontier across the East Bay. And scaring up memories of economic deprivation, and anxieties that the city would be skipped over by the latest wave of growth to sweep the region, he resisted calls to require tenant protections and affordable housing in return.[59] Oakland could have it one of two ways, he threatened, either "gentrification" or "slumification," and he was all-in on the former.[60]

But overcoming the city's reputation as a "ghost town" would require even more assertive policing. According to the investigative journalists Ali Winston and Darwin BondGraham, within months of taking office, Brown invited New York police commissioner William Bratton to Oakland, where he counseled Brown on "quality-of-life policing that targeted street-level drug dealing, homelessness, and petty crime." The OPD had never been a gentle hand. Still, Brown insisted that the "service-style" reforms implemented since the 1970s had allowed crime to run amok. So, he increased the OPD's budget and staffing, called for saturation patrols in working-class communities of color, and reinstated quotas for stops and arrests to make good on a promised, but unrealistic, 20 percent reduction in crime. According to Winston and BondGraham, this militant approach encouraged more corrupt and violent conduct toward residents of color. From 1998 to 2000, complaints about police brutality nearly doubled. This trend crescendoed in 2003, when the OPD relented to a negotiated settlement agreement after being sued by 119 men (all but one of them Black) who were terrorized by a gang of street-crime officers that called themselves the "Riders." (As of 2024, the OPD still hadn't met all of the terms of this roadmap for reform, making it the longest-running federal consent decree in the history of American policing.[61])

But drugs weren't the only blemish that Brown wanted to erase; he pushed the OPD to take a similarly unremitting approach to the sideshow and the stains that it left on the city's pavement and reputation. At times, he acted as though the sideshow was a personal affront. In some ways, it was. On more than one occasion, the mayor—who, at the time, lived in a $1.3 million loft in Jack London Square, where he had moved from San Francisco's posh Pacific Heights while preparing to resurrect his political career in the East Bay—was woken up in the middle of the night by drivers burning rubber. In addition, as he sought a path back to the Governor's Mansion through the Office of the State Attorney General, he worried that the curse of the sideshow—which, according to the OPD, had resulted in eight driving- or shooting-related deaths, and thousands of arrests—would tail him among law-and-order types on the campaign trail. "We've got to use every legitimate tool to prevent this invasion of Oakland's neighborhoods," he stumped to reporters in 2005.[62] And the man that he appointed to be his general was David Kozicki.

In December 2017, I met Kozicki at the Peet's Coffee in the Dimond District of Central East Oakland. In the 2000s, the Dimond District—perched, ambiguously, between the fortified hills and the "lawless" flats—was precisely the sort of neighborhood in which residents and business owners battled against the "crime and grime" that seemed to imperil its economic comeback. But by 2017, back it had come. The café buzzed with customers, most of them middle-class people of color, who converged to work, meet, or carry out their first dose of caffeine. In this scene, Kozicki and I stood out. Tall, White, and wearing plainclothes, he now worked for the Alameda County Sheriff's Office on its Sex Offender Task Force. Until 2010, however, this son of Oakland (but citizen of the leafy suburb of Moraga) had served on the OPD as lieutenant of the Traffic Section and, in time, deputy chief.[63]

In the late 1990s, Kozicki's increasingly aggressive campaign against the sideshow raised the status of the Traffic Section within the OPD. As the organization returned to a neighborhood-based command structure, the Traffic Section—now run out of Eastmont—was tasked with overseeing all "special events" that transcended these spatial divisions. By roaming the streets, inciting an at times massive police response, the sideshow fell squarely within Kozicki's scope. So, as anger and panic over the sideshow grew, the Traffic Section accrued legal, tactical, and financial tools to attack the problem.

At first, explained Kozicki, the Traffic Section attempted to prevent sideshows from starting through a strategy of preemption.[64] Taking a "zero tolerance" approach, officers began to roll up on any crowd of young people of color that *might*, in their view, turn into a sideshow. "We don't give them an opportunity to do anything," explained Officer George Phillips, tellingly, in a news report at the time. "Anytime an officer sees a group starting to gather, he radios up, gives their location, and everybody responds to chase them away."[65] "No crowd is too small to break up. And no ticket is too small to hand out," confirmed a reporter, who went for a ride-along. "People were pulled over for every imaginable offense, from a booming stereo, to standing up through their sunroof, to a broken brake light."[66]

In line with other aspects of broken-windows policing, this approach ran roughshod over young people's constitutional rights to assembly and normalized racial and sonic profiling. Gino Pastori-Ng remembers this time as one of "constant police harassment," "stop-and-frisk on wheels." A night of cruising around East Oakland wasn't complete without a member of the Traffic Section pulling him over and scanning for warrants against everyone in the car—perhaps even cuffing someone or writing a ticket—before releasing them with their freedom, but not their nerves, intact. It was a "traumatizing," he recalled, over two decades later. "Seeing them [the police] never equated to 'safety.'" "It pretty much only happened if I was driving with my Black friends," he added.[67]

Ultimately, this approach proved more effective at aggravating and arresting young people than stopping sideshows. So, Kozicki adopted a new tactic that he called "posting and pushing." In this maneuver, officers would pull up within range of an active sideshow ("far enough that the rocks and bottles wouldn't hit 'em," he said) and whoop their sirens. Inevitably, participants would scatter and regroup a couple of blocks away. So, the officers would do it again, disrupting the events, ad infinitum, until dawn.[68] "It pretty much always ended with the police showing up," confirmed Pastori-Ng.[69]

The second installment of *Sydewayz* is replete with scenes of posting and pushing in action. In some, the police remain in their cars, either pursuing a driver in a high-speed chase or parading by in a martial display of vehicular might. But in others, they are right up in the mix, corralling and handcuffing people, at times with guns drawn. In one particularly striking scene, three officers stalk two men by driving onto the sidewalk and nudging them along with the noses of their motorcycles. One of the men covers his ears as he walks away, indicating that the din of the police sirens, motorcycles, and helicopters created a disturbing counterpart to the noise so often ascribed to the sideshow.[70] Indeed, Yakpasua Zazaboi—who said he was targeted by the OPD for filming their sorties against the events, including his own arrests—told me that he was repeatedly cited for charges related to the volume of his music or exhaust "even though the cop was on a Harley."[71]

As the OPD reworked "Operation Soundtrap" (see ch. 4) to tackle the sideshow, then, it reinforced the dragnet-style approach to minor violations of the law that was typical of Oakland's broken-windows tactics. But maintaining this dragnet required massive numbers of police. So, the OPD increased the capacity of its "dogwatch" shift through a mix of mandatory overtime and mutual aid. In 2002, Chief Richard Word announced a plan to reassign the antisideshow sweeps, which had come to involve 60 people, taking them away from their normal responsibilities, by requisitioning off-duty officers to work overtime—an approach that cost $25,000 to $30,000 per night. In a windfall to members of the Traffic Section, between 2000 and 2005, the City spent an estimated $2 million on overtime, most of which came from the cash-strapped General Fund, to hit the sideshow.[72]

But even this increase in overtime resources didn't seem to meet the OPD's needs. So, it turned to neighboring police departments—at times enrolling one hundred additional officers from Hayward, San Leandro, and Alameda—through mutual aid agreements.[73] According to Kozicki, these cities were reluctant to participate in Oakland's antisideshow operations. But they agreed once the OPD pressured them into it. "We'd block 'em [sideshow drivers] in and put 'em on the freeway," he explained, "and block the exits down [Interstate] 880 as far as we could go." This pushed drivers from the flats into neighboring cities, attracting the attention—and ire—of law enforcement agencies across Alameda County. In response, Kozicki made his counterparts an offer they couldn't refuse. "If you don't want us to send our sideshow into Hayward," he told them, at a regional meeting, "then send us a few officers on Friday and Saturday night. We're not paying 'em. You pay 'em. But we'll do our best to keep 'em [sideshow participants] off the freeway and out of your city!"[74]

In the end, the initial stages of the antisideshow campaign, which relied upon the show-of-force method, proved as expensive as they were ineffective. The events continued to grow, often attracting over a thousand participants from around the region. In the early-to-mid-2000s, then, the City and OPD pivoted to more punitive means to control the street. "I actually wrote three State laws," said Kozicki, of this new approach. At the time, the law allowed police to place a 30-day impound on cars that were seized from street racers. But at the sideshow, where the goal was to reclaim space for revelry, rather than race through it, the OPD was restricted in its powers to a tow. This meant that cars were back on the street as soon as their owners were able to scrounge up the money to retrieve them. So, Kozicki and his political allies advocated to expand the racing law to spinning donuts. State Senator Don Perata, who represented most of Alameda County, introduced the bill in 2002. Kozicki and Larry Reid, a Black city councilmember from Deep East Oakland, rounded up residents from District 7 to testify in Sacramento.[75] This, it seemed, was critical to convincing lawmakers that the measure was meant to protect deserving and sleep-deprived people of color—who, according to Perata, who is White, were being "terrorize[d]" by the sideshows, their communities "ravaged"—rather than increase the OPD's power to target local youth.[76]

Next, Kozicki worked with City Attorney John Russo to pass "an aggressive tow policy" that allowed the OPD to take cars for "loud music." This turned out to be an even more popular tactic than the impound law. "We did a lot of towing for loud music," Kozicki told me, "because that was just a citation and a tow, whereas a 30-day impound required a crime report, which was more paperwork."[77] Amid their ongoing attempts to regulate the sonic presence of young people of color, then, the automotive soundscape—what Pastori-Ng called a "cacophony of bass"—seemed to give the OPD its most practicable means to police the sideshow.[78] According to a 2005 report to the city council, these tactics resulted in hundreds of impounds, thousands of citations, and "numerous arrests."[79] Young people took note. "Oakland police officers not only take the joy out of the joyride," wrote Pendarvis Harshaw, in his memoir, "they take the ride too."[80]

SIDESHOW LOOPS

Today, the sideshow remains a prominent site of cultural and political struggle in Oakland. If, in the 2000s, Yakpasua Zazaboi was one of the only people with the means to capture and distribute videos of these events, the spread of social media has sparked an era of viral imitation and competition. Copycats have emerged in cities across North America, including Los Angeles, Chicago, and Toronto, giving rise to a

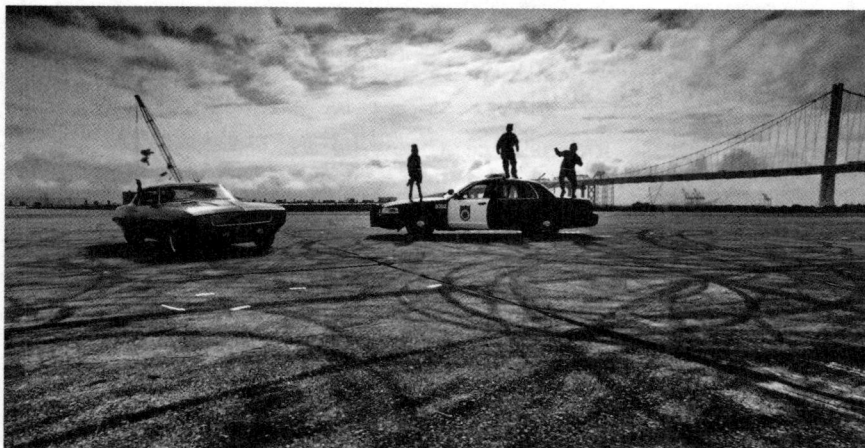

Figure 8. Kendrick Lamar spins donuts around a police cruiser on Treasure Island in San Francisco Bay, from the music video for "Alright," 2015. West Oakland and the Port of Oakland appear in the background. Credit: London Alley Entertainment.

practice that—uprooted from its origins in Oakland—is now referred to by the press and police as the "street takeover."[81]

But even as images of cars spinning in circles circulate across borders in ways that were once unimaginable, the reputation of the Oakland sideshow as an emblem of Black masculine rebellion remains indelible. Take the music video for "Alright" by Kendrick Lamar, which, released in 2015, became an anthem for the era of Black Lives Matter. As soon as the beat drops, the rapper appears in a 1968 Camaro, spinning donuts around a cop car—not in his native Compton, but on Treasure Island, in the center of San Francisco Bay, with the Port of Oakland rising in the background (see fig. 8). The rest of the video is peppered with footage of turf dancers, who perform in iconic sites like the Alameda County courthouse and Lake Merritt.[82] In this way, the video connects Oakland, sideshows, turfing, and the ongoing Black freedom struggle into a single constellation of meaning—one that continues to draw people from around the region, and even state, to the city as the mecca of these hyphy movements.

After almost three decades of roaming the streets, this cat-and-mouse game has become something of an arms race between participants and the police. On one side, drivers seek out increasingly spectacular stunts—for instance, throwing a sideshow in the middle of the San Francisco–Oakland Bay Bridge—as a means to leave their generation's (literal) mark on the landscape. On the other side, law enforcement agencies invest in new surveillance technologies, like car-mounted license-plate readers and aerial drones, to control a nuisance that has gone into overdrive. Predictably, this causes the loop to start again.

The cycle that started in the 1990s and 2000s thus continues to repeat. In the heyday of hyphy, East Bay youth created a set of wild cultural practices that both parodied and reproduced the marginalization of young people of color in the post–Civil Rights Era. And Black dance music was central to this circular struggle. Local rappers and producers converted their experiences of repression into beats, movements, and musical themes that were more and more boisterous, while young people souped up their car sound systems to blast hyphy records at late-night meetups. The OPD, in turn, used violations of the City's noise ordinances as a pretext to disrupt sideshows, tow cars, and cite or arrest participants. Rather than pipe down, however, young people responded by developing even more brazen ways to take up space, like the scream of a whistle tip, that only amplified the call of neighborhood residents for the police to secure their peace and property.

In the end, this dynamic deepened the investment of hyphy artists and audiences in locally specific expressions of defiance that—while relevant to the experiences of young people of color in other American cities—were nevertheless increasingly provincial and niche. In other words, while hyphy music was attuned to the lived realities of local listeners, it was difficult to translate for audiences outside of the Bay Area—even though it resonated, sonically, with the crunk music that would come to top the charts. In the 1990s and 2000s, then, after a period of trendsetting national success, East Bay rap drifted further into the margins of mainstream hip-hop music and culture.

Like the crackdown on rap concerts and boomboxes described in chapter 4, the antisideshow campaign represented another instance in which the city's war on nuisance targeted the cultural and sonic landscapes of Black youth. This process of regulation was especially intense because it took place in public space. But as we'll see in the next chapter, it was replicated during the same period through a municipal campaign against Black-owned nightclubs in Downtown Oakland.

6

THE CLUB

Bureaucracy and Banishment

‖‖

THE POWER OF THE CLUB

Since at least the 1950s, city planners and real-estate developers have worried about the social and economic vitality of
Downtown Oakland. Their anxieties have centered on the
intersection of Fourteenth Street and Broadway. This crossroads, where several of the city's main transportation corridors converge, has served as the geographic, economic, and
emotional heart of Oakland's preoccupation with urban
renewal (see ch. 3). All of the architectural accoutrements
are there: skyscrapers, a subway station, the aspirationally
named "City Center" complex, even a "wedding-cake" City
Hall.[1] It's as though generation after generation of civic
booster was so unsure about the city's metropolitan status
that they decided to hedge their bets, heaping all of its most
impressive amenities on the same corner. Geoffrey's Inner
Circle (GIC), a cavernous nightclub that sits a block away, at

Fourteenth and Franklin Streets, is one of those structures. Built at the turn of the twentieth century, this four-story, cornice-lined Colonial Revival is a monument of urbane refinement. Its red-and-gold awning reaches out across the sidewalk, sweeping people up in its sophistication. Or so it seemed to me in 2017 as I waited outside to meet Geoffrey Pete, its equally stylish owner.

After we ascended a majestic run of stairs, adorned with a sumptuous red carpet, Pete escorted me into the main room, where the walls were covered with photos of him—here a young man, there a bit gray, but always abidingly handsome—alongside the likes of Robert Redford, Muhammad Ali, and Busta Rhymes. It wasn't just celebrities. Politicians had come to pay their respects, too. "Feinstein's been here. Boxer's been here," said Pete, pointing out two of California's recent senators. "They need you in times of election." And as the once preeminent haunt among Black Oaklanders, he explained, using one of his most oft-repeated words, his venue had become a seat of "power."[2] Indeed, as a longtime grandee in the community, his proximity to City Hall was more than a matter of mere topography—a fact impressed upon anyone who filed past this wall of grinning dignitaries, picturing precisely Pete's "inner circle."

Pete continued to lead me through the space—past the photos, past the room named for local dance legend Ruth Beckford, past the ballroom where a crowd gathered for a repass—to his office. He offered me a seat on a chair that, once resplendent, now sagged with age. The rug beneath my feet looked worn out, too. But while the furnishings were a bit shabby, his clothing and comportment were anything but. In a city (and country) where Black people have long been policed over the "respectability" of their appearance, Pete's manner was impeccable. He was like the modern-day Slim Jenkins (see ch. 1).[3] He wore spotless tennis shoes, razor-lined khakis, and a bespoke blazer with a polka dot cravat, and peppered his sentences with superlatives like "phenomenal" and "most legendary." Standing throughout our conversation, he strode back and forth as we talked. At times, he reached down, touching me lightly, but insistently, on the elbow to stress a point—make sure that it landed—before gliding back toward the middle of the room. From my angle, I kept worrying that, at over six feet tall, he was going to crash into the chandelier that dangled over the fading opulence.

At one point in our conversation, Pete led me to the window that overlooks Franklin Street and pointed to the nearby YWCA. As secretary of the "Negro branch" in West Oakland, he told me, his mother, Dorothy Reid, had fought to integrate the White facility—now around the corner—so that he and his brothers could use the swimming pool. For Pete, Downtown Oakland was a space that still echoed with memories of Jim Crow—a landscape that molded, and was remade by, his ancestors. Indeed, he came of age amid South Berkeley's Black middle class. His father, Herman Pete, had migrated from the South around World War II. But his mother's people, the Reids, who came to California to mine for gold during the Civil War, were prominent members of the region's prewar Black community. His uncle, Paul Reid, was a gospel DJ on KWBR (later KDIA), while his cousins, Mel Reid and Betty Reid Soskin, started Reid's Records on Sacramento Street, one of the first stores to sell "race records" in the entire Bay Area. Together, the Reids promoted gospel concerts and competitions at the Oakland Auditorium. (Mel also produced a Marvin Gaye concert at the Auditorium that was released as *Marvin Gaye Live!* [1974], notching over a million record sales and a Grammy.) When Paul died in 1964, his memorial attracted thousands of mourners to the same venue where they had rejoiced to the sounds of James Cleveland, the Staple Singers, and an adolescent Aretha Franklin.[4] There were 6,500 people at the funeral, Pete told me, noting the social, if not spiritual, potency of such a flock. "*That* was a lot of power," he remarked, admiringly.[5]

In the 1960s, Pete's brothers joined the Black Panthers. One even suffered a severe beating at the hands of the Oakland Police Department

(OPD).[6] But his own path into politics had been more entrepreneurial. It began, he told me, on a childhood trip to visit relatives in Louisiana, where he marveled at not only the openness of racial oppression but also the level of property ownership among Black people forced to provide for themselves in the Jim Crow South. "Everyone owned their home," he said, his recollections gilded, perhaps, with what the political scientist Michelle Boyd calls "Jim Crow nostalgia," or a tendency to reimagine the early twentieth century as a time of Black prosperity, class solidarity, and communal uplift.[7] "Everyone had their own gardens with vegetables. They had their own cow . . . To protect yourself under segregation and terrorism, you built your own community. So, there were phenomenal communities. And the most celebrated of those venues were the clubs."[8]

Pete would get his start in nightlife when, as a grad student in theology, he was tapped to run Dock of the Bay. While named after the 1968 song by Otis Redding, this upscale, Black-owned nightspot in the once-segregated Berkeley Marina seemed, in fact, to negate the singer's lament that "nothin's gonna' change."[9] From there, Pete opened his own venue, Geoffrey's, with Cherie and John Ivey in Jack London Square. (Along with their brother, Fred, the Iveys—like Pete—went on to become fixtures of Oakland's Black nightlife.) During the Lionel Wilson and Elihu Harris administrations, Geoffrey's came to serve as one of the main rendezvous among the city's multiracial elite. In another echo of Slim Jenkins, then, Pete became involved in a mix of entertainment and politics—a cocktail of commitments that, back in his office, was evident in the file cabinets devoted to local civil rights groups like the W. E. B. Du Bois–inspired Niagara Movement Democratic Club.

But the building on Fourteenth Street was originally dedicated to a starkly different cast of power: White Power. It was commissioned in 1901 by the Athenian-Nile Club—a gentlemen's association that, modeled after San Francisco's secretive Bohemian Club, served the cabal of bankers, businessmen, and politicians that ruled Downtown Oakland

through the middle of the twentieth century. Pete—an evident collector, and collector of evidence—had the records to prove it. He passed
me tattered photos of the old tenants as we talked. While Black people
were barred from belonging to the Athenian-Nile Club, Blackness
appeared to be staged at the center of its social rituals. One image
depicted a 1950s pageant at which clubmen performed a song-and-
dance routine in blackface to the delight of the city's most eminent citizens. Colonial Revival, it seemed, was an apt description for more than
just the architectural style of the Athenian-Nile.

This history of racial exclusion was one of the reasons that Pete
decided to decamp from Jack London Square in the 1990s. After four
decades of renewal attempts, Downtown Oakland was still economically and energetically depressed. So, in keeping with national trends,
the Oakland Redevelopment Agency (ORA)—which first emerged
from a meeting at the Athenian-Nile Club in 1954—relinquished its
vision of turning the area into a replica of San Francisco, with its forest
of office towers (see ch. 3). Instead, it turned its attention to promoting
arts, culture, and entertainment. On one level, this narrative of a cultural "renaissance" served as a counterpoint to the media's persistent
coverage of Oakland as a city run amok with crime and violence. On
another, it promised to appeal to a new "creative class" of workers,
who came to be seen, in planning circles, as the rock and redeemers of
the urban renaissance creed.[10] The ORA thus pivoted to courting market-rate residential development and nightspots designed to keep
middle-class residents, workers, and visitors spending their time and
money in the district after dark.[11] If officials wanted entrepreneurs to
seed reinvestment with "diverse" entertainment, then Pete, it seemed,
would be their man. "May this venture be a successful one for you and
the City of Oakland," wrote Craig Kocian, city manager, when Pete
received his permit for GIC.[12]

The venue opened on Martin Luther King Jr. Day in 1994 with a party
for the Niagara Movement Democratic Club featuring LA congress-

woman Maxine Waters.[13] "I did a little bit of everything," said Pete, of the early days, "political functions, record-release parties, gospel brunches, talent showcases."[14] Soon, GIC became the premier place to see-and-be-seen among Oakland's Black political class. So, when Pete encountered an opportunity to purchase the building in 1997, the city council voted unanimously to lend him $270,000.[15] This was a "gamechanger," he explained, a measure of security against the continual threat of Black displacement. Otherwise, he told me, "when you amass power and visibility, they can either increase the rent or kick you out."[16]

Decades after his trip to Louisiana, Pete had finally attained his ideal of title. So, it was only right that the arresting red awning read *Geoffrey's*. This situated GIC in a long line of venues named for their African American proprietors—Esther's Orbit Room, Eli's Mile High Club, Al's House of Smiles—that apostrophe a sign of Black possession, sovereignty in a punctuation mark. And for good reason, Pete explained, as such nightspots had long served as sanctuaries from the policing that was meant to preclude Black togetherness. "Historically," he said, "when two or more Black folks were standing on the street corner, they'd hear: 'Keep it moving!'" But at a "meeting place" like GIC, he continued, "you can dress up . . . you can laugh, you can celebrate, you can mourn." "You have a *place*," he stressed. "That's *power*. And that's not accepted . . . When you're secure, America's insecure. When you're a slave, *that's* when America's secure."[17]

Despite their apparent desire to attract people to the area after dark, it wasn't long before regulators decided that the growing scene at GIC—the star-studded events, lines of revelers dressed to the nines, and crowds of rubberneckers drawn to the spectacle of it all—was more a source of "insecurity" than a "success" for the City of Oakland. "There had never been a club that had as many Black folks assembling as this one," said Pete, "because the capacity here was greater than any we'd ever had." "If two Blacks gathering together was a threat," he asked, rhetorically, "then what about 600 or 700?"[18]

In 1996, the OPD started to swarm Fourteenth Street to increase traffic and crowd control, especially during GIC's "First Saturdays" parties—which, among its cultural and political attractions, tended to draw the biggest and youngest crowds. (Importantly, Fourteenth Street is the main corridor that connects both East and West Oakland to Downtown, making it a conduit that carries residents from the margins to the center.) Over the course of the next decade, the OPD drew upon new legal and bureaucratic tools to dispatch large numbers of officers to the area, often charging, or threatening to charge, Pete for their time. Back in his office, Pete passed me another picture, this one to illustrate the police presence that his patrons would routinely encounter outside of the venue. In the photo, taken in 2007, I counted five police cruisers filling the width of Fourteenth, waiting for closing time. "It was terrorism at its *height*," he fumed, pointer finger landing on my elbow for emphasis.[19]

In 2009, Pete sued the City and several police officers for violating his civil rights. He wasn't alone. In the 2000s, all of the most prominent Black club owners in Downtown Oakland—including Fred and John Ivey and "Sweet" Jimmie Ward—sued the City and the OPD for alleged racial discrimination. But each of their cases was dismissed. In the end, it seemed, Pete's evidential and experiential records proved unconvincing to the court.

In 1990, Oakland's most prominent music venues enacted a year-long moratorium on rap concerts. As part of the plan to end the "rap ban," artists, promoters, venue owners, and city officials came to the consensus that more intense security measures were the way to manage, rather than suppress, music events that attracted large numbers of Black people and other young people of color (see ch. 4). In the 1990s and 2000s, this new approach collided with the City's campaign against renegade car parties called sideshows, which represented precisely the sort of nighttime "nuisance" that threatened to stall urban renewal once again (see ch. 5). So, at the same time that the City sought to turn parts of

Downtown Oakland into an Arts and Entertainment District, it developed new regulations and police practices that were meant to control activities on the inside and outside of nightclubs. And given the ingrained association of rap artists and audiences with recklessness and noise, in particular during the hyphy era, these regulations targeted Black-owned venues like GIC and Sweet Jimmie's. While supposedly "race-neutral," this security-oriented approach installed racist ideas about Black dance music into the day-to-day mechanisms of governance.

After the moratorium, then, Oakland's strategy of an outright ban evolved into more subtle, but no less discriminatory, measures that made it prohibitive for Black club owners to book Black dance music. In the end, GIC would be the only Black club of its generation to survive Downtown Oakland's "renaissance." To readers, this narrative of displacement might seem like a familiar process of gentrification. But this chapter of the war on nuisance reveals that—even more than economic changes—the dispossession of Black nightlife was driven by the mundane and bureaucratic regulation of Black crowds and sounds. It was the City, in this sense, rather than "the market," that was responsible for what the urban studies scholar Ananya Roy calls "racial banishment."[20]

At the same time, given the popularity of rap, R&B, dancehall, Afrobeats, and more among Black and non-Black audiences, neither residents nor regulators would stand for the wholesale displacement of Black dance music from the "New Oakland." So, the late 2000s and 2010s saw the proliferation of DJ crews and parties dedicated to what the ethnomusicologist Allie Martin calls "emancipatory soundscapes."[21] But increasingly, the profits that were produced from the cultural labor of Black musicians and nightlife workers accrued to White people.

POLICING THE LET OUT

In order to open and operate GIC, Geoffrey Pete had to navigate a tangle of permits. Like other cities, Oakland requires any public venue in which "entertainment is provided" or "dancing is permitted" to get a "cabaret permit."[22] These permits are issued and managed by the Special Activity Permits Division (SAPD) within the City Administrator's Office. Not only nightclubs fall under its purview; rather, according to Arturo Sanchez, former manager, the division is tasked with overseeing a range of businesses that, while legal, are enrolled in additional regulation because of the risk that they will "impact the quality of life of residents." Cabarets, cannabis stores, massage parlors—all of them require what Sanchez called a "nuisance permit."[23] (In fact, when I interviewed him in 2016, the SAPD and Nuisance Abatement Division were run by the same two-person staff, revealing that the regulation of nightclubs and nuisances were tied together in both theory and practice.)

At the outset, the permitting process is meant to assess and prevent the presumptive risks associated with nightlife—namely, disorder, noise, and crime—by vetting the venue's owners, investors, and operating plan. The OPD starts by running a background check on each of the applicants.[24] Then, the OPD and SAPD work together to create a risk assessment for the prospective venue. Predictably, given the association of rap music and its youthful audience with "crime and grime" (see ch. 4), regulators tend to zero in on the applicant's proposed *musical format* and *age of attendees*. While it is illegal, in the post–Civil Rights Era, to govern through overtly racial terms, these categories serve as covert stand-ins for working-class young people of color, singling out venues that intend to host rap concerts or parties dedicated to Black dance music for extra scrutiny.

When Pete sought a permit for GIC in 1993, his application was sent around to the Planning and Building Department, Fire Department, and OPD. The City had every reason to approve the venue. Pete's move from Jack London Square to Fourteenth Street would seem to advance the ORA's aim—adopted the same year—of drawing more residential and commercial investment to the area through a mix of culture and entertainment.[25] Indeed, each time the application went out for review, it returned with a seal of approval—with one catch. Like the rest of his colleagues, OPD Chief Joseph Samuels recommended approval, but only on certain conditions. He requested that a series of provisions promoting more stringent oversight be added to the permit. In line with the prevailing concerns about nuisance and violence, the contract was amended to state that it could be revoked if GIC failed to provide "adequate security," prompted "police calls-for-service," or impacted the area with "noise."[26] With little recourse, Pete signed on the dotted line.

At the time, these terms might have seemed like minor bureaucratic details. Opening with a sense of flourish and fanfare, the club attracted the same see-and-be-seen set that had made the trek to Geoffrey's in Jack London Square. Here, at last, were Downtown's long-awaited crowds of nighttime pleasure seekers. Not since the 1930s and '40s, when residents descended on swing dances at Sweet's Ballroom (see ch. 1), had the area been so lively.

But the good times weren't just confined within the walls of the club. As discussed in previous chapters, from the 1970s to the 1990s, disinvestment and the resulting war on nuisance pushed young people of color's social lives and sonic pleasures into unsanctioned spaces and times, where they were increasingly vulnerable to policing. Like the sideshow, the "let out"—the crowd that congregated outside of the club after it closed for the night—came to epitomize this landscape of last resort. Indeed, for people who met on the margins, the let out was an *outlet*. In the song "The Let Out" (2017), for instance, rapper Jidenna situates this pursuit of pleasure within anti-Black systems of poverty and policing. "Enemies tryna pack us in a prison / but we gon' pack up in that old Honda Civic." "I'm celebrating in the face of mass incarceration," he explained to an interviewer. For Jidenna—who was working as a teacher in Oakland when he was scouted to the roster of the Wondaland Arts Society by musician Janelle Monáe—the song's "party" vibe, like the scene it describes, resonates with the recognition that the good times could be snatched away at any moment. "We're free *tonight*," he said, noting the precarity of those rights.[27] Best to act like it.

In Oakland, then, spaces like the let out afforded a narrow—for some, fugitive—freedom. As with the cruise and the sideshow, this sense of action could emerge anywhere. In the 2000s, for instance, young people of color started to gather at the TGI Friday's in Jack London Square, causing the restaurant, like a music venue, to hire police officers and security guards to regulate the space.[28] But hands down, the scene outside of the clubs was the most exciting one in town. There, young people—especially straight men—could take in the spectacle of people at their sexiest, attempt to pick up a mate, and, in the case of a big-name event, bask in the aura of celebrity. For those who were too young, too poor, or—in the eyes of the bouncer—too poorly dressed to get inside the club, there was always the party outside of the party. "Can't get in the club / gotta' parkin' lot pimp," rapped Mistah F. A. B. on "Ghost Ride It" (2006).[29] And given the excitement around GIC—people on the street might catch a glimpse of Tim Hardaway or Too Short coming down the red-carpeted steps—Fourteenth and Franklin became the let out par excellence.

Soon, appealing to the conditions that were added to GIC's cabaret permit, the OPD responded to the let out with a massive and repeated police presence. In a crime report from 1996, for instance, the police painted a scene in which the street became so congested that the OPD dispatched "six patrol units and an entire squad of motorcycle officers" to disperse the crowd. As was often the case in Oakland, the OPD's attempts to intervene only escalated the chaotic situation. "In the process," read the report, "a fight broke out and bottles were thrown at officers." As the crowds kept coming, so did the cops. Eventually, in 1997, the OPD dinged Pete for violating his permit.[30] He had been put on notice, nightlife probation. Now, if he wanted to keep his permit and the doors open, he would need to comply with increasingly onerous operating conditions, imposed at the discretion of the police.

The increased oversight of GIC was in keeping with Oakland's emphasis on more intensive security measures in the wake of the rap moratorium. But over the course of the 1990s, the City came to realize that this new approach to policing nightclubs, concerts, and other "special events," which the OPD covered with overtime, was creating runaway costs. The issue stemmed, in part, from the City's entrenched, post–Proposition 13 budget woes. In the mid-1990s, the city council imposed a hiring freeze. Without enough workers to cover their essential duties, departments came to rely upon overtime to make up the gap. As a result, in fiscal year 1997–98, an estimated 2,500 of the City's 6,000 employees (42 percent) received some amount of overtime pay at a cost of $25 million, or 9.5 percent of the General Fund budget. While this workaround was used across governmental agencies, the OPD received $12.2 million, or 50 percent of all overtime wages, and a whopping 4.6 percent of general expenditures.[31] The solution, it seemed, was to strengthen the special event permitting system to compel venue owners and event promoters to pay for the OPD's attempts to regulate their crowds.

In 1999, with the support of Mayor Jerry Brown, the city council passed a law that required promoters to provide and pay for extra security measures at large sporting events, arena concerts, and block parties. At the same time, the law applied to more run-of-the-mill events, like concerts or parties at nightclubs, if the OPD determined that they would "result in impacts on public safety, health, welfare, and police resources."[32] It might have been common sense to include massive events at the Kaiser Center or Coliseum. But this second, catchall category raised two critical issues for people like Pete. First, these events occurred at nightspots that were regulated by cabaret permits, which, in theory, already authorized them to host concerts, dances, and other forms of live entertainment as a matter of course. Now, in addition to appeasing the SAPD, venue owners would have to appeal to the OPD for an event permit, which created an added burden of cost and control. Or rather, *some* venue owners. Because these conditions were only required if the OPD decided that an event would be trouble. Second, then, this vague definition gave the OPD's Special Events Unit (SEU) the power to collect intelligence on the artists, audiences, and producers associated with an event and determine whether—or under what terms—to permit it.[33]

In 2017, I asked the OPD sergeant in charge of the SEU, who didn't consent to be named, to explain this process to me. First, he reported, his team identified upcoming concerts and parties by reviewing the event calendars that were submitted once a month by venue managers. Not everyone complied with this requirement, however. So, the SEU also scanned the radio, social media, and other promotions (e.g., posters and flyers) to detect events that might otherwise escape review. Then, they researched the promoters, performers, and members of their "entourage" by consulting with the OPD's Intelligence Unit and—somewhat less sophisticated—Google. If their investigation turned up any references to crime or violence, then they either refused the permit or—in a practice that emerged in the late 1980s during the rise of rap music—required more preventative measures, like hiring additional security guards and police officers and acquiring extra liability insurance. And these requirements, which ran the risk of increasing costs to the point that an event became impractical, were made at the sole discretion of the OPD.[34]

Understandably, this approach didn't inspire a lot of confidence among artists and event producers who had suffered mistreatment at the hands of the police. For instance, Theo Aytchan Williams, the artistic director of SambaFunk!, who had produced parties in Oakland since the late 1980s, equated the SEU to the Special Weapons and Tactics (SWAT) unit—which, from the Watts Uprising to War on Drugs, was used to suppress Black communities in Los Angeles. "The special events task force," he told me, "that was created here, like SWAT was created in LA. That counterintelligence kind of surveillance—listening to the radio to see where the parties are at—that was created here in

Oakland."[35] I can't say for certain whether Oakland was the first city to use this tactic. But clearly, cultural producers like Williams saw the city's special event permitting system as part of a lineage of police practices—from SWAT to "counterintelligence," which, in Oakland, contains echoes of the OPD and FBI's repression of the Black Panther Party (see ch. 3)—meant to prevent Black people's social movements. Indeed, in 2017, the journalist Sam Lefebvre concluded that, while local rap promoters were repeatedly denied permits, or forced to cancel concerts due to onerous permit requirements, promoters who didn't book rap music rarely complied with the special event permitting system; in fact, the latter barely even knew about it.[36] In effect, then, this system represented an extraordinary form of regulation that functioned—at times, exclusively—to target Black dance music.

In addition to requiring permits for prospective events, the 1999 ordinance allowed the OPD to pass a range of costs on to venue owners, retrospectively, whenever they dispatched a large number of officers to respond to a "disturbance or potential disturbance at a cabaret site." If this occurred twice within a six-month period, then the club would be required to run all of its events—which, again, its cabaret permit supposedly covered—by the SEU for a year of probation.[37] In practice, this meant that the venues that received the most scrutiny from the police would be subject to increased surveillance and security measures, at the cost of the owner, regardless of whether the "disturbance" occurred inside of the club or on the street. And in the context of Oakland's war on nuisance and antisideshow campaign, the OPD consistently cracked down on social and sonic spaces, like the let out, that were popular among young Black people.

This approach thus reproduced racial and spatial patterns of regulation in Oakland. According to this circular logic, once a club was tagged as a "problem," it was targeted for more policing. But it was the very fact of being targeted by the police that made the club a "problem" in the first place. And as seen in chapter 4, the OPD was predisposed to see rap as a source of crime and disorder. Indeed, as Angela Woodall, a former nightlife reporter for the *Oakland Tribune*, told me, the police treated anything to do with rap as "trouble: trouble music, trouble people."[38] So, despite claims to the contrary, these decisions about "problem spaces" and "police resources" were never race-neutral. In 1995, for instance, the OPD was pilloried when some 20,000 revelers turned out for a rave at the Kaiser Center, overrunning the six officers assigned to the event. Why, wondered critics, were there so few cops at such a huge party? "I didn't want to put the guy [the promoter] in the poor house," explained Sergeant Bill McFarlane, who managed special events at the time, "so I cut a bit. I figured it was just going to be another dance."[39]

The same grace wouldn't be granted to Pete. The difference, of course, was that GIC produced events that were meant to appeal to Black residents. Over the course of the 2000s, the OPD repeatedly sent large contingents of officers to crack down on the let out at the club—in particular, on First Saturdays—and, using the new law, threatened to recoup thousands of dollars in overtime costs. In other words, the OPD decided that the crowds outside of the venue were a "disturbance or potential disturbance," determined how many officers it needed to clear the streets, and then insisted that Pete pay for their actions. The City might not have been able to "increase the rent or kick [him] out," but they could run up a massive debt to hold over his head.

These operations were often led by David Kozicki, lieutenant of the Traffic Section (see ch. 5), and Sergeant Kyle Thomas. In the mid-2000s, Thomas was put in charge of a new "club detail." The members of this unit, which was often staffed with overtime, would stake out near Black-owned venues downtown. From these command posts, they would coordinate with club owners and security, create a "visual deterrent" to crime, and crack down on the let out.

I moved to Oakland in 2009, right after this crackdown occurred. But I was able to get a glimpse of it through an unexpected source. In the last chapter, I introduced Yakpasua Zazaboi, the filmmaker who produced *Sydewayz*, a series of documentaries about the Oakland side-show. At the end of our first meeting in 2022, as we wrapped up our conversation about the City's repression of these car parties, Zazaboi mentioned—almost as an afterthought—that he had footage of the OPD carrying out similar operations against nightspots like GIC. He hadn't set out to capture the OPD's crackdown on Black-owned clubs. Instead, as he came to be known as the *Sydewayz* guy, DJs, promoters, and venue owners started to hire him to film their parties. Was he from the media? Was he shooting a music video? Patrons didn't know. So, Zazaboi and his "big-ass camera" gave the function an air of celebrity. "Half the time, we didn't do nothing with the videos except record them," he explained. "I was part of the entertainment in there." It started with Mingles, one of the Iveys's venues in Jack London Square, where he filmed their popular open mic. The Iveys then introduced Zazaboi to Pete, who hired him to work events at GIC. Eventually, as his relationship with the OPD started to deteriorate, Pete paid Zazaboi to stake out on the street, where he filmed interactions between patrons, security guards, and police officers. Pete's goal, it seemed, was to create his own record to counteract the narrative of chaos, criminality, and incompetent security perpetuated by the OPD. "Let me find the tapes," said Zazaboi, as we departed. "I'll send them to you."[40]

Viewing the reams of video, it's possible to reconstruct the arc of a First Saturdays event in the late 2000s. At the start of the night, GIC's massive security team sets up a line of metal barricades that run east along Fourteenth and wrap around the corner of Franklin. Groups of young people trickle toward the door and take their spot in line. Wearing button-down shirts, dresses, and heels—this was the era of the "no white tees" dress code—they submit to a patdown and bag check before filing up the stairs.[41] The scene is quiet, subdued. While the music inside the venue is loud—the audio of the video recordings is completely distorted from the volume—it's barely audible out on the street. From time to time, a scraper scoots by, its music echoing from the walls of the surrounding buildings, like a canyon, before fading away. Police cars pass by, as well, but rarely dwell in the vicinity of the club.

After midnight, the venue becomes completely packed with people in their 20s and 30s. On the second floor, the DJ drops "N. E. W. Oakland" by Mistah F. A. B. (2005), which celebrates camaraderie across neighborhoods that are often at odds, and the crowd—almost 100 percent Black—exuberantly sings along. The energy ramps up through a series of local slaps: "Blow the Whistle" by Too Short (2006) and "Feelin' Myself" by Mac Dre (2004). Unlike some of GIC's other events, First Saturdays is for the hyphy generation. Upstairs, there's an even larger dance floor, where partygoers are packed shoulder-to-shoulder. The selector, DJ Juice, adds popular Southern rap tracks—like "Mrs. Officer" by Lil Wayne (2008) and "Blame It" by Jamie Foxx and T-Pain (2008)—to the mix, signaling the musical connections and sonic solidarities between hyphy and crunk (see ch. 5). When "Couldn't Be a Better Player" by Lil Jon and the East Side Boyz featuring Too Short (1998) comes on, people in the crowd start doing "the bird"—flapping their arms up and down, an homage to Mac Dre—to a pioneering Oakland-Atlanta collaboration recorded in the East Bay.[42]

As 2 a.m. nears, the security team repurposes the metal barricades from the entrance to block traffic along Fourteenth and Franklin. Members of the OPD club detail arrive—at least 12 cruisers—and station themselves around the intersection. At closing time, security sweeps into action, conducting the clubgoers down the stairs, out the door, and away from the venue as quickly as possible. Their no-nonsense approach reflects the fact that Pete had been under immense pressure from the City to get people to disperse as soon as they set foot outside. "Let's go! Let's go!" chant the security guards, again and again, using flashlights to goad the dawdlers. Compared to the start of the night, the people streaming out of the club are more boisterous. Men light cigarettes. Women hobble in their heels. But the crowd is completely peaceful and, ultimately, compliant.

Eight OPD officers, accruing overtime, stand on the northeast corner of Fourteenth and Franklin, looking cold. Their demeanor is easy.
They chat and chuckle with each other. Some eye the women as they
cross the street. These cops appear to be young, no older than most of
the partygoers. Still, the display of power is stark. Most revelers avoid
the corner where the officers are posted up. After around 20 minutes,
during which a continuous stream of people is disgorged from the club,
the intersection empties out without incident. Suddenly, all is calm
again. The officers get back into their cruisers and drive away. Having
done nothing more than monitor the security team, they racked up
overtime on Pete's dime. "Y'all heading back to work, huh?" editorial-
izes Zazaboi, from off-camera. "You just had like a three-hour break."[43]

At the time that these videos were taken, the long-simmering struggle
over the costs of policing in Oakland had begun to boil over. In fiscal
year 2007–08, at the start of the Great Recession, which led to layoffs,
furloughs, and a hiring freeze, the OPD spent $25 million on overtime
pay—double what was budgeted.[44] By 2010, nearly 200 officers, or 25
percent of the force, earned more than $20,000 in overtime, many of
them from patrolling "special events" like the sideshow and the let out.
Sergeant Thomas, for instance, earned $61,000 in overtime, raising his
total income to $203,400. But even more concerning, the top recipient,
Michael Morse—who earned almost $120,000 in overtime, more than
doubling his regular income to $225,000—ran the SEU, meaning
that he controlled how much venue owners and event promoters
had to pay for overtime in the first place.[45] "There's an inherent conflict
in police overtime," protested Pete, when we met in 2017. "You're the
butcher, the baker, *and* the candlestick maker!"[46] Still, in the face
of a surging deficit, officials decided that, if they didn't rein in or recoup
these costs, Oakland could go broke.[47] In this context, Black club

owners like Pete—themselves struggling to make ends meet—got caught up in a game of fiscal hot potato.

In October 2008, Kozicki—who, by this time, had risen the ranks from lieutenant of the Traffic Section to deputy chief of police—sent an email requesting that Pete cancel First Saturdays.

> These events have established a track record as a magnet for criminal and unruly activity. The Police Department has been unable to manage these events without using overtime, and even then we have had to draw down on police resources needed in other parts of the city . . . We appreciate your efforts at bringing night life to the downtown area. However, the City is in dire financial straits . . . We need community leaders such as you to assist us through this difficult process until such time as more sustainable remedies are put in place.[48]

But in contrast to the reasoning of the special event ordinance and the OPD, Pete distanced himself from the let out. Why, he wondered, should he be responsible for people who were no longer—or never—in his club? I put this question to Kozicki. "[Pete's] got a legitimate thing: 'They weren't even in my club,'" he answered. "Well, sure they weren't. But they're here *because* of your club. And that's what the ordinance says. It doesn't say that they had to be *at* your event. It just says that your club had to be the *nexus* for this thing."[49]

The special event ordinance had, indeed, been designed to hold business owners responsible for incidents that occurred on the street so long as they were *tied* to the venue. But in an area like Downtown Oakland, where bars, restaurants, and clubs tended to cluster around one another, the science of determining this "nexus" was anything but precise. In 2006, Thomas was asked to specify exactly how far a venue's responsibility over the street extended. "They are responsible for as far as the crowd coming to [their] business," he responded.[50] Here, then, was another vague and circular form of reasoning that retrenched the policing of Black space: the club was responsible if there was a "nexus," but there was only a "nexus" if the police said that the club was responsible. And when a crime or nuisance occurred in the vicinity of multiple venues, the OPD tended almost 100 percent of the time—here, their calculations seemed more exact—to view Black businesses as the cause.

Pete refused to cancel First Saturdays or pay for the police who continued to patrol the let out along Fourteenth Street. In response, the OPD stepped up the pressure. The time for polite emails and gestures of comity had passed. In December 2008, Thomas went to the nearby Merchants Garage—which Pete had rented since he opened to provide parking for customers—and claimed that the OPD had evidence of drug deals and violence on the premises during First Saturdays events. In response, the garage manager, Gloria Verduzco, canceled her contract with GIC. Verduzco would later state, in a sworn deposition, that this had been the first time that she had received a complaint about GIC, and Thomas would admit that there was no evidence to support his allegations.[51] But without access to the garage—and facing mounting, even malicious, actions from the OPD—Pete decided to roll up the red carpet, renting the space to a church. "If you took away the Oakland Raiders' parking, they'd have to leave town," he told me in 2017 (before the Raiders did leave town). "But that was the idea."[52]

Pete tried to resist. In the aftermath of the Merchants Garage incident, he sued the City of Oakland, Thomas, Kozicki, Morse, and Pedro Espinoza—the other member of the SEU—for $5 million in damages stemming from denial of his civil rights. Pete's attorney, Amanda Metcalf, former head of the U. S. Department of Justice's Civil Rights Division in Northern California, alleged that Thomas and Kozicki made "false charges and intentional misrepresentations" that stripped Pete and his patrons of their legal protections. Moreover, she wrote in the complaint, these acts were part of a "pattern and practice of discrimination aimed at African-American owners and operators of nightclubs, cabarets and entertainment events." And all of this was "designed" to "[deny] African-Americans the constitutionally protected right of free assembly, freedom from discrimination based on race, and freedom from the abuse of police power, as well as other rights and privileges guaranteed by the United States Constitution."[53]

The task of reviewing this case fell to U. S. District Court Judge William Alsup. On paper, Alsup—a Clinton appointee who once clerked for Justice William O. Douglas, a staunch proponent of civil liberties—might have seemed like a receptive audience. But in the end, Alsup, who is White, dismissed Pete's "theory of oppression and harassment" on the grounds that it was "vague." He ruled in favor of the City's motion for summary judgment, meaning that the case never went to trial.

In his decision, Alsup took particular issue with Pete's arguments about freedom of assembly and equal protection. First, he wrote that, according to the U. S. Supreme Court's ruling in *City of Dallas v. Stanglin* (1989), the First Amendment doesn't provide a "generalized right of 'social association' that includes chance encounters in dance halls." Pete had argued that the right to assembly should be extended to "live entertainment, such as musical and dramatic works." But Alsup countered that nightclubs were specifically exempted from the Constitution. "Pete's attempt to shoehorn GIC events into another category of expressive activity is unavailing," he said.[54] In other words, since social dancing was an embodied and pleasurable—rather than a "political" or "artistic"—form of expression, it fell outside of the realm of protected rights. The power of dance music to motivate social movements among Black Oaklanders (see ch. 2), it seemed, was illegible and illegitimate to the Court.

Second, on the matter of equal protection, Alsup dismissed the notion that the OPD targeted GIC and other clubs with onerous regulations because of the race of their owners. Under civil rights law, he explained, Pete had to prove that the City and the OPD's actions were *intentionally* racist. In reviewing the case, however, Alsup saw "no evidence" that the regulation of Black-owned nightclubs in Downtown Oakland was "motivated by racial animus." After all, he said, the evidence provided by Pete didn't "mention or allude to race."[55] As critical race scholars have revealed, however, since the Civil Rights Era, overt forms of racism have been converted into covert ones that allow racial oppression to continue under cover of law. According to George Lipsitz, the maintenance of racism—this now-you-see-it, now-you-don't magic trick—operates through the "racialization of space."[56] In Oakland, this has transpired through policies and practices that target spaces associated with young people of color—cruising zones, sideshows, let outs, rap concerts, and other "nuisances"—while remaining silent on the now-protected identities of the people who are criminalized. In this sense, space—or even musical genre, in the case of rap—has provided a convenient proxy for race. Pete, in fact, attempted to expose the racism of "race-neutral" regulations like the special event ordinance, arguing that the OPD targeted Black clubs due to the racist assumption that they were the only ones that attracted "criminal or unruly behavior." In the end, however, Alsup ruled that this argument wasn't "supported by the record."[57] "Pete," he decided, "has not produced sufficient evidence to support his speculation that [the] defendants' actions were part of a coordinated racial-cleansing scheme."[58]

This was the beginning of the end for GIC. For a time, Pete stopped using the space as a club. More evenings than not, the venue remained dark and the doors locked. In effect, the party was over. But with no formal decree, and no court judgment to validate his version of events, the City could maintain that Pete's decision to shut down was just that—a choice. Never mind more than a decade of regulation. The overtime charges. The armies of officers who made Fourteenth Street seem like a cross between a checkpoint and a crime scene. Or even the duplicitous attempt to sever Pete's contract with the Merchants Garage. Never mind the maneuvers of the police and the paper pushers. "It is the City's opinion that your cabaret license is in good standing and has never been revoked," stated City Administrator Dan Lindheim in 2009.[59] This might have been literally true. But like the idea, articulated by Alsup, that officers had to be caught saying that they targeted Pete because he was Black to be considered racist, this superficial reading obscured a more profound and pernicious truth. It masked the fact that, through the routine use of race-neutral but nevertheless discriminatory regulations, operators like Pete suffered a bureaucratic "death by a thousand cuts." True, his permit was still intact. But given the web of racialized regulations he was forced to navigate—the conditions on his cabaret permit, the scrutiny of his "special events," the price tag for policing the let out—what difference did it make?

"SIDESHOW ACTIVITY"

While Judge William Alsup canned the idea that the City and the OPD's treatment of GIC was a part of a systemic pattern of discrimination against Black-owned nightclubs, Geoffrey Pete's case wasn't the first time that he had heard such concerns. In fact, in 2004, Alsup had come to a similar decision in the case of Jimmie Ward, which anticipated Pete's in terms of both its allegations and outcome.

Born near Monroe, Louisiana—where, as a child, he earned money picking cotton and driving the bus that carried his fellow students to school—Ward moved to California in 1955, part of the Second Great Migration. His pursuit of opportunity was soon rewarded when he secured work as a longshoreman and a manager at Ray's Club.[60] (For the rest of his life, he commemorated his ties to the waterfront by wearing a captain's hat emblazoned with a red heart.) In 1969, during the desegregation of the city's nightlife (see ch. 4), he bought an Italian American bar called the Lamp Post at Twenty-Third Street and Telegraph Avenue. The venue was revamped to much fanfare. According to the *Bayviewer*, a general-interest magazine that served the Black Bay Area, it hosted a visit from James Baldwin and a "dashiki party" during its opening year.[61] But Ward was soon strong-armed by Huey Newton, a distant cousin, into turning the venue over to the Black Panthers, who used it as a retreat for the Party elite and source of revenue for its survival programs.[62]

Ward's most successful venture came two decades later, when he purchased a building on a rundown stretch of San Pablo Avenue. Outfitting it with a restaurant and banquet rooms, he christened the club Jimmie's Entertainment Complex. But everyone just called it Sweet Jimmie's. If Geoffrey's was a beacon of Black progress, then Jimmie's was a relic of the blue-collar world of the West Oakland Blues. Teaming up with the aging emcee and entertainer Jay Payton—former host of the television show *Soul Is*, which had highlighted local funk bands and boogaloo crews in the 1970s (see ch. 2)—Ward booked acts like Ike Turner, Bobby "Blue" Bland, and the Chi-Lites, who attracted an older Black crowd. Still, like its hatted and sequined customers, the venue communicated a sense of class, sporting an awning and a wall-of-fame to rival even GIC. In a crowning statement, the entrance was flanked by photos of Ward and Mayor Jerry Brown locked in a bosom embrace.[63]

But this sense of fraternity turned out to be fleeting. In 2002, as Brown was working to rebrand the area around the club as the Uptown Arts and Entertainment District, the OPD repeatedly designated Sweet Jimmie's as a "disorderly house," meaning that it was linked to nuisances and other disturbances that could result in the revocation of its liquor license. According to the police report from one incident, officers arrived to find a large and chaotic crowd in front of the venue. In response, they ordered the security team to close the doors—causing, in the words of the report, a "mob" and a "sideshow" to backflow into San Pablo. The scene then allegedly descended into an "unpredictable inferno of cars, stereos, screams, and fist fights." So, the OPD shut down streets and set up "traffic posts" to control the crowd, an operation that cost the City—and now, thanks to the special event ordinance, Ward—some $4,000.[64] This incident revealed the ways that the authorities drew upon resonant ideas of improper spatial and sonic practices (note: "screams" and "stereos") to render the situation outside of Sweet Jimmie's as a "sideshow."

This, in turn, allowed the police to close streets, stop and search cars, and use other tactics developed as part of Oakland's antisideshow campaign in ways that penalized Ward and his patrons.

In fact, in the 1990s and 2000s, the OPD began to react to crowds of young people of color, especially Black men, as a potential sideshow in ways that intensified the regulation of cultural spaces and incited repeated clashes between residents and the police. In addition to reworking the organization and operations of the OPD, the moral panic over the sideshow transformed the ways that the police responded to Black and Brown crowds, cars, and sounds (see ch. 5). Amid the roll-out of new tools and tactics, everything started to seem like a sideshow in the making. And once a music venue or event was tagged with the magic words—the phrase "sideshow activity" started to appear, with more and more frequency, in media and police reports—it authorized the OPD to use extraordinary powers to disperse or arrest people whose main crime was appearing in public. Desperate times, it seemed, called for disparate measures, causing the suspension of constitutional rights to assembly and expression. According to the ethnic studies scholar Lisa Marie Cacho, people who are categorized by the state in terms of their "(il)legal status"—in this case, "sideshow participants"— "are unable to comply with the 'rule of law'" because it "targets their being and their bodies, not their behavior." These racialized groups, in turn, are "denied what the political philosopher Hannah Arendt calls 'the right to have rights.'"[65] Or as Yakpasua Zazaboi put it: "No one from the City ever said 'sideshow' without saying 'illegal sideshow.' You're labeling a whole group of people 'illegal.'"[66]

In 2004, Ward decided to resist, suing the City, OPD, Jerry Brown, and Lieutenant Edward Poulson, commander for Downtown, for violating his civil rights. Ward's complaint revealed an alternative take on the deterioration of his relationship with the authorities. In Spring 2002, at the same time as the incident discussed above, it stated, City Manager Robert Bobb—then a champion for the redevelopment of the

Uptown—approached Ward to see if he was interested in selling his property to the ORA for $1 million. Ward declined, arguing that it was worth three times as much. At that point, alleged the complaint, the City stepped up its crackdown on the venue—including, but not limited to, the disorderly house reports. The City, argued Ward, abused its governmental powers to make it so hard for him to operate that he would be compelled to sell to the ORA at below-market rate.[67]

But Ward would never get his day in court. As with Pete, Alsup granted the City's motion for a summary judgment. In fact, this ruling prefigured the one against Pete in that Alsup declared that there was "no direct evidence of racial animus" or "purposeful racial discrimination." While he admitted that discrimination might have occurred, he argued that Ward had failed to meet the burden of proof. "There is no evidence of how many or which other . . . nightclubs are owned by minorities. There is no evidence of what kinds of police enforcement actions (or lack thereof) are taken at other nightclubs," he wrote. "It is not the Court's responsibility to rummage through the record on [the] plaintiff's behalf."[68]

Ward appealed, but to no avail. Discouraged and worn down by age—he was now 70—he asked his son Dave to take on a more active role in running the club. As manager, Dave Ward steered the venue in a new direction—producing more profitable rap concerts that, according to the City, attracted a more "hyphy" audience and thus a range of nuisance and criminal activities. Ironically, then, at the same time that Brown sought to turn the area around the venue into an Arts and Entertainment District, the OPD club detail took repeated action against the revitalized crowds at Sweet Jimmie's.

On October 21, 2005, for instance, Sergeant Kyle Thomas reported that he came to monitor Sweet Jimmie's on "prior intel" (likely provided by the SEU) that rapper "Keith the Sneak [sic]" was performing to a "capacity crowd." When he arrived, Thomas saw cars circling the street—their stereos producing "very loud music, audible far in excess of 100 feet"—and other spatial and sonic practices that the OPD now tied to the sideshow. In the mid-2000s, when the music was at its height, these were the sort of "hyphy movements"—revving engines, driving with the doors open—that served as a pretext for policing young people of color who participated in Oakland's rap culture (see ch. 5). "The totality of circumstances," wrote Thomas, "required immediate action to preserve public safety . . . keep traffic flowing . . . and prevent further 'sideshow' activity." This declaration that the let out had turned into a sideshow authorized Thomas to radio for the "West End sideshow units," calling in reinforcements who could run traffic control, tow cars, and make arrests. But the people on the street weren't the only ones caught up in this enforcement action. "Based on my observations," wrote Thomas, "Sweet Jimmies [*sic*] was directly responsible for the attractable nuisance of the very large crowd and traffic." In other words, under the special event ordinance, Ward was responsible for reimbursing the OPD for the costs of policing the let out—bills that routinely topped $4,000 for a single night.[69]

Over time, this form of reasoning became formulaic: rapper → crowd → sideshow → police → bill. In comparing a number of crime reports from 2005, it's clear that Thomas copy-and-pasted the same exact text from one incident to the next:

February 27, 2005: "I knew from prior intel that the rapper 'Mac Mall' was performing at the club and that they were expecting a near capacity crowd."

April 10, 2005: "I knew from prior intel that the rapper / R&B singer 'Bobby Valintino' [*sic*] was performing at the club and that they were expecting a near capacity crowd."

May 8, 2005: "I knew from prior intel that the rapper 'Yuck Mouth' [*sic*] was performing at the club and that they were expecting a near capacity crowd."

October 22, 2005: "I knew from prior intel . . . that the rapper 'Too Short' was performing at the club and that they were expecting a near capacity crowd."

From there, each report went on to repeat the same statement regarding the need to escalate enforcement in order to "prevent further 'sideshow' activity."[70] In this manner, the reports recycled the same logic to rationalize the same enforcement activities. Now in its second decade, the OPD's antisideshow campaign produced rote representations of young people of color that echoed across the city's cultural terrain, from East Oakland to Downtown. The criminalization of the sideshow thus spurred a crackdown on more permitted cultural spaces, exposed young people to more policing, and imposed unequal regulations on Black-owned entertainment venues.

Eventually, Jimmie Ward relented to this pressure. In 2006, he attended a meeting with Mayor Brown, where officials presented an ultimatum: he could either agree to stricter operating conditions or lose his permit. The discussion revolved around two main issues. First, given the prevailing assumption that rap concerts attracted a disorderly crowd, the City pressed Ward to return to a "jazz and blues" format. Indeed, soon after the meeting, he sent a flyer to regulators stating that—at least for the next month—the venue would "cater to grown folks music."[71] This was a common rhetorical move among Black club owners who came under fire. Given the City's apparent opposition to contemporary Black popular musics—in particular, rap—it's no surprise that these owners invoked more "respectable" styles to signal older, wealthier, Whiter, and thus less "dangerous" crowds. Among the case records that I reviewed, the communications between Black venue owners and (more often than not) non-Black regulators were routinely peppered with references to "well-behaved" and "mature" audiences; expensive cover charges and exclusive dress codes; and marketing on radio stations that appealed to older audiences like KBLX ("The Soul of the Bay") rather than youth-oriented ones like KMEL ("The #1 for Hip-Hop and R&B"). White owners, by contrast, didn't seem nearly as concerned with being read as "respectable" in these ways.

Second, the City insisted that, under the terms of the 1999 ordinance, all concerts at Sweet Jimmie's would now count as "special events," meaning that Ward would need to seek permission and a dedicated police detail in advance. The process, according to Barbara Killey, who monitored cabaret permit issues at the time, would require him to confer with the SEU "regarding the size and *demographics* of the expected crowd" (italics added). The SEU would then determine the "need for private security, OPD resources, traffic control, and crowd control."[72] Most concerts would call for six officers and one sergeant at a cost of $4,000. But rap concerts, regardless of the artist, would automatically require a minimum of twenty-four officers and three sergeants, or $15,000 for a single event.[73] (As a point of comparison, in 2015, the OPD only charged the producers of Burger Boogaloo—a rock festival that drew 10,000 fans to Mosswood Park—$5,000 in police costs.[74])

Ward was trapped between a rock and hard place. In order to maintain his operating permit, he had to consent to these exceptional conditions for a six-month probation period. But even that turned out to be too long. He was forced to close the club and sell the building (albeit not to the City) before the trial period was up. Technically, he never lost his permit. He may have succumbed to the same process of bureaucratic corrosion that caused Pete to rent GIC to a church. But the City was able to maintain that this was a "private" business decision, rather than the result of a protracted municipal pressure campaign. While it may have been invisible to the court, Ward's experience proved, yet again, that Black club owners were uniquely vulnerable to an administrative "death by a thousand cuts." He passed on soon after. "A month ago, he said to me, 'I'm tired, I'm ready to go,'" Dave Ward told the *Tribune* upon Jimmie's death in 2010. "Let me tell you. If he still had a club to run, if he was still in the mix making sure everybody was having a good time, he wouldn't be tired."[75]

If this had been the end of the saga of Sweet Jimmie's, it would have been concerning enough. But what happened next revealed even more about the racialized nature of nightlife regulation in Oakland. By the time that Ward called it quits in 2006, the redevelopment of the Uptown was on the verge of takeoff. So, it wasn't long before other entrepreneurs took an interest in the venue. Soon, a group of four businessmen applied for a cabaret permit to replace the old club with a new one called Tycoons.

But upon receiving their permit application, officials opposed Tycoons for two reasons. The first was technical. According to an archaic law, it was illegal for a cabaret to locate within 300 feet of a church, library, or school. But the restrictions didn't apply in reverse. So, in 2004, as part of his agenda to open charter schools and promote the arts-led renewal of the Uptown, Jerry Brown had pushed to install the new Oakland School for the Arts right across from what was then Sweet Jimmie's. Technically, then, Tycoons would now violate the 300-foot rule.[76]

The second and more subjective concern, however, was whether the City's recent experience with Sweet Jimmie's could serve to predict, and thus prevent, the chances that a new venue would once again attract nuisance and crime. In this context, Killey, who is White, decided to deny the permit, citing the proposed Top 40 rap and R&B musical format and the dearth of "police resources" needed to address the presumed fallout of these sounds. The City's concerns were exacerbated when the OPD discovered during a background check that one of the applicants had run a club in the South Bay that, after several shootings, had been shuttered by the City of San José. "No single one of these factors, with the exception of police resources, would be grounds for denying a cabaret permit," wrote Killey in her decision. But together "they create a foreseeable risk of violence and a threat to public safety that would make permitting at this time an irresponsible act."[77]

This decision was an exceptionally rare move. In 2017, Nancy Marcus, who worked for the SAPD, told me that she hadn't seen a single permit application denied since starting the role in 2009.[78] So, the applicants appealed to the city council. Their lawyer, Zachary Wasserman, decried the fact that Killey had decided against Tycoons, in part, because of their intent to "[target] a youthful market through widespread public advertising, by radio and internet, of events combining Top 40 artists and dance." "This is precisely what any operator of a cabaret will want to do in an entertainment area," he wrote, noting the venue's location in an avowed arts and culture district:

> To suggest to the contrary is either to totally misunderstand the operation of cabarets or to unconstitutionally discriminate against Top 40 music or youthful audiences or both . . . It is very clear that the "target" that the City objects to is Top 40 music because a significant amount of Top 40 music is labeled "hip-hop" music. This objection is plainly unconstitutional and renders the denial invalid on its face.[79]

Apparently unconvinced, the city council voted to uphold the ruling 8–0.

The denial came to seem even more remarkable when, a year later, the City turned around and issued a permit for the same site to a venue called the New Parish. By this time, the city council had amended the 300-foot rule to pave the way for the redevelopment of the historic Fox Theater—which, according to Brown's own designs, was meant to become the permanent site for the Oakland School for the Arts. With this technical issue resolved, the applicants went out of their way to present their venture as the polar opposite of Sweet Jimmie's and Tycoons.

At the time, the Parish Entertainment Group (PEG) was run by Michael O'Connor and Jason Perkins, who owned and operated several nightspots in San Francisco, including, most notably, the Independent on Divisadero Street. In the mid-2000s, they realized that, given the rate of gentrification, their core market of young adults was on the verge of being priced out of San Francisco. On top of that, they recognized that the best way to succeed in running mid-sized entertainment venues was to amass enough assets to create economies of scale in booking, marketing, and artist relations. So, according to Perkins, whom I interviewed in 2017, PEG went on a growth spree—opening a series of bars, restaurants, and clubs, with the New Parish marking their first sortie into Oakland.[80] At the time, O'Connor and Perkins, who are White, searched for a local partner to aid them in navigating this new cultural and political terrain. Their sherpa turned out to be Namane Mohlabane. Born and raised in Oakland to Black South African and White Jewish parents, Mohlabane was a DJ, producer, and manager for his sister, the neo-soul singer Goapele. (He had also worked for Nancy Nadel, then city councilmember for Downtown and West Oakland, making him a valued political asset.[81]) Within a few years, however, PEG would remove him from the management team at the New Parish.

In 2008, as they moved on the old Sweet Jimmie's, PEG took pains to distinguish themselves in their cabaret permit application from men like the Wards. "WE WILL NOT BE RUNNING A DJ OR DANCE CLUB," they wrote, in all capitals. Instead, they insisted that they would draw from their experience in San Francisco—which, given the city's reputation as morally and economically superior to Oakland, was itself a selling point—to book "live music" across diverse genres. But among the thirteen styles of music listed in their application, rap and R&B were conspicuous in their absence. It wasn't that Black sounds were totally verboten. PEG included "African," reggae, soul, and spoken word alongside "Irish," indie rock, and metal. But, it seemed, Black dance musics were only acceptable if they were from another time and place. It was as though PEG sought to turn back the clock to the era of "live music" and "soul"—the era before the arrival of DJs, rap, the war on nuisance, and the securitization of nightlife (see ch. 4). "We will not be booking music which will threaten our license, our business, our restaurant, our property," they wrote.[82] In this way, they responded to regulators' entrenched anxieties about rap artists and audiences by insisting that, unlike the previous operators, they could be relied upon to manage problems before they started through their booking practices. This argument worked. Thomas, who had come out strongly against Tycoons, approved of the fact that PEG proposed "significant changes in the . . . operation" compared to Sweet Jimmie's. With his endorsement, Killey approved the permit and the New Parish opened to much acclaim.[83]

But PEG would go on to do many of the things that, in their attempt to distinguish themselves as a "responsible" venue, they said that they wouldn't. As soon as it opened, the New Parish began to book local and touring rap and R&B artists. It even became, for a time, Oakland's premier "DJ OR DANCE CLUB," as PEG rented the space to promoters for regular events like thePeople (Afro-house), Reggae Gold (dancehall), and Ships in the Night (queer trap). And their recitals of responsibility notwithstanding, PEG wasn't any more compliant than their predecessors. The SAPD's records reveal that they neglected to renew the New Parish's cabaret permit on time several years running, even after receiving several reminders. In addition, in 2011, they received a warning for operating after hours, a misstep that O'Connor blamed on Black artists. ("[It] was a reggae show with performers from Jamaica [who] obviously had little respect for local law," he wrote, in an exculpatory email to Marcus.[84]) Most egregiously, however, PEG tried to expand their operations in the East Bay even more by opening a venue called Leo's in North Oakland in 2013. But while using the space for public assembly required extensive life-safety renovations, PEG began to host concerts without a permit, putting patrons at risk in the case of an emergency. The SAPD fined O'Connor and Perkins, but the men refused to pay.[85] Eventually, rather than invest in the upgrades, they gave up on the venue and sold the property for nearly $3 million; instead of being penalized for their infractions, they flipped the building for a 250 percent profit.[86]

As discussed in this chapter, the SAPD's modus operandi is to review what a business owner has done in the past in order to predict and steer what they might do in the future. In practice, however, the ways that regulators assess management activities, as an allegedly race-neutral matter, are still colored by racial bias. So, whereas, with a Black club owner, defiance is seen as a sign of deceitfulness and danger, with a White one, it's often perceived as a sign of self-assurance and strength. Indeed, two White male club owners bragged to me that they ignored regulations that they considered unreasonable. "You have to be able to hold your ground," said Perkins, assuming a sense of persecution. "I have good lawyers," he added.[87] Indeed, unlike Pete or Ward, who had a more credible case to make for being mistreated, O'Connor and Perkins were never punished for their actions. Instead, PEG was awarded two valuable after-hours permits that allowed them to stay open until 5 a.m. at the New Parish and neighboring club the Rock Steady.[88]

In 2018, PEG was forced to relinquish control of the New Parish. But not because of the City. First, Perkins was ousted from the company when reporters revealed that he had drawn a weapon on one unhoused person and threatened several others who were camped out near PEG's properties in San Francisco's Mission District. Then, the firm came under fire from ticketing providers, who sued them for taking signing bonuses and then breaking their contracts. In need of a life raft, O'Connor sold a controlling interest in the New Parish to Allen Scott, head of concerts and festivals for Another Planet Entertainment, the largest independent concert promoter and venue manager in the Bay Area.[89] In just over a decade, then, this move completed the transfer in ownership from Jimmie Ward—a Black migrant from Jim Crow Louisiana—to one of the most powerful entertainment interests in Northern California.

BLACK SOUNDS, WHITE PROPERTY

In retrospect, 2009—the year that Geoffrey Pete sued the City and OPD, and the New Parish presented its first events—was a turning point in the long-running saga over the redevelopment of Downtown Oakland. The 650-unit Uptown Apartments and renovated Fox Theater, the centerpieces of Jerry Brown's vision of an upscale arts and culture district, opened to much razzle-dazzle. Operated by Another Planet Entertainment, the Fox came to sport the names of national touring acts—from Kylie Minogue to Modest Mouse—on its iconic and illuminated marquis. As intended, the completion of this much-anticipated reuse project—the theater had been torched by arsonists in 1973, purchased by the ORA in 1996, and revived with over $25 million in public support—prompted a wave of investment in nightspots throughout the area.[90] After a long lull, between 2007 and 2009, over 20 bars, clubs, and restaurants opened or were prepared to open in Oakland, most of them downtown.[91]

Soon, businesses like the New Parish came to replace—in this case, quite literally—ones like Sweet Jimmie's. The names (and apostrophes) of those original venues were meaningless to the visitors from Marin, San Francisco, and Walnut Creek, who streamed to the area, often for the first time, to see a concert at the Fox. Exiting the Nineteenth Street BART Station, many were surprised, if not downright relieved, to discover an ordered and attractive environment, rather than the dangerous and decrepit one that the news had trained them to dread. For the ORA, that moment—that split-second reaction among visitors—was the culmination of at least two decades' worth of work. Since the 1980s, when the area was declared a "ghost town," the City had pursued lop-sided investment in middle-class housing and nighttime entertainment (much of it White-owned) through generous subsidies and targeted policing. (The Uptown Apartments, for instance, built by national developer Forest City, received $53.5 million in public resources and an onsite OPD substation.[92]) In the process, the redevelopment of Downtown Oakland started to reverse the regional tides of cultural consumption and tax revenue. In time, longtime residents realized that, after years of traveling to San Francisco or San José, they no longer needed to leave Oakland to attend a concert or go dancing. To the contrary, residents of the region's other cities—at first the "adventurous" ones, then most everyone else—began to trek to the East Bay instead.

In the 2010s, then, revelers around the Bay Area "discovered" Downtown Oakland, which further fueled the influx of new residents and investors. This change can be seen in the number and composition of nightclubs in the area. In 2016, while starting this research, I requested data on all of the cabaret permits issued by the City since 2001, when the records began. I then used news articles, interviews, and online sources to determine the racial and gender identity of each venue owner, noting when clubs were sold but remained open under new management. The results are telling. From 2001 to 2016, the number of nightclubs in the area increased from 20 to 28, reinforcing the narrative that Downtown Oakland experienced an economic "renaissance." In the process, however, the portion of clubs owned by Black people, either in whole or in part, dropped from 55 to 36 percent. Meanwhile, the portion owned by White people soared from 20 to 61 percent.[93]

At first pass, these numbers aren't that surprising. They would seem to tell a story of economic and demographic transformation that most urban residents and scholars would readily recognize as gentrification. Indeed, amid increasing investment and rising rents, some Black club owners—who, again, rarely owned their own spaces—were driven out by the upsurge in costs and competition. But these were the exception, not the rule. In addition to examining the cabaret permit data, I also requested and reviewed the records maintained by the City for every club that closed between 2001 and 2016 to determine whether or not this closure occurred under duress from regulators. In the process, I found that 13 of 21, or 62 percent, of the Black- and Latine-owned clubs that shut down during this period did so, like Sweet Jimmie's, amid intense and expensive controls for their alleged role in causing noise, sideshows, and violence. This stands in stark contrast to the non-Black and -Latine venues that closed, of which only 2 of 15, or 13 percent, did so under municipal pressure.[94]

These disparities imply that economic displacement, or just "going out of business," is—for people like Jason Perkins—a dubious but nonetheless real privilege of Whiteness. For Black and Brown operators, on the other hand, dispossession is often a matter of public policy—the bureaucratic insistence upon "choice" notwithstanding. In a sense, then, Judge William Alsup was right: Oakland officials rarely, if ever, explained their actions in overtly racist terms. But that was because they didn't have to. Rather, using "race-neutral" policies and procedures—which embedded racist assumptions about Black dance music, audiences, and venue owners into the routine governance of nightlife—regulators remade the racial landscape of Downtown Oakland through a process of bureaucratic attrition. In a form of "racial banishment," it was the SAPD, OPD, and City Attorney's Office—more than "the market"—that transformed Downtown Oakland into a site of White pleasure, property, and profit.

But that doesn't mean that the soundtrack of the city's nightlife has become less Black. To the contrary, as the scene has come to be controlled, increasingly, by White people, rap, R&B, and other Black dance musics that were deemed menacing in the 2000s have become indispensable to marketing the "New Oakland." According to the geographer Magie Ramírez, the city's long-standing reputation as a dark and dangerous (i.e., Black) place has come to contend with a new "image problem," thanks to displacement, of no longer being Black enough.[95] The geographer Brandi Summers describes this as the politics of the "post-Chocolate City," where the "dissociation" of Black culture from intact Black communities expedites the incursion of White newcomers and capital.[96] The aestheticization of Blackness, which fuels the gentrification of areas like Downtown Oakland, agrees the performance studies scholar Kemi Adeyemi, is "produced in direct proportion to the forcible removal of actual black people."[97]

Still, these changes have presented imperfect opportunities for a new generation of DJs, dancers, and promoters of color. In the 2010s, venues like Somar and Era Art Bar (now both defunct) and 7th West, in nearby West Oakland, contributed to an emerging nightlife that spanned racial categories in terms of music, ownership, and clientele. Among some longtime Black cultural workers, like radio host and party emcee Leon "DNas" Sykes and selector and event producer Bijou McDaniel (aka DJ Kream), these spaces have served as sites that—while not always, or solely, Black-owned—nevertheless feel welcoming and safe, like little havens of the old Oakland amid the new.[98] "In conversations about displacement and dislocation," writes the ethnomusicologist Allie Martin, in her work on Washington, DC, "it is crucial to add more dimensions to our listening, because there are emancipatory soundscapes being crafted every day."[99]

In Oakland, the increase in the number of venues, events, and middle-class consumers has produced new prospects for creatives of color for whom nightlife is a source of income as well as community. "Gentrification," continues Martin, "acts more like an accordion, moving through periods of contraction and expansion."[100] So, while the road to redevelopment has been paved with racial banishment, paradoxically, it's often Black- and queer-run crews like DJ Kream's Oakhella and Soulovely—not the White EDM DJs typical of San Francisco—that are curating the sound and tending the vibe of the ostensibly "New Oakland." "I can't say that the change has hurt me," McDaniel told me in 2017. "It's helped me more than anything. "But," she added, recalling how she drove 40 miles to go dancing in San José after clubs like Sweet Jimmie's closed down, "I'm still very aware of where we came from and why these changes are happening."[101]

In the end, committed selectors and cultural organizers like Kream continue to work toward a nightlife that prioritizes the social and sonic desires of Oaklanders of color—the sort of "emancipatory soundscapes" that Martin contemplates. But the underlying map of property ownership has been completely rearranged. As of 2016, 50 percent of the venues spinning rap, R&B, and dancehall—venues like the New Parish and Starline Social Club—were owned by Whites. In 2001, none of them were.[102] Not since desegregation in the middle of the twentieth century, then, have White club owners reaped so many of the rewards created on the backs of Oakland's Black dance musicians (see ch. 4).

Back on Fourteenth Street, Pete has managed to hold onto his operating permit and his property. But First Saturdays are no more. Gone are the throngs—the get ins and let outs—that made this stretch of pavement into an enduring site of struggle over who belonged in the repopulated streets of Downtown Oakland. Instead, GIC is intermittently opened up for political meetings, memorials, and jazz concerts. In the meantime, its red carpet and gold-rimmed photos continue to fade. In December 2017, I returned to the venue to participate in a carnaval fundraiser for SambaFunk!, where I was performing a *malandro*, or "rogue," style dance with other men from the group. Sometime after midnight, I spotted Pete roaming about the space. Unlike our previous meeting, when his manner and dress gave him the air of an aristocrat, he sported a gray sweatsuit as he wandered around the room, mopping up spills and gathering empties. On this particular night, at least, he appeared to be a staff of one: simultaneously a storied club owner and a custodian. I went over to pay my regards. He gripped my hand—tapping my elbow, ever so lightly—and tipped his head toward my ear. "Keep the faith," he whispered, grimly. "Keep the faith."[103]

I left the club around 1:30 a.m. It was almost closing time—the moment that, in the 1990s and 2000s, had incited so much concern among local officials. There was no let out to speak of. Just a group of metal fans smoking cigarettes outside of a nearby rock venue called the Golden Bull. Still, members of the OPD's club detail were staked out around the block. I counted one police cruiser on Webster Street, outside of New Karibbean City, and another two at Fourteenth and Franklin. But the most alarming vehicle was the Mobile Command Unit posted outside of GIC. This sort of roving tactical center had long been used as part of the OPD's antisideshow campaign.[104] But now, according to the OPD commander for Downtown and West Oakland, it was meant to serve as a "visual deterrent" to would-be troublemakers.[105] With its swirling lights, the truck cast a menacing red glow over the desolate streetscape. Feeling a chill move down my neck, I pulled up my collar and hurried toward my car.

7

BEFORE BBQ BECKY

On Loop at Lake Merritt

VARIATION ON A MEME

On Sunday, April 29, 2018, Onsayo Abram and Kenzie Smith prepared for a cookout on the east side of Lake Merritt. Often called Oakland's "Crown Jewel," the Lake has long served as the city's central, even precious, public space. It's not much on paper. Unlike Golden Gate Park in San Francisco or Central Park in New York, it doesn't appear amid the annals of architectural greatness. But for generation after generation of Oaklander, this 140-acre tidal lagoon—ringed, in most spots, by nothing more than a thin ribbon of grass—has served as a landscape of monumental importance. It's where residents come together to celebrate, demonstrate, and mourn. And it's where Abram and Smith, like so many Black residents and relatives before them, came on Sunday, the Lord's Day, for a barbecue.[1]

Their setup was modest: two card tables stacked with meat, a couple of camp chairs, a cooler, and a charcoal grill. The scene seemed innocuous, innocent, even dull. But not to Jennifer Schulte—a White resident of the multiracial, middle-class enclave of apartments to the east. To Schulte, it looked like a violation of the City's Parks Code, which restricted the use of charcoal grills.[2] So, she reported the men to the Oakland Police Department (OPD)—"I'd like it dealt with immediately," she told dispatch—and sat patrol for two unnerving hours to see that order was restored.[3] Abram and Smith tried to remain calm. But this experience was a traumatic reminder that, for African Americans, police run-ins over misdemeanors—selling a loose cigarette for Eric Garner or failing to signal a lane change for Sandra Bland—often turn fatal. "We were scared like we were about to get killed," admitted Smith, the brother of local rapper Mistah F. A. B.[4]

This act of racial violence, a routine part of Oakland's now enduring regime of antinuisance policing (see ch. 3), might have gone unnoticed had Michelle Snider, Smith's wife, not recorded the incident on her phone. "You don't want Black people being out here?" grilled Snider, who is also White. "It has nothing to do with their race," responded Schulte, repudiating the accusation of racism with the confidence and composure of someone who is convinced they are on the side of reason and righteousness. It was simply that charcoal grills were "illegal" in that location. And for good cause, she insisted, laying out her supposedly colorblind logic: charcoal grills led to hot coals, hot coals led to hurt kids, and hurt kids led to costly lawsuits against the City of Oakland and, by extension, its taxpayers. Her cold scowl and "Terminator sunnies" gave Schulte the appearance of someone who saw herself as a responsible citizen—a noble custodian working to protect the park, kids, and Jane Q. Taxpayer from the incivilities of not the *racial*, but the *reckless*, masses.[5] Still, Snider wasn't having it. "It seems like a new Jim Crow," she said, "because . . . every time I see it, Black people are targeted regarding barbecuing at the Lake."[6]

If, by calling the cops, Schulte had sought to stop "illegal" grilling at Lake Merritt, in practice, it led to just the opposite. Once the video went viral, Black Oaklanders responded with a characteristic mix of antiracist critique, communal love, and collective presence. Drawing upon lived and ancestral experiences of caring for community in the face of racial violence and spatial exclusion, they revived a well-rehearsed repertoire of spatial and sonic practices to reclaim the Lake as a sacred and sociable terrain.

At a gathering on May 10, DJ Fuze from Digital Underground spun an impromptu mix of soul classics and Oakland slaps at the site of the standoff. The resulting video of residents, most of them Black, dancing the electric slide to "Before I Let Go" (1981) by Maze and Frankie Beverly seemed to captivate the national imagination.[7] This song is a staple of Black weddings, reunions, and cookouts, where it serves to unite people, across generations, on the dance floor. But it took on added significance when DJ Fuze dropped it at Lake Merritt because Maze— then Raw Soul—developed its sound while residing in the Bay Area in the 1970s, when the ethos of Black Power animated the funk (see ch. 2). Then, on May 20, thousands of revelers turned out for "BBQ'n While Black"—where the owners of Everett and Jones, a beloved barbecue restaurant, passed out scores of succulent ribs and the freedom fighter and philosopher Angela Davis posed for selfies with admirers.[8] Continuing throughout the season, these events restored a sense of Black custody over Lake Merritt through music, gatherings, and other cultural practices that the geographer Brandi Summers calls "reclamation aesthetics."[9]

As the original incident and its repercussions ricocheted online, news outlets, from *Newsweek* to the *New York Times*, descended on Oakland to pick up the scoop. The most resonant response, however, came from members of Black Twitter, who rebranded Schulte "BBQ Becky" and circulated memes that stuck her image—stone-faced, armed with a cell phone—into iconic images from African American history and

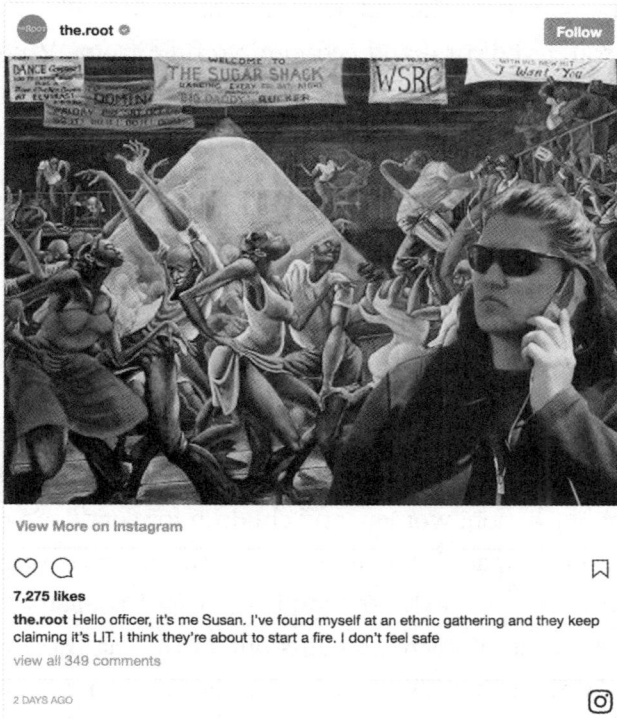

Figure 9. "BBQ Becky" meme in which Jennifer Schulte's image is inserted into a scene from the "Sugar Shack," from the cover art for Marvin Gaye's *I Want You* (1976), 2018. Credit: The Root.

culture.[10] Several of these memes commented on White ambivalence about Black dance music. Inserting Schulte into images from *Soul Train* and the video for the rapper Childish Gambino's "This Is America" (2018)—then making waves as a critique of racist violence and the coping mechanisms it encourages among Black communities—these memes called attention to the cruel ways in which White Americans have long sought to both control and consume Black soundscapes.

One meme created by the online magazine *The Root*, for instance, remixed the cover art for Margin Gaye's *I Want You* (1976) (see fig. 9). The image—a take on the painting *Sugar Shack* by Ernie Barnes (1971)—

depicts a dance hall on the "Chitlin' Circuit," where Black artists and audiences sought cultural and economic refuge from White supremacy in the time of Jim Crow. But no crowd, whether segregated or not, is innocent in the eyes and ears of BBQ Becky, who appears in the corner of the image to report on the too-liberated scene. "Hello officer," reads the caption. "I've found myself at an ethnic gathering and they keep claiming it's LIT. I think they're about to start a fire. I don't feel safe." In this parodic interaction with the police, Schulte misreads Black slang ("lit," as in lively) and calls upon the state to restore her racial entitlement to a sense of security.

The BBQ Becky incident received so much attention, in part, because it circulated amid a wave of videos that captured White people calling the cops on Black men, women, and children for conducting mundane activities in public space.[11] These repetitive attempts to control the presence of Black bodies revealed that policing Black people for trespassing on White spaces and norms remains one of the main rites / rights of American Whiteness.[12] The legal scholars Taja-Nia Henderson and Jamila Jefferson-Jones note that, throughout the Jim Crow Era, White property owners tried to prevent African Americans from moving to their neighborhoods by arguing that the mere existence of Black people in White spaces comprised a nuisance. While these "race nuisance" cases might not have won in court, they contributed to a notion of Blackness as "out of place" that reverberates in the viral #LivingWhile-Black incidents of today. According to Henderson and Jefferson-Jones, people like Schulte "weaponize the language of nuisance," thus "asserting property rights common to a white general public" and "casting . . . Blackness as a property harm."[13]

Crucially, however, as this variation on a theme (or meme) came to Oakland, most commentators read Schulte's actions as a matter of not anti-Black racism in general—as in the other events that spring—but rather an emergent crisis of gentrification in particular.[14] This explanation reached its apex in an article for the *Guardian* by journalist Sam

Levin, who wrote that, while BBQ Becky was one of many incidents to reignite a national debate about the chronic impacts of racism, in Oakland, it "triggered a more acute pain." Namely, it revealed that "while African Americans . . . have been steadily displaced by gentrification, others who remain are treated like criminals in their own hometown."[15] This account thus interpreted the policing of Black public culture within the now common, even generic, narrative of gentrification—which said that the tech-driven remaking of San Francisco had come to Oakland, turning the East Bay from a terrain of Black belonging into one of either removal or repression.

Indeed, the BBQ Becky incident occurred amid a tense moment of social, cultural, and political-economic change in Oakland—a sort of inverted mirror of the mass migration of African Americans during World War II (see ch. 1). In the Great Recession of 2007 to 2009, a devastating wave of foreclosure washed over areas that had once been redlined, stripping homes and wealth from Black and Latine residents.[16] In its wake, decades-old visions of redevelopment—spanning John Williams in the 1960s and '70s, Lionel Wilson and Elihu Harris in the 1980s and '90s, and Jerry Brown in the 2000s—began to remake the city at an alarming rate.[17] In the 2010s, amid the "renaissance" of Downtown Oakland (see ch. 6), and rising investment from corporations and speculators, the cost of residential real estate spiraled out of control—making it all but impossible for working-class people of color who suffered, but survived, the cruelties of disinvestment to stay put.

Urban studies scholars have long understood that, contrary to the arguments of free market theorists, gentrification isn't the cure to economic abandonment; rather, it feeds on it. By driving down property values and dispossessing residents, disinvestment creates the conditions of possibility for the massive profits ("buy low, sell high") that investors seek.[18] So, after decades of neglect, Oakland became, shockingly, one of the most expensive cities in the nation. In 2014 and 2015, it received the dubious distinction of the largest year-over-year increases in average rent anywhere in the U. S.[19] The growing gap between wages and rents, mixed with the predatory tactics of real-estate investors, accelerated the displacement of working-class residents, especially African Americans, who were pushed to the edge of the region, if not out of the state.[20] Others were swept into the streets. Between 2017 and 2019, as the number of unhoused residents increased by at least 47 percent, to over 4,000, Black people came to represent just 24 percent of the city's population, but 70 percent of the victims of what Summers calls its "unhousing crisis."[21] (In the 1970s, at the height of "White Flight," Black people represented 50 percent of the population.) What remained was a grievous sense of hurt and haunting. "Even though we've been gentrified out," said Jhamel Robinson, one of the organizers of BBQ'n While Black, "we're still here." Indeed, it was indicative of the times that, by 2018, Robinson had been displaced from Oakland to Sacramento, an 80-mile drive into California's scorching Central Valley.[22]

The concept of gentrification first emerged in the 1960s, when Ruth Glass, a British sociologist, noted that members of the landed elite ("the gentry") were moving from rural estates to remodeled homes in déclassé parts of London.[23] In the 1970s, however, as this provincial process of urban renewal came to be seen across the Atlantic by British Marxist geographers working in the U. S.—namely, David Harvey and Neil Smith—it transformed from a regional curiosity into a general theory of capitalist urbanization in a time of "urban crisis." This new generation of urbanists reconceptualized gentrification as a campaign by real-estate developers, corporations, and cities to recapitalize areas that had been devastated by the retreat of investors, industries, and social services in the wake of World War II.[24] In this context, "the gentry" became the growing class of service-sector workers, most of them White, who managed the "command and control" and "creative" economies of a privileged set of "global cities."[25]

In sum, this seminal research viewed the redevelopment of American cities through a political-economic lens that saw gentrification as the ruling-class solution to patterns of capital disinvestment and social disorder that appeared to peak in the 1960s and '70s. It thus created a narrative that aligned, neatly, with a litany of *neos* and *posts*—neoliberal, postmodern, postindustrial, post-Fordist, and so on—developed by Western Marxists to map the world at the turn of the millennium. In other words, the very concept of gentrification connoted a concern with a radical *rupture*—the end of one thing and the start of something new—rather than the continuation of ongoing social processes. In Oakland, the mainstream interpretation of BBQ Becky as a symptom of gentrification implied that the drive to police residents like Abram and Smith had recently arrived along with the tide of more privileged newcomers characterized (and now caricatured) by Schulte. But this narrative would seem to tune out the struggles over Black dance music, soundscapes, and spatial practices that have repeated, on loop, across the pages of this book.

So, in this chapter, I rewind the record, circling back in time to reveal the ways that the BBQ Becky incident reignited ideas, regulations, and forms of resistance that became ingrained through repetitive conflicts over Black sonic presence at Lake Merritt. By revealing the echoes and connections across three periods—picnics at Lakeside Park in the 1960s and '70s, cruising on Lakeshore Avenue in the 1980s and '90s, and Festival at the Lake in the 1990s—this spiraled account shows that both Schulte's actions and people's responses were shaped by struggles that resounded over several decades. This implies that the cultural politics of gentrification aren't new; instead, they reverberate with anti-Black anxieties and policies consolidated in the wake of Black Power. This argument resonates with the work of the ethnomusicologist Allie Martin, who writes that, rather than produce new struggles, gentrification represents an "amplification of tensions surrounding sound, music, and noise"—divides that are "deeply racialized because of the ways in which Black people have long been deemed sonically unruly and unmanageable."[26]

Indeed, the people on Black Twitter knew the score. The outpouring of BBQ Becky memes, which inserted Schulte into a vast, even comical, range of times and places, implied that her assault on Abram and Smith was as typical of 1868 and 1968 as 2018. It emerged, mimetically, out of looping attempts to criminalize and control Black crowds as deviant or dangerous rather than democratic. ("I don't feel *safe*," says Schulte, in her imagined encounter at the Sugar Shack.) But as I explain in the Conclusion, residents of color continue to draw upon a collective repertoire of musical and movement practices to reclaim the Lake as a Black terrain.

THE REVOLUTION WILL BE AMPLIFIED

In calling the OPD, Jennifer Schulte invoked the section of Oakland's Municipal Code that prohibits the use of portable charcoal grills outside of particular zones.[27] (Citing the statute, she reported Onsayo Abram and Kenzie Smith for "illegally using a charcoal grill in a non-designated area." Accustomed, perhaps, to receiving calls about more serious concerns, the dispatcher listed "charcoal grill in non-designated area" as the "weapon" in their incident log.[28]) But attempts to restrict barbecues, whether by residents or regulators, were nothing new. Rather, they emerged as a matter of public debate at a time when Lake Merritt literally echoed with calls for Black Power.

As seen in chapter 2, in the 1960s and '70s, young Black Oaklanders created "social movements" to revolutionize the spectrum of spaces and practices that oppressed them. So, while they registered voters, launched survival programs, and "policed the police," they also revamped the sounds of the city's streets, parks, radio stations, rec centers, and picnics. At times, the movement for Black Power was mundane because White Power was exactly that: casual, ordinary, and pervasive. Every effort to remix the city's public culture became an act of revolt. In this context, politics and pleasure were inseparable. The everyday sights and sounds of Black Power—dashikis, hand drums,

Figure 10. Members of the Black Panther Party conduct training exercises along the shore of Lake Merritt near the Alameda County courthouse, from the film *Black Panthers*, 1968. Credit: Ciné Tamaris.

Harley Davidsons, car stereos, and so on—became as much of an affront to the social, spatial, and sonic order of the city as the rifles and rallies taken up to tackle the "power structure." The poet and singer Gil Scott-Heron was right: the revolution would not be televised.[29] But it would be amplified, with at least a thousand watts.

Each of these priorities—politics and pleasure—converged along the edge of Lake Merritt, making it an important terrain in the struggle for self-determination. For the Black Panthers, the Lake—which abuts the Alameda County courthouse, site of countless rallies to "Free Huey" (see Intro)—became a strategic stage for public displays of resistance. The documentary *Black Panthers* (1968) by Agnès Varda, for instance, includes several shots of rank-and-file activists standing at attention, rehearsing chants, and even doing push-ups along the shore (see fig. 10).[30] These militant performances were meant to reach not just residents and reporters but also the captive ears of Huey Newton, who was incarcerated in the courthouse while awaiting trial.[31]

More often, however, this struggle over public space was animated with a sense of autonomous fun. On weekends, Lakeside Park came to attract thousands of revelers from working-class communities across the East Bay—making it a Black and Brown alternative to the more storied, but predominantly White, countercultural meccas of Golden Gate Park in San Francisco and People's Park in Berkeley. In warm weather, the area—which runs along Grand Avenue, on the northeast edge of Downtown—bloomed with residents roller-skating, barbecuing, and boogaloo dancing to funk music.[32] Like DeFremery Park in West Oakland, Lakeside Park became one of the main locations in which the cultural insurgency of Black Power came to life (see ch. 2). So, it's no surprise that in 1968—the same year the Panthers were doing push-ups by the courthouse—Sly and the Family Stone selected the park as the setting for the cover photo of their breakout album *Dance to the Music* (see fig. 11). Perched atop what is now called the "Mid-Century Monster" (1952), a sculpture by Robert Winston, the musicians—their short-cropped naturals of the 1960s turning into the more ample afros of the 1970s—seemed to personify an imagined relationship between the sound, style, and *space* of Black freedom in Oakland.

The parties at Lakeside Park defied Oakland's racial and spatial order. Located on the edge of Downtown, amid some of the most expensive apartment districts in the city, they crossed the lingering lines of segregation, which had confined African Americans to West Oakland, far from the comforts of the city's "Crown Jewel." In addition, they upset the sensibilities of old-guard residents and elites, who worried that their public spaces were being overrun by a more restive generation of Black youth with no regard for the norms of "civility." These debates over public conduct resonated with the reaction of city officials and prewar residents to the arrival of Black migrants during World War II (see ch. 1). But the intervening struggles for civil rights had reworked the discourse of racial hatred. So, whereas wartime newspapers had called for policing spaces of migrant pleasure in

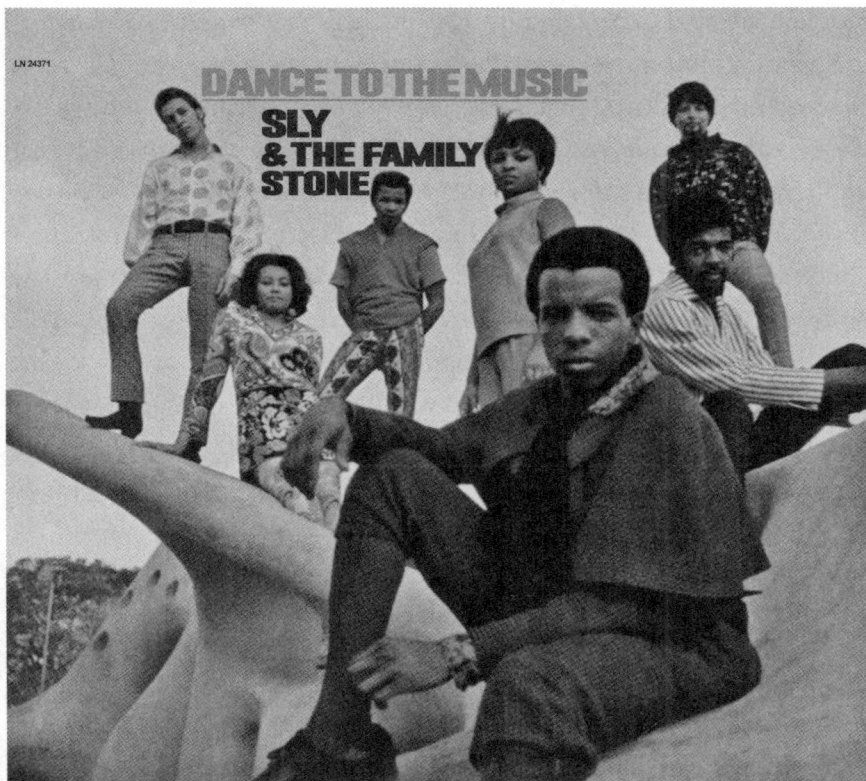

Figure 11. The members of Sly and the Family Stone pose on a sculpture at Lakeside Park for the cover art for *Dance to the Music*, 1968. Credit: Epic Records.

response to the supposed transgressions of "socially liberated or uninhibited Negroes," the *Tribune* of the more polite 1970s did the same over the threat of excessive "noise." "Ah, for yesteryear in Lakeside Park," lamented a reporter in 1979. "Where quiet families picnicked . . . where the putting green off Harrison Street was caressed by white-capped duffers—where the most serious crime was the failure to relax."[33]

The reporter added that V. Hap Smith, director of Oakland's Parks and Recreation Department, testified to the city council that the practices of the people who congregated at Lakeside Park were "neither quiet nor peaceful." They were, rather, a "noisy disruption to other more passive park users and nearby dwellers that [was] destroying . . . the park for almost everyone."[34] For Smith, the drum circles, roller discos, and other cultural practices that were popular among young people of color posed a "serious and often dangerous problem . . . where undisciplined users run roughshod over the rights of others."[35] Consistent with the post–Civil Rights Era discourses of nuisance and color-blindness, this conflict was often described in terms of sonic taste rather than race. "It comes down to this," opined the editors of the *Tribune*, "Silence or The Supremes? Pastoral peace and quiet or The Parliament Funkadelic?" But Smith, who was Black, was less oblique when it came to the racial tone of such sensibilities. "A lot of young black people like loud soul music," he stated, "and that doesn't appeal very much to a lot of older white people."[36]

While "noise" might seem as though it's an impartial matter of volume, in fact, it's a political concept imbued with a long and violent history of hierarchy (see Intro). According to the sound studies scholar Jennifer Lynn Stoever, the concept of "noise" "renders certain sounds—and the bodies that produce and consume them—as Other . . . under white supremacist epistemologies."[37] In other words, the very concept of Whiteness as a superior identity is constructed through a series of opposing categories—like proper / improper, pure / dirty, quiet / loud—that devalue Blackness as "bad sound." But the impact of these ideas isn't just conceptual. Instead, the invocation of "noise" authorizes forms of state control and racial violence that reassert White norms throughout the urban environment.[38] It loops across time and space to stigmatize the cultural practices of Black Americans as deviant, even dangerous, in ways that reproduce discriminatory patterns of regulation and policing. It may seem as though these sonic politics emerge in tandem with gentrification; but contemporary campaigns to control Black sounds reverberate with the enduring cultural politics of Whiteness. "Gentrification," argues Allie Martin, "traffics in these histories of silencing and suppression."[39]

In the late 1970s, in reaction to incessant complaints from residents about the sound of bongos and congas in Lakeside Park, the city council passed an ordinance that outlawed playing musical instruments at the Lake without a permit. This initiated a drive to restrict a wide range of pleasurable activities that were deemed nuisances to neighboring residents and property owners, including roller-skating, gambling, and barbecuing.[40] The City of Oakland thus instated some of its earliest nuisance-control measures—policies that came to remake local governance after Black Power (see ch. 3)—to manage Black crowds and sounds at Lake Merritt during the depths of disinvestment, decades before the onset of gentrification. In the process, it reactivated existing connections between race, culture, and the regulation of entertainment and recreation spaces, like the DeFremery Rec Center, that were consolidated even earlier, during the postwar period. Reiterating these legacies, Schulte's actions represented a disorienting loop that transected seemingly distinct historical eras.

In order to enforce the new rules regarding music, sound, and barbecues, the OPD introduced mounted and aerial patrols around Lakeside Park. According to Raymond Eng, who represented the neighborhood on the city council, a police helicopter soon circled the area "all day and night."[41] (Apparently, the constant chop of the propellers didn't register to officials as "noise.") This increase in policing raised real concerns about sonic profiling. At a city council meeting in 1976, African American activist Gene Hazzard reported that visitors to the part of the park where Black people congregated were cited for barbecuing, while White people continued to grill with impunity. This selective enforcement, he cautioned, was bound to erupt in a confrontation between revelers and the police.[42]

Hazzard's warning turned out, predictably, to be correct. In August 1977, just two months after Lionel Wilson took over City Hall, the OPD arrested Allan Mayeux, a resident of Richmond, for driving around Lakeside Park with a passenger on top of his car. When his brother approached the police to contest the arrest, Angelo Mayeux was wrestled to the ground and charged with "inciting a riot." In the process, one of the officers grabbed his gun. This disproportionate response sent a current of anger into the crowd of an estimated 400 onlookers, some of whom threw rocks and bottles at the cops, causing the OPD to send in reinforcements to quell the "disturbance."[43]

In the weeks to follow, indignant residents descended on the city council to indict not only the incident but also the regulatory conditions that had made it inevitable. Attorney Leon Rountree, who rallied to the cause, argued that what happened to the Mayeux brothers wasn't an isolated event; it was rather the latest in a long string of incidents in which Black people were "intimidated, harassed, and made to feel less than human" by the OPD.[44] Other residents called upon the city council to repeal the antinuisance measures that had increased tension and racial profiling at the Lake and create an oversight commission to investigate cases of police misconduct. But Wilson, who sat on the city council, demurred, revealing his reluctance to restructure—rather than just reform—the city's racist system of policing. Setting the tone for repeated struggles over the next two decades of Black political rule, he called for the creation of an ombuds role to investigate complaints against *all* government agencies, rather than the OPD in particular.[45]

CRUISE CONTROL

There was a pleasure, an indulgence, to these outdoor parties. But there was also a necessity. In the early 1970s, for instance, North Oakland's Rollerland—which, at 18,000 square feet, was the largest skating rink in Northern California—closed down after over 40 years in operation. It was once so popular that, during World War II, it was open every single day of the year, including Christmas. By 1972, however, the city had become so racked by disinvestment and poverty that the owners threw in the towel.[46] With nowhere else to turn, young people of color created

Figure 12. Young people roller-skate at an unknown outdoor location in Oakland, 1980s. Credit: African American Museum and Library at Oakland.

a skating scene at Lake Merritt (see fig. 12). But the move from indoors to outdoors, commercial rink to public park, rendered skating—a harmless pastime—a supposed threat to the public welfare. Park rangers started to issue warnings to skaters and, at one point, even considered citing them under the City's Traffic Code.[47] In this sense, disinvestment never eradicated the recreational practices of Black youth; it just pushed them into more and more precarious terrains.

This process was especially pronounced when it came to car cruising. In the 1980s, as the parties at Lakeside Park became increasingly

Figure 13. The cruising scene on Lakeshore Avenue, 1994. Credit: Courtesy of the Hayward Area Historical Society, gift of the Oakland Tribune.

policed, they were surpassed by a new generation of meetups on Lakeshore Avenue, across the water, that centered on the cruise. As discussed in chapter 5, this was a time when Oakland's postwar car culture mixed with Reagan Era cuts to youth recreation, making cruising one of the only ways for young people of color to occupy public space. At the same time, the campaign against cruising in surrounding suburbs pushed motorists into popular corridors like Lakeshore Avenue and Foothill Boulevard in East Oakland. By 1985, tens of thousands of people, most of them Black and Brown, would socialize on the east side of the Lake—the area most accessible to residents from East Oakland— on a warm-weather Sunday.[48] In a precursor to BBQ'n While Black, a parade of motorists would take over the strip, turning the park into a massive communal cookout (see fig. 13).

This is the area where Onsayo Abram and Kenzie Smith were getting ready to grill when they were confronted by Jennifer Schulte in 2018. In this sense, Schulte was echoing the complaints that residents raised against the cruise, which were, themselves, an echo of the complaints about parties at Lakeside Park in the 1970s. In the mid-1980s, a multiracial group of apartment residents organized to make noise about what they saw as nuisances in their neighborhood, from "bumper-to-bumper traffic congestion" to "nerve-shattering" stereos. One organizer reported that the cruise made residents feel like "prisoners in their own homes." "We can't open [our] windows because of boom boxes," she stated. "Polite requests to turn down the music or move cars blocking our driveways are met with violence or verbal abuse."[49]

In response, the city council called upon the ideas and practices developed during the 1970s through struggles over Lakeside Park and other public spaces to restore order to the area. Indeed, the City's censure of the cruise read like a recital of so-called "quality-of-life" crimes. One document, reported the *Tribune*, tied cruising to "public drinking, drug dealing, panhandling, littering, loud radios, harassment of women, barbecuing, and bicycles and skateboards on the sidewalks—all violations of city ordinances." In order to discourage people from gathering—and thus, it seemed, preempt all manner of chaos and crime—the city council banned parking along Lakeshore Avenue on holidays and weekends.[50]

Still, the cruising and cookouts continued. So, in 1993, residents organized again, this time registering their outrage over what a reporter compared to a "hostage" situation. The City, in turn, escalated its tactics, shutting down streets throughout the neighborhood over the Memorial Day weekend. The OPD set up a network of 17 checkpoints, where a corps of 50 officers stopped cars, checked IDs, and turned away anyone who couldn't prove that they lived in the restricted zone (see fig. 14). This prompted an outpouring of complaints from residents who were prevented from visiting friends and relatives throughout the 130-acre area, to say nothing of those who were simply expelled through this extraordinary (and illegal) act of banishment. Still, the OPD decided to continue this controversial tactic into June in order to maintain control over the territory in advance of the anticipated crowds at Festival at the Lake (see below).[51]

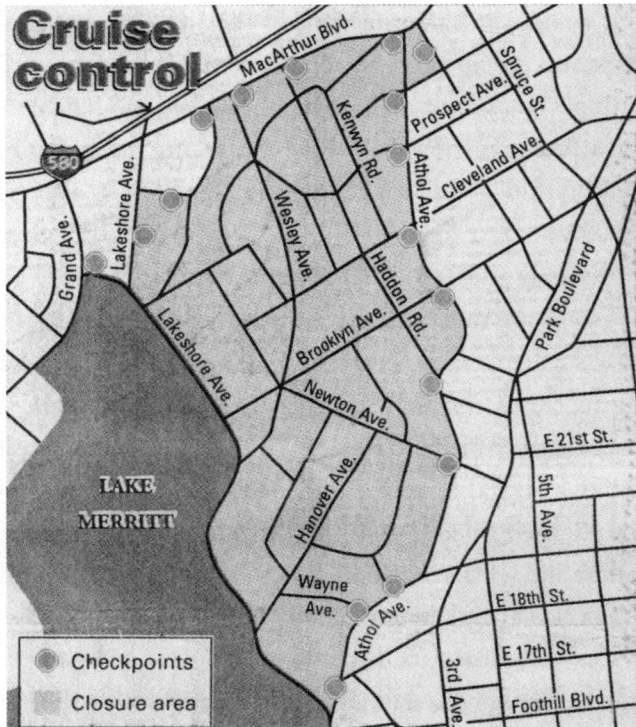

Figure 14. Map of the OPD checkpoints created to prevent cruising around Lakeshore Avenue over the Memorial Day weekend, 1993. Credit: Courtesy of the Hayward Area Historical Society, gift of the Oakland Tribune.

At the same time, the city council enacted new legal tools to toughen its campaign against the cruise. In 1992, African American councilmember Nate Miley, who represented Central East Oakland, authored an ordinance that made it illegal to drive through a "No Cruising Zone" three or more times in a given period. In line with the move toward spatial targeting, which masked the racialized nature of regulation, the law mapped out a series of cruising "hotspots," including Lakeshore and Grand Avenues by Lake Merritt and Foothill Boulevard by the Eastmont Mall, which was then becoming associated with the sideshow (see ch. 5). In order to remain silent on race, however, it was written so as to apply to any area that was, in the innocuous language of government, "affected by traffic congestion."[52]

Clearly, not all streets that were congested were considered a nuisance. Otherwise, commuters stuck on the city's slow-moving freeways would be in constant violation. So, the measure empowered the OPD to use discretionary signs to categorize otherwise normal traffic congestion as illegal "cruising." Miley, for one, insisted that the police should focus on areas populated by young people of color, telling the *Tribune* that those who cruised the streets were, in the words of the paper, "looking for drugs, selling drugs, and often armed." "It's associated with a bigger sort of problem with . . . youth out of control," he said.[53] At the apex of the crack epidemic, and amid widespread concerns about the city's descent into disorder, Miley—who now serves on the Alameda County Board of Supervisors—repeated the logic of broken-windows policing that came to reign under the Lionel Wilson and Elihu Harris administrations. He tied minor crimes, like cruising, to more grievous offenses, like violence, in ways that criminalized young people of color's presence at the Lake.

In 1995, the city council revised the anticruising law as an "emergency measure" to tighten enforcement in advance of the summer crowds. According to the police, it was too complicated and labor-intensive to track thousands of cars through a checkpoint over the course of several hours. So, the city council simplified the measure, making it illegal to loop past the same point more than once in four hours. As the ethnic studies scholar Lisa Marie Cacho argues, criminalization works through the creation of laws—like the anticruising ordinance—that "cannot be followed."[54] "There's legitimate reasons to be out there two times in four hours," protested Mayor Harris, who, after supporting the original measure, opposed the revised ordinance on the grounds that it could promote more racial profiling. Still, with Miley's support, the new restrictions passed.[55]

The OPD started to enforce the new anticruising measure in the spring and summer of 1996. From March to June, officers once again

Figure 15. OPD officers stop a muscle car at an anticruising checkpoint on Grand Avenue, 1994. Credit: Courtesy of the Hayward Area Historical Society, gift of the Oakland Tribune.

installed checkpoints around the edge of Lake Merritt and stopped every car that passed through (see fig. 15). These checkpoints were managed in teams. One officer would give the driver a notice to inform them that they were entering a "No Cruising Zone," while another would record their license plate using new computers that the OPD purchased for the purpose of tracking cruisers. If the car returned within four hours, then the officers would take down the names and ID numbers of everyone inside. If it returned again after that, the occupants could be subject to a $100 citation or arrest.[56] Long a treasured civic pastime (see Intro), looping, it seemed, was now off-limits. "I ain't hittin' the Lake," reported Keak Da Sneak in "Sunshine in the O" (1995) by 3X Krazy featuring Mike Marshall. "5–0 jackin' fools / that's a mistake."[57]

In the end, the OPD rarely enforced the anticruising law. Instead, in a practice that recurs throughout this and the previous two chapters, they used the crackdown on cruising as a form of pretextual policing. The checkpoints around the Lake increased the number of legally and politically permissible interactions between the OPD and residents—especially young people, poor people, and people of color—in ways that rummaged up charges for totally unrelated issues. This approach accorded with what the legal scholar James Forman Jr. describes as the increasing reliance on stop-and-frisk and other supposedly preventative strategies advanced by criminologists like James Q. Wilson during the 1980s and '90s (see ch. 3).[58] Incredibly, during the first several months of enforcement, the OPD didn't issue a *single citation* for cruising. Instead, by their own admission, they charged motorists with "other types of violations," like stolen goods and loud radios.[59] The anticruising campaign thus gave the OPD the rights and resources to create a dragnet that, although it didn't stop cruising, dredged up criminal charges against the people most likely to be profiled due to the color of their skin, size of their rims, and sound of their slaps. In the process, it contributed to a constant sense of surveillance—what the sociologist Victor Rios calls Oakland's "youth control complex"—converting Lake Merritt into yet another space in which young Black people were made to feel unwanted, even in an ostensible "Chocolate City."[60]

Arguing that this campaign was racist in both design and implementation, young people soon organized in opposition. These efforts were led by rapper, and now film and television director, Boots Riley of the Coup. Raised by radicals—his parents were involved in the Progressive Labor Party and Students for a Democratic Society—Riley became a vocal communist at age 14, while still a student at Oakland High, a commitment that would continue to resonate in his art and activism. In 1991, he and other hip-hop activists created the Mau Mau Rhythm Collective, which staged concerts to engage young people of color in political causes. Connecting with other artists (he met DJ Pam the Funkstress at a record release party for *2pacalypse Now* in 1991), Riley's main musical venture became the Coup. Their first full-length album, *Kill My Landlord* (1993), would play with ideological "party lines" like "rip through 'em from the tip of my Mao Tse-Tongue."[61]

In 1996, under the banner of a group called the Young Comrades, Riley threw an event at Lakeside Park called "Fuck the Police Day." Circulating among young people of color at the cruise and Festival at the Lake, he passed out flyers that called for them to reclaim space to barbecue, listen to music, and otherwise exercise their "constitutional right to hook up and kick it" in ways that were increasingly under attack.[62] (In this sense, the tactic of cookout-as-resistance preceded BBQ'n While Black by at least two decades. Longer, in fact. In April 1968, the Black Panthers Bobby Hutton and Eldridge Cleaver were driving around West Oakland, prepping for a barbecue at DeFremery Park, where residents could come together after the murder of Martin Luther King Jr., when they were ambushed by the OPD. Just 17, "Lil' Bobby" was the first member to join the Panthers and, tragically, the first to be killed by the police.[63])

In a classic strategy of community organizing, "Fuck the Police Day" turned out to be a means for the Young Comrades to mobilize young people to take collective action. In the weeks to follow, the group staged an occupation of the city council to demand a public hearing on racial profiling at Lake Merritt. At the meeting, they played a recording of a menacing message that OPD Chief Joseph Samuels had left on Riley's answering machine. "From me, and on behalf of all my officers," said the chief, "fuck you!" "*This* is the 'Sound of da Police,'" commented one of the Comrades, referencing rapper KRS-One's song about police repression.[64] "You give us no other outlets," said another, who described the cruising scene as a natural result of young people's marginalization. "You take midnight basketball away. You give us a curfew. There is nothing for youth to do at all. And we go to the park and relax in a public spot . . . and we get harassed by police." From there, his comments to Mayor Harris took on a personal tone, condemning the way that African American officials like Harris and Samuels, the city's first Black chief of police, had come to reproduce the oppressive practices of their White predecessors. "I don't appreciate getting hit with a billy club or [the police] putting a gun at my head," said the speaker. "I know when you were a youth, you didn't appreciate it either. So, don't treat us the same way you got treated."[65]

Indeed, the debate was rife with generational strife. Soon, older residents took their shots in response. According to a reporter, this protest against racial profiling was rebuffed by older residents who said that the "real issue" was "inconsiderate young people" whose gatherings had grown out of control. "Perhaps the Young Comrades are a little too young to remember what discrimination was all about," said Kieran Manjarrez. In this comment, Manjarrez discounted the youth's grievances in comparison to the aims of the Civil Rights Movement, a struggle he described in the past tense ("what discrimination *was* all about"). "I find it offensive . . . to have the banner of discrimination waved as a cover for what is just anti-social behavior."[66] In a manner consistent with colorblind ideology, Manjarrez reiterated a discourse that would repeat, on loop, from struggles over Lakeside Park in the 1970s to BBQ Becky in 2018, which rationalized the regulation of people of color as a logical response to their own "misconduct." This perspective missed the fact that, in the post–Civil Rights Era, anti-Black policing had come to center on the censure of young people's culture and comportment (see ch. 3). In this context, cries of structural racism were moot / mute.

MANAGING DIVERSITY

The struggle over the cruise was so intense, in part, because—in the minds of many residents and administrators—it was tied to the fate of Festival at the Lake (FAL), a beloved annual event. Officially, the Lake Merritt Garden Society launched FAL in 1982 to fête the flora of Lakeside Park. But it was impossible to ignore the fact that the parties at Lakeside Park in the 1970s, which had prompted new regulations and racial profiling by the OPD, had been nothing if not a "festival at the Lake." Moreover, starting in 1979, Black-serving radio station KDIA produced a series of free concerts by pop musicians like Patrice Rushen called "Project Pride," which were meant to discourage revelers from littering and other quality-of-life violations at Lakeside Park.[67] Unofficially, then, FAL emerged out of these earlier attempts to manage the sonic presence and spatial practices of Black youth in this marquee public space.

In line with the policies and politics of the Lionel Wilson administration, FAL represented an attempt to remake Lake Merritt—and Oakland at large—into a space that could attract wary visitors, corporations, and investors (see ch. 3). This occurred, in particular, through the talk of "diversity." At the time, and still today, many residents saw Lake Merritt as a mecca of liberal multiculturalism. According to the cultural studies scholar Jodi Melamed, multiculturalism arose in the 1970s as a "counterinsurgency" against the antiracist revolts of the 1960s. In this context, the notion of diversity diverted attempts to dismantle racism into the consumption of racialized aesthetics in ways that reinforced White power and privilege through a desire, rather than a distaste, for difference.[68]

This new way of talking about race was taken up in cities like Oakland, which sought to recover from the legacies of racial redlining by recruiting capital back to the urban core. In her research on redevelopment in Washington, DC, the geographer Brandi Summers—who came of age in Oakland during the 1980s—argues that the talk of diversity serves to transform Blackness from a sign of danger to a source of market value. It also treats African Americans as comparable to every other group—just one of many "ethnicities" to make up the "diverse" metropolis—in ways that undercut Black claims to space and expedite displacement. In the process, the commodification of Blackness "create[s] a new medium of racial representation, consumption, and commercial growth, which conceal[s] the violence of dispossession and highlight[s] the illusion of inclusion within the culture of modern capital."[69]

In Oakland, many residents worried that the increasing investment in diversity was a not-so-covert way to cover over the imprint of Blackness. (In 1996, for instance, Black residents criticized the move to turn East Fourteenth Street into "International Boulevard" as an attempt to erase African Americans from East Oakland.) Still, others saw the idea of diversity as a means to appreciate the city's working-class communities of color—whether cynically or sincerely—as a source of value instead of its perpetual inverse. And Lake Merritt, named the first wildlife refuge in North America in 1869, came to represent an urban space that flourished through cohabitation rather than segregation. It was, in the romantic musings of a reporter from 1985, a model of the "urban dream." It served not only "yuppies in running shoes" but also "homeless people" and "inner city teenagers." "It all works in the way that a fully integrated, tolerant, culturally diverse and forward-looking city dreams of working . . . There are no second class citizens at the lake."[70]

In the 1980s, FAL came to epitomize these impassioned reveries. For at least one weekend a year, the media would marvel at the city's exciting, if not exotic, multiculturalism in a way that suburbanites—long accustomed to seeing Oakland with a mix of fear and loathing—could appreciate. In 1985, when the event attracted an estimated 15,000 people, the *Tribune* touted FAL for its breakdancers, blues, and barbecues rather than its bougainvillea.[71] Most readers refused to live amid these markers of Blackness. But they made for an exciting excursion from time to time. Still, Oakland's recalcitrant "image problem" was never far from view. "For a few days each year," wrote a reporter for the *East Bay Express* in 1997, reminiscing about the event of the 1980s, "pictures of smiling fairgoers and stories about the good time they were having replaced the standard-issue prattle about Oakland's drugs, guns, and crime. Maybe it was just too good to last."[72]

The turning point arrived, unsurprisingly, when young Black Oaklanders began to take an interest in FAL as a place to be embodied, rather than exhibited for tourists. In the late 1980s and early 1990s, participants in the cruising scene along Lakeshore relocated to Grand Avenue during the festival weekend. As in the early days of the side-show, the more controlled activities inside of the event were mirrored by the crowds that staked out their own independent terrain on the margins (see ch. 5). For many young people of color, the event didn't begin or end at the gates of Lakeside Park; it unfurled, instead, through-out the area. "I never even went to the festival," admitted Travis Watts, producer of Fam Bam, a more recent music event at Lake Merritt, who extolled the festivities, not FAL, in 2018. "It wasn't even about the festi-val for me."[73]

While longtime residents often reminisce about the event, it's hard to find recordings that capture the social and sonic environment that surrounded Festival at the Lake. But one compilation of footage shot by Mario Bobino and Ramasses Head, some of which was used for Bobino's video for 3X Krazy's "Sunshine in the O" (1995), gives a sense of the scene in 1995 and 1996.[74] The compilation actually starts inside of the official event, where visitors stroll among the food stands and sprawl across the lawns to lounge and listen to music. But it's the out-side of the event that commands the most camera time. On Grand Ave-nue, the atmosphere is more boisterous. Groups of men and women, running from their teens to their thirties, meander and mingle on the sidewalk, revealing what Keak Da Sneak meant when he rapped: "In the O-A-K / we chill and parlay / in the sunshine."[75]

The soundscape of the scene, audible underneath the music in the video, is a steady din of excitement and exchange. It centers on the voices of men, who call out their sets and their cities, comment on women's appearances, and taunt the police officers who cruise up and down the street. It's important to note that, created by men according to the conventions of 1990s rap videos, the edit expresses a heteromas-culine gaze. Indeed, to the extent that they appear at all, most women are depicted silently and from the rear, while, off-camera, men offer a running commentary on their bodies. Clearly, the pleasures of the cruise among young men could reproduce the marginalization of Black women and girls.

Given the repetitive attempts to regulate the sonic presence and spatial practices of young Black Oaklanders, it was only a matter of time before neighborhood residents, event organizers, and officials started to take issue with the scene on Grand Avenue. It appeared as though the aspiration to include "inner city teenagers" in Lake Merritt's "urban dream" was interrupted by a widespread concern about the ways that young Black people remade the space according to their own social priorities. By posting up and partying outside of FAL, rather than participating in a sanctioned way, they resisted what Summers describes as the "dissociation of blackness from Black embodiment."[76]

Predictably, the City's response was to send in the police. In 1994, as the sun began to set on the festival, over 200 officers—and more called up on reserve—moved in to expel the remaining crowds from the area around Lakeside Park. When some of the revelers refused, the OPD applied more muscle. In an echo of the case of the Mayeux brothers, which occurred in the exact same spot, the scene turned tumultuous when the police tried, according to news reports, to "arrest an unruly man." "Lakeside Park," in the words of a reporter, "turned from a fairground into a battlefield." As the crowd became restive, the OPD sent more riot-ready officers to the scene, where, armed with pepper spray and M-80 explosives, they tried to force the now hostile masses to disperse. In the end, 22 people were treated for injuries, only two of them police, and over 100 were arrested.[77]

The battle along Grand died down that night. But a war of words and recrimination soon began to rage. At a press conference the next day, Mayor Elihu Harris and OPD Chief Joseph Samuels attributed the melee to what Harris called a "mob mentality" and a "breakdown of law and order." "There will be those who will say that the cops were at fault," added Samuels. "They will try to make a black and white issue out of it." "But it is not a racist or racial issue," he insisted. "The issue is lawlessness and rowdy behavior."[78] In a prelude to the debate over the anticruising campaign, then, Black officials sought to rationalize the repressive policing and collective punishment of young Black people by condemning their individual "misconduct."

As the reporters trained their microphones on the mayor and the chief, however, a few voices managed to break through the "law and order" narrative to present an alternative view of the supposed "riot." "Whenever young people gather to socialize," Joseph Boon, 18, told the *Tribune*, "we are broken up by the police. Just like everybody else, we . . . want places to go so we can listen to music, relax, and have fun. But where are we supposed to go?"[79] Raymond Brooks, 19, challenged the idea that young people were the "rowdy" ones. After being clubbed and pepper-sprayed by the police as he tried to flee the scene, he spent the rest of the night crying in anger and dismay. "[The police] made me feel kind of dirty," he said. "It's like they invited us down there to beat us up."[80]

Officials soon wondered whether they could rescue FAL for the coming year. Given its economic and emotional import to residents and promoters alike, most worried that—if the event died, whether due to unruliness or repression—the result would be another stain on the city's already tainted reputation. So, in the run-up to 1995, the OPD tried to set the tone for a "respectful" event by saturating Lake Merritt with park patrols. As with the anticruising and antibarbecuing campaigns of the previous decades, they cracked down on minor crimes, issuing citations for public drinking, urination, and other misdemeanors. According to one lieutenant, this "zero tolerance" approach was meant to prevent the creeping spread of disorder that supposedly led to the disturbance at FAL in 1994. "We'd like to nip this in the bud," he told a reporter. "We are going to be courteous, we are going to be sensitive, and we are going to enforce the law." "People are going to go to jail for those things."[81]

Meanwhile, city officials and festival organizers spent the entire year preparing—even bracing—for the return of the event. Harris convened a Youth Advisory Board, which, arguing that young people's refusal to participate stemmed from the lack of age-appropriate activities, recommended a suite of changes to the festival. These included replacing an area for community organizations with carnival rides; selling discounted tickets in high schools; creating a zone dedicated to youth music, dance, and visual art; and sponsoring a late-night basketball tournament at Laney College. Then, in 1996, organizers simply moved all of the youth-centered activities to Laney. If, in 1995, promoters tried to recuperate the image of FAL as a model of liberal multiculturalism under the theme of "Bringing Us All Together," then, in 1996, they reverted to a strategy of separate-but-equal, removing young people of color from their post along Grand Avenue to a segregated reserve on the opposite side of the Lake.[82]

The much-feared repeat of the melee never occurred. But the preventative measures themselves contributed to FAL's eventual demise. In addition to creating a secondary site, organizers ramped up security measures—recruiting, according to the *Tribune*, a "small army of volunteers . . . to blanket the festival and keep the peace." While this group, some 500 strong, was meant to create a sense of "amiable security," 200 police officers were mustered to deal with more criminal concerns. The multiplication of venues, activities, and security measures, in turn, increased production costs. In 1995, when it spent hundreds of thousands of dollars on police services, FAL wound up with a $281,000 deficit from which it never recovered. Moreover, even with these "enhancements"—or, perhaps, because of them—attendance started to crater. In 1997, when organizers threw in the towel, turnout hit a 15-year low.[83]

BACK TO BLACK

Looping back to the start, it's now clear that the BBQ Becky incident reprised these repetitive struggles over Lake Merritt. As memories of previous periods of gathering—some traumatic, others triumphant—

Figure 16. A vendor sells T-shirts that mock Jennifer Schulte by connecting BBQ'n While Black to Festival at the Lake, 2018. Credit: Used with permission of the Oakland Tribune.

rippled through Black Oakland in 2018, residents recalled the fugitive pleasures of roller-skating, cruising, sideshows, and other forms of circling and circulation. But none of these memories reverberated with as much force as those of Festival at the Lake. To many, the renewed assertion of the right to social gatherings seemed to revive the sense of collective presence—of Black people seeing themselves, and each other, as belonging in the heart of the city—that had reached its peak at FAL.

At BBQ'n While Black, for instance, a vendor sold T-shirts that blended the image of Jennifer Schulte with a crowd of revelers at Lakeside Park in the 1990s (see fig. 16). This blurring technique—which dissolved the distance between these two events across the decades—revealed that, for Black Oaklanders, BBQ Becky represented what Amiri Baraka (Leroi Jones) once called the "changing same."[84] But like Baraka, the vendor wasn't just concerned with the looping nature of anti-Black racism; instead, he seemed more interested in how the resurgent commitment to gathering at the Lake resurrected the city's vibrant, but criminalized, Black public cultures. The joke, then, was on Schulte. "Hi police," read the caption, "I'd like to call on myself. I just brought back Festival at the Lake."

In order to get the meaning, and thus the joke, memes invoke insider references that only some viewers will understand. In the process, explains the musicologist Braxton Shelley, they reproduce the boundaries of community.[85] Indeed, with regard to BBQ Becky, local and national commentators—who were caught up reading the event as an example of gentrification—failed to appreciate the echoic reservoir of trauma and joy stirred up in the incident's wake. Like the people who circulated memes on Black Twitter, however, Black Oaklanders knew that this was nothing new. For decades, residents and regulators who targeted them had stated, like Schulte, that this had "nothing to do with their race." But Black residents recognized that talk about noise, trash, traffic, and other nuisances had long served to mask campaigns to silence and erase the imprint of Black life from Lake Merritt and the city at large.

While, at times, critiques of gentrification treat the policing of Black communities and displacement of Black public culture as a sign of the *end* of Black time, this prehistory of BBQ Becky reveals that the current moment in Oakland resounds with the sonic politics of a "past that is not past."[86] Reverberating across the campaigns to regulate bongos and congas at Lakeside Park in the 1970s, suppress the sounds of stereos at the cruise along Lakeshore Avenue in the 1980s, and curate and contain the embodiment of Blackness at Festival at the Lake in the 1990s, the script was set long before Jennifer Schulte picked up the phone to dial 911.

Repetition, in this sense, can be violent. But the loop can also provide a path out of oppression. As they faced repeated attempts at policing and displacement, Black Oaklanders returned, again and again, to inherited forms of gathering, from parties at Lakeside Park to Fuck the

Police Day and BBQ'n While Black, that reinstated a sense of belonging. Moreover, in each of these moments, they took up musical and movement practices—from funk grooves to the cruise, from DJ sets to electric slides—that used looping as a means to remediate and reclaim spaces that were adverse to Black life. In the Conclusion, I'll explore some of these practices in more detail and provide three core reflections on the significance of Black sonic politics in Oakland and beyond.

CONCLUSION

Black Sound, Unbound

The listener begins to anticipate the return of the beginning as the end approaches.

JOSEPH SCHLOSS, *Making Beats* (2004)[1]

IT SEEMS ONLY RIGHT to end a book about loops in the same place that it started. From hip-hop beats to house music, producers and DJs reorder linear sound recordings into repeating grooves, encoding them with a Black sense of time rooted in Afro-Diasporic practices of "cyclic motion, call and response, [and] repetition and variation."[2] In this circular form, the end of one loop marks the beginning of another. Time is bent over on itself. Moving ahead means moving back, but in a way that's pleasurable.

The same is true for the experience of time that emerged from my routine walks around Lake Merritt; the end of one stroll was only ever an interlude until my next trip around the water. In that spirit, I want to end *On Loop* with an echo—a repetition with a difference—of the walk that I recounted in the Introduction. This final account details a walk that occurred in the wake of the BBQ Becky incident, when the living legacies of Oakland's Black dance music and sound cultures underwent a resurgence (see ch. 7). Attuning to these practices, I reflect upon what this space has taught me about Black sonic politics and why I think it matters to Oakland and other cities engaged in the ongoing struggle for Black freedom.

⁕⁕⁕⁕⁕⁕⁕⁕⁕⁕⁕⁕⁕⁕⁕⁕⁕⁕⁕⁕

On June 24, 2018, I parked my car, cruised past the pergola—there was no drum circle today—and set out on my Sunday ritual of a walk around Lake Merritt before Samba Church (see Intro). In a reflection of the communal resolve to repudiate Jennifer Schulte's attempt to stop "illegal" grilling, the area along Lakeshore Avenue—the site of the original incident—brimmed with barbecues. Black residents circled around pop-up tents, smokers, and, resolutely, charcoal grills. (On the margins of this scene, by contrast, a solitary group of White people huddled around a gas-operated device, marking them as both in obeyance of the law and oblivious to custom.)

The space pulsated with the sound of cans cracking, dominoes slapping, and, everywhere, laughter. At one end of the grounds, a mobile DJ bumped a mix of past and present rap hits. But like at the sideshow, the musical selection wasn't centralized (see ch. 5). This wasn't a concert or festival, with the crowd oriented toward a single stage. Instead, each party managed a portable speaker, cultivating its own vibe while contributing to the vitality of the collective soundscape.

Uncontained, in open air, songs crashed into one another. It was often hard to know which beat to nod along to. But the overall effect was one of relentless groove and movement. At moments, the rhythms and tempos of different songs seemed to magically sync. In one memorable instance, the crisp claps of "More Bounce to the Ounce" (1980) by electro-funk outfit Zapp melded with "The Motto" (2011) by rappers Drake and Lil Wayne to convey a serendipitous sense of oneness. "Rest in peace, Mac Dre / I'ma do it for the Bay," rapped

Drake, in a rare case of recognition of the region's impact on hip-hop culture at large.[3]

In his research on mobile tape and CD players, the sound studies scholar Michael Bull describes the use of personal stereos as a solipsistic means to control unwanted encounters and "colonize" public space for private experience.[4] Building upon the embrace of boomboxes by the hip-hop generation (see ch. 4), however, the sound culture along Lakeshore converted the personal curation of recorded music into a communal and creative act. Each individual song was offered to the collective, crafting a commons of polyrhythmic potential. People amplified their own music (often loudly) not to compete with or wall off their neighbors, but rather to create opportunities for outsiders to come in. Over the course of the day, I saw many people break away from their parties to bond with the members of other groups, often drawn in by a beloved song or a particularly good beat.

At one point, a sudden cheer emerged from amid the crowd. I turned toward the excitement to see over a thousand young people of color, mostly boys and men, stream past in a parade of bicycles. This sort of procession—which, in a teenager's version of the cruise, typically involves young men on dirt bikes and ATVs, revving their engines and popping wheelies—is common around the Lake on Sundays. But this particular event was so massive that, at one point, it stretched all the way around the water, from Lakeshore to Grand Avenue.

I would come to learn that the "Oakland Rideout," as it was called, had been organized by NFL stars Josh Johnson and Marshawn Lynch. Raised in Oakland, the two men came up amid the city's deeply rooted cultures of self-determined circulation. The Rideout thus revealed that these predominantly Black practices, from the cruise to the sideshow, lived on as vital, everyday tactics to reclaim public space for Black belonging. "It's not a protest, or a demonstration," explained the journalist Pendarvis Harshaw, who also grew up in Oakland and participated in the parade. "In a year when people of color have had the police called on them for BBQing, selling water, being a firefighter, checking out of an Airbnb, sleeping in their own dorm—the list goes on—simply taking up space and celebrating together is an act of liberation."[5] And as in the park, where the party came to a standstill, as picnickers stared in awe, the riders carried mobile speakers that crackled with local slaps—demonstrating, once again, the power of amplified music and looping movements to transform a hostile terrain into a space for Black freedom and pleasure.

As the parade rounded the pergola, and the sounds of the riders trailed off, I set out in the opposite direction, toward the amphitheater, to continue my walk. As I moved south along Lakeshore, the already thin ribbon of grass between the water and the street became even thinner, narrowing to almost nothing. There was no more room to grill—with charcoal or otherwise—except across the street at Pine Knoll Park, where another contingent tended their barbecues. Still, there were other ways to use sound to contour and occupy this space. In a practice that dated back decades, people of color—especially older African American men, who likely participated in the cruise in the 1980s and '90s—parked their cars along the west side of Lakeshore Avenue. Throwing open their doors, windows, and trunks, they let the music from their stereos spill out and envelop the path.

This spot was popular, in part, because it provided sweeping views of Downtown Oakland's modest (but expanding) skyline and—if the afternoon fog didn't roll in—sunset. In fact, it was so iconic that it became a go-to spot for the cover art of local rap albums, including Too Short's *Get in Where You Fit In* (1993) and Mistah F. A. B.'s *Son of a Pimp* (2005). But people were also attracted to this area because they could park within spitting distance of the path, allowing them to participate in the pedestrian scene from the partial seclusion of their cars. Cars, in this way, served as a roving counterpart to the barbecues near the pergola. They provided a semiprivate space that was parked, literally, in the middle of the street, creating a zone of comfort and retreat, but also opportunities to connect with others as they strolled past.

In Western thought, cars are often seen as a sealed-off "cocoon"—a source of isolation, privacy, and other modern problems. But according to the sound studies scholar Gavin Steingo, among Black South Africans, they often serve as vehicles for social encounter. They create a porous edge where the people, events, and sounds on the inside and outside become open and exposed to each other.[6] As with the barbecues, then, this commitment to dwelling in the parking spaces along Lakeshore Avenue occasioned spontaneous connections between acquaintances and strangers.

Indeed, as music poured from their speakers, the motorists immersed the area with the colliding sounds of soul, funk, trap, soca, and—as was everywhere the case in Oakland that season—Afrobeats by Nigerian pop artists like Mr Eazi and Burna Boy. One song after another washed over me as I strolled past, momentarily wrapping me in its groove before releasing me into the next. It was like scrolling through the dial of a radio devoted to dance music from around the postwar Black Atlantic. Composed of songs that crossed oceans of time and space, and centered on individual desire and expression, the soundscape still made coherent sense. It fashioned a feeling of commonality out of the mixed multitudes and deep crates of Afro-Diasporic musical roots and routes.

I continued on in this manner—my body a crossfader—until I arrived at the amphitheater. Here, at the site of the drum circle incident described in the Introduction, I came upon another sort of ring ritual.[7] Someone had rolled a portable speaker into the middle of the space, creating an impromptu cypher, where a group of dancers took turns freestyling to a prerecorded mix of house music.[8] Adding to the swirl of movement, a crowd of Black and Brown bicyclists—who regularly congregated along the path—looped past the dancers on their fixed-gears, often toting speakers of their own, popping wheelies and other tricks. The occasional roller skater cruised past, too, bopping to the different beats that animated the scene unfurling at the foot of 1200

Lakeshore. In stark contrast to this churn, the apartments towered overhead, stoic and still, standing watch, ever vigilant, like a sentry.[9]

ııııııııııııııııııııııııııııııı

So, here we are again: the amphitheater. The departure point is also the destination. Since our last stop, so many pages ago, we have traveled across the city, from Seventh Street to Downtown, Eastmont to Lake Merritt, and back again. We have traversed a century of recursive struggles to defend spaces of Black belonging from policing and displacement. What can we learn from these looping trajectories? To end, I want to amplify three main points that I have taken from my time attuning to Black sonic politics in Oakland. I hope that these reflections provide insights to readers about the relationship between race, space, and sound in their own cities, or at least give them something to react to and revise.

First, sound in general, and Black dance music in particular, is a charged site of racialized struggle—one with real and significant consequences. Sound is neither good nor bad; instead, it represents a potent and often polarizing site of contention within power-laden contests over the right to control, define, and enjoy urban space. While it tends to be treated as ephemeral, invisible, or trivial, sound is a tangible medium through which the social, spatial, and legal order of the city is forged and resisted.

In Oakland, sound has become entangled in struggles over segregation, redevelopment, antinuisance campaigns, broken-windows policing, nightlife, the management of public space, and more. Born from within hierarchies of race, class, gender, and age, the reception and regulation of sound has tended to reiterate these enduring inequalities. At the same time, however, everyday sound cultures—especially the aural-kinesthetic qualities of Black dance music—have served as one of the most powerful and preferred means to oppose precisely those regimes. Through the constant (re)invention of sonic practices—from slap bass to bass-driven slaps, boogaloo routines to sideshow "bars," funk grooves to the cruise—Black Oaklanders have created a range of "social movements" that challenge oppressive norms and, at times, motivate more traditional political organizing. In Oakland, then, Black dance music has helped to make and remake the very fabric of the city. Whether in terms of forms of repression or resistance—and, in fact, it has been central to both—we can't understand the ways that Oakland has come to feel or function without centering struggles over its Black soundscapes.

Second, sound embeds different cultural logics and politics. The Black sonic practices at Lake Merritt, for instance, embody the properties of openness, porosity, and relationship. They resist individuation and enclosure. As with other aspects of Oakland's Black performance practices, like looping grooves and boogaloo crews, they reflect the interdependence of the self and the social (see ch. 2). In my experience, Black people were more likely than others to use their own personal means of sound amplification, whether in terms of boomboxes, mobile speakers, or car stereos. But these expressions of sonic individualism didn't function to dominate or foreclose other sounds. Rather, in the Afro-Diasporic traditions of call-and-response, polyrhythm, and improvisation, they served as occasions for participation and engagement.

Sound, in its nature, is unbounded. Especially at the Lake—where it reverberates off the water, speeding, unimpeded, over a vast terrain—it doesn't respect the apparent divisions of borders or bodies.[10] Rather than try to reimpose a sense of separation and sovereignty, Black sonic politics tend to embrace the relational, nondualistic qualities of sound—to be moved by that which comes from beyond the self, without being subsumed into it. Thinking back to the comments made by the dancer and steelpanist at the meeting about drumming at Lake Merritt (see Intro), it tends to embed a "frequency of love" that, if they are open to it, allows people to "connect with [their] neighbors."

But not everyone is open to it. Indeed, it's a frequency that not everyone "can hear." In particular, Whiteness has been constructed through a different set of cultural logics and politics, which entail a distinct, often diametric, relationship to sound. Like other aspects of Whiteness, White sonic politics are rooted in the capitalist and colonialist concepts of private property and personhood. In these constructs, the self is made through processes of individual possession, exclusion, and control.[11] In its essence, however, the unbounded and social nature of sound in general, and Black sonic practices in particular, transgresses and trespasses upon this model of property. This is reflected in the law and logic of "nuisance," which, as explained throughout this book, has become the basis of so much of contemporary governance in Oakland and other American cities.

In this sense, White sonic politics have become entrenched in the regulation of urban space and cultural life. While ideas of private property and nuisance are only one of many ways to relate to sound, they have been invested with the power of the state, which has the authority to define what counts as legitimate and, as we have seen, again and again, enforce these norms with violence. This means that—even if carried out by a civilian, like Sean McDonald or Jennifer Schulte— attempts to suppress Black sound as nuisance are backed, in the final instance, by the force of the police.

Here, again, it is important to note that racial identities aren't determinative or monolithic. In other words, by describing these cultural logics as "Black" and "White," I don't mean to argue that all Black people or White people will subscribe to them or follow their precepts. To the contrary, Black people may be unsettled by the porous or public aspects of certain soundscapes, while non-Black people may be drawn in by them. Instead, I use these terms to indicate that different sound cultures are unequally situated vis-à-vis the power of law and legitimacy. And this colors commonsense perceptions of people's sonic practices in ways that reproduce America's White / Black racial hierarchy.

In Oakland, for instance, the city's noise ordinances are meant to prevent sounds from repeating, reaching beyond a narrow radius, and impacting other people. This automatically positions the Black sonic practices described above as illegitimate, a violation of law and norm, and thus vulnerable to regulation and policing. This framework is built on top of a foundation of sonic racism. Namely, as we have seen at various points, the treatment of Black sound as unwanted and unruly "noise"—or what the poet and performance studies scholar Fred Moten calls the "always already improper voice or instrument"—has long served to reinforce the notion of Whiteness as normal and Blackness as nuisance or "out of place."[12]

This leads to my third and final reflection. Contrary to the linear notion of time that prevails in Western thought, Black dance music embodies a logic of the loop. This requires us to reckon with the history and future of Oakland and other (post-)Chocolate Cities according to a different rhythm than the one that animates mainstream accounts. Like the circular pattern of the musical and movement practices described in this book, from looping records to spinning donuts, Oakland's Black geographies tend to be structured by an experience of repetition rather than progression. This loop can be both good and bad. On one side, it reflects the recurrent nature of anti-Black racism and regulation. On the other, it points to the ways that Black Oaklanders have recovered and remixed long-standing sonic and spatial practices to free themselves from these constraints.

Ultimately, thinking, acting, and *moving* in time with Black dance music requires us to listen for the loops, layers, and echoes that live within the deep grooves of America's racist order and antiracist Black geographies. In contrast to linear theories, stories, and song structures, it calls for us to rethink struggles over urban space in terms of what the hip-hop scholar Tricia Rose calls the dance of "repetition and rupture."[13] The notion of time as an arrow provides a view of the present that is too narrow to grasp the historically entrenched nature of racism and the extent of the work needed to repair it. But by the same token, the notion of time as a never-ending loop is too mechanistic to recognize the ever-present potential for escape. In between these two ends of the pendulum, Black dance music insists that in the loop there lives, always, the prospect for improvisation, transformation, and transcendence.

Acknowledgments

I HAVE A LOVE for books that borders on reverence. Otherwise, I wouldn't have been able to devote a decade to writing one. But a book is a strange thing. The research, rumination, and struggle—the moments of insight and moments of uncertainty—unfold over many years. Then, at some point, this seemingly infinite, open-ended process comes to a close. What was molten for so long finally hardens. What was relational and collaborative, intuitive and embodied, becomes frozen text on the page or screen. So, it feels important to refuse this ossification by expressing my deepest gratitude for the web of people who've supported this work—however invisible or inaudible in its present form.

Thank you, first, to my dance teachers. You attuned me to the reverberations that tied Afro-Diasporic histories and movement lineages to the embodied politics of race and belonging during my time in Oakland. I'm no longer in your midst, but you remain in mine. I move differently in the world because of you. Thank you to Theo Aytchan Williams, Ezra Bristow, Joy Broussard, Halima Mahdee, and Alicia Langlais. I also want to give a special dedication to my teacher, collaborator, and friend Baba Rashad Pridgen, may his memory be a blessing. Rashad, you gifted me the title of "sound geographer" while working together on the Global Street Dance Masquerade. You saw and celebrated me before I could sense myself in the resonances between these categories. I always assumed that it was just a matter of time before we would dance and write together again—or, at least, that I would get to share these pages with you. You are loved and deeply missed.

In addition to my dance teachers, I was shaped in profound ways—ones reflected in these pages—by the community of artistic, intellectual, and political co-conspirators who took me in while I lived in the East Bay. Thank you to Eric Arnold, Roberto Bedoya, Sarolta Cump, Julián Delgado Lopera, Jahan Khalighi, Alexis Madrigal, Desi Mundo, Liam O'Donoghue, Ndidi Okwelogu, Michael Orange, Kiki Poe, Jasmine Saavedra Fuego, Zoé Samudzi, Vanessa Whang, Marvin K. White, and Spencer Wilkinson. I'm also grateful to the many people who participated in this research, generously sharing their time, insights, and stories. I especially want to thank those who sat for multiple interviews, commented on excerpts, or otherwise went above-and-beyond, including Gino Pastori-Ng, Steve Snider, Spencer Wilkinson, and Yakpasua Zazaboi. In addition, I received immense support from the staff at local libraries and archives, including John Christian at the Hayward Area Historical Society, Sean Heyliger at the African American Museum and Library at Oakland, and Dorothy Lazard and Emily Foster at the Oakland History Center of the Oakland Public Library.

Most of this research and writing occurred while I was in graduate school at UC Berkeley. Thank you to the members of my dissertation committee— Teresa Caldeira, Jake Kosek, Donald Moore, and Jovan Scott Lewis—each of whom brought such distinct ideas and aesthetics to bear upon my maturation as a scholar. Roaming between disciplines, my interest in the intersections of race, culture, and urbanism was rounded out by Sharad Chari, Paul Groth, James Holston, Shannon Jackson, Leigh Raiford, Ananya Roy, and Richard Walker. I was also especially blessed by my relationships with Brandi Summers and Christina Zanfagna, who I met just as I was "leaving" academia. Thank you, Brandi and Christina, for your wisdom, kindness, and camaraderie, and for demonstrating a form of community-rooted, collaborative cultural politics that I deeply admire. In addition, my graduate studies were supported by grants from the UC Berkeley Graduate Division, Department of Geography, Designated Emphasis in Global Metropolitan Studies, and Bancroft Library; the UC Humanities Research Institute; and the Mellon Foundation / American Council of Learned Societies.

The open secret about graduate school is that the other students are often the greatest teachers, and my experience was no different. Thank you to Javier Arbona, Alexander Arroyo, miyuki baker, Trisha Barua, Hannah Birnbaum, Evan Bissell, Peter Ekman, John Elrick, Zöe Friedman-Cohen, april l. graham-jackson, Terra Graziani, Katy Guimond, Camilla Hawthorne, Kaily Heitz, Juan Herrera, Chris Herring, Savannah Kilner, Andrea Marston, Erin McElroy, Chris Mizes, Diana Negrín da Silva, Meredith Palmer, Magie Ramírez, Jen Rose Smith, Gil Rothschild Elyassi, Alex Schafran, Emma Shaw Crane, John Stehlin, Divya Sundar, Erin Torkelson, Ashton Wesner, and Leonora Zonin-sein. This research never would have come to be without the prolific influence of my dear friend Eli Marienthal. I followed him to the East Bay, where his mother, Penny, gave me my first home. I followed him to Berkeley Geography. And I followed him into the basement of a barber shop on Telegraph Avenue, where we joined a group of artists, vendors, and activists trying to organize a self-governed street party. This detour changed the course of my research and relationship to Oakland's public culture in ways that echo to this day. Thank you, Eli, for always opening my eyes and ears to what's over the next horizon.

Since returning to New England in 2022, when I started working on this book, I have received support from many old friends from my time at Brown University. Sandy Zipp welcomed me back to Providence, providing me with a desk, library card, and thoughtful group of undergraduate students at the precise moment that I needed to remember how to write. Micah Salkind, Nate Sloan, and Charlie Harding entertained my most arcane music questions, sharing deep thoughts and often deep cuts. Leora Fridman continued to serve as a valued thought partner about writing in ways that are both political and personal, sincere but not too self-serious. And since 2006, when we sat next to each other in a postwar history course taught by Robert Self—author of *American Babylon*, one of the classic books about Oakland—Robert Smith III has been a constant teacher, inspiration, and companion.

This book wouldn't exist in its current form without the team at UC Press. Thank you to my editor, Kim Robinson, for your constant encouragement, calm guidance, and sage counsel. Thank you to editorial assistant Aline Dolinh for tending to all of the sacred details with clarity and grace; you took a murky process and made it manageable. And thank you to Jessica Moll, Paul Tyler, Chloe Wong, and the many workers whose names I will never know. I also want to thank Kevin Millham for his careful work on the index and Stephen Loewinsohn for sharing his captivating image of a local sideshow for the cover.

This book was immeasurably improved thanks to the careful scrutiny of two anonymous reviewers and several not-so-anonymous ones, including Kaily Heitz, Nate Sloan, Robert Smith III, Barry Werth, and Christina Zanfagna. It also benefited from a workshop with an incisive group of students at Mount Holyoke College, with whom I connected thanks to an invitation from Phillip Campanile.

In truth, all of this is a prelude to my gratitude for my family. This work is dedicated to my mom and dad, Kathy and Barry, the dancer and the writer, who imparted to me their love of people, craft, and a good political debate. Thank you for modeling what it means to be curious, compassionate, and of service. Thank you to my sister, Emily, whose commitment to cities and people continues to intersect with my own in potent and inspiring ways. Thank you to my child, Malka, for arriving on this earth eager to dance. It inspires and uplifts me to see how the loop begins again with you. And thank you, a thousand times, to my partner, Ellie, who suffered through early drafts, soothed my worries and disappointments, celebrated my wins, and offered extra childcare when I needed more focus to write than parenting a toddler typically afforded. You call me back when my politics and ethics become too abstract, reminding me to be gentle and golden-hearted. I love you for that, and so much more.

Notes

PREFACE

1. Here, "the deep" is a reference to the low-frequency sound-waves that make up bass tones in music. But it's also an invocation of "Deep East Oakland," or "The Deep East," the easternmost stretch of the East Oakland flats, which, since the 1960s, has been predominantly Black. In this sense, the "deepness" of the city's sound ties the prominence of synthesized bass within local rap music to its specific Black geographies, which are considered remote, mysterious, and impenetrable, but also rooted, soulful, and profound. The geographer Kaily Heitz relates this to what Katherine McKittrick calls the "ungeographic" nature of Blackness. For Heitz, "the deep" "links the violence of policing, structural abandonment, and illicit gang economies of survival to a conceptual geography of the city as a non-space (no there there) that has endured and intensified through decades of racialized displacement." Kaily Heitz, "Back against the Mall: Caring for Deep East Oakland" (unpublished manuscript, 2023). See also Katherine McKittrick, *Demonic Grounds: Black Women and the Cartographies of Struggle* (University of Minnesota Press, 2006).

2. Clyde Carson featuring The Team, "Slow Down," *Slow Down*, Universal Republic Records, 2012, no catalog no., MP3, single.

3. The term "yadadamean?" ("you know what I mean?") is accredited to Oakland's gravel-voiced rapper Keak Da Sneak, along with many other popular phrases, including "hyphy," the name for the East Bay's signature style of party rap (see ch. 5). Keak Da Sneak, "Super Hyphy," *That's My Word*, Rah Records, 2005, RTE 131, CD, album. In African and Afro-Diasporic cultures, there is a custom of investing the very sound of words with a sense of mystical or spiritual power. According to the Black studies scholar Louis Chude-Sokei, for instance, Jamaican Rastafarians treat certain words as potent because of how they sound, and are sounded, rather than their "logocentric meaning." Louis Chude-Sokei, "The Sound of Culture: Dread Discourse and Jamaican Sound Systems," in *Language, Rhythm, and Sound: Black Popular Cultures into the Twenty-First Century*, ed. Joseph K. Adjaye and Adrianne R. Andrews (University of Pittsburgh Press, 1997).

4. Quoted in Joel Selvin, *Sly & The Family Stone: An Oral History* (Permuted Press, 1998), 28–29. See also Greg Bridges, "Reflections with Larry Graham," *Reflections in Rhythm*, August 10, 2010, online.

5. Sly and the Family Stone, "Thank You (Falettinme Be Mice Elf Agin)," *Thank You (Falettinme Be Mice Elf Agin) / Everybody Is a Star*, Epic, 1969, 5–10555, vinyl, 7", single; Graham Central Station, "The Jam," *Ain't No 'Bout-a-Doubt It*, Warner Bros. Records, 1975, BS 2876, vinyl, LP, album.

6. Rickey Vincent, interview by author, November 30, 2017; Digital Underground, "The Humpty Dance," *Sex Packets*, Tommy Boy, 1990, TBCD 1026, CD, album.

7. Leigh Raiford, *Imprisoned in a Luminous Glare: Photography and the African American Freedom Struggle* (University of North Carolina Press, 2011), 136–37, 144–45.

8. Tina M. Campt, *Listening to Images* (Duke University Press, 2017), 7.

9. James Brown, "Say It Loud—I'm Black and I'm Proud," *Say It Loud—I'm Black and I'm Proud*, King Records, 1968, 45–6187, vinyl, 7", single; Marvin Gaye, "Inner City Blues (Make Me Wanna Holler)," *What's Going On*, Tamla, 1971, TS-310, vinyl, LP, album.

10. Brandi T. Summers, *Black in Place: The Spatial Aesthetics of Race in a Post-Chocolate City* (University of North Carolina Press, 2019).

INTRODUCTION

1. Michael E. Veal, *Dub: Soundscapes and Shattered Songs in Jamaican Reggae* (Wesleyan University Press, 2007), 198.

2. Quoted in Katherine McKittrick, "Rebellion / Invention / Groove," *Small Axe: A Caribbean Journal of Criticism* 20, no. 1 (2016): 79–91, at 87.

3. James A. Snead, "On Repetition in Black Culture," *Black American Literature Forum* 15, no. 4 (1981): 146–54, at 150.

4. For more on Congo Square, see Ned Sublette, *The World That Made New Orleans: From Spanish Silver to Congo Square* (Lawrence Hill Books, 2008).

5. Hanif Abdurraqib, *A Little Devil in America: Notes in Praise of Black Performance* (Random House, 2021), 18.

6. Author field notes from walk around Lake Merritt, November 25, 2017.

7. The anthropologist Joel Streicker comes to a similar conclusion about the spatial politics of *champeta* parties in Cartagena, Colombia. "The sound systems at these semi-open air dances are so powerful that the music can be heard at least two kilometers away . . . This music speaks of—and is—a presence that the rich cannot avoid, a nearly dusk-to-dawn siege reminding the wealthy of the popular class's otherness. The sound systems provide a nonspatial way of appropriating space." Joel Streicker, "Spatial Reconfigurations, Imagined Geographies, and Social Conflicts in Cartagena, Colombia," *Cultural Anthropology* 12, no. 1 (1997): 109–28, at 116.

8. Oakland, originally known as Huchiun, is the unceded and unrecognized home of the Lisjan Ohlone people, who continue to organize for cultural, political, and territorial sovereignty. Those interested in learning more about the history of Indigenous dispossession and supporting the ongoing struggle for land "rematriation" should visit www.sogoreate-landtrust.com.

9. Crowned the winner of a dance contest at Carnaval San Francisco in 2001, Williams is known by many people in Oakland as "King Theo." While I refer to most individuals by their last name, I choose to refer to him by the artist name that he uses within Oakland's cultural and political scenes, including SambaFunk!, of which I was a member from 2016 to 2019. This is not meant to diminish him in comparison to the other figures in the book, but rather to honor him.

10. Ali Winston and Darwin BondGraham, *The Riders Come Out at Night: Brutality, Corruption, and Cover-Up in Oakland* (Atria Books, 2023), 134–35.

11. This account is based on audio recordings of 911 calls related to OPD Incident #15–051796, September 27, 2015 (public records requested by author).

12. Ibid.

13. In the days to come, Williams charged McDonald with assault for his aggressive behavior, as well. In the end, the Alameda County District Attorney's Office decided to drop the charges against both parties. Sam Levin, "OPD Responds to Noise Complaints by White Man against Black Drummers at Lake Merritt, Sparks Concerns about Racial Profiling," *East Bay Express*, September 29, 2015, online; Sam Levin, "No Charges in Lake Merritt Drumming Incident, OPD Says Noise Complaint Was Not a Priority," *East Bay Express*, October 26, 2015, online.

14. For more on the local origins of the Black Lives Matter Movement, see Julia C. Wong, "The Bay Area Roots of Black Lives Matter," *SFWeekly*, November 11, 2015, online.

15. Comment posted by Sean McDonald on October 10, 2015, in response to Levin, "OPD Responds to Noise Complaints."

16. Quoted in Tulio Ospina, "Racially Profiled, Drummers Make Noise about Gentrification in Oakland," *Oakland Post*, October 4, 2015, online.

17. Author field notes from PRAC meeting, September 14, 2016.

18. Ibid.

19. Nina Sun Eidsheim, *The Race of Sound: Listening, Timbre, and Vocality in African American Music* (Duke University Press, 2019), 24.

20. Plastic Ono Band, "Give Peace a Chance," *Give Peace a Chance / Remember Love*, Apple Records, 1969, APPLE 13, vinyl, 7", single; Public Enemy, "Fight the Power," *Fight the Power*, Motown, 1989, ZB 42877, vinyl, 7", single.

21. For examples of studies that center on the role of politicized artists and lyrics in the context of organized social movements, see Olaf Kaltmeier and Wilfried Raussert, eds., *Sonic Politics: Music and Social Movements in the Americas* (Routledge, 2021); Joe Mulhall, *Rebel Sounds: Music as Resistance* (Footnote, 2024); Shana L. Redmond, *Anthem: Social Movements and the Sound of Solidarity in the African Diaspora* (New York University Press, 2014); Pat Thomas, *Listen, Whitey!: The Sights and Sounds of Black Power, 1965–1975* (Fantagraphics, 2012).

22. Matt Sakakeeny, "Music, Sound, Politics," *Annual Review of Anthropology* 53, no. 1 (2024): 309–29, at 311.

23. Lilian Radovac, "The 'War on Noise': Sound and Space in La Guardia's New York," *American Quarterly* 63, no. 3 (2011): 733–60, at 744.

24. Oakland Planning Department, *Noise: An Element of the Oakland Comprehensive Plan* (City of Oakland, 1974), 3, Main Branch, Oakland Public Library, Oakland, CA.

25. Jennifer Lynn Stoever, *The Sonic Color Line: Race and the Cultural Politics of Listening* (New York University Press, 2016), 12.

26. Matthew D. Morrison, "Race, Blacksound, and the (Re)Making of Musicological Discourse," *Journal of the American Musicological Society* 72, no. 3 (2019): 781–823, at 794. See also Matthew D. Morrison, *Blacksound: Making Race and Popular Music in the United States* (University of California Press, 2024).

27. Stoever, *Sonic Color Line*, 11.

28. For more on the "American audio-racial imagination," see Josh Kun, *Audiotopia: Music, Race, and America* (University of California Press, 2005), 20–26.

29. For more on American anti-Black racism as a system of caste oppression, see Isabel Wilkerson, *Caste: The Origins of Our Discontents* (Random House, 2020).

30. Alexander Weheliye, *Phonographies: Grooves in Sonic Afro-Modernity* (Duke University Press, 2005), 38.

31. Paul Gilroy, *The Black Atlantic: Modernity and Double Consciousness* (Harvard University Press, 1993), 36–40. There is often a gendered dimension to the production of sound as a freedom practice. The visual studies scholar Tina Campt describes a form of "black feminist futurity" in which "both quiet and the quotidian are mobilized as everyday practices of refusal." "It's not always loud and demanding. It is frequently quiet and opportunistic, dogged and disruptive," she writes. Campt, *Listening to Images*, 4, 17.

32. Gayle Wald, "Soul Vibrations: Black Music and Black Freedom in Sound and Space," *American Quarterly* 63, no. 3 (2011): 673–96, at 675.

33. Julian Henriques, *Sonic Bodies: Reggae Sound Systems, Performance Techniques and Ways of Knowing* (Continuum, 2011), xxviii, 13, 20, 53–54.

34. Wald, "Soul Vibrations," 675.

35. McKittrick, "Rebellion / Invention / Groove," 81.

36. Kun, *Audiotopia*, 17.

37. Matt Sakakeeny, "'Under the Bridge': An Orientation to Soundscapes in New Orleans," *Ethnomusicology* 54, no. 1 (2010): 1–27.

38. Cheryl Harris, "Whiteness as Property," *Harvard Law Review* 106 (1993): 1709–91; George Lipsitz, *How Racism Takes Place* (Temple University Press, 2011); K-Sue Park, "Money, Mortgages, and the Conquest of America," *Law & Social Inquiry* 41, no. 4 (2016): 1006–35.

39. Here, my interpretation resonates with the work of the geographer Magie Ramírez, who has written about Sean MacDonald's attack on SambaFunk! and other cultural political struggles in Oakland. See Margaret Ramírez, "Decolonial Ruptures: Art-Activism amid Racialized Dispossession in Oakland" (PhD diss., University of Washington, 2017); Margaret M. Ramírez, "City as Borderland: Gentrification and the Policing of Black and Latinx Geographies in Oakland," *Environment and Planning D: Society and Space* 38, no. 1 (2020): 147–66.

40. Leroi Jones, *Black Music* (Da Capo Press, 1998 [1967]).

41. Stoever, *Sonic Color Line*, 3.

42. Saidiya Hartman, *Lose Your Mother: A Journey along the Atlantic Slave Route* (Farrar, Straus and Giroux, 2007), 8.

43. Soyica Diggs Colbert, Douglas A. Jones Jr., and Shane Vogel, "Introduction: Tidying Up after Repetition," in *Race and Performance after Repetition*, ed. Soyica Diggs Colbert, Douglas A. Jones Jr., and Shane Vogel (Duke University Press, 2020), 16.

44. McKittrick, *Demonic Grounds*, 1–2.

45. Anna Livia Brand, "Today Like Yesterday, Tomorrow Like Today: Black Geographies in the Breaks of the Fourth Dimension," in *The Black Geographic: Praxis, Resistance, Futurity*, ed. Camilla Hawthorne and Jovan Scott Lewis (Duke University Press, 2023), 268. See also Rasheedah Phillips, *Dismantling the Master's Clock: On Race, Space, and Time* (AK Press, 2025).

46. For more on the role of "repe[tition] with a difference" in African American literary and vernacular culture, see Henry Louis Gates Jr., *The Signifying Monkey: A Theory of African American Literary Criticism* (Oxford University Press, 1988). For more on the importance of "echo" in "Black Atlantic expression," see Tsitsi Ella Jaji, *Africa in Stereo: Modernism, Music, and Pan-African Solidarity* (Oxford University Press, 2014).

47. Snead, "On Repetition in Black Culture," 147–48. For more on Hegel's views of geography, culture, and racial hierarchy, see Georg Wilhelm Friedrich Hegel, "Geographical Basis of World History," in *Race and the Enlightenment: A Reader*, ed. Emmanuel Chukwudi Eze (Blackwell, 1997 [1837]).

48. Snead, "On Repetition in Black Culture," 149–50.

49. Snead, "On Repetition in Black Culture," 150.

50. Henriques, *Sonic Bodies*, 147. Henriques also notes that repetition is intrinsic to the materiality of soundwaves: "The cyclical movement of repeating is . . . inseparable from the material vibrations of sounding with its rhythms, pulses, beats, waves, rotations, oscillations, vibrations and frequencies" (165).

51. Snead, "On Repetition in Black Culture," 150–51. See also Anne Danielsen, "Time and Time Again: Repetition and Difference in Repetitive Music," in *Over and Over: Exploring Repetition in Popular Music*, ed. Olivier Julien and Cristophe Levaux (Bloomsbury, 2018); Samuel A. Floyd Jr., "Ring Shout!: Literary Studies, Historical Studies, and Black Music Inquiry," *Black Music Research Journal* 11, no. 2 (1991): 265–87.

52. Veal, *Dub*, 246.

53. Mark V. Campbell, *Afrosonic Life* (Bloomsbury, 2022), 36.

54. Quoted in Jeff Chang, *Can't Stop Won't Stop: A History of the Hip-Hop Generation* (St. Martin's Press, 2005), 78.

55. Chang, *Can't Stop Won't Stop*, 78.

56. Mark Katz, *Groove Music: The Art and Culture of the Hip-Hop DJ* (Oxford University Press, 2012), 31–32.

57. Joseph G. Schloss, *Making Beats: The Art of Sample-Based Hip-Hop* (Wesleyan University Press, 2014 [2004]), 33.

58. Patricia Herrera, "A Sonic Treatise of Futurity: Universes' *Party People*," in *Race and Performance after Repetition*, ed. Soyica Diggs Colbert, Douglas A. Jones Jr., and Shane Vogel (Duke University Press, 2020), 72.

59. Katz, *Groove Music*, 36.

60. Tim Lawrence, *Love Saves the Day: A History of American Dance Music Culture, 1970–1979* (Duke University Press, 2003), 107, 217, 384.

61. Oliver Wang, *Legions of Boom: Filipino American Mobile DJ Crews in the San Francisco Bay Area* (Duke University Press, 2015), 33–34.

62. Lawrence, *Love Saves the Day*, 212–20.

63. Veal, *Dub*, 246.

64. For more on the relationship between disco and house music, see Micah E. Salkind, *Do You Remember House?: Chicago's Queer of Color Undergrounds* (Oxford University Press, 2019).

65. James Baldwin, "Of the Sorrow Songs: The Cross of Redemption," in *The Cross of Redemption: Uncollected Writings*, ed. Randall Kenan (Pantheon Books, 2010 [1979]), 153.

66. For more on the marketing of hip-hop culture to White suburban audiences, see Tricia Rose, *Black Noise: Rap Music and Black Culture in Contemporary America* (Wesleyan University Press, 1994), 6–7, 17.

67. For more on the history of Afro-Diasporic dance in Oakland, see Halifu Osumare, *Dancing in Blackness: A Memoir* (University Press of Florida, 2018).

68. Jafari S. Allen, "For 'the Children' Dancing the Beloved Community," *Souls* 11, no. 3 (2009): 311–26, at 317.

69. Steve King, *Who Owns Your Neighborhood?: The Role of Investors in Post-Foreclosure Oakland* (Urban Strategies Council, 2012), online; Erin McElroy and Alex Werth, "Deracinated Dispossessions: On the Foreclosures of 'Gentrification' in Oakland, CA," *Antipode* 51, no. 3 (2019): 878–98.

70. For more on the marketing of Blackness as a redevelopment strategy, see Kaily Heitz, "Oakland Is a Vibe: Blackness, Cultural Framings, and Emancipations of The Town" (PhD diss., University of California, Berkeley, 2021).

71. Juan Herrera, *Cartographic Memory: Social Movement Activism and the Production of Space* (Duke University Press, 2022), 4–5, 18.

72. For more on gender and urban public space in the United States, see Sarah Deutsch, *Women and the City: Gender, Space, and Power in Boston, 1870–1940* (Oxford University Press, 2000).

1. OAKLAND BLUES

1. This song, by blues singer Dave Alexander, appears to have been written to score "The People and the Police: Oakland," an episode of the KRON-TV television program *Assignment 4*. See Ira Eisenberg, dir., "The People and the Police: Oakland," *Assignment 4*, television series episode, Young Broadcasting, 1974, Internet Archive.

2. For more on the settlement and incorporation of Oakland, see Beth Bagwell, *Oakland: The Story of a City* (Oakland Heritage Alliance, 1996 [1982]).

3. Quoted in Joshua Jelly-Schapiro, "High Tide, Low Ebb," in *Infinite City: A San Francisco Atlas*, ed. Rebecca Solnit (University of California Press, 2010), 60.

4. Marilynn S. Johnson, *The Second Gold Rush: Oakland and the East Bay in World War II* (University of California Press, 1993), 52.

5. Bagwell, *Oakland*; Richard Walker, "Industry Builds Out the City: The Suburbanization of Manufacturing in the San Francisco Bay Area, 1850–1940," in *Manufacturing Suburbs: Building Work and Home on the Metropolitan Fringe*, ed. Robert Lewis (Temple University Press, 2004). For more on West Oakland and trans-Pacific trade, see Alexis Madrigal, *The Pacific Circuit: A Globalized Account of the Battle for the Soul of an American City* (Foster, Straus and Giroux, 2025).

6. Robert Self, *American Babylon: Race and the Struggle for Postwar Oakland* (Princeton University Press, 2003), 43.

7. Lawrence P. Crouchett, Lonnie Bunch III, and Martha Kendall Winnacker, *Visions toward Tomorrow: The History of the East Bay Afro-American Community, 1852–1977* (Northern California Center for Afro-American History and Life, 1989). For more on the ironic "freedom" to sell one's labor power, see Karl Marx, *Capital, Volume 1* (Penguin Books, 1990 [1867]). For more on the settlement and segregation of Chinese immigrants in Oakland during the late nineteenth century, see L. Eve Armentrout Ma, *Hometown Chinatown: The History of Oakland's Chinese Community* (Garland, 2000).

8. By World War II, the Northern European and Protestant workers who had first migrated to West Oakland in the nineteenth century had moved to new racially restrictive subdivisions in East Oakland. See Chris Rhomberg, *No There There: Race, Class, and Political Community in Oakland* (University of California Press, 2004), chap. 3. In response to the declaration of war with Japan in 1941, the United States forcibly relocated and incarcerated an estimated 120,000 Japanese Americans—two thirds of whom were U. S. citizens—to a network of ten concentration camps. In West Coast cities like San Francisco and Oakland, where most people of Japanese descent lived, entire communities were displaced for the remainder of World War II.

9. Quoted in Jacqueline Cogdell DjeDje, "The California Black Gospel Music Tradition: A Confluence of Musical Styles and Cultures," in *California Soul: Music of African Americans in the West*, ed. Jacqueline Cogdell DjeDje and Eddie S. Meadows (University of California Press, 1998), 145.

10. Oakland's Chinatown was displaced multiple times between the 1850s and 1870s before arriving at its long-term location around Eighth and Webster

Streets. Still, it was consistently located in the downtown area. See Ma, *Hometown Chinatown*.

11. Crouchett, Bunch III, and Winnacker, *Visions toward Tomorrow*, chaps. 2–3.

12. Rhomberg, *No There There*, 77–78.

13. Bagwell, *Oakland*, 234.

14. Jelly-Schapiro, "High Tide, Low Ebb," 60.

15. Crouchett, Bunch III, and Winnacker, *Visions toward Tomorrow*, 43; Johnson, *Second Gold Rush*, 32–38, 52.

16. Johnson, *Second Gold Rush*, chaps. 3–4.

17. Johnson, *Second Gold Rush*, 95.

18. Quoted in Johnson, *Second Gold Rush*, 150, 168.

19. For more on migration, class, and respectability politics in African American urban communities, see Hazel V. Carby, "Policing the Black Woman's Body in an Urban Context," in *Cultures in Babylon: Black Britain and African America* (Verso, 1999 [1992]); Isabel Wilkerson, *The Warmth of Other Suns: The Epic Story of America's Great Migration* (Vintage Books, 2010), 289–91.

20. Quoted in Johnson, *Second Gold Rush*, 170.

21. Quoted in Wilkerson, *Warmth of Other Suns*, 291; Stoever, *Sonic Color Line*, 189.

22. Quoted in Johnson, *Second Gold Rush*, 147.

23. Johnson, *Second Gold Rush*, 159–63.

24. Quoted in Johnson, *Second Gold Rush*, 154.

25. Donna J. Murch, *Living for the City: Migration, Education, and the Rise of the Black Panther Party in Oakland, California* (University of North Carolina Press, 2010), 21–22.

26. Wilkerson, *Warmth of Other Suns*, 261–62.

27. Johnson, *Second Gold Rush*, 155–57, 265n34.

28. Phil McArdle, *A History of the Oakland Police Department* (City of Oakland, 1980), 12, Institute for Governmental Studies Library, University of California, Berkeley, CA.

29. Johnson, *Second Gold Rush*, 162–63.

30. Johnson, *Second Gold Rush*, 168.

31. Walter Green, "Oral History with Walter Green," interviewed by Nadine Wilmot, 1999, BANC MSS 2006/112, Box 1, Oakland Oral History Project, Bancroft Library, University of California, Berkeley, CA.

32. Wilkerson, *Warmth of Other Suns*, 211.

33. Quoted in Marcus Anthony Hunter and Zandria F. Robinson, *Chocolate Cities: The Black Map of American Life* (University of California Press, 2018), 2.

34. Hunter and Robinson, *Chocolate Cities*, 4.

35. Ishmael Reed, *Blues City: A Walk in Oakland* (Crown, 2003).

36. Oakland City Planning Commission, *Shoreline Development: A Part of the Master Plan* (City of Oakland, 1951), 69, Environmental Design Library, University of California, Berkeley, CA.

37. Residents and boosters of San Francisco's Fillmore District claimed this title, too. See Elizabeth Pepin and Lewis Watts, *The Harlem of the West: The San Francisco Fillmore Jazz Era* (Chronicle Books, 2006).

38. The Classic Archives Old Time Radio Channel, "One Night Stand 440604 0329 Lionel Hampton Civic Auditorium Oakland," June 1, 2019, YouTube.

39. Quoted in Willie R. Collins, "Jazzing Up Seventh Street: Musicians, Venues, and Their Social Implications," in *Sights and Sounds: Essays in Celebration of West Oakland*, ed. Suzanne Stewart and Mary Praetzellis (California Department of Transportation, 1997), 315.

40. Collins, "Jazzing Up Seventh Street," 315–16.

41. Quoted in Collins, "Jazzing Up Seventh Street," 314.

42. "City Officials Probe Riot Here; Preventative Measures Planned," *Oakland Tribune*, March 8, 1944, 11; "Transportation Is Blamed for Riot; Remedies Sought," *Oakland Tribune*, March 10, 1944, 5; Bill Tobitt, "Here's News from Home," *Oakland Tribune*, March 11, 1944, 7, California Digital Newspaper Collection.

43. Quoted in Bagwell, *Oakland*, 240; Crouchett, Bunch III, and Winnacker, *Visions toward Tomorrow*, 51.

44. Johnson, *Second Gold Rush*, 169.

45. Lance Boos, "Raymond E. Jackson and Segregation in the American Federation of Musicians, 1900–1944" (MA thesis, State University of New York, Buffalo State College, 2015), 20.

46. Leta E. Miller, "Racial Segregation and the San Francisco Musicians' Union, 1923–60," *Journal of the Society for American Music* 1, no. 2 (2007): 161–206, at 173–75.

47. Quoted in Miller, "Racial Segregation," 172.

48. Miller, "Racial Segregation," 185–86.

49. Earl Watkins, "Oral History with Earl Watkins," interviewed by Donna J. Murch, 1998, BANC MSS 2006/112, Box 1, Oakland Oral History Project, Bancroft Library, University of California, Berkeley, CA.

50. Miller, "Racial Segregation," 197–98.

51. Name illegible, *Oakland Tribune*, June 18, 1957, Music Federation, American, San Francisco Bay Area, Calif. Local 6, Hayward Area Historical Society, Hayward, CA.

52. For a classic study of Black urban life under segregation, see St. Clair Drake and Horace R. Cayton, *Black Metropolis: A Study of Negro Life in a Northern City* (University of Chicago Press, 1993 [1945]).

53. For more on the racial and sexual politics of "slumming," see Kevin J. Mumford, *Interzones: Black / White Sex Districts in Chicago and New York in the Early Twentieth Century* (Columbia University Press, 1997).

54. Jelly-Schapiro, "High Tide, Low Ebb," 62.

55. Miller, "Racial Segregation," 191.

56. Collins, "Jazzing Up Seventh Street," 296–97.

57. Crouchett, Bunch III, and Winnacker, *Visions toward Tomorrow*, 37.

58. Lee Hildebrand, "West Side Story," *East Bay Express*, September 28, 1979, 1, Magazine and Newspaper Room, Main Branch, Oakland Public Library, Oakland, CA.

59. Collins, "Jazzing Up Seventh Street," 297.

60. Ray Astbury, "Oakland," in *Encyclopedia of the Blues*, ed. Edward Komara (Routledge, 2006).

61. Quoted in Lee Hildebrand and James C. Moore Sr., "Oakland Blues," in *California Soul: Music of African Americans in the West*, ed. Jacqueline Cogdell DjeDje and Eddie S. Meadows (University of California Press, 1988), 109.

62. Hildebrand and Moore Sr., "Oakland Blues," 106–10.

63. Quoted in Hildebrand and Moore Sr., "Oakland Blues," 108. In the 1940s, the more uptempo boogie woogie and jump blues were also popular among African American musicians and audiences on the West Coast. This makes the emphasis on sadness in early Oakland blues recordings even more remarkable.

64. Hildebrand and Moore Sr., "Oakland Blues," 109–10; Michael Point, "Lowell Fulson," in *Encyclopedia of the Blues*, ed. Edward Komara (Routledge, 2006).

65. Lowell Fulson, "Three O'Clock Blues," *Three O'Clock Blues / I'm Wild about You Baby*, Down Town Recording, 1948, shellac, 10", single.

66. Point, "Lowell Fulson," 350.

67. B. B. King, "Three O'Clock Blues," *Three O'Clock Blues / That Ain't the Way to Do It*, RPM Records, 1951, 339, shellac, 10", single.

68. Hildebrand and Moore Sr., "Oakland Blues," 110. See also Jelly-Schapiro, "High Tide, Low Ebb," 62.

69. Hildebrand and Moore Sr., "Oakland Blues," 108.

70. Maureen Mahon, "Listening for Willie Mae 'Big Mama' Thornton's Voice: The Sound of Race and Gender Transgressions in Rock and Roll," *Women and Music: A Journal of Gender and Culture* 15, no. 1 (2011): 1–17.

71. Quoted in Marlon Riggs and Peter Webster, dirs., *Long Train Running: A History of the Oakland Blues*, film recording, University of California, Berkeley, School of Journalism, 1981, Media Services and Collections, University of California, Berkeley, CA.

72. Astbury, "Oakland."

73. In histories of West Oakland, Slim Jenkins' Club is referred to by many names, whether because it went through several name changes or because it was known in more colloquial terms. Some of these names include: Slim Jenkins' Café, Slim Jenkins' Corner, Slim Jenkins' Place, Slim Jenkins' Restaurant and Bar, and Slim Jenkins' Supper Club.

74. Wilkerson, *Warmth of Other Suns*, 186–87.

75. Steven A. Jones, Bill Jersey, Sharon Wood, and Marshall Crutcher, dirs., *Crossroads: A Story of West Oakland*, film recording, Quest Productions, 1996, Media Services and Collections, University of California, Berkeley, CA.

76. Murch, *Living for the City*, 27; "Slim Jenkins Dies in West Oakland," *Oakland Tribune*, May 24, 1967, Jenkins, "Slim" Harold, Hayward Area Historical Society, Hayward, CA.

77. Watkins, "Oral History with Earl Watkins"; Jim Goggin, *Earl Watkins: The Life of a Jazz Drummer* (Trafford, 2005), 33.

78. Stoever, *Sonic Color Line*, 13–16.

79. Hildebrand, "West Side Story"; Esther Mabry, "Oral History with Esther Mabry," interviewed by Gay Rich, 2002, MS 191, African American Museum and Library at Oakland Oral History Collection, African American Museum and Library at Oakland, Oakland Public Library, Oakland, CA.

80. Willie R. Collins, "California Rhythm and Blues Recordings, 1942–1972: A Diversity of Styles," in *California Soul: Music of African Americans in the West*, ed. Jacqueline Cogdell DjeDje and Eddie S. Meadows (University of California Press, 1998), 228–30; Jimmy McCracklin, "Too Late to Change," *I Just Gotta Know*, Imperial, 1963, LP 9219, vinyl, LP, album; Jimmy Wilson, "Tin Pan Alley," *Tin Pan Alley / Big Town Jump*, Big Town, 1953, 101, vinyl, 10", single; Lowell Fulson, "Blue Shadows," *Blue Shadows / Low Society Blues*, Swing Time, 1950, 226, shellac, 10", single.

81. Christina Zanfagna, *Holy Hip Hop in the City of Angels* (University of California Press, 2017), 86.

82. Collins, "Jazzing Up Seventh Street," 297, 314.

83. Johnny Heartsman, the Rhythm Rocker, and the Gaylarks, "Johnny's House Party, Parts 1 & 2," *Johnny's House Party, Parts 1 & 2*, Music City, 1957, 45–807, vinyl, 7", single.

84. Goerge Lipsitz, *Midnight at the Barrelhouse: The Johnny Otis Story* (University of Minnesota Press, 2010), 9.

85. Watkins, "Oral History with Earl Watkins."

86. Rashad Shabazz, *Spatializing Blackness: Architectures of Confinement and Black Masculinity in Chicago* (University of Illinois Press, 2015), chap. 1. See also Mumford, *Interzones*.

87. Watkins, "Oral History with Earl Watkins." The same tactics were used to stop interracial mixing in Los Angeles in the 1950s. See Collins, "California Rhythm and Blues Recordings," 234; Anthony Macías, "Bringing Music to the People: Race, Urban Culture, and Municipal Politics in Postwar LA," *American Quarterly* 56, no. 3 (2004): 693–717.

88. Nancy Barr Mavity, "Get Definite Recommendation for Oakland within 60 Days," *Oakland Tribune*, April 20, 1944, Curfew Law, Oakland History Room, Main Branch, Oakland Public Library, Oakland, CA.

89. "Council Rejects Curfew Plan," *Oakland Tribune*, November 17, 1943, Curfew Law, Oakland History Room, Main Branch, Oakland Public Library, Oakland, CA.

90. Dorothy W. Pitts, *A Special Place for Special People: The DeFremery Story* (Better Communications, 1993), 20, 33.

91. Ruth Beckford, "Oral History with Ruth Beckford," interviewed by Rick Moss, 2007, MS 191, African American Museum and Library at Oakland

Oral History Collection, African American Museum and Library at Oakland, Oakland Public Library, Oakland, CA.

92. Quoted in Pitts, *Special Place*, 22.

93. Judith May, "Struggle for Authority: A Comparison of Four Social Change Programs in Oakland, California" (PhD diss., University of California, Berkeley, 1973), 132–36; Pitts, *Special Place*, 88–91.

94. The data on arrests is from James Q. Wilson, *Varieties of Police Behavior: The Management of Law and Order in Eight Communities* (Harvard University Press, 1978 [1968]), 114.

95. Murch, *Living for the City*, 68.

96. Renaming turned out to be one aspect of that conversion process. After Black Panther Bobby Hutton was murdered by the OPD in 1968, Black Oaklanders began to refer to DeFremery as Lil' Bobby Hutton Park. Today, using this name situates residents within the spatial and epistemological legacy of Black radicalism in Oakland.

2. SOCIAL MOVEMENTS

1. Stokely Carmichael, "Speech at University of California, Berkeley," October 29, 1966, Greek Theatre, University of California, Berkeley, CA, recording and transcript accessed online through American Public Media Reports.

2. Sly and the Family Stone, "I Want to Take You Higher," *Stand! / I Want to Take You Higher*, Epic Records, 1969, 5–10450, vinyl, 7", single.

3. Carmichael, "Speech."

4. Stokely Carmichael and Charles V. Hamilton, *Black Power: The Politics of Liberation* (Random House, 1967), 44.

5. Carmichael, "Speech."

6. Joshua Bloom and Waldo E. Martin, *Black against Empire: The History and Politics of the Black Panther Party* (University of California Press, 2012), 19–23, 30–32.

7. For more on "sousveillance," or surveillance of the authorities "from below," see Simone Browne, *Dark Matters: On the Surveillance of Blackness*. Duke University Press, 2015).

8. Bloom and Martin, *Black against Empire*, 34, 38–39, 43–44.

9. Bloom and Martin, *Black against Empire*, 2–3, 47–48, 57–61, 159.

10. Beckford, "Oral History with Ruth Beckford."

11. Bloom and Martin, *Black against Empire*, 184.

12. Bloom and Martin, *Black against Empire*; Murch, *Living for the City*; Rhomberg, *No There There*; Ananya Roy, Stuart Schrader, and Emma Shaw Crane, "Gray Areas: The War on Poverty at Home and Abroad," in *Territories of Poverty: Rethinking North and South*, ed. Ananya Roy and Emma Shaw Crane (University of Georgia Press, 2015); Self, *American Babylon*.

13. Avery F. Gordon, "Something More Powerful than Skepticism," in *Keeping Good Time: Reflections on Knowledge, Power, and People* (Routledge, 2015 [2004]), 187.

14. In 2020, Barrows Hall—home to the Departments of African American Studies and Ethnic Studies—was unnamed in light of the fact that David Prescott Barrows, university president from 1919 to 1923, was an outspoken racist and agent of colonization in the Philippines. As of 2025, the building was referred to as the Social Sciences Building.

15. Rickey Vincent, *Party Music: The Inside Story of the Black Panthers' Band and How Black Power Transformed Soul Music* (Lawrence Hill Books, 2013), xiv.

16. For more on the role of "funkateers" in the mythic, extraterrestrial narrative of Parliament Funkadelic, see Tony Bolden, "Groove Theory: A Vamp on the Epistemology of Funk," *American Quarterly* 52, no. 4 (2013): 9–34.

17. Vincent, interview by author.

18. Self, *American Babylon*, 223.

19. Vincent, interview by author. This line is a reference to Parliament, "Give Up the Funk (Tear the Roof Off the Sucker)," *Mothership Connection*, Casablanca, 1975, NBLP 7022, vinyl, LP, album. Oakland's MC Hammer sampled Parliament in MC Hammer, "Turn This Mutha Out," *Let's Get It Started*, Capitol Records, 1988, C1–90924, vinyl, LP, album.

20. Vincent, interview by author.

21. Clyde Woods, "'Sittin' on Top of the World': The Challenges of Blues and Hip Hop Geographies," in *Black Geographies and the Politics of Place*, ed. Katherine McKittrick and Clyde Woods (South End Press, 2007), 54. See also Clyde Woods, *Development Arrested: The Blues and Plantation Power in the Mississippi Delta* (Verso, 2017 [1998]).

22. Murch, *Living for the City*, 11.

23. Vincent, *Party Music*, 3.

24. Vincent, interview by author.

25. Ibid.

26. Vincent, *Party Music*, xv.

27. Vincent, *Party Music*, xiv.

28. Greg Bridges, interview by author, January 19, 2018.

29. Vincent, *Party Music*, 20–31.

30. Vincent, *Party Music*, 220–21; The Lumpen, *Free Bobby Now / No More, Seize the Time*, 1970, BPP-4501-A, vinyl, 7", single.

31. Vincent, *Party Music*, 37–42.

32. Vincent, *Party Music*, 32.

33. Quoted in Vincent, *Party Music*, 33; Sly and the Family Stone, "Dance to the Music," *Dance to the Music*, Epic, 1967, 5–10256, vinyl, 7", single.

34. Bridges, interview by author; The Impressions, "We're a Winner," *We're a Winner*, ABC Records, 1967, 45–11022, vinyl, 7", single; The Staple Singers, "Respect Yourself," *Respect Yourself*, Stax, 1971, STA-0104, vinyl, 7", single.

35. This account is based on an audio recording of a Lumpen concert at Merritt College in November 1970, Box 4, Folders 5–6, Huey P. Newton Foundation Inc. Collection, Department of Special Collections and University Archives, Stanford University Libraries, Stanford, CA; The Impressions, "People Get Ready," *People Get Ready / I've Been Trying*, ABC-Paramount, 1965, 45–10622, vinyl, 7", single.

36. Ibid.

37. Vincent, *Party Music*, 95–96.

38. The Temptations, "My Girl," *My Girl / (Talkin' 'Bout) Nobody but My Baby*, Gordy, 1964, Gordy-7038, vinyl, 7", single.

39. James Brown, "Papa's Got a Brand New Bag," *Papa's Got a Brand New Bag*, King Records, 1965, 938, vinyl, LP, album.

40. Veal, *Dub*, 246.

41. Rickey Vincent, *Funk: The Music, the People, and the Rhythm of the One* (St. Martin's Press, 1996), 37; James Brown, "Get Up (I Feel Like Being a) Sex Machine," *Get Up (I Feel Like Being a) Sex Machine*, King Records, 1970, 45–6318, vinyl, 7", single; James Brown, "The Payback," *The Payback*, Polydor, 1973, PD 14223, vinyl, 7", single; James Brown, "Papa Don't Take No Mess," *Papa Don't Take No Mess*, Polydor, 1974, PD 14255, vinyl, 7", single.

42. Quoted in Vincent, *Party Music*, 95–96.

43. Quoted in Selvin, *Sly & The Family Stone*, 1–3.

44. Quoted in Selvin, *Sly & The Family Stone*, 17.

45. Quoted in Selvin, *Sly & The Family Stone*, 21, 31.

46. While many of the East Bay's blues musicians would continue to record and perform for decades, their listeners became increasingly young and White rather than Black. Big Mama Thornton, for instance, enjoyed some of the greatest commercial success of her career playing for White audiences in San Francisco and Europe as part of the 1960s "blues revival" that took off among members of the White counterculture and folk scene, who found, in African American blues, a sound of racial authenticity that they were craving. See Mahon, "Listening for Willie Mae." To remain relevant to young Black audiences, other musicians updated their sound. In 1972, for instance, Jimmy McCracklin released a new recording of his 1961 hit "Just Got to Know." While the original, released on Bob Geddins's Art-Tone Records, is a classic 12-bar blues with blaring saxophone and boogie woogie piano, the 1972 version—which appeared on the appropriately titled *Yesterday Is Gone*, put out by Stax Records—is driven by prominent percussion that's organized around "the One" and a funky horn section. His vocal performance goes from resonating with sadness to something more like sex. See Jimmy McCracklin, "Just Got to Know," *The Drag / Just Got to Know*, Art-Tone Records, 1961, 825, vinyl, 7", single; Jimmy McCracklin, "Just Got to Know," *Yesterday Is Gone*, Stax, 1972, STS-2047, vinyl, LP, album.

47. Sly and the Family Stone, "Everyday People," *Everyday People*, Epic, 1968, 5–10407, vinyl, 7", single; Sly and the Family Stone, "Stand!," *Stand!*, Epic, 1969, BN 26456, vinyl, LP, album.

48. Vincent, *Party Music*, 51–52, 59; Sly and the Family Stone, "Dance to the Music."

49. Naomi Macalalad Bragin, "Black Power of Hip Hop Dance: On Kinesthetic Politics" (PhD diss., University of California, Berkeley, 2015), 32.

50. Selvin, *Sly & The Family Stone*, 28–30, 40, 47–48.

51. Sly and the Family Stone, "Thank You (Falettinme Be Mice Elf Agin")"; Sly and the Family Stone, "Thank You for Talkin' to Me Africa," *There's a Riot Goin' On*, Epic, 1971, KE 30986, vinyl, LP, album.

52. Veal, *Dub*, 13.

53. Braxton D. Shelley, "Analyzing Gospel," *Journal of the American Musicological Society* 72, no. 1 (2019): 181–243; Sly and the Family Stone, "I Want to Take You Higher."

54. Bolden, "Groove Theory," 9, 15–16.

55. Imani K. Johnson, "Music Meant to Make You Move: Considering the Aural Kinesthetic," *Sounding Out!*, June 18, 2012, online.

56. Eric Arnold, "The Bay Area Was Hip-Hop before There Was Hip-Hop," *KQED*, February 1, 2023, online. The Bay Area's role in the advent of hip-hop dance is largely overlooked due to the fact that popping first reached a national audience when a Fresno-based group called the Electric Boogaloos performed on *Soul Train* in 1979. At the time, host Don Cornelius credited the group with the style. But according to the filmmaker Spencer Wilkinson, who is working with Arnold on a documentary about Bay Area street dance in the 1960s and '70s, the Electric Boogaloos likely derived their name, costume, and choreography from an encounter with West Oakland's Derrick and Company at a battle in Sacramento in 1976. Thanks to recent advocacy from surviving practitioners of the Oakland boogaloo, the city's role in the invention of popping is now in the process of being restored. Spencer Wilkinson, interview by author, January 4, 2023.

57. Thomas Guzman-Sanchez, *Underground Dance Masters: Final History of a Forgotten Era* (Praeger, 2012), 8–9.

58. Wilkinson, interview by author.

59. Ibid. The concert—part of the most elaborate, expensive tour ever produced for a Black musical artist at that time—was recorded and released as *Live: P. Funk Earth Tour* (1977). The album contains a mix of songs from the Oakland Coliseum and a previous stop at the Los Angeles Forum.

60. Macalalad Bragin, *Black Power of Hip Hop Dance*, 1–2, 23–24, 35–36.

61. Quoted in Naomi Macalalad Bragin, *Kinethic California: Dancing Funk and Disco Era Kinships* (University of Michigan Press, 2024), 109.

62. Wilkinson, interview by author.

63. Agnès Varda, dir., *Black Panthers*, film recording, 1968, Ciné Tamaris, Kanopy.

64. For more on the politics of "insurgent visibility," see Raiford, *Imprisoned in a Luminous Glare*.

65. Parlet, *Pleasure Principle*, Casablanca, 1978, NBLP 7094, vinyl, LP, album.

66. Robin D. G. Kelley, *Yo' Mama's Disfunktional!: Fighting the Culture Wars in Urban America* (Beacon Press, 1997), 16–17, 41.

67. Bolden, "Groove Theory," 10.

3. INTO THE CRACK

1. Bloom and Martin, *Black against Empire*, 199–200, 209–11.
2. Bloom and Martin, *Black against Empire*, 367–69, 380.
3. Carmichael, "Speech."
4. Murch, *Living for the City*, 227.
5. Quoted in Self, *American Babylon*, 313.
6. Lionel J. Wilson, *Lionel Wilson: Athlete, Judge, and Oakland Mayor*, Black Alumni Club, University of California, Berkeley, 1995, Bancroft Library, University of California, Berkeley, CA, 9–10.
7. Self, *American Babylon*, 312–14.
8. Adolph Reed Jr., *Stirrings in the Jug: Black Politics in the Post-Segregation Era* (University of Minnesota Press, 1999).
9. Parliament, "Chocolate City," *Chocolate City*, Casablanca, 1975, NBLP 7014, vinyl, LP, album.
10. Rhomberg, *No There There*, 183; Self, *American Babylon*, 312–14.
11. Wilson, *Varieties of Police Behavior*, 123–26.
12. Wilson, *Varieties of Police Behavior*, 193.
13. Wilson, *Varieties of Police Behavior*, 172, 180–84.
14. Charles Fain Lehman, "Contra 'Root Causes': What the Work of James Q. Wilson Can Teach Us about the Fight over Criminal Justice Today," *City Journal*, Summer 2021, online.
15. James Q. Wilson and George L. Kelling, "Broken Windows: The Police and Neighborhood Safety," *Atlantic Monthly* 249, no. 3 (1982): 29–38. See also Bernard E. Harcourt, *Illusion of Order: The False Promise of Broken Windows Policing* (Harvard University Press, 2001).
16. Quoted in Elaine Woo, "James Q. Wilson Dies at 80; Pioneer in 'Broken Windows' Approach to Improve Policing," *Los Angeles Times*, March 3, 2021, online.
17. Rudolph Giuliani, "What New York Owes James Q. Wilson," *City Journal*, Spring 2012, online.
18. Alex S. Vitale and Brian J. Jefferson, "The Emergence of Command and Control Policing in Neoliberal New York," in *Policing the Planet: Why the Policing Crisis Led to Black Lives Matter*, ed. Jordan T. Camp and Christina Heatherton (Verso, 2016).
19. Rhomberg, *No There There*, 102.

20. Crouchett, Bunch III, and Winnacker, *Visions toward Tomorrow*, 53.

21. Huey P. Newton, *Revolutionary Suicide* (Penguin Books, 2009 [1973]), 249.

22. Johnson, *Second Gold Rush*, 54, 200–201.

23. Nathan McClintock, "From Industrial Garden to Food Desert: Demarcated Devaluation in the Flatlands of Oakland, California," in *Cultivating Food Justice: Race, Class, and Sustainability*, ed. Alison Hope Alkon and Julian Agyeman (MIT Press, 2011), 103.

24. Self, *American Babylon*, 171.

25. Richard Rothstein, *The Color of Law: A Forgotten History of How Our Government Segregated America* (Liveright, 2018).

26. Mitchell Schwarzer, *Hella Town: Oakland's History of Development and Disruption* (University of California Press, 2021), 244.

27. Will D. Tate, *The New Black Urban Elites* (R&E Research Associates, 1976), 7, Environmental Design Library, University of California, Berkeley, CA.

28. Murch, *Living for the City*, 8.

29. Self, *American Babylon*, 172–74.

30. Edith K. Hill, "Oral History with Edith Katherine Hill," interviewed by Nadine Wilmot, 1998, BANC MSS 2006/112, Box 1, Oakland Oral History Project, Bancroft Library, University of California, Berkeley, CA.

31. Self, *American Babylon*, 166–67.

32. Self, *American Babylon*, 156, 165.

33. Jordan T. Camp and Christina Heatherton, eds., *Policing the Planet: Why the Policing Crisis Led to Black Lives Matter* (Verso, 2016); Jamie Peck and Adam Tickell, "Neoliberalizing Space," *Antipode* 34, no. 3 (2002): 380–404. The figures on War on Poverty spending in Oakland are cited in Herrera, *Cartographic Memory*, 63.

34. Ruth W. Gilmore, *Golden Gulag: Prisons, Surplus, Crisis, and Opposition in Globalizing California* (University of California Press, 2007). For more on the ways that Oakland's empowerment programs became a site of political organizing, see Rhomberg, *No There There*, chap. 7; Self, *American Babylon*, chap. 5.

35. Quoted in Dan Baum, "Legalize It All: How to Win the War on Drugs," *Harper's*, April 22, 2016, online.

36. Robert S. Oden, *From Blacks to Brown and Beyond: The Struggle for Progressive Politics in Oakland, California, 1966–2011* (Cognella, 2012), 41–43.

37. Proposition 13 capped property taxes at one percent of assessed value and then limited the rate at which that value, and thus an owner's tax bill, could be reassessed. This giveaway to the ownership class applied not only to single-family homes but also to multi-family, commercial, and industrial properties.

38. Quoted in Self, *American Babylon*, 316.

39. Roger L. Kemp, *Coping with Proposition 13* (Lexington Books, 1980), 4; Self, *American Babylon*, 316–25. Meanwhile, voters in suburban Alameda County were more than 70 percent in favor.

40. Kemp, *Coping with Proposition 13*, 1–5.

41. Kemp, *Coping with Proposition 13*, 119–23.

42. Newton, *Revolutionary Suicide*, 202.

43. For more on the role of the CIA in the rise of the crack epidemic, see Gary Webb, *Dark Alliance: The CIA, the Contras, and the Crack Cocaine Explosion* (Seven Stories Press, 1998).

44. University–Oakland Metropolitan Forum, *Oakland's Economy in the 1990's: A Sourcebook of Planning and Community Development Issues Facing the City, Its Neighborhoods, and the Region* (Institute of Urban and Regional Development, University of California, Berkeley, 1990), 1A2, 1–2, Environmental Design Library, University of California, Berkeley, CA.

45. While the people criminalized during the War on Drugs were overwhelmingly boys and men, girls, women, and queer and trans people of color have also long confronted exploitation and criminalization via the production and policing of sex work. Oakland consistently ranks as one of the foremost centers of sex trafficking in the U. S.

46. Mark Michaels, "Crackdown," *East Bay Express*, July 25, 1986, 1, Institute for Governmental Studies Library, University of California, Berkeley, CA.

47. Bridges, interview by author.

48. Dashka Slater, "The Other Epidemic: Fatal Encounters with Crack," *East Bay Express*, October 9, 1998, 14, Magazine and Newspaper Room, Main Branch, Oakland Public Library, Oakland, CA.

49. Urban Strategies Council, *Call to Action: An Oakland Blueprint for Youth Development* (Urban Strategies Council, 1996), 32, Institute for Governmental Studies Library, University of California, Berkeley, CA.

50. Winston and BondGraham, *The Riders*, 175.

51. Michelle Alexander, *The New Jim Crow: Mass Incarceration in the Age of Colorblindness* (New Press, 2010); Gilmore, *Golden Gulag*.

52. Tanya Maria Golash-Boza, *Before Gentrification: The Creation of DC's Racial Wealth Gap* (University of California Press, 2023).

53. Edwin Meese III, "Address of the Honorable Edwin Meese III, Attorney General of the United States, before the San Diego Crime Commission," September 27, 1985, San Diego, California, transcript accessed online through U.S. Department of Justice.

54. Winston and BondGraham, *The Riders*, 169.

55. Alexander, *New Jim Crow*, 98.

56. Winston and BondGraham, *The Riders*, 175.

57. Urban Strategies Council, *Call to Action*, 43.

58. Winston and BondGraham, *The Riders*, 175.

59. Self, *American Babylon*, 25–28, 138–39.

60. Newton, *Revolutionary Suicide*, 13–14.

61. Self, *American Babylon*, 150–55.

62. Moriah Ulinskas, "Imagining a Past Future: Photographs from the Oakland Redevelopment Agency," *Places Journal*, January 2019, online.

63. Quoted in Schwarzer, *Hella Town*, 274.

64. Mitchell Schwarzer, "Oakland City Center: The Plan to Reposition Downtown within the Bay Region," *Journal of Planning History* 14, no. 2 (2015): 88–111. One of these blocks remained a hole in the earth all the way until 2018, when record-low commercial vacancies finally convinced the developer Shorenstein Properties to "break ground."

65. Richard Walker, "Oakland: Dark Star in an Expanding Universe" (unpublished manuscript, 1997).

66. Michael D. Spear, "Investor Perceptions of Downtown Oakland," Symposium for Business Leaders, Holy Names College, Oakland, CA, October 17, 1986, Institute for Governmental Studies Library, University of California, Berkeley, CA.

67. Cynthia Kroll, *Downtown Oakland and the Regional Economy* (University–Oakland Metropolitan Forum, 1987), 5–6, 84–88, Environmental Design Library, University of California, Berkeley, CA.

68. Jay D. Starling, *Municipal Coping Strategies: "As Soon as the Dust Settles"* (Sage Publications, 1985), 53, Environmental Design Library, University of California, Berkeley, CA.

69. Theo Aytchan Williams, interview by author, September 5, 2017.

70. Oakland Interagency Council on Drugs, *Report to the City of Oakland, Covering the Period September 1, 1984 to December 31, 1984* (City of Oakland, 1985), app. I, p. 8, Institute for Governmental Studies Library, University of California, Berkeley, CA.

71. Oakland Interagency Council on Drugs, *Report to the City of Oakland*, app. I, p. 4.

72. Oden, *From Blacks to Brown*, 136–37.

73. These statistics are based on U.S. Census data from www.bayareacensus.ca.gov. While immigration from Asia and Latin America increased after 1965, Oakland had long been home to significant communities of Chinese, Japanese, and Mexican American residents. See Herrera, *Cartographic Memory;* Ma, *Hometown Chinatown.*

74. Jennifer Tilton, *Dangerous or Endangered?: Race and the Politics of Youth in Urban America* (New York University Press, 2010), 174.

75. Victor M. Rios, *Punished: Policing the Lives of Black and Latino Boys* (New York University Press, 2011), 18. See also Tilton, *Dangerous or Endangered*, 173–75.

76. Emerson Street, "Nightstick Justice in Oakland," *New Republic*, February 20, 1950, 15, Institute for Governmental Studies Library, University of California, Berkeley, CA.

77. Vitale and Jefferson, "Emergence of Command and Control Policing," 158, 160.

78. Robin D.G. Kelley, "Thug Nation: On State Violence and Disposability," in *Policing the Planet: Why the Policing Crisis Led to Black Lives Matter*, ed. Jordan T. Camp and Christina Heatherton (Verso, 2016), 21.

79. Tilton, *Dangerous or Endangered*, 55–56.

80. Eisenberg, "The People and the Police."

81. In 2004, following the passage of Measure Y, a parcel tax that funded community policing, Community Policing Officers were rebranded Problem Solving Officers. They are now known as Community Resource Officers.

82. Wilson and Kelling, "Broken Windows."

83. Tilton, *Dangerous or Endangered*, 33–35, 60–66.

84. Tom DeVries, "The New Urban Guerillas," *California*, September 1989, 62, Institute for Governmental Studies Library, University of California, Berkeley, CA.

85. Quoted in Julian Lucas, "Ishmael Reed Gets the Last Laugh," *New Yorker*, July 19, 2021, online.

86. Reed, *Blues City*, 26–28.

87. Lucas, "Ishmael Reed."

88. Ishmael Reed, "Noise Torture Thrives in Oakland," *Oakland Tribune*, February 3, 2004, Local 5; Ishmael Reed, "The Peace-and-Quiet Bandits," *Oakland Tribune*, September 21, 2005, Local 6, Magazine and Newspaper Room, Main Branch, Oakland Public Library, Oakland, CA. See also Ishmael Reed, *Mumbo Jumbo* (Scribner, 2022 [1972]).

4. BLACK NOISE

1. Margurite Fuller, "Letter: Obnoxious Boom Boxes," *Oakland Tribune*, September 22, 2005, Magazine and Newspaper Room, Main Branch, Oakland Public Library, Oakland, CA.

2. Watkins, "Oral History with Earl Watkins."

3. Collins, "Jazzing Up Seventh Street," 322.

4. For more on the impact of disco parties and DJing techniques on popular music and nightlife, see Lawrence, *Love Saves the Day*.

5. Steven Waksman, *Live Music in America: A History from Jenny Lind to Beyoncé* (Oxford University Press, 2022), 482.

6. Lawrence, *Love Saves the Day*, 128.

7. For more on the advent of new audio technologies as a means to enhance the experience of dancers at disco and house music clubs, see Salkind, *Do You Remember House*, chap. 2.

8. Lee Hildebrand, interview by author, April 20, 2017.

9. Carl Greene and Edward Hawthorne, interview by author, March 4, 2017.

10. Lee Hildebrand, "Juke Joint Rambles, Midnight Crawls," in *Bay Area Blues*, photographs by Michelle Vignes (Pomegranate, 1993), 10–11, African American Museum and Library at Oakland, Oakland Public Library, Oakland, CA.

11. Rose, *Black Noise*, 63.

12. For more on the lineage of funk music in hip-hop, see Chang, *Can't Stop Won't Stop*; Vincent, *Funk*, chaps. 20–21.

13. George Ciccariello-Maher and Jeff St. Andrews, "Between Macks and Panthers: Hip Hop in Oakland and San Francisco," in *Hip Hop in America: A Regional Guide*, ed. Mickey Hess (Greenwood Press, 2010), 267.

14. Eric Arnold, *Hip-Hop Atlas of the Bay* (Oakland Museum of California, 2018), 7; Ciccariello-Maher and St. Andrews, "Between Macks and Panthers," 268; Digital Underground, "Same Song," *This Is an E.P. Release*, Tommy Boy, 1991, TBCD 964, CD, EP; Parliament, "Theme from the Black Hole," *Theme from the Black Hole*, Casablanca, 1979, NB 2235, vinyl, 7", single; Tupac, "I Get Around," *I Get Around*, Interscope Records, 1993, 0–96036, vinyl, 12", single.

15. Alec Banks, "The Oakland Police Lawsuit, the Gangsta Rap Defense, and Chokeholds," *Rock the Bells*, August 20, 2020, online.

16. Lavar Pope, *Rap and Politics: A Case Study of Panther, Gangster, and Hyphy Discourses in Oakland, CA (1965–2010)* (Palgrave Macmillan, 2020).

17. Wilkinson, interview by author.

18. Arnold, *Hip-Hop Atlas*, 3.

19. The Oakland Coliseum also turned out to be a crucial site in the career of Too Short, who started hawking tapes from the parking lot in 1981 at age 15. Ciccariello-Maher and St. Andrews, "Between Macks and Panthers," 261.

20. Quoted in Jeffrey Ressner, "Hammer Time: America's Most Popular Rapper Is Also a Demanding Taskmaster," *Rolling Stone*, September 6, 1990, online; MC Hammer, "Ring 'Em," *Feel My Power*, Bustin' Records, 1987, BR-LP-001, vinyl, LP, album.

21. Larry Kelp, "Oaktown Revival," *Oakland Tribune*, August 19, 1990, Music Rap Dec 1985–Dec 1990, Hayward Area Historical Society, Hayward, CA.

22. Arnold, *Hip-Hop Atlas*, 11.

23. Ressner, "Hammer Time."

24. For more on the transition of KMEL from a rock station to one of the most influential rap stations in the country, see Arnold, *Hip-Hop Atlas*, 4; Chang, *Can't Stop Won't Stop*, 440–41.

25. Waksman, *Live Music in America*, 500–502.

26. Arnold, *Hip-Hop Atlas*, 3; Larry Kelp, 1989, "Welcome to 'Oaktown,' Rap Capital U.S.A.," *Oakland Tribune*, October 8, 1989, Music Rap Dec 1985–Dec 1990, Hayward Area Historical Society, Hayward, CA.

27. C. J. Clemmons and Craig Anderson, "Shooting Reports Conflict at Rap Concert," *Oakland Tribune*, October 15, 1989, Music Rap Dec 1985–Dec 1990, Hayward Area Historical Society, Hayward, CA.

28. Hildebrand, interview by author.

29. C. J. Clemmons and Harry Harris, "Coliseum Will Screen Rap Acts to Avert Concert Violence," *Oakland Tribune*, October 17, 1989, A7, Magazine and Newspaper Room, Main Branch, Oakland Public Library, Oakland, CA.

30. Kevin Fagan, "Oakland to Host First Major Concert in a Year," *Oakland Tribune*, November 18, 1990, A1, Magazine and Newspaper Room, Main Branch, Oakland Public Library, Oakland, CA.

31. Fagan, "Oakland to Host."

32. Ressner, "Hammer Time."

33. Arnold, *Hip-Hop Atlas*, 13.

34. Rose, *Black Noise*, 124–39.

35. Chuck Phillips, "Beating the Rap of Concert Violence," *Los Angeles Times*, February 10, 1991, online; N. W. A., "Fuck the Police," *Straight Outta Compton*, Ruthless Records, 1988, SL 57102, vinyl, LP, album.

36. Phillips, "Beating the Rap."

37. Murray Forman, *The 'Hood Comes First: Race, Space, and Place in Rap and Hip-Hop* (Wesleyan University Press, 2002), 141–42.

38. Waksman, *Live Music in America*, 513.

39. Ronald Brooks, David Elliot, and Neil Johnson, "Media Distorts Rap-Music Violence," *Oakland Tribune*, November 18, 1990, Music Rap Dec 1985–Dec 1990, Hayward Area Historical Society, Hayward, CA.

40. Phillips, "Beating the Rap."

41. Quoted in Fagan, "Oakland to Host."

42. Quoted in William Brand, "Rap on Trial: Event Outcome to Decide Future Policy," *Oakland Tribune*, December 28, 1990, A1, Magazine and Newspaper Room, Main Branch, Oakland Public Library, Oakland, CA.

43. Quoted in Robert J. Lopez, "Rappers Return with Safe Show: Tight Security Keeps Night Peaceful," *Oakland Tribune*, December 30, 1990, A1, Magazine and Newspaper Room, Main Branch, Oakland Public Library, Oakland, CA.

44. Dave Becker, "Promoters, Rappers Debate Future of Concerts," *Oakland Tribune*, May 19, 1996, Music Rap 1996, Hayward Area Historical Society, Hayward, CA.

45. Karin Bijsterveld, "The Diabolical Symphony of the Mechanical Age: Technology and Symbolism of Sound in European and North American Noise Abatement Campaigns, 1900–40," *Social Studies of Science* 31, no. 1 (2001): 37–70; Radovac, "The 'War on Noise.'"

46. Oakland Police Department, *Rules and Regulations for the Government of the Police Department, Oakland, Cal* (City of Oakland, 1912), Bancroft Library, University of California, Berkeley, CA.

47. Chang, *Can't Stop Won't Stop*.

48. Joseph G. Schloss and Bill Bahng Boyer, "Urban Echoes: The Boombox and Sonic Mobility in the 1980s," in *The Oxford Handbook of Mobile Music Studies* ed. Sumanth Gopinath and Jason Stanyek (Oxford University Press, 2014).

49. Schloss and Bahng Boyer, "Urban Echoes," 407.

50. For more on the cultural impact of the Walkman, see Michael Bull, *Sounding Out the City: Personal Stereos and the Management of Everyday Life* (Berg, 2000).

51. Editorial, "Striking the Wrong Note," *Oakland Tribune*, July 9, 1978, Oakland, Calif. Noise Legislation, Hayward Area Historical Society, Hayward, CA.

52. City of Oakland Ordinances #10029 C. M. S. (1981) and #11200 C. M. S. (1990), public records requested by author.

53. "Council to Study Measure to End Noise Pollution," *Oakland Tribune*, August 29, 1971, Oakland, Calif. Noise Legislation, Hayward Area Historical Society, Hayward, CA. The law was based on a model ordinance developed by the League of California Cities.

54. City of Oakland Municipal Code Section 8.18.010, "Excessive and Annoying Noises Prohibited."

55. City of Oakland Ordinance #11200 C. M. S.

56. Joel F. Brenner, "Nuisance Law and the Industrial Revolution," *Journal of Legal Studies* 3, no. 2 (1974): 403–33; Mariana Valverde, "Seeing Like a City: The Dialectic of Modern and Premodern Ways of Seeing in Urban Governance," *Law and Society Review* 45, no. 2 (2011): 277–312.

57. Schloss and Bahng Boyer, "Urban Echoes," 408.

58. Peter Marks, "Street Crackdown's Aim: Turn Down That Stereo!," *New York Times*, June 13, 1993, sec. 1, p. 39; Nick Ravo, "The Noise Police Take the Boom Out of the Bronx," *New York Times*, October 6, 1991, sec. 1, p. 32, online.

59. Quoted in Marks, "Street Crackdown's Aim."

60. Mike Fitelson, "City Moves to Bolster Noise Rules," *Montclarion*, February 23, 1996, 3; Nancy L. Valcke, "Noise Hotline: Oakland Quieter than Expected," *Montclarion*, May 16, 1997, 1, Magazine and Newspaper Room, Main Branch, Oakland Public Library, Oakland, CA; Judith Scherr, "City Requests Stricter Noise Pollution Law," *Montclarion*, December 21, 1993, 1, Noise, Oakland, Calif., Hayward Area Historical Society, Hayward, CA.

61. Greene and Hawthorne, interview by author.

62. Ed Blakely, interview by author, June 24, 2017.

63. Blakely, interview by author.

64. Rose, *Black Noise*, 64–65, 81.

65. Rose, *Black Noise*, 63.

66. E-40 featuring Keak Da Sneak, "Tell Me When to Go," *My Ghetto Report Card*, Reprise Records, 2006, 49963–2, CD, album.

67. Andrea L. Smith, "Hyphy Intellect: The Formation of Bay Area Hip Hop Identities in the Realm of Commercial Culture" (PhD diss., University of California, Davis, 2011), 208–15. See also Ciccariello-Maher and St. Andrews, "Between Macks and Panthers."

5. THE SIDESHOW

1. E-40 featuring Keak Da Sneak, "Tell Me When to Go."

2. Material from this chapter was first published in French; Alex Werth, "Le Rodéo Sauvage," in *Nos Lieux Communs: Une Géographie du Monde Contemporain*, ed. Michel Bussi, Martine Drozdz, and Fabrice Argounès (Fayard, 2024). Used with permission.

3. John G. Stehlin, *Cyclescapes of the Unequal City: Bicycle Infrastructure and Uneven Development* (University of Minnesota Press, 2019), chap. 5.

4. Author field notes from October 19, 2015.

5. Campbell, *Afrosonic Life*, 36.

6. Quoted in Yakpasua Zazaboi, dir., *Sydewayz*, film recording, Sydewayz Media, 2006 (access provided by Yakpasua Zazaboi).

7. Yakpasua Zazaboi, interviews by author, July 6, 2022, and February 22, 2023.

8. Lipsitz, *How Racism Takes Place*, 64. See also Zanfagna, *Holy Hip Hop*, 16.

9. Watkins, "Oral History with Earl Watkins."

10. Brandon LaBelle, *Acoustic Territories: Sound Culture and Everyday Life* (Continuum, 2010), 142.

11. This account is based on a review of *Oakland Tribune* articles filed under Cruising at the Hayward Area Historical Society, Hayward, CA.

12. Cf. James Forman Jr., *Locking Up Our Own: Crime and Punishment in Black America* (Farrar, Straus and Giroux, 2017), 53.

13. Zazaboi, interviews by author.

14. Christina Cielo, "Civic Sideshows: Communities and Publics in East Oakland" (Institute for the Study of Social Change, University of California, Berkeley, 2005), 16–20, online.

15. Arnold, *Hip-Hop Atlas*, 4. For more on the importance of Soul Beat, see Eric Ducker, "The Untold History of Oakland's Soul Beat, a Pioneer among Black-Owned TV Networks," *Medium*, May 12, 2020, online.

16. Gaye T. Johnson, *Spaces of Conflict, Sounds of Solidarity: Music, Race, and Spatial Entitlement in Los Angeles* (University of California Press, 2013), 156.

17. Johnson, *Spaces of Conflict*, xi.

18. Zazaboi, interviews by author.

19. Quoted in Sean Maher, "Summer without Sideshows Celebrated in Oakland," *Oakland Tribune*, October 19, 2010, online.

20. Mike Davis, *City of Quartz: Excavating the Future in Los Angeles* (Vintage Books, 1992 [1990]), 242–44.

21. Quoted in Chauncey Bailey, "Reviving Eastmont Challenges Manager," *Oakland Tribune*, June 6, 1993, Eastmont Shopping Center, Oakland, Calif. 1991–, Hayward Area Historical Society, Hayward, CA.

22. Harry Harris, "140 Cops Get New Base at Eastmont," *Oakland Tribune*, October 19, 2004, News 1; Deborah S. Kim, "Oakland Police Go to the People," *Oakland Tribune*, August 14, 1992, A3, Magazine and Newspaper Room, Main Branch, Oakland Public Library, Oakland, CA.

23. Gino Pastori-Ng, interviews by author, February 3 and February 10, 2023, and July 23, 2024.

24. Pastori-Ng, interviews by author; Yukmouth, "City of Dope," *Thugged Out: The Albulation*, Rap-A-Lot Records, 1998, 7243 8 46720 2 7, CD, album.

25. Pendarvis Harshaw, *OG Told Me* (self-pub., 2017), 49.

26. Zazaboi, interviews by author.

27. Pascal Menoret, *Joyriding in Riyadh: Oil, Urbanism, and Road Revolt* (Cambridge University Press, 2014), 166.

28. For more on representations of masculinity, sex, and violence in rap music, see Rose, *Black Noise*; Tricia Rose, *The Hip Hop Wars: What We Talk About When We Talk About Hip Hop—and Why It Matters* (Basic Books, 2008). For a queer reading of masculinity and homophobia in dancehall culture, see Nadia Ellis, "Out and Bad: Toward a Queer Performance Hermeneutic in Jamaican Dancehall," *Small Axe: A Caribbean Journal of Criticism* 15, no. 2 (2011): 7–23.

29. Zazaboi, interviews by author.

30. Roberto Bedoya, "Spatial Justice: Rasquachification, Race and the City," *Creative Time Reports*, September 15, 2014, online.

31. Pastori-Ng, interviews by author; Sirealz, "4 15's in the Trunk," *Save Some 4 Later*, 2011, no label, no catalog no., CD, album.

32. Pastori-Ng, interviews by author.

33. Weheliye, *Phonographies*, 107.

34. Boots Riley, dir., "You a Big Muthaf***a," *I'm a Virgo*, television series, season 1, episode 1, Media Res and Amazon Studios, 2023, Prime Video; Mac Dre, "Feelin' Myself," *Ronald Dregan: Dreganomics*, Thizz Entertainment, 2004, THZ 1065, CD, album; Mount Westmore, "Big Subwoofer," *Snoop Cube 40 $hort*, MNRK Music Group, 2002, MNK-CD-46871, CD, album.

35. 3X Krazy, "Keep It on the Real," *Keep It on the Real*, Noo Trybe Records, 1997, 7243 8 38584 2 2, CD, single; Luniz, "I Got 5 on It," *I Got 5 on It*, Noo Trybe Records, 1995, 7243 8 38474 2 6, CD, single.

36. Quoted in Laurence Madrigal, dir., *We Were Hyphy*, film recording, Castle G Productions, 2022, PBS Online.

37. Pendarvis Harshaw and Olivia Allen-Price, "'It's Pure Energy': How Hyphy Came to Define Bay Area Hip-Hop," *KQED*, July 22, 2021, online.

38. Andrea L. S. Moore, "Hyphy Sparked a Social Movement," *Ethnic Studies Review* 37, no. 1 (2017): 45–62, at 45.

39. Quoted in Madrigal, *We Were Hyphy*.

40. See Rios, *Punished*, 118.

41. Pope, *Rap and Politics*, 254.

42. Traxamillion featuring Too Short and Mistah F. A. B., "Sideshow," *The Slapp Addict*, Slapp Addict Productions, 2006, 5, CD, album.

43. Naomi Macalalad Bragin, "Shot and Captured: Turf Dance, YAK Films, and the Oakland, California, R. I. P. Project," *TDR / The Drama Review* 58, no. 2 (2014): 99–114.

44. Quoted in DJ Vlad, dir., *Ghostride the Whip*, film recording, Rugged Entertainment, 2008, Prime Video.

45. E-40 featuring Keak Da Sneak, "Tell Me When to Go."

46. Harshaw, *OG Told Me*, 26; Smith, *Hyphy Intellect*, 42.

47. Terror Squad featuring Fat Joe and Remy Ma, "Lean Back," *True Story*, Universal Records, 2004, B0002806–02, CD, album.

48. Quoted in Madrigal, *We Were Hyphy*.

49. E-40 featuring Keak Da Sneak, "Tell Me When to Go."

50. Lil Jon also produced "Blow the Whistle" by Too Short. Released one week apart, these two anthems marked the peak of hyphy's commercial success. Too Short, "Blow the Whistle," *Blow the Whistle*, Jive, 2006, 82876–83501–2, CD, album.

51. While acknowledging the sonic similarities between hyphy and crunk, which were cemented through the Atlanta-to-Oakland connection, Lavar Pope argues that hyphy—as a descendant of Oakland's Black radical discourses, and steeped in spatial struggles with the OPD—retained more political messages than its Southern counterpart. Pope, *Rap and Politics*, 230. But the ethnomusicologist Kevin Holt argues that the cultural politics of crunk were also a response to the surveillance and policing of Black youth in Atlanta's public space during the 1990s. Kevin C. Holt, "Get Crunk!: The Performative Resistance of Atlanta Hip-Hop Party Music" (PhD diss., Columbia University, 2018).

52. Fairfield is in Solano County, the most remote part of the Bay Area.

53. Bernard Gourley, dir., "Tell Me When to Go," music video, Immigrant Films, 2006, YouTube.

54. Beyoncé, "Get Me Bodied," *B'Day*, Columbia, 2006, 82876 88132 2, CD, album; Missy Elliott featuring Ciara and Fatman Scoop, "Lose Control," *The Cookbook*, Atlantic, 2005, 83779–2, CD, album; Usher featuring Lil Jon and Ludacris, "Yeah!," *Confessions*, Arista, 2004, 82876–52141–2, CD, album.

55. Philip A. Jamison, "Square Dance Calling: The African-American Connection," *Journal of Appalachian Studies* 9, no. 2 (2003): 387–98.

56. J. Douglas Allen-Taylor, "Showing Their Side," *East Bay Express*, March 12, 2003, online.

57. Tilton, *Dangerous or Endangered*, 156–58.

58. Oden, *From Blacks to Brown*, 205–6, 243–44.

59. Tilton, *Dangerous or Endangered*, 163–64.

60. Quoted in Jim DuPont, Elissa Dennis, and Tom Csekey, "Oakland for the Elite Only? As City Officials Urge Housing Downtown, Don't Forget the Others," *San Francisco Chronicle*, November 23, 1999, online.

61. Winston and BondGraham, *The Riders*, 37–39, 54, 78–79.

62. Quoted in Heather MacDonald, "Brown Wants to Criminalize 'Sideshow' Spectating," *Oakland Tribune*, May 27, 2005, online.

63. David Kozicki, interview by author, December 7, 2017.

64. Ibid.

65. Quoted in Mike Martinez, "Police Feel They Have Handle on Sideshow Cruisers," *Oakland Tribune*, August 19, 2001, Local 1, Magazine and Newspaper Room, Main Branch, Oakland Public Library, Oakland, CA.

66. Angela Buenning, "Sideshow Makes Problems for Community," *Oakland Post*, April 26, 1998, 2, Magazine and Newspaper Room, Main Branch, Oakland Public Library, Oakland, CA.

67. Pastori-Ng, interviews by author.

68. Kozicki, interview by author.

69. Pastori-Ng, interviews by author.

70. Zazaboi, *Sydewayz*.

71. Zazaboi, interviews by author.

72. Harry Harris and Laura Counts, "Extra Police to Monitor 'Sideshows,'" *Oakland Tribune*, March 17, 2002, Local 1; Brenda Payton, "Oakland Can No Longer Tolerate 'Sideshow' Dangers," *Oakland Tribune*, July 3, 2001, Local 1, Magazine and Newspaper Room, Main Branch, Oakland Public Library, Oakland, CA; Oakland Police Department, *A Report Regarding Two Alternatives to Address Sideshow Activities* (City of Oakland, June 7, 2005), public records requested by author.

73. Martinez, "Police Feel They Have Handle."

74. Kozicki, interview by author.

75. Kozicki, interview by author. The other two laws developed by Kozicki instituted new regulations and increased penalties meant to reduce noise from whistle tips, motorized scooters, and "pocket bikes."

76. Quoted in Steve Geissinger and Michael Geissinger, "Sideshow Law Lapse Blamed on the Bay Area," *Oakland Tribune*, February 18, 2007, online.

77. Kozicki, interview by author.

78. Pastori-Ng, interviews by author.

79. Oakland Police Department, *Report Regarding Two Alternatives*, 4.

80. Harshaw, *OG Told Me*, 50.

81. Nathan Solis and Melissa Hernandez, "Inside L. A.'s Deadly Street Take-over Scene: 'A Scene of Lawlessness,'" *Los Angeles Times*, August 22, 2022, online.

82. Kendrick Lamar, "Alright," *To Pimp a Butterfly*, Interscope Records, 2015, AFTMB002295802CD, CD, album; Colin Tilley and the Little Homies, dirs., "Alright," music video, London Alley Entertainment, 2015, YouTube.

6. THE CLUB

1. Construction of Oakland's City Hall, the city's first skyscraper, began in 1911, the same year that Mayor Frank Mott was married. Commentators thus nicknamed the beaux-arts building—at the time, the tallest west of the Mississippi River—"Mayor Mott's wedding cake." Bagwell, *Oakland*, 184.

2. Geoffrey Pete, interview by author, October 17, 2017.

3. According to the drummer Earl Watkins, Slim Jenkins "had pride in his race." "He wanted to show the people that he was a businessman in every sense of the word . . . His clothes were tailor made. His wife—they'd get the same material . . . They'd have matching suits, matching Cadillacs." Watkins, "Oral History with Earl Watkins."

4. DjeDje, "California Black Gospel Music Tradition," 151; Lee Hildebrand, "Sell a Joyful Noise," *East Bay Express*, December 1, 1989, Magazine and Newspaper Room, Main Branch, Oakland Public Library, Oakland, CA.

5. Pete, interview by author.

6. Liza Veal, "Talking to Geoffrey Pete Is Hearing Oakland's History in Microcosm," *Oakland Local*, March 2, 2014, online.

7. Michelle R. Boyd, *Jim Crow Nostalgia: Reconstructing Race in Bronzeville* (University of Minnesota Press, 2008).

8. Pete, interview by author.

9. Otis Redding, "(Sittin' on) The Dock of the Bay," *(Sittin' on) The Dock of the Bay*, Volt, 1968, 45–157, vinyl, 7", single.

10. For more on redevelopment strategies that are meant to attract the "creative class," see Richard Florida, *The Rise of the Creative Class Revisited* (Basic Books, 2012).

11. The 1992 Strategic Plan called for promoting market-rate and affordable housing development in the area to support the growth of "retailing, dining, entertainment, commercial recreation, and cultural activities." Oakland—Sharing the Vision Inc., *The Oakland Strategic Plan* (Oakland—Sharing the Vision Inc., 1992), 10–14, Institute for Governmental Studies Library, University of California, Berkeley, CA.

12. Letter from Craig G. Kocian to Geoffrey Pete, December 17, 1993 (public records requested by author).

13. Ikimulisa Sockwell, "Oakland Club to Cater to a New Crowd," *Oakland Tribune*, December 9, 1993, Pete, Geoffrey, Hayward Area Historical Society, Hayward, CA.

14. Pete, interview by author.

15. Diana M. Williams, "City Loan Bolsters 14th St. Upgrade," *Oakland Tribune*, July 10, 1997, Pete, Geoffrey, Hayward Area Historical Society, Hayward, CA.

16. Pete, interview by author.

17. Ibid.

18. Ibid.

19. Ibid.

20. Ananya Roy, "Dis / possessive Collectivism: Property and Personhood at City's End," *Geoforum* 80 (2017): A1–11.

21. Allie Martin, *Intersectional Listening: Gentrification and Black Sonic Life in Washington, DC* (Oxford University Press, 2025), 24. Martin describes an emancipatory soundscape as a "process in which sonic space is created and maintained in the service of Black life." "Emancipatory soundscapes oscillate in a queer space between the grounded 'already otherwise' and the utopian 'not yet' . . . Emancipatory soundscapes . . . are both already here and yet always signaling to the possibility of what could be."

22. City of Oakland Municipal Code Section 5.12, "Cabarets."

23. Arturo Sanchez, interview by author, November 11, 2016.

24. According to Oakland Municipal Code Section 5.12.010 ("Definitions"), applicants can be rejected if they have a conviction or plea bargain for fraud, selling drugs, or violent crime.

25. Oakland Community and Economic Development Agency, *Request for Proposals: Uptown Oakland Fox Theater* (City of Oakland, 1997), 2, Oakland. Theaters. Fox., Oakland History Room, Main Branch, Oakland Public Library, Oakland, CA.

26. Letter from Joseph Samuels to Larry Carroll, December 13, 1993 (public records requested by author).

27. Jidenna featuring Quavo, "The Let Out," *The Chief*, Epic, 2017, 88985303062, CD, album; "Jidenna Breaks Down 'The Let Out' on Genius' Video Series 'Verified,'" *Genius*, March 8, 2017, online.

28. Kara Platoni, "Where the Cops Don't Say 'TGIF,'" *East Bay Express*, April 16, 2003, online.

29. Mistah F.A.B, "Ghost Ride It," *Top Secret!—September 2006 Reloaded*, Strictly Hits Vinyl Service, 2006, ts-077, vinyl, 12", EP.

30. Reports related to OPD Incident (no. unknown), March 3, 1996, and OPD Incident #162, April 27, 1997 (public records requested by author).

31. Stacey Wells, "Oakland's Tab for OT: $25 Million," *Oakland Tribune*, November 8, 1998, News 1, Magazine and Newspaper Room, Main Branch, Oakland Public Library, Oakland, CA.

32. City of Oakland Ordinance #12132 C.M.S. (1999), public records requested by author.

33. Ordinance #12132 C.M.S. In the aftermath of the murder of George Floyd in 2020, and amid calls from local organizers to reduce the role of the OPD in noncriminal matters, the city council voted to "civilianize" special event permitting by turning it over to the Economic and Workforce Development Department. It also moved to remove this vague language to "avoid disparate impacts resulting from unequal implementation of special event requirements" and "[eliminate] confusion over whether an event at an already licensed facility must obtain a special event permit." Oakland Economic and Workforce Development Department, *Launch of Updated Special Events Permitting Process*, City of Oakland, January 27, 2023 (public records requested by author).

34. Ordinance #12132 C.M.S. OPD Sergeant, Special Events Unit, interview by author, February 16, 2017.

35. Williams, interview by author.

36. Sam Lefebvre, "Blacklisted: How the Oakland Police Department Discriminates against Rappers and Music Venues," *East Bay Express*, April 26, 2017, online.

37. Oakland City Manager's Office, *A Follow-Up Report from the City Manager Regarding Proposed Amendments to Special Event, Park Area Use, Pool Room and Cabaret Ordinances to Allow Recovery of Extraordinary Police Costs*, City of Oakland, March 23, 1999 (public records requested by author).

38. Angela Woodall, interview by author, October 7, 2016.

39. Quoted in Diana M. Williams, "City Admits Lapse in Rave Party Permit," *Oakland Tribune*, November 29, 1995, A9, Magazine and Newspaper Room, Main Branch, Oakland Public Library, Oakland, CA.

40. Zazaboi, interviews by author.

41. During the 2000s, a cheap, oversized white tee-shirt was the standard uniform for young men involved in the Hyphy Movement. According to Andrea Smith, among working-class youth with little disposable income, this look was valued for its ease and affordability. Packages of white tees were often sold in corner stores, which represented the main retail outlets in some disinvested Black neighborhoods. Smith, *Hyphy Intellect*, 108–14. The white tee thus became a raced, classed, gendered, and aged marker of youth style. Under explicit pressure from officials, Oakland club owners routinely banned white tees from their dress codes as a supposed security measure. For more on nightclub dress codes and racial exclusion, see Reuben A. Buford May, "Velvet Rope Racism, Racial Paranoia, and Cultural Scripts: Alleged Dress Code Discrimination in Urban Nightlife, 2000–2014," *City & Community* 17, no. 1 (2018): 44–64.

42. Jamie Foxx featuring T-Pain, "Blame It," *Intuition*, J Records, 2008, 88697–41294–2-RE2, CD, album; Lil Jon and the East Side Boyz featuring Too Short, "Couldn't Be a Better Player," *More Freaky Tales*, Short Records, 1988, 01241–42571–2, CD, single; Lil Wayne, "Mrs. Officer," *Tha Carter III*, Cash Money Records, 2008, B0011232–72, CD, album; Mac Dre, "Feelin' Myself"; Mistah F.A.B., "N.E.W. Oakland," *Son of a Pimp*, Thizz Entertainment, 2005, THN 6004, CD, album; Too Short, "Blow the Whistle."

43. Unpublished footage provided by Yakpasua Zazaboi.

44. Kelly Rayburn, "Oakland Mayor Lifts Police Overtime Restrictions," *Oakland Tribune*, November 25, 2008, online.

45. Robert Gammon, "Oakland Cops Make Bank on Overtime," *East Bay Express*, March 9, 2011, online.

46. Pete, interview by author.

47. Overtime pay wasn't the only aspect of policing that drained Oakland's coffers during this time. Between 2002 and 2011, the City paid more than $46 million to settle police misconduct claims, "far outstripping similar costs in larger cities like San Jose and San Francisco." In addition, between 2003 and 2012, it spent more than $8 million on court monitoring costs associated with the federal consent decree, which stemmed from systemic abuse. Winston and BondGraham, *The Riders*, 298.

48. Email from David Kozicki to Geoffrey Pete, October 30, 2008 (public records requested by author).

49. Kozicki, interview by author.

50. Report on administrative hearing for Mingles, May 15, 2006 (public records requested by author). Cf. Matt Sakakeeny, *Roll with It: Brass Bands in the Streets of New Orleans* (Duke University Press, 2013), 34.

51. Robert Gammon, "Cops Charging Overtime to Clubs," *East Bay Express*, March 2, 2011, online.

52. Pete, interview by author.

53. Complaint in Pete v. City of Oakland et al., 2009, No. C 09–06097 WHA, Document 1, United States District Court, Northern District California, December 31, PACER.

54. Decision in Pete v. City of Oakland et al., 2011, No. C 09–06097 WHA, Document 143, United States District Court, Northern District California, March 10, PACER.

55. Ibid.

56. Lipsitz, *How Racism Takes Place*, 35. See also David T. Goldberg, *The Threat of Race: Reflections on Racial Neoliberalism* (Blackwell, 2009); Jodi Melamed, *Represent and Destroy: Rationalizing Violence in the New Racial Capitalism* (University of Minnesota Press, 2011); Michael Omi and Howard Winant, *Racial Formation in the United States*, 3rd ed. (Routledge, 2014).

57. Decision in Pete v. City of Oakland et al.

58. Ibid.

59. Letter from Dan Lindheim to Geoffrey Pete, January 13, 2009 (public records requested by author).

60. "'Sweet Jimmie' Ward, 74," *Oakland Post*, February 10, 2010, 1, Magazine and Newspaper Room, Main Branch, Oakland Public Library, Oakland, CA.

61. This account is based on reporting in the February 1970 issue of the *Bayviewer*, MS 201, Bayviewer Magazine Collection, African American Museum and Library at Oakland, Oakland Public Library, Oakland, CA.

62. Elaine Brown, *A Taste of Power: A Black Woman's Story* (Pantheon Books, 1992), 329–33.

63. Katy St. Clair, "Jimmie's Sour Grapes," *East Bay Express*, February 26, 2003, online.

64. Report related to OPD Incident #2758, April 1, 2002 (public records requested by author).

65. Lisa M. Cacho, *Social Death: Racialized Rightlessness and the Criminalization of the Unprotected* (New York University Press, 2012), 6.

66. Zazaboi, interviews by author.

67. Complaint in Jimmie's Limousine Service, Inc. v. City of Oakland et al., 2004, No. C 04–3321 WHA, Document 1, United States District Court, Northern District California, August 13, PACER.

68. Decision in Jimmie's Limousine Service, Inc. v. City of Oakland et al., 2005, No. C 04–3321 WHA, Document 54, United States District Court, Northern District California, August 18, PACER.

69. This account is based on records maintained by the City of Oakland as part of its case file on Jimmie's Entertainment Complex (public records requested by author).

70. Ibid.

71. Ibid.

72. Barbara Killey, *Decision, after Reconsideration, of Hearing Officer on Application of Oakland Partner Group LLC for a Permit to Operate a Cabaret under the Name Tycoons at 1731 San Pablo Avenue*, City of Oakland, March 7, 2007, 3 (public records requested by author).

73. Ibid.

74. Lefebvre, "Blacklisted."

75. Quoted in Cecily Burt and Sean Maher, "Salute to Legendary Oakland Bar Owner," *Oakland Tribune*, February 11, 2010, A3, Magazine and Newspaper Room, Main Branch, Oakland Public Library, Oakland, CA.

76. Report on proposal to amend the 300-foot rule, November 13, 2007 (public records requested by author).

77. Barbara Killey, *A Public Hearing on the Appeal of the Administrative Hearing Officer's Decision to Deny the Application of Oakland Partners Group LLC for a Permit to Operate a Cabaret under the Name Club O (Application Submitted to Operate a Cabaret Under the Name Tycoons) and Adopting a Resolution Affirming Hearing Officer's Denial of the Permit*, City of Oakland, April 17, 2007, 6 (public records requested by author).

78. Nancy Marcus, interview by author, August 15, 2017.

79. Letter from Zachary Wasserman to Oakland City Council, March 19, 2007 (public records requested by author).

80. Jason Perkins, interview by author, June 5, 2017.

81. Rachel Swan, "Goapele Gets Closer to Home," *East Bay Express*, August 5, 2009, online.

82. Cabaret permit application for the New Parish, October 29, 2008 (public records requested by author).

83. Cabaret permit approval for the New Parish, November 25, 2009 (public records requested by author).

84. This account is based on records maintained by the City of Oakland as part of its case file on the New Parish (public records requested by author).

85. Greg Minor, interview by author, March 2, 2017.

86. Perkins, interview by author. The sale records are based on data from www.propertyshark.com.

87. Perkins, interview by author.

88. See note 84.

89. Dave Brooks, "After Rough Spell, Oakland's New Parish Sold to Allen Scott from Another Planet Entertainment," *Billboard*, September 5, 2018, online; Sam Lefebvre, "Parish Entertainment Group Dissolves amid Allegations against Jason Perkins," *East Bay Express*, June 27, 2018.

90. Kathleen Richards, "Out Foxed? The City of Oakland Is Banking on the Fox Theater to Revive Uptown, but Where Will That Leave the Paramount?" *East Bay Express*, July 25, 2007, 9, Oakland. Theaters. Fox., Oakland History Room, Main Branch, Oakland Public Library, Oakland, CA.

91. Angela Woodall, "An Entertainment Commission Could Open the Door for Many," *Oakland Tribune*, March 12, 2009, online.

92. Richard Parks, "The Uptown Apartments Look Nice, but Are Still Mostly Empty," *East Bay Express*, April 8, 2009, online.

93. I derived these figures from an analysis of the City of Oakland's list of licensed cabarets from 2001 (the earliest year for which data are available) to 2016, news reports, and case files related to individual clubs (public records requested by author).

94. Ibid.

95. Ramírez, *Decolonial Ruptures*, 135–45.

96. Summers, *Black in Place*, 3–4, 22–23. See also Kaily Heitz, "Sunflower's Oakland: The Black Geographic Image as a Site of Reclamation," *Antipode* 54, no. 1 (2022): 19–43.

97. Kemi Adeyemi, *Feels Right: Black Queer Women and the Politics of Partying in Chicago* (Duke University Press, 2022), 2.

98. Bijou McDaniel, interview by author, July 5, 2017; Leon "DNas" Sykes, interview by author, August 17, 2016.

99. Martin, *Intersectional Listening*, 203.

100. Ibid.

101. McDaniel, interview by author.

102. See note 93.

103. Author field notes from SambaFunk! Joy Funkraiser, December 9, 2017.

104. See, for instance, Buenning, "Sideshow Makes Problems."

105. OPD Special Resource Commander, Area 1, interview by author, November 28, 2017.

7. BEFORE BBQ BECKY

1. Material from this chapter was first published by University of California Press as Alex Werth, "Before BBQ Becky: Racial Reverberations at Oakland's Lake Merritt," *Journal of Popular Music Studies* 33, no. 4 (2021): 78–103 (used with permission).

2. According to City rules, charcoal grilling was only allowed in the stationary pits installed in "designated areas" on the Grand Avenue side of Lake Merritt. People were allowed to use portable grills on the east side of the water, but not charcoal ones.

3. Quoted in Simone Aponte, "2 Investigates Obtains 'BBQ Becky's' Viral 911 Calls," *KTVU*, September 2, 2018, online.

4. Quoted in Momo Chang, "Kenzie Smith Speaks Out," *East Bay Express*, May 31, 2018, online.

5. Online critics took issue with Schulte's image, including her sunglasses, which seemed styled for a ruthless sort of efficacy rather than fashion.

6. Michelle Dione, "Original BBQ Meme Video—the First Viral 'Karen,'" April 30, 2018, YouTube.

7. Maze featuring Frankie Beverly, "Before I Let Go," *Before I Let Go*, Capitol Records, 1981, A-5031, vinyl, 7", single. Within a week, the electric slide video was viewed over 750,000 times on Facebook.

8. Jonathan Kauffman, "Anti-Racist Barbecuers Take Back Oakland's Communal Backyard at Lake Merritt," *San Francisco Chronicle*, May 20, 2018, online.

9. Brandi T. Summers, "Reclaiming the Chocolate City: Soundscapes of Gentrification and Resistance in Washington, DC," *Environment and Planning D: Society and Space* 39, no. 1 (2021): 30–46.

10. For more on "Black Twitter," see Roderick Graham and 'Shawn Smith, "The Content of Our #Characters: Black Twitter as Counterpublic," *Sociology of Race and Ethnicity* 2, no. 4 (2016): 433–49. Twitter is now X.

11. These included a girl selling water in San Francisco, a graduate student napping in the common room of her dorm at Yale, two men attending a meeting at a Starbucks in Philadelphia, and many more.

12. Lipsitz, *How Racism Takes Place*; McKittrick, "Rebellion / Invention / Groove."

13. Taja-Nia Y. Henderson and Jamila Jefferson-Jones, "#LivingWhileBlack: Blackness as Nuisance," *American University Law Review* 69, no. 3 (2020): 863–914, at 870, 878.

14. Erin Baldassari, "'BBQing While Black' Festival Draws Huge Crowd to Oakland's Lake Merritt," *East Bay Times*, May 20, 2018, online; Laura M. Holson, "Hundreds in Oakland Turn Out to BBQ While Black," *New York Times*, May 21, 2018, online.

15. Sam Levin, "'We're Being Pushed Out': The Displacement of Black Oakland," *The Guardian*, June 1, 2018, online.

16. See Introduction, note 69.

17. Brandi T. Summers and Desiree Fields, "Speculative Urban Worldmaking: Meeting Financial Violence with a Politics of Collective Care," *Antipode* 56, no. 3 (2024): 821–40; Alex Werth and Eli Marienthal, "'Gentrification' as a Grid of Meaning: On Bounding the Deserving Public of Oakland First Fridays," *City* 20, no. 5 (2016): 719–36.

18. Neil Smith, *The New Urban Frontier: Gentrification and the Revanchist City* (Routledge, 1996).

19. Robert Gammon, "Time Is Running Out for Oakland," *East Bay Express*, December 9, 2015, online; Sam Levin, "Oakland Readies for the Housing Boom," *East Bay Express*, December 24, 2014, online.

20. The Anti-Eviction Mapping Project, "Oakland Unlawful Detainers, 2005–2015," in *Counterpoints: A San Francisco Bay Area Atlas of Displacement and Resistance* (PM Press, 2021); Lauren Hepler, "The Hidden Toll of California's Black Exodus," *CalMatters*, July 15, 2020, online.

21. Brandi T. Summers, "Untimely Futures," *Places Journal*, November 2021, online.

22. Quoted in Pendarvis Harshaw, "'We're Still Here': 'BBQ'n While Black' Draws Oaklanders Out in Force," *KQED*, May 21, 2018, online.

23. Ruth L. Glass, *London: Aspects of Change* (MacGibbon & Kee, 1964).

24. David Harvey, "From Managerialism to Entrepreneurialism: The Transformation of Urban Governance in Late Capitalism," *Geografiska Annaler: Series B, Human Geography* 71, no. 1 (1989): 3–17; Neil Smith, "Toward a Theory of Gentrification: A Back to the City Movement by Capital, Not People," *Journal of the American Planning Association* 45, no. 4 (1989): 538–48; Smith, *New Urban Frontier*.

25. Saskia Sassen, *The Global City: New York, London, Tokyo*, 2nd ed. (Princeton University Press, 2001 [1996]); Sharon Zukin, *The Cultures of Cities* (Wiley-Blackwell, 1996).

26. Alison Martin, "Plainly Audible: Listening Intersectionally to the Amplified Noise Act in Washington, DC," *Journal of Popular Music Studies* 33, no. 4 (2021): 104–25, at 105.

27. See note 2.

28. Aponte, "2 Investigates"; "Oakland Police Release Log of Events from BBQ Controversy at Lake Merritt," *KTVU*, May 27, 2018, online.

29. Gil Scott-Heron, "The Revolution Will Not Be Televised," *The Revolution Will Not Be Televised*, Flying Dutchman, 1974, BDL1–0613, vinyl, LP, album.

30. Varda, *Black Panthers*.

31. In his memoir, Newton mentions that, while in jail, he spent time looking out at Lake Merritt, where he witnessed both quotidian activities ("people walking") and demonstrations, including a rally following the funeral of Lil' Bobby Hutton in 1968. Newton, *Revolutionary Suicide*, 299.

32. Filmmaker Spencer Wilkinson confirmed that, according to William Randolph of the Black Resurgents, young people would walk around Lake Merritt after church in their Sunday best, often in order to impress and flirt with each other. Dance, including boogaloo, was part of that ritual. Spencer Wilkinson, email to author, December 10, 2024.

33. Lloyd Boles, "'Lifestyle' Intrusion in the Park," *Oakland Tribune*, August 21, 1979, Oakland, Calif. Park, Lake Merritt Park, General, 1978–1983, Hayward Area Historical Society, Hayward, CA.

34. Ibid.

35. Quoted in "Council Told Park Woes," *Oakland Tribune*, August 22, 1979 Oakland, Calif. Park, Lake Merritt Park, General, 1978–1983, Hayward Area Historical Society, Hayward, CA.

36. "No Harmony on Park Rock," *Oakland Tribune*, August 23, 1979, Oakland, Calif. Park, Lake Merritt Park, General, 1978–1983, Hayward Area Historical Society, Hayward, CA.

37. Stoever, *Sonic Color Line*, 13.

38. Ramírez, "City as Borderland"; Summers, "Reclaiming the Chocolate City."

39. Martin, "Plainly Audible," 108.

40. "Move to Ease Park Problems," *Oakland Tribune*, May 12, 1976; "Park Rules Approved," *Oakland Tribune*, June 2, 1976, Oakland, Calif. Park, Lake Merritt Park, General, 1960–1977, Hayward Area Historical Society, Hayward, CA.

41. Quoted in "Move to Ease."

42. "Parks Rules Approved."

43. "Cops Surrounded by Angry Crowd," *Oakland Tribune*, August 29, 1977; "Park Dispute Unresolved," *Oakland Tribune*, September 30, 1977, Oakland, Calif., Lake Merritt Park, General, 1960–1977, Hayward Area Historical Society, Hayward, CA.

44. "Police Harassment Charged," *Oakland Tribune*, September 7, 1977, Oakland, Calif. Park, Lake Merritt Park, General, 1960–1977, Hayward Area His-

torical Society, Hayward, CA. For more on Rountree's connections to Black nightlife, see Hildebrand, "West Side Story."

45. "Police Harassment Charged."

46. Karen Emerson, "Memories of Rollerland," *Oakland Tribune*, February 12, 1972, Rollerland, Hayward Area Historical Society, Hayward, CA.

47. "Lakeside Skaters Warned," *Oakland Tribune*, May 30, 1979, Oakland, Calif. Roller Skating, Hayward Area Historical Society, Hayward, CA.

48. Del Lane, "Lake Shore Avenue Parking Ban Begins," *Oakland Tribune*, August 2, 1985, Oakland, Calif. Park, Lake Merritt Park, General, 1985–, Hayward Area Historical Society, Hayward, CA.

49. Cecily Burt, "Lakeshore Cruising Triggers Complaints," *Oakland Tribune*, May 24, 1993, Cruising, 1990–, Hayward Area Historical Society, Hayward, CA; Amanda Covarrubias, "Lakeside Park's Duck Area Reclaimed for the Law-Abiding," *Oakland Tribune*, July 29, 1985, Oakland, Calif. Park, Lake Merritt Park, General, 1985–, Hayward Area Historical Society, Hayward, CA.

50. Lane, "Lake Shore Avenue."

51. Yasmin Anwar, "Responses Mixed to Curtailed Cruising," *Oakland Tribune*, May 30, 1993; Harry Harris and Craig Staats, "Police to Attempt Cruising Control," *Oakland Tribune*, May 29, 1993; Harry Harris and Craig Staats, "Police Will Rely on Cruising Law to Control Traffic," *Oakland Tribune*, June 5, 1993, Cruising, 1990–, Hayward Area Historical Society, Hayward, CA; William Wong, "An Oakland Dilemma: Whose Lake Is It?," *Oakland Tribune*, May 28, 1993, Oakland, Calif. Park, Lake Merritt Park, General, 1985–, Hayward Area Historical Society, Hayward, CA.

52. City of Oakland Ordinance #11504 C.M.S. (1992), public records requested by author.

53. Quoted in Jacqueline Cutler, "Council Member Wants to Curb Cruising," *Oakland Tribune*, May 27, 1992, Cruising, 1990–, Hayward Area Historical Society, Hayward, CA.

54. Cacho, *Social Death*, 6.

55. Quoted in David K. Li, "Council OKs Curb on Lake Cruising," *Oakland Tribune*, April 20, 1995; Craig Staats, "City Seeks to Stall Cruising Near Lake," *Oakland Tribune*, April 18, 1995, Oakland, Calif. Park, Lake Merritt Park, General, 1985–, Hayward Area Historical Society, Hayward, CA.

56. Oakland Police Services Agency, *Report Re: Cruising around Lake Merritt* (City of Oakland, July 23, 1996), public records requested by author.

57. 3X Krazy featuring Mike Marshall, "Sunshine in the O," *Sick-O*, Str8 Game Records, 1995, STG 1202, CD, EP.

58. Forman Jr., *Locking Up Our Own*, 197–98.

59. Oakland Police Services Agency, *Report Re: Cruising*, 3.

60. Rios, *Punished*.

61. Pope, *Rap and Politics*, 275; The Coup, "Dig It!," *Kill My Landlord*, EMI, 1993, E2–89047, CD, album.

62. Riley displays the flyer for the camera in RamHistoryMaker, "Festival at the Lake Oakland, CA," November 11, 2010, YouTube.

63. Newton, *Revolutionary Suicide*, 126.

64. KRS-One, "Sound of da Police," *Return of the Boom Bap*, Jive, 1993, 01241–41517–2, CD, album.

65. HipHopSlam, "1996 Oakland Mayor vs. Boots Riley, Young Comrades, and Callers re: OPD at Lake Merritt," January 9, 2022, YouTube.

66. Quoted in Diana M. Williams, "Cruising Law May Take a Turn for the Better," *Oakland Tribune*, July 24, 1996, Oakland, Calif. Park, Lake Merritt Park, General, 1985–, Hayward Area Historical Society, Hayward, CA.

67. Editorial, "Taking Pride in Lakeside Park," *Oakland Tribune*, October 16, 1979, Oakland, Calif. Park, Lake Merritt Park, General, 1978–1983, Hayward Area Historical Society, Hayward, CA.

68. Melamed, *Represent and Destroy*, 91–97.

69. Summers, *Black in Place*, 3.

70. Mary Ann Hogan, "The Shores of Lake Merritt Reflect Oakland at Its Best," *Oakland Tribune*, May 26, 1985, Oakland, Calif. Park, Lake Merritt Park, General, 1985–, Hayward Area Historical Society, Hayward, CA.

71. Ed Levitt, "Oakland Event Lures Big, Happy Crowd," *Oakland Tribune*, June 2, 1985, A1, Magazine and Newspaper Room, Main Branch, Oakland Public Library, Oakland, CA.

72. Bill O'Brien, "The Magic Is Gone: Farewell to Festival at the Lake," *East Bay Express*, October 9, 1997, 36, Magazine and Newspaper Room, Main Branch, Oakland Public Library, Oakland, CA.

73. Quoted in Sandhya Dirks, "When Oakland Was a 'Chocolate City': A Brief History of Festival at the Lake," *KQED*, September 14, 2018, online.

74. RamHistoryMaker, "Festival at the Lake."

75. 3X Krazy featuring Mike Marshall, "Sunshine in the O."

76. Summers, *Black in Place*, 3.

77. Harry Harris and Craig Staats, "Violence Leads City to Reconsider Lake Site," *Oakland Tribune*, June 7, 1994, A1; Lola Smallwood, "Festival Programs to Curtail Rowdiness," *Oakland Tribune*, February 19, 1995, A15; Diana M. Williams, "Festival Ends in Violence," *Oakland Tribune*, June 6, 1994, A1, Magazine and Newspaper Room, Main Branch, Oakland Public Library, Oakland, CA.

78. Quoted in Harris and Staats, "Violence Leads City."

79. Quoted in Daniel Velasquez, "Officials Vow to Listen to Youth," *Oakland Tribune*, June 10, 1994, A1, Magazine and Newspaper Room, Main Branch, Oakland Public Library, Oakland, CA.

80. Quoted in Diana M. Williams, "Rioting Over, Oakland Assesses the Damage," *Oakland Tribune*, June 7, 1994, A1, Magazine and Newspaper Room, Main Branch, Oakland Public Library, Oakland, CA.

81. Quoted in Dashka Slater, "CALM Prevails at Lake Merritt," *East Bay Express*, April 28, 1995, 2, Magazine and Newspaper Room, Main Branch, Oakland Public Library, Oakland, CA.

82. David K. Li, "Organizers Spread Out Festival Gala," *Oakland Tribune*, November 1, 1995, A9; Smallwood, "Festival Programs," Magazine and Newspaper Room, Main Branch, Oakland Public Library, Oakland, CA.

83. Pete Hodgdon, "Volunteers to Help with Light Security at Festival at the Lake," *Oakland Tribune*, March 29, 1996, A13; Kathleen Kirkwood, "Panel OKs Cash Rescue of Festival," *Oakland Tribune*, September 25, 1996, A11, Magazine and Newspaper Room, Main Branch, Oakland Public Library, Oakland, CA; Thaai Walker, "Festival at the Lake Discontinued: Debt from Oakland Fete Proved Insurmountable," *San Francisco Chronicle*, November 11, 1997, online.

84. Jones, *Black Music*.

85. Braxton D. Shelley, " 'I Had to Flip This One': Music, Memes, and Digital Antiphony," lecture at the Radcliffe Institute for Advanced Study, Cambridge, MA, March 23, 2020, YouTube.

86. Christina Sharpe, *In the Wake: On Blackness and Being* (Duke University Press, 2016), 9.

CONCLUSION

1. Epigraph from Joseph G. Schloss, *Making Beats: The Art of Sample-Based Hip-Hop* (Wesleyan University Press, 33), used with permission.

2. Schloss, *Making Beats*, 138.

3. Drake featuring Lil Wayne, "The Motto," *Take Care*, Cash Money Records, 2011, AAC, album, deluxe edition; Zapp, "More Bounce to the Ounce," *Zapp*, Warner Bros. Records, 1980, WBS49534, vinyl, 7", single.

4. Bull, *Sounding Out the City*, 24, 35, 153.

5. Pendarvis Harshaw, "The Power of Taking Up Space: Marshawn Lynch's Oakland Rideout," *KQED*, June 24, 2018, online.

6. Gavin Steingo, "Another Resonance: Africa and the Study of Sound," in *Remapping Sound Studies*, ed. Gavin Steingo and Jim Sykes (Duke University Press, 2019), 48, 51.

7. The ring shout is an African American spiritual practice, which was derived from a diverse set of music and performance rituals carried by enslaved people from Africa to the Americas. According to the music scholar Samuel A. Floyd Jr., the ring—with its unique traits of call-and-response, polyrhythm, improvisation, and more—became the basis for most later genres of Black popular music, including jazz, blues, and rock 'n' roll. See Samuel A. Floyd Jr., *The Power of Black Music: Interpreting Its History from Africa to the United States* (Oxford University Press, 1995).

8. For more on open-air house dance, including cyphering, as a way to "reimagine the social," see Kavita Kulkarni, " 'Like a Cosmic, Invisible Umbilical Cord': Soul Summit and the Haptic Arrangements of Black Social Life," *Journal of Popular Music Studies* 33, no. 4 (2021): 171–202.

9. Author field notes from walk around Lake Merritt, June 24, 2018.

10. In part, Black dance music tends to embody a logic of relative borderlessness because—for a range of contextually specific reasons, rooted in both African-descended customs and anti-Black racism—Black sound cultures are more likely to occur in tight quarters and / or open air. This aspect of Black sounding has been taken up in more detail by scholars of a range of musical styles and scenes, including hip-hop (Chang, *Can't Stop Won't Stop*; Rose, *Black Noise*), reggae and dancehall (Henriques, *Sonic Bodies*), second lining (Sakakeeny, *Roll with It*), *champeta* (Streicker, "Spatial Reconfigurations"), and more.

11. My interpretation of White sonic politics as rooted in the qualities of private property is inspired, in part, by the ways that the critical race scholar George Lipsitz has theorized the "White spatial imaginary." Lipsitz, *How Racism Takes Place*, 28–30.

12. Fred Moten, *Stolen Life* (Duke University Press, 2018), 131.

13. Rose, *Black Noise*, 70.

Bibliography

||||||||||||||||||||||||||||||||||||||||||||||||||||||||||||||||||||||||||||||||||||||||||||||||||||||||||||||||||||||||||||||||||||||||||||||||||

BOOKS AND BOOK CHAPTERS

Abdurraqib, Hanif. *A Little Devil in America: Notes in Praise of Black Performance*. Random House, 2021.

Adeyemi, Kemi. *Feels Right: Black Queer Women and the Politics of Partying in Chicago*. Duke University Press, 2022.

Alexander, Michelle. *The New Jim Crow: Mass Incarceration in the Age of Colorblindness*. New Press, 2010.

The Anti-Eviction Mapping Project. "Oakland Unlawful Detainers, 2005–2015." In *Counterpoints: A San Francisco Bay Area Atlas of Displacement and Resistance*. PM Press, 2021.

Arnold, Eric. *Hip-Hop Atlas of the Bay*. Oakland Museum of California, 2018.

Astbury, Ray. "Oakland." In *Encyclopedia of the Blues*, edited by Edward Komara. Routledge, 2006.

Bagwell, Beth. *Oakland: The Story of a City*. Oakland Heritage Alliance, 1996 [1982].

Baldwin, James. "Of the Sorrow Songs: The Cross of Redemption." In *The Cross of Redemption: Uncollected Writings*, edited by Randall Kenan. Pantheon Books, 2010 [1979].

Bloom, Joshua, and Waldo E. Martin. *Black against Empire: The History and Politics of the Black Panther Party*. University of California Press, 2012.

Boyd, Michelle R. *Jim Crow Nostalgia: Reconstructing Race in Bronzeville*. University of Minnesota Press, 2008.

Brand, Anna Livia. "Today Like Yesterday, Tomorrow Like Today: Black Geographies in the Breaks of the Fourth Dimension." In *The Black Geographic: Praxis, Resistance, Futurity*, edited by Camilla Hawthorne and Jovan Scott Lewis. Duke University Press, 2023.

Brown, Elaine. *A Taste of Power: A Black Woman's Story*. Pantheon Books, 1992.

Browne, Simone. *Dark Matters: On the Surveillance of Blackness*. Duke University Press, 2015.

Bull, Michael. *Sounding Out the City: Personal Stereos and the Management of Everyday Life*. Berg, 2000.

Cacho, Lisa M. *Social Death: Racialized Rightlessness and the Criminalization of the Unprotected*. New York University Press, 2012.

Camp, Jordan T., and Christina Heatherton, eds. *Policing the Planet: Why the Policing Crisis Led to Black Lives Matter*. Verso, 2016.

Campbell, Mark V. *Afrosonic Life*. Bloomsbury, 2022.

Campt, Tina M. *Listening to Images*. Duke University Press, 2017.

Carby, Hazel V. "Policing the Black Woman's Body in an Urban Context." In *Cultures in Babylon: Black Britain and African America*. Verso, 1999 [1992].

Carmichael, Stokely, and Charles V. Hamilton. *Black Power: The Politics of Liberation*. Random House, 1967.

Chang, Jeff. *Can't Stop Won't Stop: A History of the Hip-Hop Generation*. St. Martin's Press, 2005.

Chude-Sokei, Louis. "The Sound of Culture: Dread Discourse and Jamaican Sound Systems." In *Language, Rhythm, and Sound: Black Popular Cultures into the Twenty-First Century*, edited by Joseph K. Adjaye and Adrianne R. Andrews. University of Pittsburgh Press, 1997.

Ciccariello-Maher, George, and Jeff St. Andrews. "Between Macks and Panthers: Hip Hop in Oakland and San Francisco." In *Hip Hop in America: A Regional Guide*, edited by Mickey Hess. Greenwood Press, 2010.

Colbert, Soyica Diggs, Douglas A. Jones Jr., and Shane Vogel. "Introduction: Tidying Up after Repetition." In *Race and Performance after Repetition*, edited by Soyica Diggs Colbert, Douglas A. Jones Jr., and Shane Vogel. Duke University Press, 2020.

Collins, Willie R. "California Rhythm and Blues Recordings, 1942–1972: A Diversity of Styles." In *California Soul: Music of African Americans in the West*, edited by Jacqueline Cogdell DjeDje and Eddie S. Meadows. University of California Press, 1998.

Collins, Willie R. "Jazzing Up Seventh Street: Musicians, Venues, and Their Social Implications." In *Sights and Sounds: Essays in Celebration of West Oakland*, edited by Suzanne Stewart and Mary Praetzellis. California Department of Transportation, 1997.

Crouchett, Lawrence P., Lonnie Bunch III, and Martha Kendall Winnacker. *Visions toward Tomorrow: The History of the East Bay Afro-American Community, 1852–1977*. Northern California Center for Afro-American History and Life, 1989.

Danielsen, Anne. "Time and Time Again: Repetition and Difference in Repetitive Music." In *Over and Over: Exploring Repetition in Popular Music*, edited by Olivier Julien and Cristophe Levaux. Bloomsbury, 2018.

Davis, Mike. *City of Quartz: Excavating the Future in Los Angeles*. Vintage Books, 1992 [1990].

Deutsch, Sarah. *Women and the City: Gender, Space, and Power in Boston, 1870–1940*. Oxford University Press, 2000.

DjeDje, Jacqueline Cogdell. "The California Black Gospel Music Tradition: A Confluence of Musical Styles and Cultures." In *California Soul: Music of African Americans in the West*, edited by Jacqueline Cogdell DjeDje and Eddie S. Meadows. University of California Press, 1998.

Drake, St. Clair, and Horace R. Cayton. *Black Metropolis: A Study of Negro Life in a Northern City*. University of Chicago Press, 1993 [1945].

Eidsheim, Nina Sun. *The Race of Sound: Listening, Timbre, and Vocality in African American Music*. Duke University Press, 2019.

Florida, Richard. *The Rise of the Creative Class Revisited*. Basic Books, 2012.

Floyd Jr., Samuel A. *The Power of Black Music: Interpreting Its History from Africa to the United States*. Oxford University Press, 1995.

Forman, Murray. *The 'Hood Comes First: Race, Space, and Place in Rap and Hip-Hop*. Wesleyan University Press, 2002.

Forman Jr., James. *Locking Up Our Own: Crime and Punishment in Black America*. Farrar, Straus and Giroux, 2017.

Gates Jr., Henry Louis. *The Signifying Monkey: A Theory of African American Literary Criticism*. Oxford University Press, 1988.

Gilmore, Ruth W. *Golden Gulag: Prisons, Surplus, Crisis, and Opposition in Globalizing California*. University of California Press, 2007.

Gilroy, Paul. *The Black Atlantic: Modernity and Double Consciousness*. Harvard University Press, 1993.

Glass, Ruth L. *London: Aspects of Change*. MacGibbon & Kee, 1964.

Goggin, Jim. *Earl Watkins: The Life of a Jazz Drummer*. Trafford, 2005.

Golash-Boza, Tanya Maria. *Before Gentrification: The Creation of DC's Racial Wealth Gap*. University of California Press, 2023.

Goldberg, David T. *The Threat of Race: Reflections on Racial Neoliberalism*. Blackwell, 2009.

Gordon, Avery F. "Something More Powerful than Skepticism." In *Keeping Good Time: Reflections on Knowledge, Power, and People*. Routledge, 2016 [2004].

Guzman-Sanchez, Thomas. *Underground Dance Masters: Final History of a Forgotten Era*. Praeger, 2012.

Harcourt, Bernard E. *Illusion of Order: The False Promise of Broken Windows Policing*. Harvard University Press, 2001.

Harshaw, Pendarvis. *OG Told Me*. Self-published, 2017.

Hartman, Saidiya. *Lose Your Mother: A Journey along the Atlantic Slave Route*. Farrar, Straus and Giroux, 2007.

Hegel, Georg Wilhelm Friedrich. "Geographical Basis of World History." In *Race and the Enlightenment: A Reader*, edited by Emmanuel Chukwudi Eze. Blackwell, 1997 [1837].

Henriques, Julian. *Sonic Bodies: Reggae Sound Systems, Performance Techniques and Ways of Knowing*. Continuum, 2011.

Herrera, Juan. *Cartographic Memory: Social Movement Activism and the Production of Space*. Duke University Press, 2022.

Herrera, Patricia. "A Sonic Treatise of Futurity: Universes' *Party People*." In *Race and Performance after Repetition*, edited by Soyica Diggs Colbert, Douglas A. Jones Jr., and Shane Vogel. Duke University Press, 2020.

Hildebrand, Lee. "Juke Joint Rambles, Midnight Crawls." In *Bay Area Blues*, photographs by Michelle Vignes. Pomegranate, 1993.

Hildebrand, Lee, and James C. Moore Sr. "Oakland Blues." In *California Soul: Music of African Americans in the West*, edited by Jacqueline Cogdell DjeDje and Eddie S. Meadows. University of California Press, 1998.

Hunter, Marcus Anthony, and Zandria F. Robinson. *Chocolate Cities: The Black Map of American Life*. University of California Press, 2018.

Jaji, Tsitsi Ella. *Africa in Stereo: Modernism, Music, and Pan-African Solidarity*. Oxford University Press, 2014.

Jelly-Schapiro, Joshua. "High Tide, Low Ebb." In *Infinite City: A San Francisco Atlas*, edited by Rebecca Solnit. University of California Press, 2010.

Johnson, Gaye T. *Spaces of Conflict, Sounds of Solidarity: Music, Race, and Spatial Entitlement in Los Angeles*. University of California Press, 2013.

Johnson, Marilynn S. *The Second Gold Rush: Oakland and the East Bay in World War II*. University of California Press, 1993.

Jones, Leroi. *Black Music*. Da Capo Press, 1998 [1967].

Kaltmeier, Olaf, and Wilfried Raussert, eds. *Sonic Politics: Music and Social Movements in the Americas*. Routledge, 2021.

Katz, Mark. *Groove Music: The Art and Culture of the Hip-Hop DJ*. Oxford University Press, 2012.

Kelley, Robin D. G. "Thug Nation: On State Violence and Disposability." In *Policing the Planet: Why the Policing Crisis Led to Black Lives Matter*, edited by Jordan T. Camp and Christina Heatherton. Verso, 2016.

Kelley, Robin D. G. *Yo' Mama's Disfunktional!: Fighting the Culture Wars in Urban America*. Beacon Press, 1997.

Kemp, Roger L. *Coping with Proposition 13*. Lexington Books, 1980.

Kun, Josh. *Audiotopia: Music, Race, and America*. University of California Press, 2005.

LaBelle, Brandon. *Acoustic Territories: Sound Culture and Everyday Life*. Continuum, 2010.

Lawrence, Tim. *Love Saves the Day: A History of American Dance Music Culture, 1970–1979*. Duke University Press, 2003.

Lipsitz, George. *How Racism Takes Place*. Temple University Press, 2011.

Lipsitz, George. *Midnight at the Barrelhouse: The Johnny Otis Story*. University of Minnesota Press, 2010.

Ma, L. Eve Armentrout. *Hometown Chinatown: The History of Oakland's Chinese Community*. Garland, 2000.

Macalalad Bragin, Naomi. *Kinethic California: Dancing Funk and Disco Era Kinships*. University of Michigan Press, 2024.

Madrigal, Alexis. *The Pacific Circuit: A Globalized Account of the Battle for the Soul of an American City*. Foster, Straus and Giroux, 2025.

Martin, Allie. *Intersectional Listening: Gentrification and Black Sonic Life in Washington, DC*. Oxford University Press, 2025.

Marx, Karl. *Capital, Volume 1*. Penguin Books, 1990 [1867].

McClintock, Nathan. "From Industrial Garden to Food Desert: Demarcated Devaluation in the Flatlands of Oakland, California." In *Cultivating Food Justice: Race, Class, and Sustainability*, edited by Alison Hope Alkon and Julian Agyeman. MIT Press, 2011.

McKittrick, Katherine. *Demonic Grounds: Black Women and the Cartographies of Struggle*. University of Minnesota Press, 2006.

Melamed, Jodi. *Represent and Destroy: Rationalizing Violence in the New Racial Capitalism*. University of Minnesota Press, 2011.

Menoret, Pascal. 2014. *Joyriding in Riyadh: Oil, Urbanism, and Road Revolt*. Cambridge University Press.

Morrison, Matthew D. *Blacksound: Making Race and Popular Music in the United States*. University of California Press, 2024.

Moten, Fred. *Stolen Life*. Duke University Press, 2018.

Mulhall, Joe. *Rebel Sounds: Music as Resistance*. Footnote, 2024.

Mumford, Kevin J. *Interzones: Black / White Sex Districts in Chicago and New York in the Early Twentieth Century*. Columbia University Press, 1997.

Murch, Donna J. *Living for the City: Migration, Education, and the Rise of the Black Panther Party in Oakland, California*. University of North Carolina Press, 2010.

Newton, Huey P. *Revolutionary Suicide*. Penguin Books, 2009 [1973].

Oden, Robert S. *From Blacks to Brown and Beyond: The Struggle for Progressive Politics in Oakland, California, 1966–2011*. Cognella, 2012.

Omi, Michael, and Howard Winant. *Racial Formation in the United States*, 3rd ed. Routledge, 2014.

Osumare, Halifu. 2018. *Dancing in Blackness: A Memoir*. University Press of Florida, 2018.

Pepin, Elizabeth, and Lewis Watts. *The Harlem of the West: The San Francisco Fillmore Jazz Era*. Chronicle Books, 2006.

Phillips, Rasheedah. *Dismantling the Master's Clock: On Race, Space, and Time.* AK Press, 2025.

Pitts, Dorothy W. *A Special Place for Special People: The DeFremery Story.* Better Communications, 1993.

Point, Michael. "Lowell Fulson." In *Encyclopedia of the Blues*, edited by Edward Komara. Routledge, 2006.

Pope, Lavar. *Rap and Politics: A Case Study of Panther, Gangster, and Hyphy Discourses in Oakland, CA (1965–2010).* Palgrave Macmillan, 2020.

Raiford, Leigh. *Imprisoned in a Luminous Glare: Photography and the African American Freedom Struggle.* University of North Carolina Press, 2011.

Redmond, Shana L. *Anthem: Social Movements and the Sound of Solidarity in the African Diaspora.* New York University Press, 2014.

Reed, Ishmael. *Blues City: A Walk in Oakland.* Crown, 2003.

Reed, Ishmael. *Mumbo Jumbo.* Scribner, 2022 [1972].

Reed Jr., Adolph. *Stirrings in the Jug: Black Politics in the Post-Segregation Era.* University of Minnesota Press, 1999.

Rhomberg, Chris. *No There There: Race, Class, and Political Community in Oakland.* University of California Press, 2004.

Rios, Victor M. *Punished: Policing the Lives of Black and Latino Boys.* New York University Press, 2011.

Rose, Tricia. *Black Noise: Rap Music and Black Culture in Contemporary America.* Wesleyan University Press, 1994.

Rose, Tricia. *The Hip Hop Wars: What We Talk About When We Talk About Hip Hop—and Why It Matters.* Basic Books, 2008.

Rothstein, Richard. *The Color of Law: A Forgotten History of How Our Government Segregated America.* Liveright, 2018.

Roy, Ananya, Stuart Schrader, and Emma Shaw Crane. "Gray Areas: The War on Poverty at Home and Abroad." In *Territories of Poverty: Rethinking North and South*, edited by Ananya Roy and Emma Shaw Crane. University of Georgia Press, 2015.

Sakakeeny, Matt. *Roll with It: Brass Bands in the Streets of New Orleans.* Duke University Press, 2013.

Salkind, Micah E. *Do You Remember House?: Chicago's Queer of Color Undergrounds.* Oxford University Press, 2019.

Sassen, Saskia. *The Global City: New York, London, Tokyo*, 2nd ed. Princeton University Press, 2001 [1996].

Schloss, Joseph G. *Making Beats: The Art of Sample-Based Hip-Hop*. Wesleyan University Press, 2014 [2004].

Schloss, Joseph G., and Bill Bahng Boyer. "Urban Echoes: The Boombox and Sonic Mobility in the 1980s." In *The Oxford Handbook of Mobile Music Studies*, edited by Sumanth Gopinath and Jason Stanyek. Oxford University Press, 2014.

Schwarzer, Mitchell. *Hella Town: Oakland's History of Development and Disruption*. University of California Press, 2021.

Self, Robert. *American Babylon: Race and the Struggle for Postwar Oakland*. Princeton University Press, 2003.

Selvin, Joel. *Sly & The Family Stone: An Oral History*. Permuted Press, 1998.

Shabazz, Rashad. *Spatializing Blackness: Architectures of Confinement and Black Masculinity in Chicago*. University of Illinois Press, 2015.

Sharpe, Christina. *In the Wake: On Blackness and Being*. Duke University Press, 2016.

Smith, Neil. *The New Urban Frontier: Gentrification and the Revanchist City*. Routledge, 1996.

Stehlin, John G. *Cyclescapes of the Unequal City: Bicycle Infrastructure and Uneven Development*. University of Minnesota Press, 2019.

Steingo, Gavin. "Another Resonance: Africa and the Study of Sound." In *Remapping Sound Studies*, edited by Gavin Steingo and Jim Sykes. Duke University Press, 2019.

Stoever, Jennifer Lynn. *The Sonic Color Line: Race and the Cultural Politics of Listening*. New York University Press, 2016.

Sublette, Ned. *The World That Made New Orleans: From Spanish Silver to Congo Square*. Lawrence Hill Books, 2008.

Summers, Brandi T. *Black in Place: The Spatial Aesthetics of Race in a Post-Chocolate City*. University of North Carolina Press, 2019.

Thomas, Pat. *Listen, Whitey!: The Sights and Sounds of Black Power, 1965–1975*. Fantagraphics, 2012.

Tilton, Jennifer. *Dangerous or Endangered?: Race and the Politics of Youth in Urban America*. New York University Press, 2010.

Veal, Michael E. *Dub: Soundscapes and Shattered Songs in Jamaican Reggae*. Wesleyan University Press, 2007.

Vincent, Rickey. *Funk: The Music, the People, and the Rhythm of the One.* St. Martin's Press, 1996.

Vincent, Rickey. *Party Music: The Inside Story of the Black Panthers' Band and How Black Power Transformed Soul Music.* Lawrence Hill Books, 2013.

Vitale, Alex S., and Brian J. Jefferson. "The Emergence of Command and Control Policing in Neoliberal New York." In *Policing the Planet: Why the Policing Crisis Led to Black Lives Matter,* edited by Jordan T. Camp and Christina Heatherton. Verso, 2016.

Waksman, Steven. *Live Music in America: A History from Jenny Lind to Beyoncé.* Oxford University Press, 2022.

Walker, Richard. "Industry Builds Out the City: The Suburbanization of Manufacturing in the San Francisco Bay Area, 1850–1940." In *Manufacturing Suburbs: Building Work and Home on the Metropolitan Fringe,* edited by Robert Lewis. Temple University Press, 2004.

Wang, Oliver. *Legions of Boom: Filipino American Mobile DJ Crews in the San Francisco Bay Area.* Duke University Press, 2015.

Webb, Gary. *Dark Alliance: The CIA, the Contras, and the Crack Cocaine Explosion.* Seven Stories Press, 1998.

Weheliye, Alexander. *Phonographies: Grooves in Sonic Afro-Modernity.* Duke University Press, 2005.

Werth, Alex. "Le Rodéo Sauvage." In *Nos Lieux Communs: Une Géographie du Monde Contemporain,* edited by Michel Bussi, Martine Drozdz, and Fabrice Argounès. Fayard, 2024.

Wilkerson, Isabel. *Caste: The Origins of Our Discontents.* Random House, 2020.

Wilkerson, Isabel. *The Warmth of Other Suns: The Epic Story of America's Great Migration.* Vintage Books, 2010.

Wilson, James Q. *Varieties of Police Behavior: The Management of Law and Order in Eight Communities.* Harvard University Press, 1978 [1968].

Winston, Ali, and Darwin BondGraham. *The Riders Come Out at Night: Brutality, Corruption, and Cover-Up in Oakland.* Atria Books, 2023.

Woods, Clyde. *Development Arrested: The Blues and Plantation Power in the Mississippi Delta.* Verso, 2017 [1998].

Woods, Clyde. "'Sittin' on Top of the World': The Challenges of Blues and Hip Hop Geographies." In *Black Geographies and the Politics of Place,* edited by Katherine McKittrick and Clyde Woods. South End Press, 2007.

Zanfagna, Christina. *Holy Hip Hop in the City of Angels*. University of California Press, 2017.

Zukin, Sharon. 1996. *The Cultures of Cities*. Wiley-Blackwell, 1996.

JOURNAL ARTICLES AND UNPUBLISHED MANUSCRIPTS

Allen, Jafari S. "For 'the Children' Dancing the Beloved Community." *Souls* 11, no. 3 (2009): 311–26.

Bedoya, Roberto. "Spatial Justice: Rasquachification, Race and the City." *Creative Time Reports*, September 15, 2014. Online.

Bijsterveld, Karin. "The Diabolical Symphony of the Mechanical Age: Technology and Symbolism of Sound in European and North American Noise Abatement Campaigns, 1900–40." *Social Studies of Science* 31, no. 1 (2001): 37–70.

Bolden, Tony. "Groove Theory: A Vamp on the Epistemology of Funk." *American Quarterly* 52, no. 4 (2013): 9–34.

Brenner, Joel F. "Nuisance Law and the Industrial Revolution." *Journal of Legal Studies* 3, no. 2 (1974): 403–33.

Cielo, Christina. "Civic Sideshows: Communities and Publics in East Oakland." Institute for the Study of Social Change, University of California, Berkeley, 2005. Online.

Ellis, Nadia. "Out and Bad: Toward a Queer Performance Hermeneutic in Jamaican Dancehall." *Small Axe: A Caribbean Journal of Criticism* 15, no. 2 (2011): 7–23.

Floyd Jr., Samuel A. "Ring Shout!: Literary Studies, Historical Studies, and Black Music Inquiry." *Black Music Research Journal* 11, no. 2 (1991): 265–87.

Graham, Roderick, and 'Shawn Smith. "The Content of Our #Characters: Black Twitter as Counterpublic." *Sociology of Race and Ethnicity* 2, no. 4 (2016): 433–49.

Harris, Cheryl. "Whiteness as Property." *Harvard Law Review* 106 (1993): 1709–91.

Harvey, David. "From Managerialism to Entrepreneurialism: The Transformation of Urban Governance in Late Capitalism." *Geografiska Annaler: Series B, Human Geography* 71, no. 1 (1989): 3–17.

Heitz, Kaily. "Back against the Mall: Caring for Deep East Oakland." Unpublished manuscript, 2023.

Heitz, Kaily. "Sunflower's Oakland: The Black Geographic Image as a Site of Reclamation." *Antipode* 54, no. 1 (2022): 19–43.

Henderson, Taja-Nia Y., and Jamila Jefferson-Jones. "#LivingWhileBlack: Blackness as Nuisance." *American University Law Review* 69, no. 3 (2020): 863–914.

Jamison, Philip A. "Square Dance Calling: The African-American Connection." *Journal of Appalachian Studies* 9, no. 2 (2003): 387–98.

Johnson, Imani K. "Music Meant to Make You Move: Considering the Aural Kinesthetic." *Sounding Out!*, June 18, 2012. Online.

Kulkarni, Kavita. " 'Like a Cosmic, Invisible Umbilical Cord': Soul Summit and the Haptic Arrangements of Black Social Life." *Journal of Popular Music Studies* 33, no. 4 (2021): 171–202.

Macalalad Bragin, Naomi. "Shot and Captured: Turf Dance, YAK Films, and the Oakland, California, R. I. P. Project." *TDR / The Drama Review* 58, no. 2 (2014): 99–114.

Macías, Anthony. "Bringing Music to the People: Race, Urban Culture, and Municipal Politics in Postwar LA." *American Quarterly* 56, no. 3 (2004): 693–717.

Mahon, Maureen. "Listening for Willie Mae 'Big Mama' Thornton's Voice: The Sound of Race and Gender Transgressions in Rock and Roll." *Women and Music: A Journal of Gender and Culture* 15, no. 1 (2011): 1–17.

Martin, Alison. "Plainly Audible: Listening Intersectionally to the Amplified Noise Act in Washington, DC." *Journal of Popular Music Studies* 33, no. 4 (2021): 104–25.

May, Reuben A. Buford. "Velvet Rope Racism, Racial Paranoia, and Cultural Scripts: Alleged Dress Code Discrimination in Urban Nightlife, 2000–2014." *City & Community* 17, no. 1 (2018): 44–64.

McElroy, Erin, and Alex Werth. "Deracinated Dispossessions: On the Foreclosures of 'Gentrification' in Oakland, CA." *Antipode* 51, no. 3 (2019): 878–98.

McKittrick, Katherine. "Rebellion / Invention / Groove." *Small Axe: A Caribbean Journal of Criticism* 20, no. 1 (2016): 79–91.

Miller, Leta E. "Racial Segregation and the San Francisco Musicians' Union, 1923–60." *Journal of the Society for American Music* 1, no. 2 (2007): 161–206.

Moore, Andrea L. S. "Hyphy Sparked a Social Movement." *Ethnic Studies Review* 37, no. 1 (2017): 45–62.

Morrison, Matthew D. "Race, Blacksound, and the (Re)Making of Musicological Discourse." *Journal of the American Musicological Society* 72, no. 3 (2019): 781–823.

Park, K-Sue. "Money, Mortgages, and the Conquest of America." *Law & Social Inquiry* 41, no. 4 (2016): 1006–35.

Peck, Jamie, and Adam Tickell. "Neoliberalizing Space." *Antipode* 34, no. 3 (2002): 380–404.

Radovac, Lilian. "The 'War on Noise': Sound and Space in La Guardia's New York." *American Quarterly* 63, no. 3 (2011): 733–60.

Ramírez, Margaret M. "City as Borderland: Gentrification and the Policing of Black and Latinx Geographies in Oakland." *Environment and Planning D: Society and Space* 38, no. 1 (2020): 147–66.

Roy, Ananya. "Dis / possessive Collectivism: Property and Personhood at City's End." *Geoforum* 80 (2017): A1–11.

Sakakeeny, Matt. "Music, Sound, Politics." *Annual Review of Anthropology* 53, no. 1 (2024): 309–29.

Sakakeeny, Matt. "'Under the Bridge': An Orientation to Soundscapes in New Orleans." *Ethnomusicology* 54, no. 1 (2010): 1–27.

Schwarzer, Mitchell. "Oakland City Center: The Plan to Reposition Downtown within the Bay Region." *Journal of Planning History* 14, no. 2 (2015): 88–111.

Shelley, Braxton D. "Analyzing Gospel." *Journal of the American Musicological Society* 72, no. 1 (2019): 181–243.

Smith, Neil. "Toward a Theory of Gentrification: A Back to the City Movement by Capital, Not People." *Journal of the American Planning Association* 45, no. 4 (1979): 538–48.

Snead, James A. "On Repetition in Black Culture." *Black American Literature Forum* 15, no. 4 (1981): 146–54.

Streicker, Joel. "Spatial Reconfigurations, Imagined Geographies, and Social Conflicts in Cartagena, Colombia." *Cultural Anthropology* 12, no. 1 (1997): 109–28.

Summers, Brandi T. "Reclaiming the Chocolate City: Soundscapes of Gentrification and Resistance in Washington, DC." *Environment and Planning D: Society and Space* 39, no. 1 (2021): 30–46.

Summers, Brandi T. "Untimely Futures." *Places Journal*, November 2021. Online.

Summers, Brandi T., and Desiree Fields. "Speculative Urban Worldmaking: Meeting Financial Violence with a Politics of Collective Care." *Antipode* 56, no. 3 (2024): 821–40.

Ulinskas, Moriah. "Imagining a Past Future: Photographs from the Oakland Redevelopment Agency." *Places Journal*, January 2019. Online.

Valverde, Mariana. "Seeing Like a City: The Dialectic of Modern and Premodern Ways of Seeing in Urban Governance." *Law and Society Review* 45, no. 2 (2011): 277–312.

Wald, Gayle. "Soul Vibrations: Black Music and Black Freedom in Sound and Space." *American Quarterly* 63, no. 3 (2011): 673–96.

Walker, Richard. "Oakland: Dark Star in an Expanding Universe." Unpublished manuscript, 1997.

Werth, Alex. "Before BBQ Becky: Racial Reverberations at Oakland's Lake Merritt." *Journal of Popular Music Studies* 33, no. 4 (2021): 78–103.

Werth, Alex, and Eli Marienthal. "'Gentrification' as a Grid of Meaning: On Bounding the Deserving Public of Oakland First Fridays." *City* 20, no. 5 (2016): 719–36.

Wilson, James Q., and George L. Kelling. 1982. "Broken Windows: The Police and Neighborhood Safety." *Atlantic Monthly* 249, no. 3 (1982): 29–38.

DISSERTATIONS, THESES, AND LECTURES

Boos, Lance. "Raymond E. Jackson and Segregation in the American Federation of Musicians, 1900–1944." MA thesis, State University of New York, Buffalo State College, 2015.

Heitz, Kaily. "Oakland Is a Vibe: Blackness, Cultural Framings, and Emancipations of The Town." PhD diss., University of California, Berkeley, 2021.

Holt, Kevin C. "Get Crunk!: The Performative Resistance of Atlanta Hip-Hop Party Music." PhD diss., Columbia University, 2018.

Macalalad Bragin, Naomi. "Black Power of Hip Hop Dance: On Kinesthetic Politics." PhD diss., University of California, Berkeley, 2015.

May, Judith V. "Struggle for Authority: A Comparison of Four Social Change Programs in Oakland, California." PhD diss., University of California, Berkeley, 1973.

Ramírez, Margaret M. "Decolonial Ruptures: Art-Activism amid Racialized Dispossession in Oakland." PhD diss., University of Washington, 2017.

Shelley, Braxton D. "'I Had to Flip This One': Music, Memes, and Digital Antiphony." Lecture at the Radcliffe Institute for Advanced Study, Cambridge, MA, March 23, 2020. YouTube.

Smith, Andrea L. "Hyphy Intellect: The Formation of Bay Area Hip Hop Identities in the Realm of Commercial Culture." PhD diss., University of California, Davis, 2011.

NEWSPAPER, MAGAZINE, AND ONLINE ARTICLES

Allen-Taylor, J. Douglas. "Showing Their Side." *East Bay Express*, March 12, 2003. Online.

Anwar, Yasmin. "Responses Mixed to Curtailed Cruising." *Oakland Tribune*, May 30, 1993. Cruising. 1990–. Hayward Area Historical Society, Hayward, CA.

Aponte, Simone. "2 Investigates Obtains 'BBQ Becky's' Viral 911 Calls." *KTVU*, September 2, 2018. Online.

Arnold, Eric. "The Bay Area Was Hip-Hop before There Was Hip-Hop." *KQED*, February 1, 2023. Online.

Bailey, Chauncey. "Reviving Eastmont Challenges Manager." *Oakland Tribune*, June 6, 1993. Eastmont Shopping Center. Oakland, Calif. 1991–. Hayward Area Historical Society, Hayward, CA.

Baldassari, Erin. "'BBQing While Black' Festival Draws Huge Crowd to Oakland's Lake Merritt." *East Bay Times*, May 20, 2018. Online.

Banks, Alec. "The Oakland Police Lawsuit, the Gangsta Rap Defense, and Chokeholds." *Rock the Bells*, August 20, 2020. Online.

Baum, Dan. "Legalize It All: How to Win the War on Drugs." *Harper's*, April 22, 2016. Online.

Becker, Dave. "Promoters, Rappers Debate Future of Concerts." *Oakland Tribune*, May 19, 1996. Music. Rap. 1996. Hayward Area Historical Society, Hayward, CA.

Boles, Lloyd. "'Lifestyle' Intrusion in the Park." *Oakland Tribune*, August 21 1979. Oakland, Calif. Park. Lake Merritt Park. General. 1978–1983. Hayward Area Historical Society, Hayward, CA.

Brand, William. "Rap on Trial: Event Outcome to Decide Future Policy." *Oakland Tribune*, December 28, 1990, A1. Magazine and Newspaper Room, Main Branch, Oakland Public Library, Oakland, CA.

Brooks, Dave. "After Rough Spell, Oakland's New Parish Sold to Allen Scott from Another Planet Entertainment." *Billboard*, September 5, 2018. Online.

Brooks, Ronald, David Elliot, and Neil Johnson. "Media Distorts Rap-Music Violence." *Oakland Tribune*, November 18, 1990. Music. Rap. Dec 1985–Dec 1990. Hayward Area Historical Society, Hayward, CA.

Buenning, Angela. "Sideshow Makes Problems for Community." *Oakland Post*, April 26, 1998, 2. Magazine and Newspaper Room, Main Branch, Oakland Public Library, Oakland, CA.

Burt, Cecily. "Lakeshore Cruising Triggers Complaints." *Oakland Tribune*, May 24, 1993. Cruising. 1990–. Hayward Area Historical Society, Hayward, CA.

Burt, Cecily, and Sean Maher. "Salute to Legendary Oakland Bar Owner." *Oakland Tribune*, February 11, 2010, A3. Magazine and Newspaper Room, Main Branch, Oakland Public Library, Oakland, CA.

Chang, Momo. "Kenzie Smith Speaks Out." *East Bay Express*, May 31, 2018. Online.

"City Officials Probe Riot Here; Preventative Measures Planned." *Oakland Tribune*, March 8, 1944, 11. California Digital Newspaper Collection.

Clemmons, C.J., and Craig Anderson. "Shooting Reports Conflict at Rap Concert." *Oakland Tribune*, October 15, 1989. Music. Rap. Dec 1985–Dec 1990. Hayward Area Historical Society, Hayward, CA.

Clemmons, C.J., and Harry Harris. "Coliseum Will Screen Rap Acts to Avert Concert Violence." *Oakland Tribune*, October 17, 1989, A7. Magazine and Newspaper Room, Main Branch, Oakland Public Library, Oakland, CA.

"Cops Surrounded by Angry Crowd." *Oakland Tribune*, August 29, 1977. Oakland, Calif. Park. Lake Merritt Park. General. 1960–1977. Hayward Area Historical Society, Hayward, CA.

"Council Rejects Curfew Plan." *Oakland Tribune*, November 17, 1943. Curfew Law. Oakland History Room, Main Branch, Oakland Public Library, Oakland, CA.

"Council to Study Measure to End Noise Pollution." *Oakland Tribune*, August 29, 1971. Oakland, Calif. Noise Legislation. Hayward Area Historical Society, Hayward, CA.

"Council Told Park Woes." *Oakland Tribune*, August 22, 1979. Oakland, Calif. Park. Lake Merritt Park. General. 1978–1983. Hayward Area Historical Society, Hayward, CA.

Covarrubias, Amanda. "Lakeside Park's Duck Area Reclaimed for the Law-Abiding." *Oakland Tribune*, July 29, 1985. Oakland, Calif. Park. Lake Merritt Park. General. 1985–. Hayward Area Historical Society, Hayward, CA.

Cutler, Jacqueline. "Council Member Wants to Curb Cruising." *Oakland Tribune*, May 27, 1992. Cruising. 1990–. Hayward Area Historical Society, Hayward, CA.

DeVries, Tom. "The New Urban Guerillas." *California*, September 1989, 62. Institute for Governmental Studies Library, University of California, Berkeley, CA.

Dirks, Sandhya. "When Oakland Was a 'Chocolate City': A Brief History of Festival at the Lake." *KQED*, September 14, 2018. Online.

Ducker, Eric. "The Untold History of Oakland's Soul Beat, a Pioneer among Black-Owned TV Networks." *Medium*, May 12, 2020. Online.

DuPont, Jim, Elissa Dennis, and Tom Csekey. "Oakland for the Elite Only? As City Officials Urge Housing Downtown, Don't Forget the Others." *San Francisco Chronicle*, November 23, 1999. Online.

Editorial. "Striking the Wrong Note." *Oakland Tribune*, July 9, 1978. Oakland, Calif. Noise Legislation. Hayward Area Historical Society, Hayward, CA.

Editorial. "Taking Pride in Lakeside Park." *Oakland Tribune*, October 16, 1979. Oakland, Calif. Park. Lake Merritt Park. General. 1978–1983. Hayward Area Historical Society, Hayward, CA.

Emerson, Karen. "Memories of Rollerland." *Oakland Tribune*, February 12, 1972. Rollerland. Hayward Area Historical Society, Hayward, CA.

Fagan, Kevin. "Oakland to Host First Major Concert in a Year." *Oakland Tribune*, November 18, 1990, A1. Magazine and Newspaper Room, Main Branch, Oakland Public Library, Oakland, CA.

Fitelson, Mike. "City Moves to Bolster Noise Rules." *Montclarion*, February 23, 1996, 3. Magazine and Newspaper Room, Main Branch, Oakland Public Library, Oakland, CA.

Fuller, Margurite. "Letter: Obnoxious Boom Boxes." *Oakland Tribune*, September 22, 2005. Magazine and Newspaper Room, Main Branch, Oakland Public Library, Oakland, CA.

Gammon, Robert. "Cops Charging Overtime to Clubs." *East Bay Express*, March 2, 2011. Online.

Gammon, Robert. "Oakland Cops Make Bank on Overtime." *East Bay Express*, March 9, 2011. Online.

Gammon, Robert. "Time Is Running Out for Oakland." *East Bay Express*, December 9, 2015. Online.

Geissinger, Steve, and Michael Geissinger. "Sideshow Law Lapse Blamed on the Bay Area." *Oakland Tribune*, February 18, 2007. Online.

Giuliani, Rudolph W. "What New York Owes James Q. Wilson." *City Journal*, Spring 2012. Online.

Harris, Harry. "140 Cops Get New Base at Eastmont." *Oakland Tribune*, October 19, 2004, News 1. Magazine and Newspaper Room, Main Branch, Oakland Public Library, Oakland, CA.

Harris, Harry, and Laura Counts. "Extra Police to Monitor 'Sideshows.'" *Oakland Tribune*, March 17, 2002, Local 1. Magazine and Newspaper Room, Main Branch, Oakland Public Library, Oakland, CA.

Harris, Harry, and Craig Staats. "Police to Attempt Cruising Control." *Oakland Tribune*, May 29, 1993. Cruising. 1990–. Hayward Area Historical Society, Hayward, CA.

Harris, Harry, and Craig Staats. "Police Will Rely on Cruising Law to Control Traffic." *Oakland Tribune*, June 5, 1993. Cruising. 1990–. Hayward Area Historical Society, Hayward, CA.

Harris, Harry, and Craig Staats. "Violence Leads City to Reconsider Lake Site." *Oakland Tribune*, June 7, 1994, A1. Magazine and Newspaper Room, Main Branch, Oakland Public Library, Oakland, CA.

Harshaw, Pendarvis. "The Power of Taking Up Space: Marshawn Lynch's Oakland Rideout." *KQED*, June 24, 2018. Online.

Harshaw, Pendarvis. "'We're Still Here': 'BBQ'n While Black' Draws Oaklanders Out in Force." *KQED*, May 21, 2018. Online.

Harshaw, Pendarvis, and Olivia Allen-Price. "'It's Pure Energy': How Hyphy Came to Define Bay Area Hip-Hop." *KQED*, July 22, 2021. Online.

Hepler, Lauren. "The Hidden Toll of California's Black Exodus." *CalMatters*, July 15, 2020. Online.

Hildebrand, Lee. "Sell a Joyful Noise." *East Bay Express*, December 1, 1989. Magazine and Newspaper Room, Main Branch, Oakland Public Library, Oakland, CA.

Hildebrand, Lee. "West Side Story." *East Bay Express*, September 28, 1979, 1. Magazine and Newspaper Room, Main Branch, Oakland Public Library, Oakland, CA.

Hodgdon, Pete. "Volunteers to Help with Light Security at Festival at the Lake." *Oakland Tribune*, March 29, 1996, A13. Magazine and Newspaper Room, Main Branch, Oakland Public Library, Oakland, CA.

Hogan, Mary Ann. "The Shores of Lake Merritt Reflect Oakland at Its Best." *Oakland Tribune*, May 26, 1985. Oakland, Calif. Park. Lake Merritt Park. General. 1985–. Hayward Area Historical Society, Hayward, CA.

Holson, Laura M. "Hundreds in Oakland Turn Out to BBQ While Black." *New York Times*, May 21, 2018. Online.

"Jidenna Breaks Down 'The Let Out' on Genius' Video Series 'Verified.'" *Genius*, March 8, 2017. Online.

Kauffman, Jonathan. "Anti-Racist Barbecuers Take Back Oakland's Communal Backyard at Lake Merritt." *San Francisco Chronicle*, May 20, 2018. Online.

Kelp, Larry. "Oaktown Revival." *Oakland Tribune*, August 19, 1990. Music. Rap. Dec 1985–Dec 1990. Hayward Area Historical Society, Hayward, CA.

Kelp, Larry. "Welcome to 'Oaktown,' Rap Capital U.S.A." *Oakland Tribune*, October 8, 1989. Music. Rap. Dec 1985–Dec 1990. Hayward Area Historical Society, Hayward, CA.

Kim, Deborah S. "Oakland Police Go to the People." *Oakland Tribune*, August 14, 1992, A3. Magazine and Newspaper Room, Main Branch, Oakland Public Library, Oakland, CA.

Kirkwood, Kathleen. "Panel OKs Cash Rescue of Festival." *Oakland Tribune*, September 25, 1996, A11. Magazine and Newspaper Room, Main Branch, Oakland Public Library, Oakland, CA.

"Lakeside Skaters Warned." *Oakland Tribune*, May 30, 1979. Oakland, Calif. Roller Skating. Hayward Area Historical Society, Hayward, CA.

Lane, Del. "Lake Shore Avenue Parking Ban Begins." *Oakland Tribune*, August 2, 1985. Oakland, Calif. Park. Lake Merritt Park. General. 1985–. Hayward Area Historical Society, Hayward, CA.

Lefebvre, Sam. "Blacklisted: How the Oakland Police Department Discriminates against Rappers and Music Venues." *East Bay Express*, April 26, 2017. Online.

Lefebvre, Sam. "Parish Entertainment Group Dissolves amid Allegations against Jason Perkins." *East Bay Express*, June 27, 2018. Online.

Lehman, Charles Fain. "Contra 'Root Causes': What the Work of James Q. Wilson Can Teach Us about the Fight over Criminal Justice Today." *City Journal*, Summer 2021. Online.

Levin, Sam. "No Charges in Lake Merritt Drumming Incident, OPD Says Noise Complaint Was Not a Priority." *East Bay Express*, October 26, 2015. Online.

Levin, Sam. "Oakland Readies for the Housing Boom." *East Bay Express*, December 24, 2014. Online.

Levin, Sam. "OPD Responds to Noise Complaints by White Man against Black Drummers at Lake Merritt, Sparks Concerns about Racial Profiling." *East Bay Express*, September 29, 2015. Online.

Levin, Sam. "'We're Being Pushed Out': The Displacement of Black Oakland." *The Guardian*, June 1, 2018. Online.

Levitt, Ed. "Oakland Event Lures Big, Happy Crowd." *Oakland Tribune*, June 2, 1985, A1. Magazine and Newspaper Room, Main Branch, Oakland Public Library, Oakland, CA.

Li, David K. "Council OKs Curb on Lake Cruising." *Oakland Tribune*, April 20, 1995. Oakland, Calif. Park. Lake Merritt Park. General. 1985–. Hayward Area Historical Society, Hayward, CA.

Li, David K. "Organizers Spread Out Festival Gala." *Oakland Tribune*, November 1, 1995, A9. Magazine and Newspaper Room, Main Branch, Oakland Public Library, Oakland, CA.

Lopez, Robert J. "Rappers Return with Safe Show: Tight Security Keeps Night Peaceful." *Oakland Tribune*, December 30, 1990, A1. Magazine and Newspaper Room, Main Branch, Oakland Public Library, Oakland, CA.

Lucas, Julian. "Ishmael Reed Gets the Last Laugh." *New Yorker*, July 19, 2021. Online.

MacDonald, Heather. "Brown Wants to Criminalize 'Sideshow' Spectating." *Oakland Tribune*, May 27, 2005. Online.

Maher, Sean. "Summer without Sideshows Celebrated in Oakland." *Oakland Tribune*, October 19, 2010. Online.

Marks, Peter. "Street Crackdown's Aim: Turn Down That Stereo!" *New York Times*, June 13, 1993, sec. 1, 39. Online.

Martinez, Mike. "Police Feel They Have Handle on Sideshow Cruisers." *Oakland Tribune*, August 19, 2001, Local 1. Magazine and Newspaper Room, Main Branch, Oakland Public Library, Oakland, CA.

Mavity, Nancy Barr. "Get Definite Recommendation for Oakland within 60 Days." *Oakland Tribune*, April 20, 1944. Curfew Law. Oakland History Room, Main Branch, Oakland Public Library, Oakland, CA.

Michaels, Mark. "Crackdown." *East Bay Express*, July 25, 1986, 1. Institute for Governmental Studies Library, University of California, Berkeley, CA.

"Move to Ease Park Problems." *Oakland Tribune*, May 12, 1976. Oakland, Calif. Park. Lake Merritt Park. General. 1960–1977. Hayward Area Historical Society, Hayward, CA.

Name Illegible. *Oakland Tribune*, June 18, 1957. Music Federation, American. San Francisco Bay Area, Calif. Local 6. Hayward Area Historical Society, Hayward, CA.

"No Harmony on Park Rock." *Oakland Tribune*, August 23, 1979. Oakland, Calif. Park. Lake Merritt Park. General. 1978–1983. Hayward Area Historical Society, Hayward, CA.

"Oakland Police Release Log of Events from BBQ Controversy at Lake Merritt." *KTVU*, May 27, 2018. Online.

O'Brien, Bill. "The Magic Is Gone: Farewell to Festival at the Lake." *East Bay Express*, October 9, 1997, 36. Magazine and Newspaper Room, Main Branch, Oakland Public Library, Oakland, CA.

Ospina, Tulio. "Racially Profiled, Drummers Make Noise about Gentrification in Oakland." *Oakland Post*, October 4, 2015. Online.

"Park Dispute Unresolved." *Oakland Tribune*, September 30, 1977. Oakland, Calif. Park. Lake Merritt Park. General. 1960–1977. Hayward Area Historical Society, Hayward, CA.

"Park Rules Approved." *Oakland Tribune*, June 2, 1976. Oakland, Calif. Park. Lake Merritt Park. General. 1960–1977. Hayward Area Historical Society, Hayward, CA.

Parks, Richard. "The Uptown Apartments Look Nice, but Are Still Mostly Empty." *East Bay Express*, April 8, 2009. Online.

Payton, Brenda. "Oakland Can No Longer Tolerate 'Sideshow' Dangers." *Oakland Tribune*, July 3, 2001, Local 1. Magazine and Newspaper Room, Main Branch, Oakland Public Library, Oakland, CA.

Phillips, Chuck. "Beating the Rap of Concert Violence." *Los Angeles Times*, February 10, 1991. Online.

Platoni, Kara. "Where the Cops Don't Say 'TGIF.'" *East Bay Express*, April 16, 2003. Online.

"Police Harassment Charged." *Oakland Tribune*, September 7, 1977. Oakland, Calif. Park. Lake Merritt Park. General. 1960–1977. Hayward Area Historical Society, Hayward, CA.

Ravo, Nick. "The Noise Police Take the Boom out of the Bronx." *New York Times*, October 6, 1991, Section 1, 32. Online.

Rayburn, Kelly. "Oakland Mayor Lifts Police Overtime Restrictions." *Oakland Tribune*, November 25, 2008. Online.

Reed, Ishmael. "Noise Torture Thrives in Oakland." *Oakland Tribune*, February 3, 2004, Local 5. Magazine and Newspaper Room, Main Branch, Oakland Public Library, Oakland, CA.

Reed, Ishmael. "The Peace-and-Quiet Bandits." *Oakland Tribune*, September 21, 2005, Local 6. Magazine and Newspaper Room, Main Branch, Oakland Public Library, Oakland, CA.

Ressner, Jeffrey. "Hammer Time: America's Most Popular Rapper Is Also a Demanding Taskmaster." *Rolling Stone*, September 6, 1990. Online.

Richards, Kathleen. "Out Foxed? The City of Oakland Is Banking on the Fox Theater to Revive Uptown, but Where Will That Leave the Paramount?" *East Bay Express*, July 25, 2007, 9. Oakland. Theaters. Fox. Oakland History Room, Main Branch, Oakland Public Library, Oakland, CA.

Scherr, Judith. "City Requests Stricter Noise Pollution Law." *Montclarion*, December 21, 1993, 1. Noise. Oakland, Calif. Hayward Area Historical Society, Hayward, CA.

Slater, Dashka. "CALM Prevails at Lake Merritt." *East Bay Express*, April 28, 1995, 2. Magazine and Newspaper Room, Main Branch, Oakland Public Library, Oakland, CA.

Slater, Dashka. "The Other Epidemic: Fatal Encounters with Crack." *East Bay Express*, October 9, 1998, 14. Magazine and Newspaper Room, Main Branch, Oakland Public Library, Oakland, CA.

"Slim Jenkins Dies in West Oakland." *Oakland Tribune*, May 24, 1967. Jenkins, "Slim" Harold. Hayward Area Historical Society, Hayward, CA.

Smallwood, Lola. "Festival Programs to Curtail Rowdiness." *Oakland Tribune*, February 19, 1995, A15. Magazine and Newspaper Room, Main Branch, Oakland Public Library, Oakland, CA.

Sockwell, Ikimulisa. "Oakland Club to Cater to a New Crowd." *Oakland Tribune*, December 9, 1993. Pete, Geoffrey. Hayward Area Historical Society, Hayward, CA.

Solis, Nathan, and Melissa Hernandez. "Inside L. A.'s Deadly Street Takeover Scene: 'A Scene of Lawlessness.'" *Los Angeles Times*, August 22, 2022. Online.

St. Clair, Katy. "Jimmie's Sour Grapes." *East Bay Express*, February 26, 2003. Online.

Staats, Craig. "City Seeks to Stall Cruising Near Lake." *Oakland Tribune*, April 18, 1995. Oakland, Calif. Park. Lake Merritt Park. General. 1985–. Hayward Area Historical Society, Hayward, CA.

Street, Emerson. "Nightstick Justice in Oakland." *New Republic*, February 20, 1950, 15. Institute for Governmental Studies Library, University of California, Berkeley, CA.

Swan, Rachel. "Goapele Gets Closer to Home." *East Bay Express*, August 5, 2009. Online.

"'Sweet Jimmie' Ward, 74." *Oakland Post*, February 10, 2010, 1. Magazine and Newspaper Room, Main Branch, Oakland Public Library, Oakland, CA.

Tobitt, Bill. "Here's News from Home." *Oakland Tribune*, March 11, 1944, 7. California Digital Newspaper Collection.

"Transportation Is Blamed for Riot; Remedies Sought." *Oakland Tribune*, March 10, 1944, 5. California Digital Newspaper Collection.

Valcke, Nancy L. "Noise Hotline: Oakland Quieter than Expected." *Montclarion*, May 16, 1997, 1. Magazine and Newspaper Room, Main Branch, Oakland Public Library, Oakland, CA.

Veal, Liza. "Talking to Geoffrey Pete Is Hearing Oakland's History in Microcosm." *Oakland Local*, March 2, 2014. Online.

Velasquez, Daniel. "Officials Vow to Listen to Youth." *Oakland Tribune*, June 10, 1994, A1. Magazine and Newspaper Room, Main Branch, Oakland Public Library, Oakland, CA.

Walker, Thaai. "Festival at the Lake Discontinued: Debt from Oakland Fete Proved Insurmountable." *San Francisco Chronicle*, November 11, 1997. Online.

Wells, Stacey. "Oakland's Tab for OT: $25 Million." *Oakland Tribune*, November 8, 1998, News 1. Magazine and Newspaper Room, Main Branch, Oakland Public Library, Oakland, CA.

Williams, Diana M. "City Admits Lapse in Rave Party Permit." *Oakland Tribune*, November 29, 1995, A9. Magazine and Newspaper Room, Main Branch, Oakland Public Library, Oakland, CA.

Williams, Diana M. "City Loan Bolsters 14th St. Upgrade." *Oakland Tribune*, July 10, 1997. Pete, Geoffrey. Hayward Area Historical Society, Hayward, CA.

Williams, Diana M. "Cruising Law May Take a Turn for the Better." *Oakland Tribune*, July 24, 1996. Oakland, Calif. Park. Lake Merritt Park. General. 1985–. Hayward Area Historical Society, Hayward, CA.

Williams, Diana M. "Festival Ends in Violence." *Oakland Tribune*, June 6, 1994, A1. Magazine and Newspaper Room, Main Branch, Oakland Public Library, Oakland, CA.

Williams, Diana M. "Rioting Over, Oakland Assesses the Damage." *Oakland Tribune*, June 7, 1994, A1. Magazine and Newspaper Room, Main Branch, Oakland Public Library, Oakland, CA.

Wong, Julia C. "The Bay Area Roots of Black Lives Matter." *SFWeekly*, November 11, 2015. Online.

Wong, William. "An Oakland Dilemma: Whose Lake Is It?" *Oakland Tribune*, May 28, 1993. Oakland, Calif. Park. Lake Merritt Park. General. 1985–. Hayward Area Historical Society, Hayward, CA.

Woo, Elaine. "James Q. Wilson Dies at 80; Pioneer in 'Broken Windows' Approach to Improve Policing." *Los Angeles Times*, March 3, 2012. Online.

Woodall, Angela. "An Entertainment Commission Could Open the Door for Many." *Oakland Tribune*, March 12, 2009. Online.

INTERVIEWS BY AUTHOR

Blakely, Ed. June 24, 2017.

Bridges, Greg. January 19, 2018.

Greene, Carl, and Edward Hawthorne. March 4, 2017.

Hildebrand, Lee. April 20, 2017.

Kozicki, David. December 7, 2017.

Marcus, Nancy. August 15, 2017.

McDaniel, Bijou. July 5, 2017.

Minor, Greg. March 2, 2017.

OPD Sergeant, Special Events Unit. February 16, 2017.

OPD Special Resource Commander, Area 1. November 28, 2017.

Pastori-Ng, Gino. February 3, 2023, February 10, 2023, and July 23, 2024.

Perkins, Jason. June 5, 2017.

Pete, Geoffrey. October 17, 2017.

Sanchez, Arturo. November 11, 2016.

Sykes, Leon "DNas." August 17, 2016.

Vincent, Rickey. November 30, 2017.

Wilkinson, Spencer. January 4, 2023.

Williams, Theo Aytchan. September 5, 2017.

Woodall, Angela. October 7, 2016.

Zazaboi, Yakpasua. July 6, 2022 and February 22, 2023.

ORAL HISTORIES

Beckford, Ruth. "Oral History with Ruth Beckford." Interviewed by Rick Moss, 2007. MS 191, African American Museum and Library at Oakland Oral History Collection, African American Museum and Library at Oakland, Oakland Public Library, Oakland, CA.

Green, Walter. "Oral History with Walter Green." Interviewed by Nadine Wilmot, 1999. BANC MSS 2006/112, Box 1, Oakland Oral History Project, Bancroft Library, University of California, Berkeley, CA.

Hill, Edith K. "Oral History with Edith Katherine Hill." Interviewed by Nadine Wilmot, 1998. BANC MSS 2006/112, Box 1, Oakland Oral History Project, Bancroft Library, University of California, Berkeley, CA.

Mabry, Esther. "Oral History with Esther Mabry." Interviewed by Gay Rich, 2002. MS 191, African American Museum and Library at Oakland Oral History Collection, African American Museum and Library at Oakland, Oakland Public Library, Oakland, CA.

Watkins, Earl. "Oral History with Earl Watkins." Interviewed by Donna J. Murch, 1998. BANC MSS 2006/112, Box 1, Oakland Oral History Project, Bancroft Library, University of California, Berkeley, CA.

Wilson, Lionel J. *Lionel Wilson: Athlete, Judge, and Oakland Mayor.* Black Alumni Club, University of California, Berkeley, 1995. Bancroft Library, University of California, Berkeley, CA.

SPEECHES

Carmichael, Stokely. "Speech at University of California, Berkeley," October 29, 1966. Greek Theatre, University of California, Berkeley, CA. Recording and transcript accessed online through American Public Media Reports.

Meese III, Edwin. "Address of the Honorable Edwin Meese III, Attorney General of the United States, before the San Diego Crime Commission," September 27, 1985. San Diego, CA. Transcript accessed online through U. S. Department of Justice.

Spear, Michael D. "Investor Perceptions of Downtown Oakland," October 17, 1986. Symposium for Business Leaders, Holy Names College, Oakland, CA. Transcript accessed at Institute for Governmental Studies Library, University of California, Berkeley, CA.

PLANNING AND GOVERNMENTAL REPORTS

King, Steve. *Who Owns Your Neighborhood?: The Role of Investors in Post-Foreclosure Oakland.* Urban Strategies Council, 2012. Online.

Kroll, Cynthia. *Downtown Oakland and the Regional Economy.* University–Oakland Metropolitan Forum, 1987. Environmental Design Library, University of California, Berkeley, CA.

McArdle, Phil. *A History of the Oakland Police Department.* City of Oakland, 1980. Institute for Governmental Studies Library, University of California, Berkeley, CA.

Oakland City Planning Commission. *Shoreline Development: A Part of the Master Plan.* City of Oakland, 1951. Environmental Design Library, University of California, Berkeley, CA.

Oakland Community and Economic Development Agency. *Request for Proposals: Uptown Oakland Fox Theater.* City of Oakland, 1997. Oakland. Theaters. Fox. Oakland History Room, Main Branch, Oakland Public Library, Oakland, CA.

Oakland Interagency Council on Drugs. *Report to the City of Oakland, Covering the Period September 1, 1984 to December 31, 1984*. City of Oakland, 1985. Institute for Governmental Studies Library, University of California, Berkeley, CA.

Oakland Planning Department. *Noise: An Element of the Oakland Comprehensive Plan*. City of Oakland, 1974. Main Branch, Oakland Public Library, Oakland, CA.

Oakland Police Department. *Rules and Regulations for the Government of the Police Department, Oakland, Cal*. City of Oakland, 1912. Bancroft Library, University of California, Berkeley, CA.

Oakland—Sharing the Vision Inc. *The Oakland Strategic Plan*. Oakland—Sharing the Vision Inc., 1992. Institute for Governmental Studies Library, University of California, Berkeley, CA.

Starling, Jay D. *Municipal Coping Strategies: "As Soon as the Dust Settles."* Sage Publications, 1985. Environmental Design Library, University of California, Berkeley, CA.

Tate, Will D. *The New Black Urban Elites*. R&E Research Associates, 1976. Environmental Design Library, University of California, Berkeley, CA.

University–Oakland Metropolitan Forum. *Oakland's Economy in the 1990's: A Sourcebook of Planning and Community Development Issues Facing the City, Its Neighborhoods, and the Region*. Institute of Urban and Regional Development, University of California, Berkeley, 1990. Environmental Design Library, University of California, Berkeley, CA.

Urban Strategies Council. *Call to Action: An Oakland Blueprint for Youth Development*. Urban Strategies Council, 1996. Institute for Governmental Studies Library, University of California, Berkeley, CA.

COURT CASES

Complaint in Jimmie's Limousine Service, Inc. v. City of Oakland et al. No. C 04–3321 WHA, Document 1. United States District Court, Northern District California, August 13, 2004. PACER.

Decision in Jimmie's Limousine Service, Inc. v. City of Oakland et al. No. C 04–3321 WHA, Document 54. United States District Court, Northern District California, August 18, 2005. PACER.

Complaint in Pete v. City of Oakland et al. No. C 09–06097 WHA, Document 1. United States District Court, Northern District California, December 31, 2009. PACER.

Decision in Pete v. City of Oakland et al. No. C 09–06097 WHA, Document 143. United States District Court, Northern District California, March 10, 2011. PACER.

MUSICAL RECORDINGS

3X Krazy. "Keep It on the Real." *Keep It on the Real*. Noo Trybe Records, 1997, 7243 8 38584 2 2, CD, single.

3X Krazy featuring Mike Marshall. "Sunshine in the O." *Sick-O*. Str8 Game Records, 1995, STG 1202, CD, EP.

B. B. King. "Three O'Clock Blues." *Three O'Clock Blues / That Ain't the Way to Do It*. RPM Records, 1951, 339, shellac, 10", single.

Beyoncé. "Get Me Bodied." *B'Day*. Columbia, 2006, 82876 88132 2, CD, album.

Clyde Carson featuring The Team. "Slow Down." *Slow Down*. Universal Republic Records, 2012, No Catalog Number, MP3, single.

The Coup. "Dig It!" *Kill My Landlord*. EMI, 1993, E2–89047, CD, album.

Digital Underground. "The Humpty Dance." *Sex Packets*. Tommy Boy, 1990, TBCD 1026, CD, album.

Digital Underground. "Same Song." *This Is an E. P. Release*. Tommy Boy, 1991, TBCD 964, CD, EP.

Drake featuring Lil Wayne. "The Motto." *Take Care*. Cash Money Records, 2011, AAC, album, deluxe edition.

E-40 featuring Keak Da Sneak. "Tell Me When to Go." *My Ghetto Report Card*. Reprise Records, 2006, 49963–2, CD, album.

Gil Scott-Heron. "The Revolution Will Not Be Televised." *The Revolution Will Not Be Televised*. Flying Dutchman, 1974, BDL1–0613, vinyl, LP, album.

Graham Central Station. "The Jam." *Ain't No 'Bout-a-Doubt It*. Warner Bros. Records, 1975, BS 2876, vinyl, LP, album.

The Impressions. "People Get Ready." *People Get Ready / I've Been Trying*. ABC-Paramount, 1965, 45–10622, vinyl, 7", single.

The Impressions. "We're a Winner." *We're a Winner*. ABC Records, 1967, 45–11022, vinyl, 7", single.

James Brown. "Get Up (I Feel Like Being a) Sex Machine." *Get Up (I Feel Like Being a) Sex Machine*. King Records, 1970, 45–6318, vinyl, 7", single.

James Brown. "Papa Don't Take No Mess." *Papa Don't Take No Mess*. Polydor, 1974, PD 14255, vinyl, 7", single.

James Brown. "The Payback." *The Payback*. Polydor, 1973, PD 14223, vinyl, 7", single.

James Brown. "Papa's Got a Brand New Bag." *Papa's Got a Brand New Bag*. King Records, 1965, 938, vinyl, LP, album.

James Brown. "Say It Loud—I'm Black and I'm Proud." *Say It Loud—I'm Black and I'm Proud*. King Records, 1968, 45–6187, vinyl, 7", single.

Jamie Foxx featuring T-Pain. "Blame It." *Intuition*. J Records, 2008, 88697–41294–2-RE2, CD, album.

Jidenna featuring Quavo. "The Let Out." *The Chief*. Epic, 2017, 88985303062, CD, album.

Jimmy McCracklin. "Just Got to Know." *The Drag / Just Got to Know*. Art-Tone Records, 1961, 825, vinyl, 7", single.

Jimmy McCracklin. "Just Got to Know." *Yesterday Is Gone*. Stax, 1972, STS-2047, vinyl, LP, album.

Jimmy McCracklin. "Too Late to Change." *I Just Gotta Know*. Imperial, 1963, LP 9219, vinyl, LP, album.

Jimmy Wilson. "Tin Pan Alley." *Tin Pan Alley / Big Town Jump*. Big Town, 1953, 101, vinyl, 10", single.

Johnny Heartsman, the Rhythm Rocker, and the Gaylarks. "Johnny's House Party, Parts 1 & 2." *Johnny's House Party, Parts 1 & 2*. Music City, 1957, 45–807, vinyl, 7", single.

Keak Da Sneak. "Super Hyphy." *That's My Word*. Rah Records, 2005, RTE 131, CD, album.

Kendrick Lamar. "Alright." *To Pimp a Butterfly*. Interscope Records, 2015, AFT-MB002295802CD, CD, album.

KRS-One. "Sound of da Police." *Return of the Boom Bap*. Jive, 1993, 01241–41517–2, CD, Album.

Lil Jon and the East Side Boyz featuring Too Short. "Couldn't Be a Better Player." *More Freaky Tales*. Short Records, 1998, 01241–42571–2, CD, single.

Lil Wayne. "Mrs. Officer." *Tha Carter III*. Cash Money Records, 2008, B0011232–72, CD, album.

Lowell Fulson. "Blue Shadows." *Blue Shadows / Low Society Blues*. Swing Time, 1950, 226, shellac, 10", single.

Lowell Fulson. "Three O'Clock Blues." *Three O'Clock Blues / I'm Wild about You Baby*. Down Town Recording, 1948, shellac, 10", single.

The Lumpen. *Free Bobby Now / No More*. Seize the Time, 1970, BPP-4501-A, vinyl, 7", single.

Luniz. "I Got 5 on It." *I Got 5 on It*. Noo Trybe Records, 1995, 7243 8 38474 2 6, CD, single.

Mac Dre. "Feelin' Myself." *Ronald Dregan: Dreganomics*. Thizz Entertainment, 2004, THZ 1065, CD, album.

Marvin Gaye. "Inner City Blues (Make Me Wanna Holler)." *What's Going On*. Tamla, 1971, TS-310, vinyl, LP, album.

Maze featuring Frankie Beverly. "Before I Let Go." *Before I Let Go*. Capitol Records, 1981, A-5031, vinyl, 7", single.

MC Hammer. "Ring 'Em." *Feel My Power*. Bustin' Records, 1987, BR-LP-001, vinyl, LP, album.

MC Hammer. "Turn This Mutha Out." *Let's Get It Started*. Capitol Records, 1988, C1–90924, vinyl, LP, album.

Missy Elliott featuring Ciara and Fatman Scoop. "Lose Control." *The Cookbook*. Atlantic, 2005, 83779–2, CD, album.

Mistah F. A. B. "Ghost Ride It." *Top Secret!—September 2006 Reloaded*. Strictly Hits Vinyl Service, 2006, ts-077, vinyl, 12", EP.

Mistah F. A. B. "N. E. W. Oakland." *Son of a Pimp*. Thizz Entertainment, 2005, THN 6004, CD, album.

Mount Westmore. "Big Subwoofer." *Snoop Cube 40 $hort*. MNRK Music Group, 2002, MNK-CD-46871, CD, album.

N. W. A. "Fuck the Police." *Straight Outta Compton*. Ruthless Records, 1988, SL 57102, vinyl, LP, album.

Otis Redding. "(Sittin' on) The Dock of the Bay." *(Sittin' on) The Dock of the Bay*. Volt, 1968, 45–157, vinyl, 7", single.

Parlet. *Pleasure Principle*. Casablanca, 1978, NBLP 7094, vinyl, LP, album.

Parliament. "Chocolate City." *Chocolate City*. Casablanca, 1975, NBLP 7014, vinyl, LP, album.

Parliament. "Give Up the Funk (Tear the Roof Off the Sucker)." *Mothership Connection*. Casablanca, 1975, NBLP 7022, vinyl, LP, album.

Parliament. "Theme from the Black Hole." *Theme from the Black Hole.* Casablanca, 1979, NB 2235, vinyl, 7", single.

Plastic Ono Band. "Give Peace a Chance." *Give Peace a Chance / Remember Love.* Apple Records, 1969, APPLE 13, vinyl, 7", single.

Public Enemy. "Fight the Power." *Fight the Power.* Motown, 1989, ZB 42877, vinyl, 7", single.

Sirealz. "4 15's in the Trunk." *Save Some 4 Later.* No label, 2011, no catalog no., CD, album.

Sly and the Family Stone. "Dance to the Music." *Dance to the Music.* Epic, 1967, 5–10256, vinyl, 7", single.

Sly and the Family Stone. "Everyday People." *Everyday People.* Epic, 1968, 5–10407, vinyl, 7", single.

Sly and the Family Stone. "I Want to Take You Higher." *Stand! / I Want to Take You Higher.* Epic, 1969, 5–10450, vinyl, 7", single.

Sly and the Family Stone. "Stand!" *Stand!* Epic, 1969, BN 26456, vinyl, LP, album.

Sly and the Family Stone. "Thank You (Falettinme Be Mice Elf Agin)." *Thank You (Falettinme Be Mice Elf Agin) / Everybody Is a Star.* Epic, 1969, 5–10555, vinyl, 7", single.

Sly and the Family Stone. "Thank You for Talkin' to Me Africa." *There's a Riot Goin' On.* Epic, 1971, KE 30986, vinyl, LP, album.

The Staple Singers. "Respect Yourself." *Respect Yourself.* Stax, 1971, STA-0104, vinyl, 7", single.

The Temptations. "My Girl." *My Girl / (Talkin' 'Bout) Nobody but My Baby.* Gordy, 1964, Gordy-7038, vinyl, 7", single.

Terror Squad featuring Fat Joe and Remy Ma. "Lean Back." *True Story.* Universal Records, 2004, B0002806–02, CD, album.

Too Short. "Blow the Whistle." *Blow the Whistle.* Jive, 2006, 82876–83501–2, CD album.

Traxamillion featuring Too Short and Mistah F. A. B. "Sideshow." *The Slapp Addict.* Slapp Addict Productions, 2006, 5, CD, album.

Tupac. "I Get Around." *I Get Around.* Interscope Records, 1993, 0–96036, vinyl, 12", single.

Usher featuring Lil Jon and Ludacris. "Yeah!" *Confessions.* Arista, 2004, 82876–52141–2, CD, album.

Yukmouth. "City of Dope." *Thugged Out: The Albulation*. Rap-A-Lot Records, 1998, 7243 8 46720 2 7, CD, album.

Zapp. "More Bounce to the Ounce." *Zapp*. Warner Bros. Records, 1980, WBS49534, vinyl, 7", single.

FILM RECORDINGS, TELEVISION EPISODES, AND MUSIC VIDEOS

DJ Vlad, dir. *Ghostride the Whip*. Film recording. Rugged Entertainment, 2008. Prime Video.

Eisenberg, Ira, dir. "The People and the Police: Oakland." *Assignment 4*. Television series episode. Young Broadcasting, 1974. Internet Archive.

Gourley, Bernard, dir. "Tell Me When to Go." Music video. Immigrant Films, 2006. YouTube.

Jones, Steven A., Bill Jersey, Sharon Wood, and Marshall Crutcher, dirs. *Crossroads: A Story of West Oakland*. Film recording. Quest Productions, 1996. Media Services and Collections, University of California, Berkeley, CA.

Madrigal, Laurence, dir. *We Were Hyphy*. Film recording. Castle G Productions, 2022. PBS Online.

Riggs, Marlon, and Peter Webster, dirs. *Long Train Running: A History of the Oakland Blues*. Film recording. University of California, Berkeley, School of Journalism, 1981. Media Services and Collections, University of California, Berkeley, CA.

Riley, Boots, dir. "You a Big Muthaf***a." *I'm a Virgo*. Television series, season 1, episode 1. Media Res and Amazon Studios, 2023. Prime Video.

Tilley, Colin, and the Little Homies, dirs. "Alright." Music video. London Alley Entertainment, 2015. YouTube.

Varda, Agnès, dir. *Black Panthers*. Film recording. Ciné Tamaris, 1968. Kanopy.

Zazaboi, Yakpasua, dir. *Sydewayz*. Film recording. Sydewayz Media, 2006. Access provided by Yakpasua Zazaboi.

Index

Page references followed by italicized *fig.* indicate illustrations or material contained in their captions.

ence with, 24–29, 31; borderless logic of, 312n10; connection fostered by, 12, 134, 252–53, 254–55, 257; looping in, 19–20, 133–34, 259–60; masculinity and, 158; "New Oakland" and, 185, 214; political impact of, xv–xvi, 11, 87–88; popularity of, 31; prohibited at Black-owned nightclubs, 185, 209–10; war on nuisance against, 96, 133–34, 185; White ambivalence about, 221

Black Lives Matter Movement, 5, 175

Black men: crack epidemic and, 102–3; masculinity and, 158, 175, 244–45; policing of, 42, 57, 111, 169, 202; stereotypes about, 128

Black Messengers, 84

Black middle class: Black migrants and, 40; education levels of, 98; law-and-order policing supported by, 95, 117; social movement of, 110–11, 110 *fig. 5*; unions and early growth of, 38; as "urban guerillas," 115; White Flight and, 99

Black migrants: Black middle class and, 40; the blues and, 20, 37, 48, 55, 59, 68; education levels of, 41; motivations of, 34–35; negative reactions to sight/sound of, 40–41, 56; Oakland segregation and, 39, 40; post-WWII job losses affecting, 96–98; Southern customs of, 43, 49, 59–60

Black musicians: unionization of, 45–46; West Oakland opportunities for, 47–48, 52–56, 119

Black nationalism, 63, 77, 137

Black nightlife: dispossession of, 23, 185; policing of, 136. *See also* nightclubs

Black Noise (T. Rose), 121

Black Oaklanders: BBQ Becky incident and, 248–50; civic/religious organizations of, 37–38; electoral successes of, 91–92; entrepreneurship of, 47; incarceration rates, 104; murder rate, 103; population of, 31, 39, 97, 111, 224; repetition and, 249–50; "social movements" of, 257; street dance performances of, 79; unemployment rate, 102–3; war on nuisance against, 96; White antipathy to cultural practices of, 36–37

Black Panther (newspaper), 70, 71

Black Panther Party for Self-Defense (BPP): black homeowners and, 115; Black-owned nightclubs and, 200–201; crack epidemic and, 156; cultural effect of, 65–66, 69, 84; DeFremery Park and, 85–86, 87, 240, 279n96; establishment of, 64; FBI campaign against, 89–90, 191; 50th anniversary museum exhibit, xiii–xiv, 84–85, 86 *fig. 3*; funk culture and, 20–21; growth of, 64–65; Lake Merritt events, 226, 227 *fig. 10*; newspaper of, 70, 71; Oakland electoral campaigns of, 90; OPD and, 64, 93, 180–81, 240; soul band of, 69, 70–73, 76; survival programs of, 65, 84, 89, 90, 200–201; Tupac and, 123; Vincent and, 69; visual identity of, xiv, 70, 86–87

Black Panthers (documentary film; 1968), 85–86, 86 *fig. 3*, 227, 227 *fig. 10*

Black Power: boogaloo culture and, 83–84, 165; call for, 61–63, 66; crack and, 101–2; cultural effects of, 65–66, 67–70; dance music and, 78–79; emancipatory imagination of, 68;

complaints about, 234–35; repetition and, 248; resistance to anticruising measures, 239–41; sideshows and, 157; as "social movement," 257; TV portrayals of, 160

crunk, 165–66, 176, 296n51

dance breaks, 166–67
dance circles, 2–3, 255
dance music: aural-kinesthetic relationship in, 79; Black Power and, 78–79; Brown (James) as revolutionizer of, 73–74; political impact of, 11, 68–69; recorded vs. live, 119–20. *See also* Black dance music
"Dance to the Music" (Sly and the Family Stone), 72, 73
Dance to the Music (Sly and the Family Stone), 228, 229 *fig. 11*
dancehall, 24, 158, 185
Davis, Angela, 220
Davis, Mike (A's player), 124
Davis, Mike (urbanist), 152
DeFremery, James, 58
DeFremery Park (West Oakland, CA): BPP use of, 84–85, 86 *fig. 3*, 228, 240, 279n96; OPD migrant youth control experiments at, 57–58
DeFremery Recreation Center (DRC; West Oakland, CA), 58–60, 65, 85
Dell Graham Trio, xii
Dellums, Ron, 91, 136
Denton (TX), 75
DeSanto, Sugar Pie, 52, 121
desegregation, 95, 118, 200, 216
Detroit (MI), xi, 43, 91
Digital Underground: BBQ Becky incident and, 220; danceable sound of,

161; East Bay as home to, 121; funk influence on, xii, 22, 122, 161; on security at rap concerts, 129; Shock G as frontman for, 122; success of, 21–22, 127, 143, 161; Tupac and, 123
Dinkins, David, 94, 95
disco: looping in, 18–19; mainstream acceptance of, 119; sonic technologies and development of, 17, 289n7
disinvestment: Black middle class and, 114, 117, 142; Black youth recreational practices and, 232–33; crack epidemic and, 102–3; entertainment venue closures as result of, 148, 187; gentrification and, 223–25; as intentional racist process, 109; war on nuisance and, 131, 138; Wilson (Lionel) redevelopment efforts and, 92
displacement: African American, 168, 223; of Black dance music, 185; of Black nightlife, 23, 214; of Black public life, 249; Black resistance to, 249–50; of Chinatown, 273–74n10; diversity discourse and, 242; "emancipatory soundscapes" and, 215; gentrification and, 29, 185, 223, 224; of Japanese Americans, 273n8; repetition and, 15; schisms resulting from, 26; of sideshows, 152–53; in West Oakland, 118
diversity discourse, 242–43. *See also* multiculturalism
DJs: author's experience, 26, 27; Black/queer aesthetics developed by, 19; boomboxes and, 132; disco and, 17, 18; Downtown redevelopment and, 26, 215; dub as used by, 17; hip-hop and, 17, 132; in "New Oakland," 215;

Ohlone people, 34, 267n8

"Okies," 42

Oklahoma, 39

Omni (Oakland, CA), 127

"One, the" (downbeat), 73–75, 282n46

Operation Soundtrap, 134–35, 172

Otis, Johnny, 52, 56

Pacific Islanders, 31, 111, 154

Palestine (TX), 35, 54

Pam the Funkstress, 239

"Papa's Got a Brand New Bag" (J. Brown), 74–75

Parish Entertainment Group (PEG), 208–11. *See also* New Parish (Oakland, CA)

Parliament, 92, 123. *See also* Parliament-Funkadelic (P-Funk)

Parliament-Funkadelic (P-Funk), xii, 87, 122; Mothership, 80, 83, 283n59

partner dancing, 81

Party Music (Vincent), 69

Pastori-Ng, Gino, 153–57, 159–60, 171–72

Payton, Jay, 82 *fig. 2*, 84, 201

"People Get Ready" (Impressions), 72

"People Get Ready" (Lumpen), 72–73

People's Park (Berkeley, CA), 228

Perata, Don, 174

Perkins, Jason, 208–9, 210, 211, 214

Perry, Lee ("Scratch"), 16

Pete, Geoffrey: author's final visit with, 216; civil rights lawsuit filed by, 184, 197–99, 211; decision to close GIC, 199–200; family background of, 180–81; as GIC owner, 179–80, 181; Merchants Garage rented by, 197; permit violation of, 188. *See also* Geoffrey's Inner Circle (GIC; Oakland, CA)

Petrillo, James, 46–47

Pilate, Felton, 124–25

Pittman, Tarea Hall, 91

Pitts, Dorothy, 58–59

Please Hammer Don't Hurt 'Em (Hammer), 125, 127

pleasure principle, 87, 151–52, 162, 187, 228

"pocket bikes," 297n75

Point, Michael, 50

Pointer Sisters, 80

policing: community style of, 113; law-and-order style of, 109–10, 142; "legalistic" style of, 93; legitimacy crisis in, 113; pretextual style of, 238–39; racial politics of, 28. *See also* broken-windows policing; Oakland Police Department (OPD)

polyrhythm, 257, 312n7

Pope, Lavar, 33, 162–63, 296n51

popping, 79, 82, 283n56

popular music: Black, 2, 205, 312n7; Black Power Movement and, 65, 69; Black youth culture and, 73; marketing of, 24; rap domination of, 21, 121; recorded vs. live, 119; sonic technologies and temporal structure of, 17, 74–75

popular music industry, 24

Port of Oakland, 106, 141, 175 *fig. 8*

post–Civil Rights Era: anti-Black policing during, 241; "colorblind" discrimination forms during, 21, 96, 137, 162, 186, 230, 241; conflicts during, 111, 139; marginalization of young people of color during, 176, 241; middle-class neighborhoods of color during, 110–11; police/community relations during, 113–14

and, 142; East Bay, 22, 138–39, 143, 150–51, 176–77; first major acts, 122–25, 161; gangster, xii, 128, 156–57, 161; hyphy, 32, 161, 266n3, 296n51 (*see also* Hyphy Movement); marketing of, 24; music videos, 125, 142, 150, 158, 163, 166, 175 *fig. 8,* 244; Oakland ban on, 21–22, 120–22, 126–30, 150, 184, 189; party, xi–xii (*see also* slaps); popularity of, 21, 117, 120, 131, 185; presence of, in the "New Oakland," 214; prohibited at Black-owned nightclubs, 209–10; radio stations, 290n24; repetition in, 134; rhythms of, 137–38; sideshows and, 159–61; sound of, 21, 121, 137–38

rasquachismo, 159

Rastafarians, 266n3

Raw Fusion, 123

Ray Luv, 123

Ray-Lynch, Leopold, 152

Ray's Club (Oakland, CA), 200

Reading, John, 91, 107

Reagan, Nancy, 110 *fig. 5*

Reagan, Ronald, 100, 102

real estate costs, 223–24

"reclamation aesthetics," 220

redlining, 37, 38, 67, 120

Reed, Adolph, 91

Reed, Carla, 115

Reed, Ishmael, 43, 115–17

reggae, 11, 16–17, 78

Reggae Gold, 210

Reid, Dorothy, 180

Reid, Larry, 174

Reid, Mel, 180

Reid, Paul, 180

Reid's Records (South Berkeley, CA), 180

rent parties, 48

repetition: in African/Afro-Diasporic musics, 15–16, 75, 251; BBQ Becky incident and, 247–50; in disco, 18–19; in funk, 75; in hip-hop, 17–18; in improvisation, 2; as Oakland feature, 14, 259; in rap, 134; rewinds and, 142; soundwaves and, 271n50; violence of, 19, 249. *See also* looping

Republican Party, 38, 53, 91

Revolutionary Action Movement (RAM), 63, 64

rewinds, 142

rhythm, 15–16, 73–78

Richmond (CA), 34, 41–42, 79, 83, 123

Richmond Merchants Committee, 41–42

"Riders, The" (OPD vigilante group), 169, 302n47

Riggs, Marlon, 52

Riley, Boots, 69, 160, 239–40, 240

Riley, Terry Christian, 80

"Ring 'Em" (Hammer), 124–25

ring shout, 255–56, 312n7

Rios, Victor, 239

"RIP Oscar Grant" (short film; 2010), 164, 164 *fig. 7*

Rishell, Clifford, 53

Robinson, Cynthia, 76. *See also* Sly and the Family Stone

Robinson, Jhamel, 224

Robinson, L. C. ("Good Rockin'"), 53

Robinson, Zandria, 42–43

robotting, 79, 83

Rock, Rick, 166

rock concerts, 128–29, 206

rock íní roll, 52, 312n7

Rock Steady (Oakland, CA), 211

roda (dance circle), 2–3

roller discos, 230

Shakur, Afeni, 123

Shakur, Assata, 123

Shakur, Tupac. *See* Tupac

Shelley, Braxton, 78, 249

Ships in the Night, 210

Shock G, 122, 123. *See also* Digital
Underground

Shorenstein Properties, 287n64

Showcase Club (Oakland, CA), 71, 76, 120

Siano, Nicky, 18

"Sideshow" (Too Short and Mistah
F.A.B.), 163

sideshows: Black freedom/pleasure and,
144; as "Black noise," 152; boogaloo
culture and, 155; changing locations
of, 155; complaints about, 134;
criminalization of, 205; defined, 21,
148–49; demonization of, 167;
displacement of, 152–53; donut
spinning as feature of, 142; at
Eastmont Mall, 151–52, 155, 236; goal
of, 173; Hyphy Movement and, 139,
162, 163; international spread of,
174–75; looping and, 176; marginal
sites of, 150, 162; masculinity and, 32,
175 *fig. 8*; media coverage of, 155–56,
160, 175; nightclub policing and, 201–2;
origins of, 79–80, 146–48; policing of,
139, 145, 163; popularity of, 167; racist
coding of, 156; repetition and, 248; as
resistance, 167–68; soundscape of,
159–61; turfing and, 163–64; violence
at, 155–56, 170; war on nuisance
against, 21, 22, 42, 168–74

Silk's (Emeryville, CA), 125

Sirealz, 159

slap-bass style, xii, 77

Slapp Addict, The (Traxamillion), 163

"slaps": anticruising campaign and, 239;
in Black nightclubs, 143; Black sonic
politics and, 22, 254, 257; defined, xi;
history of, xii; hyphy and, 143; as San
Francisco Bay Area rap type, xi–xii,
xiv–xv, 220

slavery, 13, 14, 68

Slim Jenkins' Club (West Oakland, CA),
53, 54, 54 *fig. 1*, 55, 277n73

Sly and the Family Stone, 61; Graham
(Larry) as bassist for, xii; Graham
(Larry) departs from, 80; influence of,
xii, 122; Lakeside Park album cover of,
228, 229 *fig. 11*; Lumpen covers of,
71–72, 73; mixed-race/mixed-gender
composition of, 76–77; origins of, 76;
political impact of, 76–78; slap-bass
style in, xii, 77, 78

Smith, Andrea, 139, 162, 165, 301n41

Smith, Kenzie, 218–19, 226, 234. *See also*
BBQ Becky incident (2018)

Smith, Neil, 224

Smith, V. Hap, 229–30

Snead, James, 2, 15, 16, 19–20

Snider, Michelle, 219. *See also* BBQ Becky
incident (2018)

Sobrante Park (East Oakland, CA), 79–80

social dance, 81

social media, 174–75. *See also* Black
Twitter

"social movements": dance and, 81;
defined, 66; music and, 77; political
response to, 87–88

Sol House, 27

Somar (Oakland, CA), 215

Son of a Pimp (Mistah F.A.B.), 254

community policing and, 113–15; cruising policies, 147–48; Kozicki and, 170–74, 297n75; "post-racial" ideology and, 112–13; as racist, 138, 185, 187; "rap ban," 21–22, 120–22, 125–30, 138, 150, 184, 189; sideshows and, 134, 143, 168–74, 176–77; urban renewal and, 184–85. *See also* nuisance

War on Poverty, 91, 92, 98, 99, 148

Ward, Dave, 203–5, 206

Ward, Jimmie ("Sweet Jimmie"), 184; as Black migrant, 200; Brown (Jerry) and, 201, 205; civil rights lawsuit filed by, 202–3; death of, 206; fines paid by, 201, 204; nightclubs opened by, 200–201. *See also* Sweet Jimmie's (Oakland, CA)

Warden, Donald, 63

Washington (DC), 91, 92, 128, 242

Wasserman, Zachary, 208

Waters, Maxine, 182–83

Watkins, Earl, 44, 46, 118–19, 146, 298n3

Watts, Travis, 244

Watts Community Action Patrol (CAP), 63–64

Watts Uprising (1965), 63

Webster, Peter, 52

Weheliye, Alexander, 10, 160–61

West Oakland (CA): Black civic/religious organizations in, 37–38; Black entrepreneurs in, 47, 107; blockbusting and, 99; as "ghost town," 105; industrial development in, 36; local music industry, 49; as multiethnic community, 37; in music videos, 175, 175 *fig. 8*; nightlife in, 47–48, 49, 52–56, 54 *fig. 1*, 118; Northern European immigrants in, 273n8; OPD policing

of, 42, 59–60, 135; railroad connections to, 35–36; segregation in, 39, 47, 228; transportation to, 184; urban renewal in, 105, 106 *fig. 4*, 118

wheelback, 17

whistle tips, 297n75

White Flight: Oakland nightlife and, 118–19; Oakland tax revenues and, 92, 100–101; real estate values and, 105; residential segregation and, 98–99

White Power: Black nightclub owners and, 53, 181–82; Black urban regime and, 92; impact of, in Oakland, 34, 36; mundane aspects of, 226; Oakland power structure, 53, 107, 181–82

White sonic politics, 24, 258, 313n11

White supremacy, 65, 230

Whiteness: as cultural construct, 9, 230, 258; economic displacement as privilege of, 214; literacy as privilege of, 10; masculinity and, 158; as norm in urban governance, 259; segregation and, 222; sound and, 258–59

Wiggins, D'Wayne, 80

Wilkerson, Isabel, 40, 41

Wilkinson, Spencer, 283n56, 308n32

Williams, John B., 107, 223

Williams, LaVerne, 65

Williams, Theo Aytchan ("King Theo"), 3–4, 5, 26, 109, 190, 267n9, 268n13

Wilson, James Q., 92–95, 104, 113, 239

Wilson, Jimmy, 55

Wilson, Lionel: advisers to, 136; antidrug campaigns of, 110 *fig. 5*; arrest of son of, 104; Black nightclubs under, 181; as Black urban regime leader, 91, 120; education of, 91; elected Oakland mayor, 90, 91–92, 231; Harris as

Wilson, Lionel *(continued)*
  successor of, 113; inner circle of, 101;
  migrant background of, 90–91; as
  Oakland mayor, 21, 99, 168–69;
  policing style under, 109–10, 113, 120,
  232, 237; political career of, 91, 100;
  urban renewal and, 107, 110, 136,
  168–69, 223; war on nuisance initiated
  by, 21, 95–96
Winston, Ali, 104, 169
Winston, Robert, 228, 229 *fig. 11*
Wolf's Records (West Oakland, CA), 49
"(Won't Be) No More" (Lumpen), 71
Woodall, Angela, 192
Woods, Clyde, 68
Word, Richard, 172–73
World War I, 90
World War II: African American mass
  migration during, 20, 31, 34–35, 36,
  38–39, 223 (*see also* Black migrants;
  Great Migration); American entrance
  into, 38; Bay Area shipbuilding

industry during, 38–39; Black social/
  cultural life during, 58; car culture
  following, 146; economic decline
  following, 105, 148; Japanese intern-
  ment during, 273n8; job losses
  following, 96–98; policing/regulation
  of migrants during, 41–42
Wynter, Sylvia, 2, 11

"yadadamean?" xi, 266n3
Yesterday Is Gone (McCracklin), 282n46
Young Comrades, 240–41
youth culture, 154, 161. *See also* Black
  youth culture; Hyphy Movement
Youth UpRising (East Oakland, CA), 164
Yukmouth, 156, 157, 159, 204
YWCA (Downtown Oakland, CA), 180

Zanfagna, Christina, 55
Zazaboi, Yakpasua, 143–46, 151–52, 157,
  158, 172, 192–93, 195, 202
"zigzagging," 157

Founded in 1893,
UNIVERSITY OF CALIFORNIA PRESS
publishes bold, progressive books and journals
on topics in the arts, humanities, social sciences,
and natural sciences—with a focus on social
justice issues—that inspire thought and action
among readers worldwide.

The UC PRESS FOUNDATION
raises funds to uphold the press's vital role
as an independent, nonprofit publisher, and
receives philanthropic support from a wide
range of individuals and institutions—and from
committed readers like you. To learn more, visit
ucpress.edu/supportus.